Natural Disaster Hotspots
Case Studies

Disaster Risk Management Series

Natural Disaster Hotspots
Case Studies

Edited by

Margaret Arnold[1]
Robert S. Chen[2]
Uwe Deichmann[3]
Maxx Dilley[4]
Arthur L. Lerner-Lam[5]
Randolph E. Pullen[6]
Zoe Trohanis[7]

The World Bank
Hazard Management Unit
2006
Washington, D.C.

[1] Hazard Risk Management Team, World Bank
[2] Center for International Earth Science Information Network (CIESIN), Columbia University
[3] Development Economics Research Group, World Bank
[4] United Nations Development Programme
[5] Center for Hazards and Risk Research (CHRR) and Lamont-Doherty Earth Observatory (LDEO), Columbia University
[6] Center for Inernational Earth Science Invormation Network (CIESIN), and Center for Hazards and Risk Research (CHRR), Columbia University
[7] Hazard Risk Management Team, World Bank

1818 H Street NW
Washington DC 20433
Telephone: 202-473-1000
Internet: www.worldbank.org
E-mail: feedback@worldbank.org

1 2 3 4 5 09 08 07 06

ISBN-10: 0-8213-6332-8
ISBN-13: 978-0-8213-6332-4
eISBN-10: 0-8213-6333-6
eISBN-13: 978-0-8213-6333-1
DOI: 10.1596/978-0-8213-6332-4

Cover photo: Margaret Arnold

Library of Congress Cataloging-in-Publication Data

Natural disaster risk hotspots case studies / edited by Margaret Arnold ... [et al.].
p. cm. -- (Disaster risk management series)
Includes bibliographical references.
ISBN 0-8213-6332-8
1. Natural disasters--Risk assessment. I. Arnold, Margaret, 1965- II. Series.

BG5014.N35 2006
363.34--dc22

2005050448

Contents

Figures

Preface

This second volume of the Natural Disaster Hotspots project presents a series of case studies undertaken to support the global analysis, published in 2005 as *Natural Disaster Hotspots: A Global Risk Analysis*. The Hotspots initiative aims to provide information to inform development strategies and investments and to prioritize actions for reducing disaster risk. The initiative began in 2001 under the umbrella of the ProVention Consortium as a collaborative effort of the World Bank, Columbia University's Earth Institute, and a number of international partners.

The core study team for the Hotspots initiative included staff from the World Bank's Disaster Management Facility (now the Hazard Risk Management Team) and the Development Economics Research Group (DECRG) and from the Center for Hazards and Risk Research (CHRR), the Center for International Earth Science Information Network (CIESIN), the International Research Institute for Climate and Society (IRI), and the Lamont Doherty Earth Observatory (LDEO) at Columbia University. The project also benefited from close collaboration with the Norwegian Geotechnical Institute (NGI), the United Nations Development Programme (UNDP), the United Nations Environment Programme (UNEP), the United Nations Office for the Coordination of Humanitarian Affairs (OCHA), the United Nations World Food Programme (WFP), the U.S. Geological Survey (USGS), the United Nations International Strategy for Disaster Reduction (ISDR), and others.

Key contributors to the initiative were the authors of the case studies, each listed below with their affiliations:

Chapter One—Drought Disaster in Asia

Written by Mathew Barlow of the University of Massachusetts, Lowell (formerly Atmospheric and Environmental Research, Inc. and IRI), Heidi Cullen of the Weather Channel (formerly National Center for Atmospheric Research (NCAR)), Brad Lyon of IRI, and Olga Wilhelmi of NCAR.

Chapter Two—Global Landslides Risk Case Study

Written by Farrokh Nadim of the International Center for Geohazards at the Norwegian Geotechnical Institute (ICG/NGI); Oddvar Kjekstad, Ulrik Domaas, and Ramez Rafat of NGI; and Pascal Peduzzi of the UNEP Early Warning Unit DEWA/GRID-Europe. The Annex to Chapter Two was written by Christian Herold and Pascal Peduzzi of UNEP/DEWA/GRID-Europe.

Chapter Three—Storm Surges in Coastal Areas

Written by Robert J. Nicholls of the School of Civil Engineering and the Environment at the University of Southampton (formerly the Flood Hazard Research Centre, Middlesex University, London).

Chapter Four—Natural Disaster Risks in Sri Lanka: Mapping Hazards and Risk Hotspots

Written by Vidhura Ralapanawe of Ralapanawe Associates and Lareef Zubair of IRI with Upamala Tennakoon of Natural Resources Management Services and Ruvini Perera of IRI. Much of the analysis for the case study was carried out using the resources of IRI and its collaborative project with the Mahaweli Authority of Sri Lanka, conducted by the Foundation for Environment,

Climate, and Technology (FECT). Samitha Jayamaha, Brad Lyon, and Benno Blumenthal also contributed expertise and guidance to the study. Amara Samarasinghe and Mahadevan Ramachandran provided background of the work of the World Food Programme in Sri Lanka. C.M. Madduma Bandara of the Interim National Water Resources Authority of Sri Lanka also provided guidance to the project.

Chapter Five—Multihazard Risks in Caracas, República de Bolivariana Venezuela

Written by Kristina R. Czuchlewski, Klaus H. Jacob, Arthur L. Lerner-Lam, and Kevin Vranes of the Lamont-Doherty Earth Observatory and the Center for Hazards and Risk Research of the Earth Institute at Columbia University, and students and faculty of the Urban Planning Studio: "Disaster Resilient Caracas," of the Graduate School of Architecture, Planning, and Preservation of Columbia University.

Chapter Six—Reducing the Impacts of Floods through Early Warning and Preparedness: A Pilot Study for Kenya

Written by Hussein Gadain of the USGS Famine Early Warning System Network; Nicolas Bidault, Linda Stephen, and Ben Watkins of the World Food Programme, Vulnerability Assessment and Mapping Unit; Maxx Dilley of UNDP (formerly IRI); and Nancy Mutunga of the Famine Early Warning System Network Kenya.

In addition to the contributors listed above, the study team would like to thank Jeffrey Sachs, Director of the Earth Institute; Katherine Sierra, World Bank Vice President for Infrastructure; Maryvonne Plessis-Fraissard, Director of the World Bank's Transport and Urban Development Department; and Eleoterio Codato, Sector Manager for the Bank's Urban Unit, for their support of the Hotspots initiative. The team is also grateful to Kathy Boyer of the U.S. Federal Emergency Management Agency (formerly of the CHRR) for her extensive help with project management and implementation, particularly relating to the case studies. Thanks are also due to David Peppiatt, Manager of the ProVention Consortium Secretariat, for his continued encouragement and support of the project. Funding for the initiative was provided by the United Kingdom's Department for International Development (DFID) and the Norwegian Ministry of Foreign Affairs. Their support is greatly appreciated. The team is also grateful to the CHRR, the Earth Institute, and the Lamont-Doherty Earth Observatory of Columbia University for providing complementary support to the project and support to the Caracas case study. The support of the U.S. Agency for International Development (USAID) for the Kenya case study is gratefully acknowledged.

Introduction

Natural disasters made 2005 an unforgettable year of tragedy. It began in the aftermath of the December 26, 2004, tsunami in the Indian Ocean that devastated countries from Indonesia to Somalia, killing an estimated 300,000 people and leaving 1.5 million people homeless. In March 2005, another strong earthquake took the lives of almost 2,000 people on the island of Nias in Indonesia. The year inaugurated a record hurricane season, with storms causing severe damages throughout the Caribbean, Mexico, and the United States' Gulf Coast. On October 8, 2005, the world witnessed the devastating impacts of another major earthquake in the Kashmir region, which claimed more than 73,000 lives in Pakistan, and over 1,300 more in India. And these were just a few major catastrophes that grabbed the headlines for brief periods. All told, there were 360 natural disasters that killed more than 90,000 people and affected more than 150 million lives in 2005.

Given the devastating losses of 2005, it would at least be a small comfort to consider the year an anomaly unlikely to be repeated. However, the number of disaster events seemingly continues to rise, as do the social and economic costs. Disasters in 2005 caused some US$159 billion in damage (of which US$125 billion were losses caused by Hurricane Katrina in the United States), a 71 percent increase from the total losses of US$93 billion in 2004. And although the number of overall deaths caused by natural disasters is decreasing, the number of those affected in terms of disruptions to daily life, loss of livelihoods, and deepening poverty continues to increase. The impacts of population and economic growth, rapid urbanization, environmental degradation and climate change are a few of the factors that will continue to fuel this trend unless something is done to reduce disaster risks.

The Hotspots initiative aims to contribute to efforts to reduce disaster losses by identifying geographic areas that are most vulnerable to hazards and encouraging development agencies and policy makers to incorporate disaster risk management into investment plans and decisions. The project began in early 2001, when the World Bank's Disaster Management Facility (DMF; now the Hazard Risk Management Team-HRMT), initiated discussions with the newly established Center for Hazards and Risk Research (CHRR) at Columbia University to conduct a global-scale, multi-hazard risk analysis focused on identifying key "hotspots" where the risks of natural disasters are particularly high. Discussions culminated in the formulation of a project, implemented jointly by several departments within both the World Bank and Columbia University, with the participation of numerous other international partners.

The project results consist of a global analysis of disaster risks associated with six major natural hazards—cyclones, droughts, earthquakes, floods, landslides, and volcanoes—accompanied by a series of case studies. The global analysis, described in a separate volume, assessed the estimated spatial distribution of relative risks of mortality and economic losses associated with each hazard and all hazards combined. Risk levels are estimated by combining hazard exposure with historical vulnerability for two indicators of elements at risk—gridded population and gross domestic product (GDP) per unit area. Calculating relative risks for each grid cell rather than for countries as a whole allows risk levels to be compared at subnational scales.

The resolution of the global analysis is relatively coarse, however, and global datasets inadequately capture important factors affecting local risk levels. Specific limitations of the global analysis include the following:

- Global spatial datasets on vulnerability characteristics of the major sets of elements at risk to each hazard do not exist, although vulnerability may be inferred from existing data on a limited basis in some cases.
- Existing global spatial datasets on major hazards and elements at risk are of coarse resolution, sufficient for resolving only relatively broad spatial patterns of risk.
- Existing global spatial datasets on major hazards cover only limited time periods that may not fully characterize the probability of recurrence of hazardous events.
- Global data on socioeconomic "outcome" variables—for example, mortality, morbidity, economic losses, and impoverishment—are universally available only at the country level in the form of national statistics. Yet such data are needed to verify the global risk assessment (that is, assessed spatial patterns of disaster risk hotspots should correspond to historical patterns of actual human and economic losses to some degree).

To partially address these limitations, the case studies in this volume were undertaken as the second component of the Hotspots project to complement the global-scale analysis. Each case study was implemented by a different set of researchers within a general framework provided by the project. The case studies use the same theory of disaster causality as the global analysis—namely, that the risks of a specified type of disaster-related loss to a set of elements at risk over a given period are a function of the exposure of the specified set of elements to natural hazards and their degree of vulnerability to the hazards to which they are exposed.

Three case studies address specific hazards: landslides, storm surges, and drought. Three other case studies address regional multihazard situations in Sri Lanka, the Tana River basin in Kenya, and the city of Caracas, Repúblic Bolivariana de Venezuela. This small number of geographically limited case studies was designed to:

- provide "ground truthing" for particular regions identified as potential hotspots;
- explore specific cases where there are more detailed loss probability data and models compared with what is available globally;
- ascertain what finer scale data may exist locally, for example, on vulnerability, response capacity, and poverty;
- identify cross-hazard dependencies and interactions among hazards, exposure, vulnerability, and multihazard risk management at subnational scales;
- examine the policy context for risk management and the degree to which multiple hazards are recognized and addressed in an integrated manner;
- engage national- to local-level stakeholders; and
- demonstrate that the theory and methods that guide the global analysis can be applied on a more regional or local geographic scale.

Key findings from the case studies are:

Scale matters. Geographic areas that are identified as hotspots at the global scale may have a highly variable spatial distribution of risk at finer scales.

Scale affects data availability and quality. Hazard, exposure, and vulnerability data are available at subnational resolutions for individual countries and even cities, as the analyses for Sri Lanka and Caracas show. More comprehensive, better quality data permit more complete, accurate, and reliable identification of multihazard hotspots at finer scales of resolution.

Scale affects the utility of the results. Better data resolution and a richer set of variables contribute to results that are more relevant for national-to-local scale risk management planning, as illustrated in the case study from Caracas. This is very important, as decisions made at local and national scales have perhaps the greatest potential to directly affect risk levels, both positively and negatively.

The global- and local-scale analyses are complementary. In some instances, national-to-local level risk assessors and planners may be able to "downscale" global data for finer-scale risk assessment to compensate for a lack of local data. Ideally, however, global analyses would be scaled up—generalized from more detailed larger-scale data. In practice, many barriers still remain. The global infrastructure for systematically assembling and integrating relevant datasets for disaster risk assessment at multiple scales remains inadequate. Nonetheless, the fact that relevant datasets can be obtained and integrated at various scales creates the hope that data eventually can be collected and shared routinely to improve disaster risk assessment globally and locally.

Taken together, the global analysis and case studies provide strong evidence of the importance of employing multihazard approaches in disaster risk management. Given resource constraints and the multiple roles played by key infrastructure—such as roads, railroads, and ports in disaster preparedness, emergency response, reconstruction, and ongoing economic activity—it is vital that planners and decision makers at all levels have a sound appreciation of the hazards prevalent in their specific regions of concern, along with associated vulnerabilities. Moreover, they need to understand the potential interactions among these hazards, whether direct—for example, storms that initiate both floods and landslides—or indirect—such as consecutive hazards that deplete resources and strain response capacities. We hope that in addition to providing interesting and useful results, the global analysis and case studies will stimulate additional research, particularly at national and local levels, increasingly linked to disaster risk reduction policy making and practice.

Chapter 1

Drought Disaster in Asia

Mathew Barlow, Heidi Cullen, Brad Lyon, and Olga Wilhelmi

Drought ranks as the natural hazard with the greatest negative impact on human livelihood. Due to the complexities of drought disasters, however, investigations of drought have been limited primarily to local case studies. As global climate data are operationally monitored and forecast, a more regional-to-global scale perspective on the climatic signature of drought disasters could enhance ongoing efforts in drought monitoring, early warning, and mitigation efforts. This investigation undertakes a preliminary examination of the climatic aspects of drought disasters across a broad geographic range—the countries of Asia and the maritime continent (Indonesia and Malaysia)—with data and methodology that may be easily extended to global consideration.

A drought disaster is caused by the combination of both a climate hazard—the occurrence of deficits in rainfall and snowfall—and a societal vulnerability—the economic, social, and political characteristics that render livelihoods susceptible in the region influenced by the deficits. Global disaster databases such as the Emergency Events Database (EM-DAT), maintained by the Center for Research on the Epidemiology of Disasters, include global information on recorded drought disasters at the country level. The corresponding climate information is not readily available, however, because, although several climate-based measures of drought exist, their general relevance to the incidence of drought disasters is not well known.

Both the climate dynamics and the societal impacts of drought are highly complex, poorly understood, and difficult to generalize. Drought is commonly divided into meteorological, agricultural, hydrologic, or socioeconomic categories, and there is great variation in both the climatic and the socio-political-economic character between and within these categories. Droughts involving persistent, severe deficits in rain or snow, however, can be reflected in all four categories and so may be more amenable to generalization. The recent exceptionally severe drought in Central-Southwest Asia provides a motivating example, where a clear signal is seen in both the climate and societal data across a wide variety of sectors—including agriculture, livestock, water resources, and environmental management—as well as across several countries (Agrawala et al. 2001; Barlow et al. 2002; Lautze et al. 2002). The first key question for the present investigation is whether there is a relationship between severe and persistent precipitation deficits and the reported incidence of drought disaster at the country level. It may be that the disasters are too dependent on the local economic, political, and social circumstances to show a clear and consistent link to the climate data, and it may be that the country-averaged climate data do not have sufficient resolution in space or time to capture the relevant climate fluctuations. The second key question is whether such a relationship could be generalized across the range of climatic and societal characteristics of multiple countries.

The EM-DAT database, which was used in this study, contains drought disaster reports that meet at least one of four criteria: 10 or more people reported killed, 100 or more people reported affected, a call for international assistance, or a declaration of a state of disaster. The basic spatial unit of the data is countries, although more specific geographic information is given when available. Clearly, the identification of events based on these criteria depends strongly on the quality of reporting and may be critically influenced by political, social, and economic conditions. To avoid some of these complexities for this preliminary analysis, the disasters are considered only in terms of whether one appears or does not appear in the disaster database for a given country, unweighted by any other factor. The data are further restricted to reports that include a month (some specify only a year), for unambiguous comparison to the monthly climate data. The enhanced version of the EM-DAT natural disaster database, which includes data from 1975 to 2001, is used to provide incidence of drought disaster for the 27 countries in the "Asia" category. The Asia region was chosen for this pilot effort because of the large-scale, exceptionally severe drought that occurred from 1999 to 2001 as well as the availability of some geo-referenced data for the region.

For the analysis of climate data, two estimates are used based only on precipitation deficits and emphasizing multiple months of severe precipitation deficits. The first, Persistent Deficits of Precipitation (PDP), which was also used in the World Vulnerability Report, tracks the number of consecutive months that the observed precipitation falls below a given threshold (for example, 75 percent of median). The second, the Weighted Anomaly of Standardized Precipitation (WASP), is an average of weighted (relative to the local annual cycle) and standardized (relative to the local standard deviation) precipitation over a set number of months—12 for this investigation. This index is similar to the Standardized Precipitation Index (SPI) and, for averages in the 6- to 12-month range, correlates well with the Palmer Drought Severity Index (PDSI). (See Annex I.A for a discussion of the calculation of the PDP and WASP.) Although many estimates of drought are available and would be high priorities in future analyses, we begin here with two that are used in climate monitoring by the International Research Institute for Climate Prediction (IRI). The climatic drought estimates are analyzed as country averages for consistency with the disaster data, starting in 1979 (the beginning of consistently available satellite data to supplement the station data for precipitation). These country averages are particularly problematic for large countries such as China and India, which range over vast areas and encompass multiple climate zones, as evident in the range of annual average precipitation (see figure 1.1). The quality of the precipitation data in the region is also marginal in some areas, particularly in the north and west. The emphasis on severe, widespread events may be expected to alleviate these problems somewhat.

The results demonstrate a correspondence between severe, persistent precipitation deficits observed in the available climate data and reported drought disasters for 14 of the 27 countries during the 1979–2001 period. Global-scale climate fluctuations in 1982–1983 and 1999–2001 strongly affected the occurrence of widespread precipitation deficits in the region and were also reflected in the disaster data, particularly in the later period, which encompassed the largest values in both climate and disaster data. There is some suggestion that the relationship is particularly strong in the semiarid countries. The relationship is present in other climatic zones, however; Laos, for instance, shows a relationship over multiple drought events.

Asian Drought Disasters in EM-DAT

The spatial distribution of the number of disaster reports for each country over the 1975–2001 period is shown in figure 1.2 (Unfortunately, geo-referenced data are not yet available for all the countries in the region. Although EM-DAT reporting began in 1975, no reports specify a month until 1977.) Figure 1.3 shows the number of reports for all countries in the region, with the further restriction that only reports associated with a specific month are shown. These are the data that will be compared with the climate data. Note that the countries with the largest area and population (China and India) dominate the reports.

The year-to-year variation of the drought disaster reports for the region is shown in figure 1.4 for all reports and in figure 1.5 for only the reports that specify a month. Although there is modest variability throughout the period, the number of reports over the last three years is notably larger. This increase is expected to some degree due to the severity of the recent drought in the region, which is one of the motivating factors for the study. However, the larger number of reports also raises questions about changes in reporting over the period. As a first check on this, the time variation of drought disaster reports in all countries outside of Asia is shown in figure 1.6. Although there is still a maximum for the recent period in the non-Asian reports, the largest values for the period occur during 1983. Thus there does not appear to be a general bias in the EM-DAT reporting

Figure 1.1. Total Annual Precipitation, in millimeters. Due to the unavailability of geo-referenced data, this plot does not show several countries in the west and north of the study region: Israel, Jordan, Uzbekistan, Mongolia, Iraq, Tajikistan, Armenia, and Georgia. These countries all have annual averages of less than 500 mm, except for Georgia, which has an annual average of 720 mm.

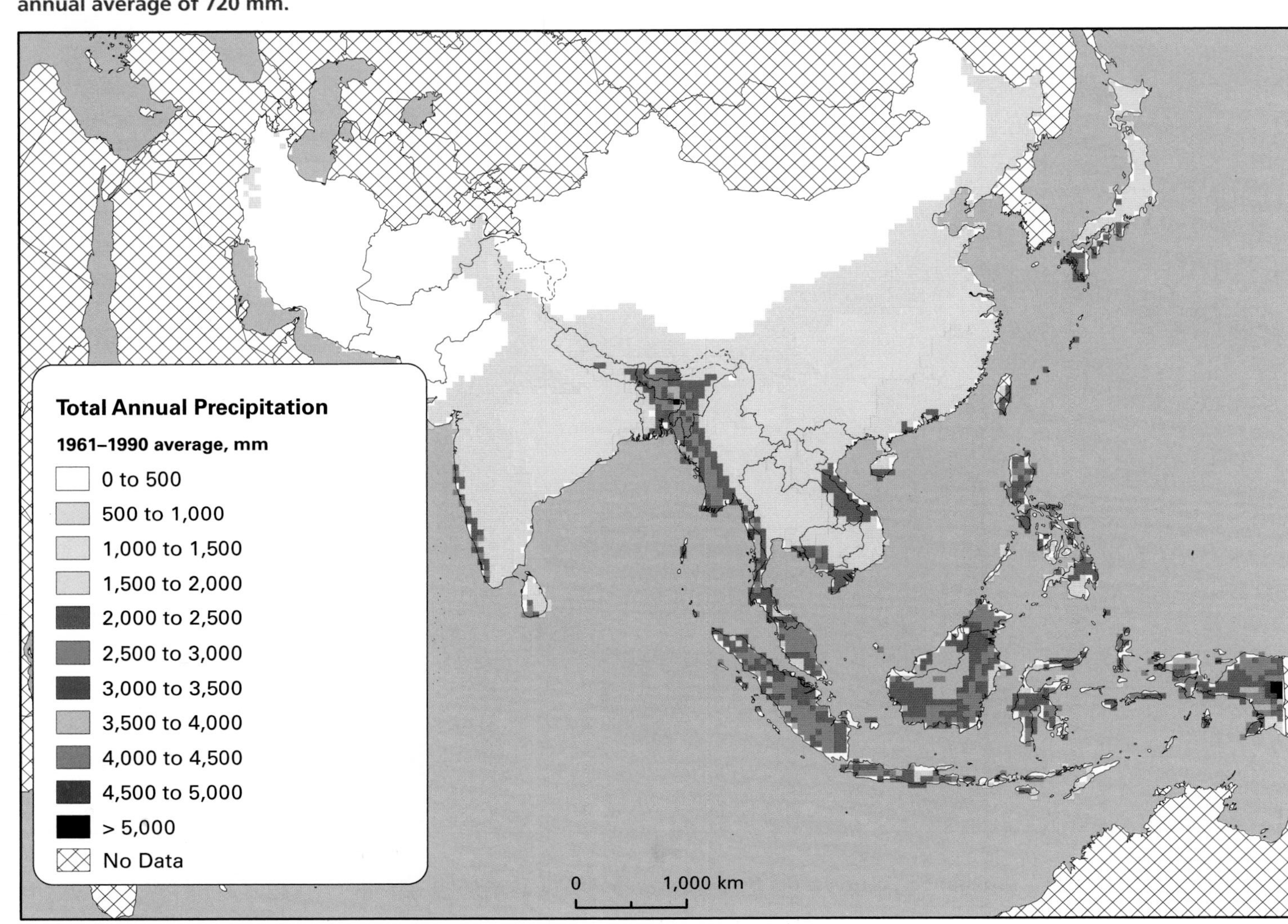

Figure 1.2. Total number of drought disasters for all Asian countries with geo-referenced boundaries available

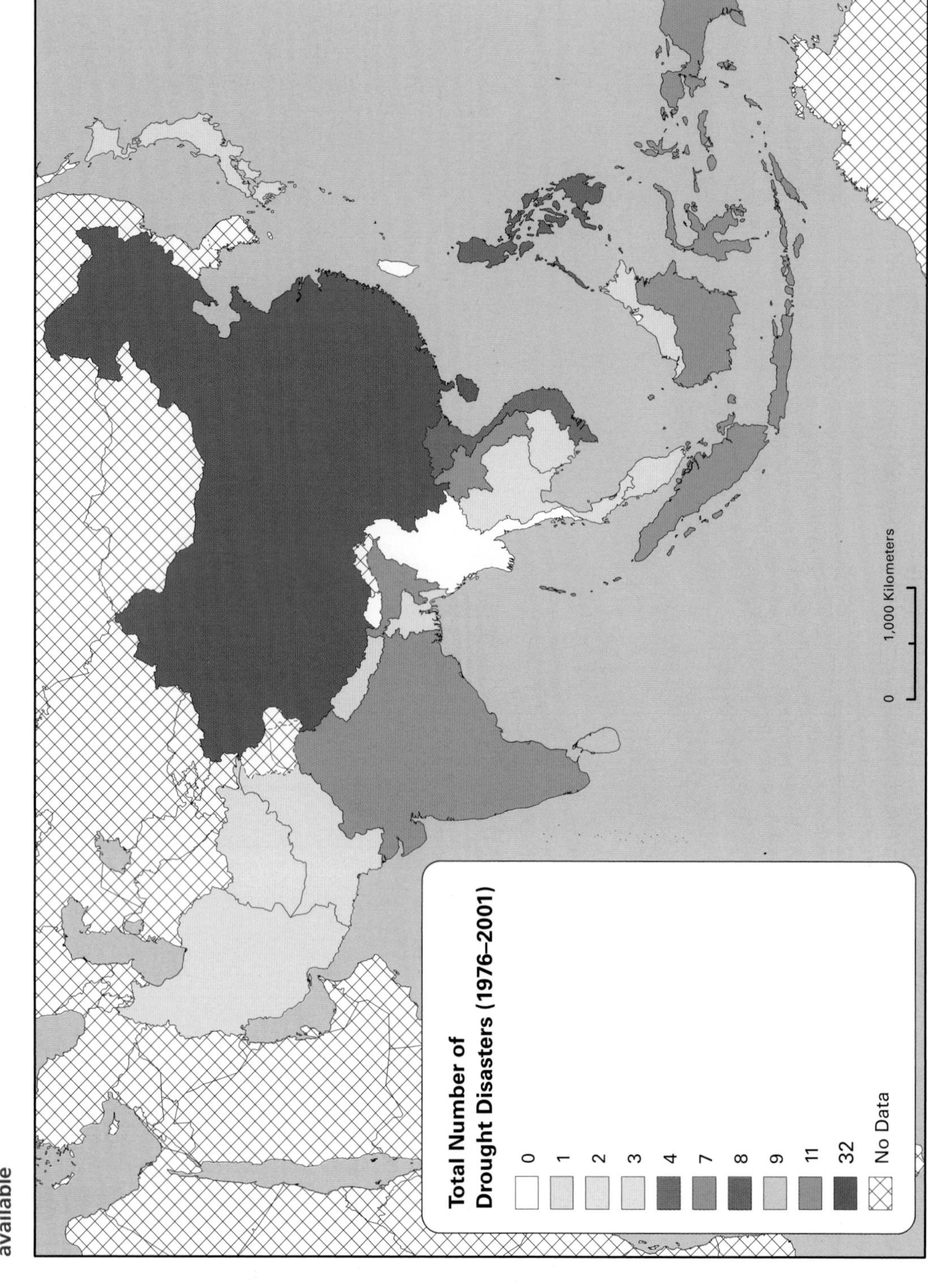

Figure 1.3. Number of drought disasters with month specified, for all countries listed in the Asia category in EM-DAT

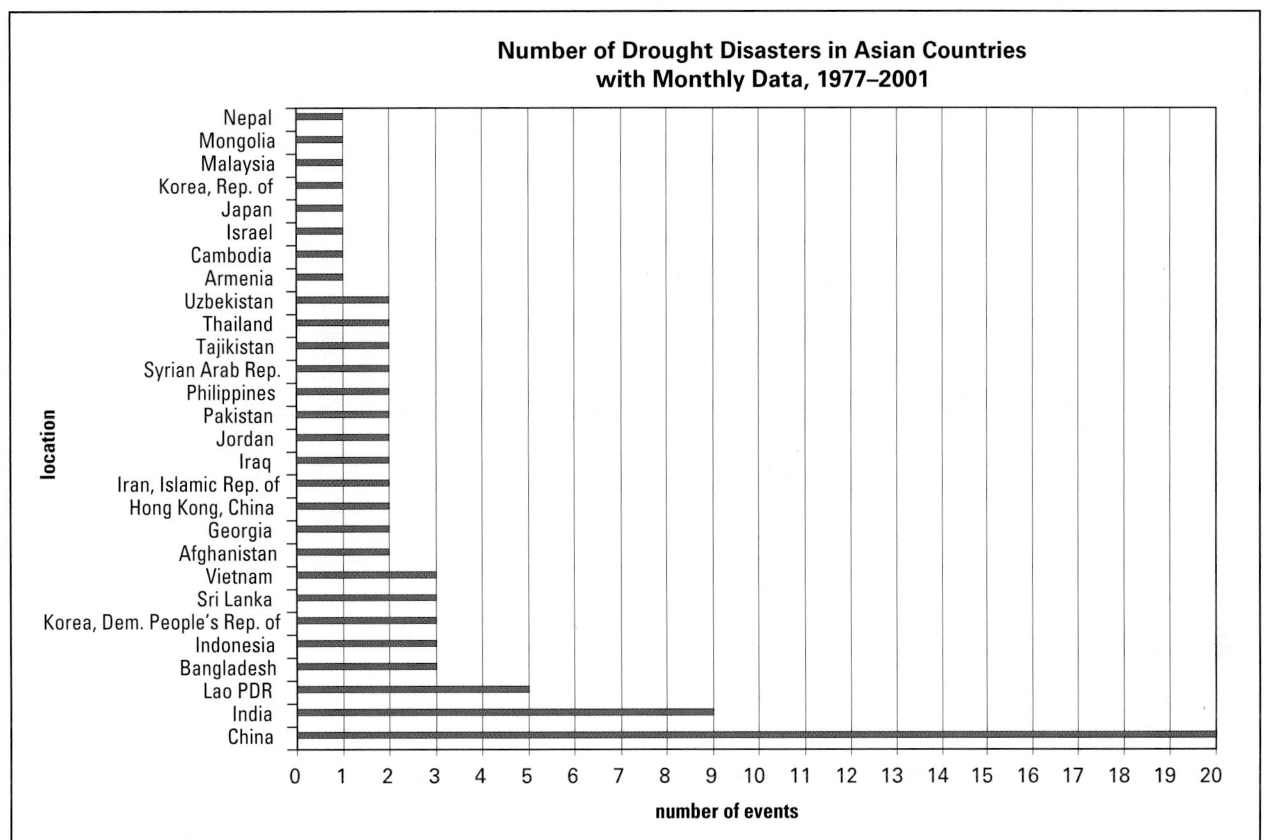

Figure 1.4. Number of drought disasters for Asia and the maritime continent, summed by year and over all countries in the region

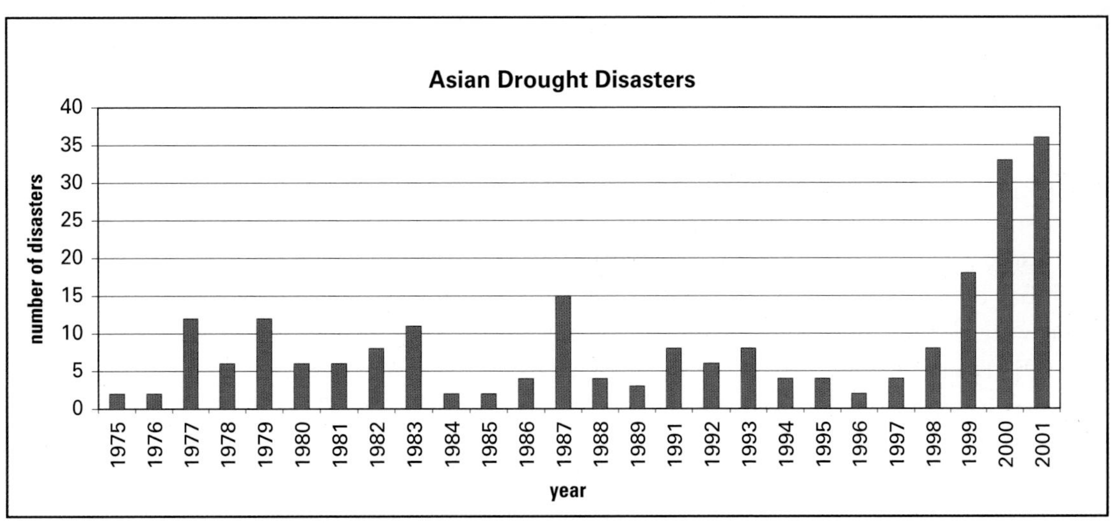

Figure 1.5. Number of drought disasters with months specified for Asia and the maritime continent

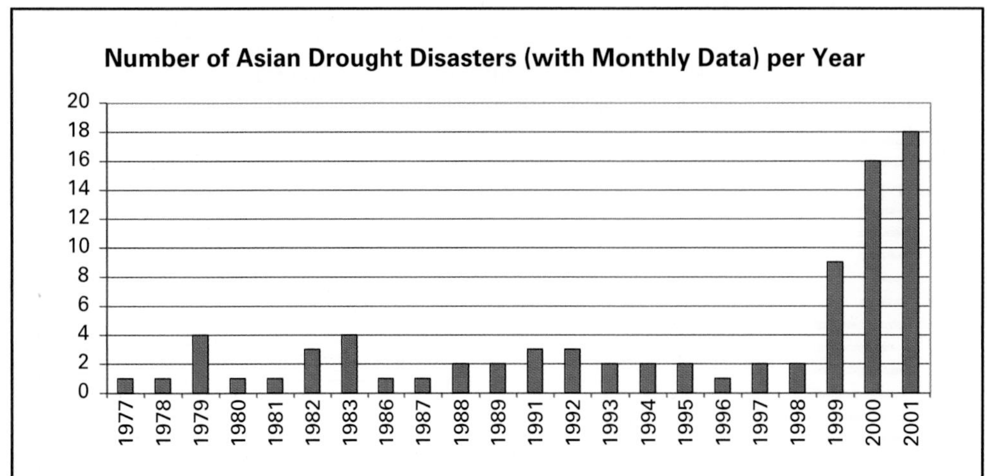

Figure 1.6. Number of drought disasters for non-Asia countries in the EM-DAT database

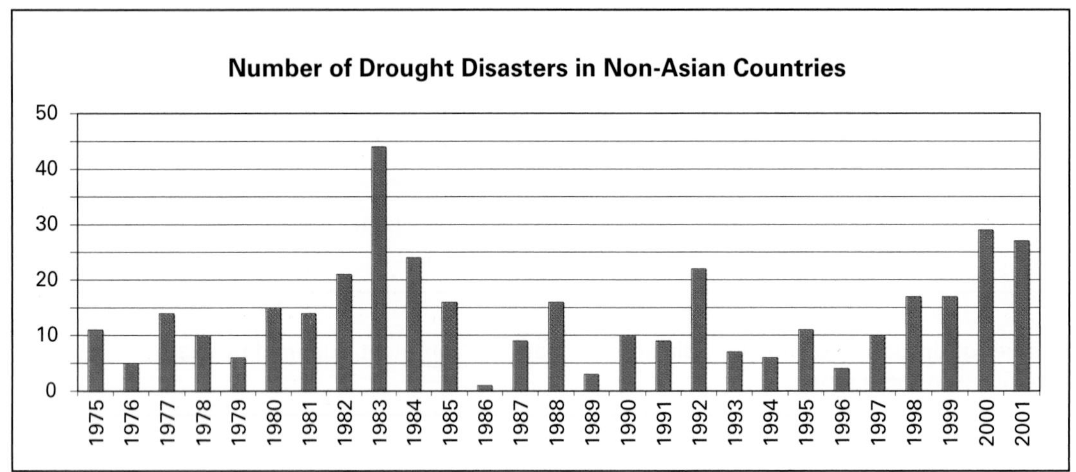

toward the end of the period. While the variations in the non-Asian reports are outside the scope of this analysis, we note that an exceptionally strong El Niño was associated with global climate anomalies during 1982–1983 and there were global-scale drought anomalies during 1999–2001 (Hoerling and Kumar 2003).

The precipitation deficits for Asia in the 1999–2000 period are shown in figure 1.7. The precipitation deficits have been normalized by the yearly standard deviation to account for the dramatic changes in average precipitation across the region (see figure 1.1). Severe deficits occurred during this period across the mid-latitudes and subtropics of the entire region, except for parts of southern China. (This highlights the problem of averages for large countries such as China, which in this case has precipitation deficits that average to near zero for the country as a whole due to offsetting contributions from wet and dry regions.) Apart from Indochina, the severe precipitation deficits are well represented by the incidence of drought disaster for this recent period, from 1999–2001 (see figure 1.8).

Climate-Based Drought Estimates and Drought Disaster Reports

Persistent Precipitation Deficits

To look for severe and persistent events as they occur in the climate data, a tally may be kept of the number of consecutive months that precipitation deficits exceed a

Figure 1.7. Precipitation anomalies for the 1999-2001 period, divided by yearly standard deviation to facilitate comparison over diverse climate regimes

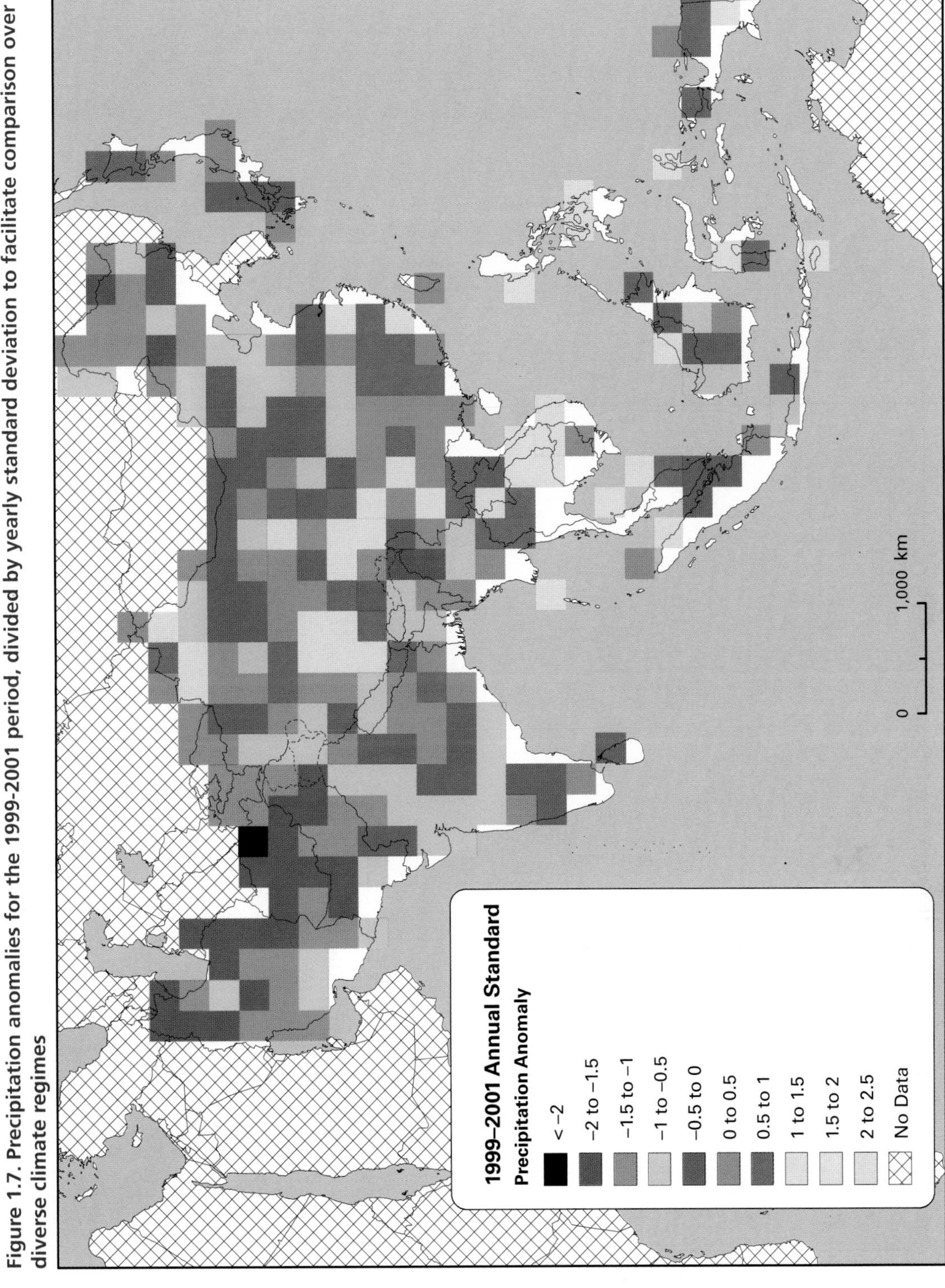

Figure 1.8. Reported drought disasters, 1999–2001

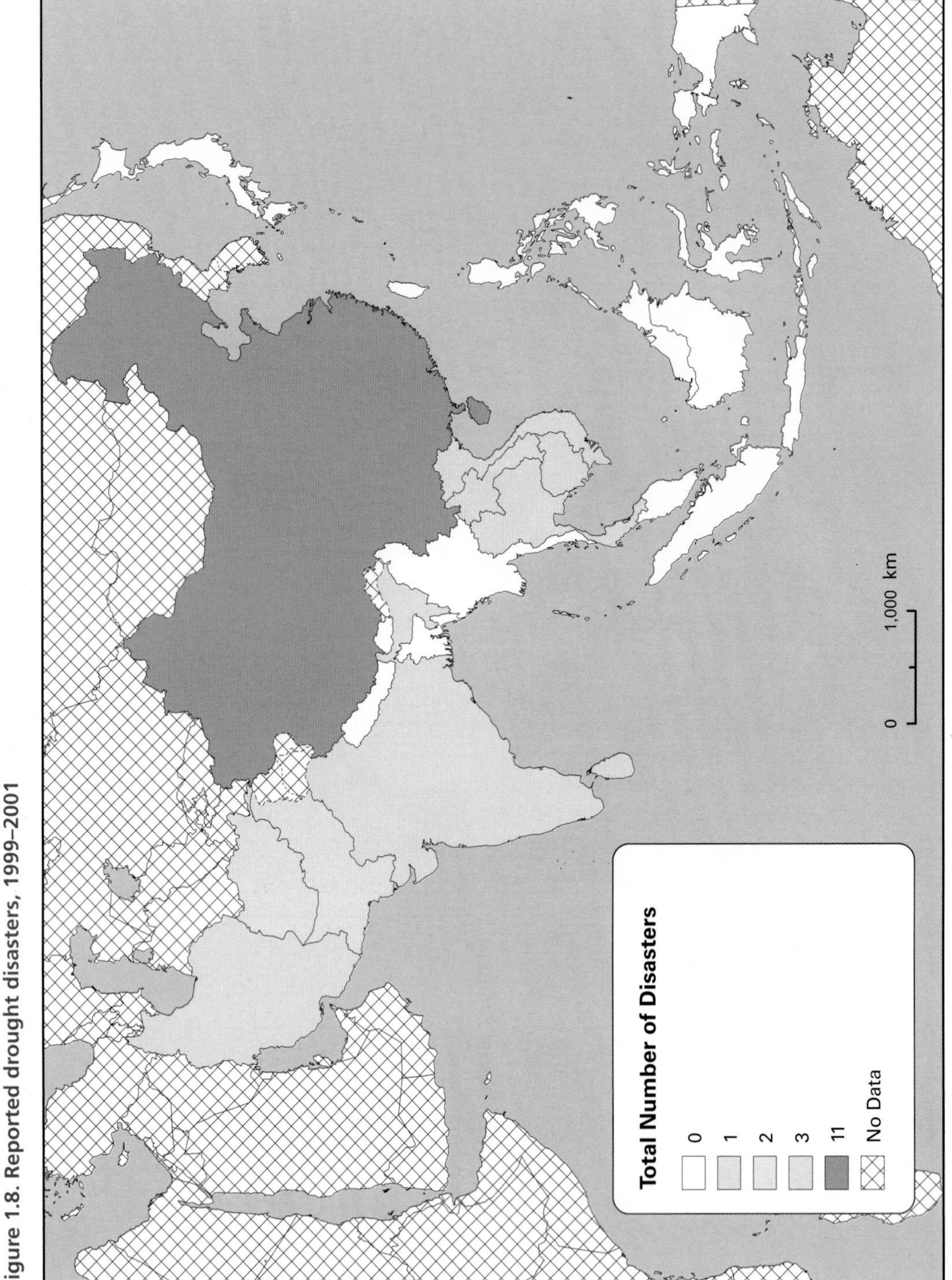

given threshold. As a starting point, we consider three variations in the calculation of persistent precipitation deficits. For each, the threshold is set to be 75 percent of median (by calendar month), while the number of months considered is variously taken to be 3, 6, and 4 out of 6. (See Annex 1.A for a description of this calculation.) These criteria are applied to the gridded precipitation data, and then averaged to the country level, necessitating the choice of another threshold, here taken to be the requirement that a minimum of 50 percent of the gridboxes within a country meet the criteria. Multiple instances of meeting the climate criteria within a single 12-month period are taken to represent a single climate event. For each observed climate event, the disaster reports are then searched to see if a disaster is reported within three months.

The precipitation data are from the Climate Prediction Center Merged Analysis of Precipitation (CMAP) (Xie and Arkin 1996, 1997), which began in 1979.

Figure 1.9 shows the number of matches (climate event and subsequent disaster report) and nonmatches (climate event but no disaster report) between the three-month criteria and the disaster reports. Several countries show matches, and both Afghanistan and Pakistan have matches with no nonmatches—that is, there is a one-to-one correspondence between climate events and reported drought disasters. The countries have been ordered left to right based on their average annual precipitation, and there is some suggestion that the matches are more frequent in the semiarid countries.

It is important to note that all the matches in the semiarid countries occur during the recent extended drought period (1999–2001), so it is difficult to assess the reproducibility of this relationship. However, this drought period encompasses 40 distinct drought disaster reports from 20 different countries that represent a diverse array of political, social, and economic conditions as well as a range of quality in climate data. So, the broad agreement even for a single drought period is likely to be meaningful.

The results for the six-month criteria are similar (with a smaller fraction of gridboxes required per country) and are not shown.

Figure 1.10 shows the results where deficits are required to meet the threshold in any four out of six consecutive months. Several more matches are present with little increase in nonmatches. It appears that the comparison works better in semiarid countries.

Weighted Anomaly of Standardized Precipitation

Main Findings

Another approach to estimating drought is to simply average the precipitation anomalies over a set number of months. In order to make such a calculation easier to interpret across different climate regimes and different seasons, the anomalies can be normalized and weighted according to the average local magnitude and seasonality. IRI uses the WASP for climate monitoring (see Annex 1.A for details of calculation). It is similar to another standard monitoring product, the SPI. Here, drought is identified in the climate data when the country average of the WASP is less than –1. As shown in figure 1.11, more than half the countries show a correspondence between 12-month WASP and drought disasters. The number of matches is compared with the total number of disaster reports (with a month specified) in figure 1.12. The climate drought estimate, based on the 12-month WASP, identifies all reported drought disasters for Israel, Afghanistan, Syria, Pakistan, Armenia, and Malaysia (seven matches total) while also generating 10 nonmatches (identified climatic drought without a corresponding disaster report).

Statistical analysis, conducted by taking the observed WASP-identified drought episodes, randomly shuffling them in time, and then recounting the matches with the disaster data, shows that in 1,000 random reshufflings the same number of matches (18) over all countries did not ever occur by chance. This is consistent with the relatively few number of months where the WASP threshold is exceeded and the relatively few number of months with a disaster report (one to two months for most of the countries) over the 276 months and 27 countries considered. Random matches are rare for each country (Afghanistan, for instance, would get two random matches only about 2 percent of the time), and the chances of randomly getting such matches in at least 14 of the 27 countries are highly unlikely (less than 1 in 1,000).

The WASP estimate picks up many of the same droughts as the PDP, but there are some differences as well; a more sophisticated analysis could refine the util-

Figure 1.9. Match between drought disaster and climatic measure of drought (3 consecutive months with precipitation deficits meeting a set threshold). Number of matches (climatic drought events with subsequent disaster) are in red and non-matches (climatic drought events with no subsequent disaster) are in yellow. Countries have been ordered left to right based on annual average precipitation (green line, in mm).

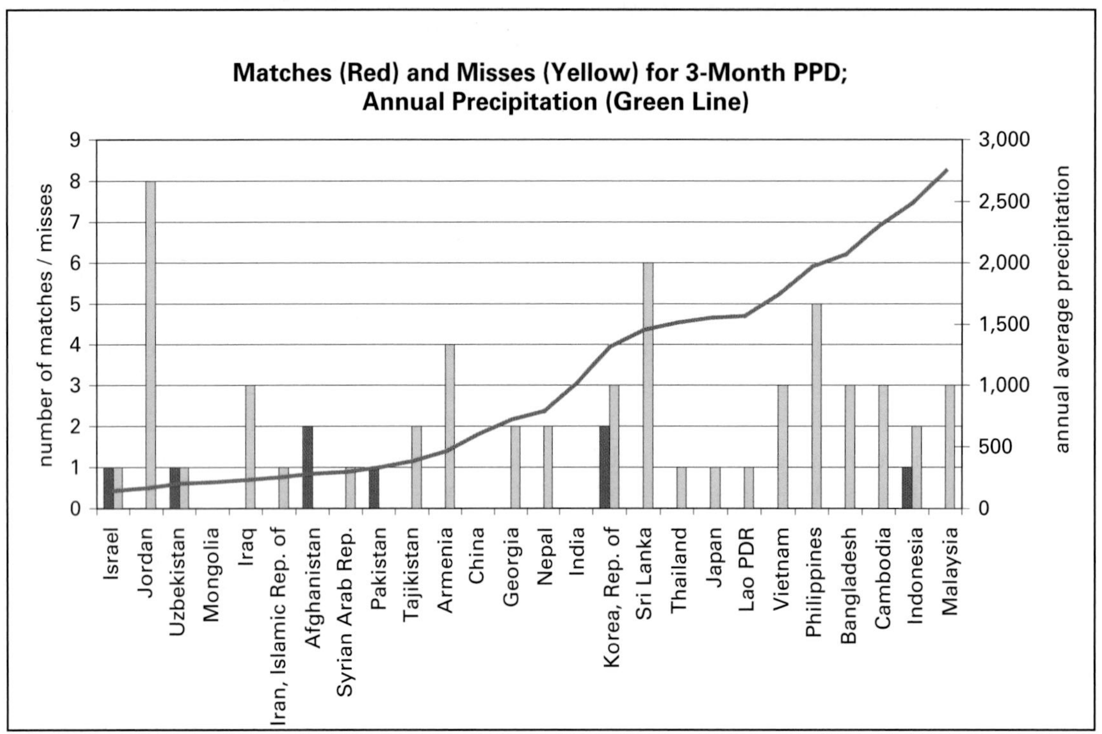

Figure 1.10. Match between drought disaster and climatic measure of drought (4 out of 6 months with precipitation deficits meeting a set threshold). Countries have been ordered left to right based on annual average precipitation (green line, in mm).

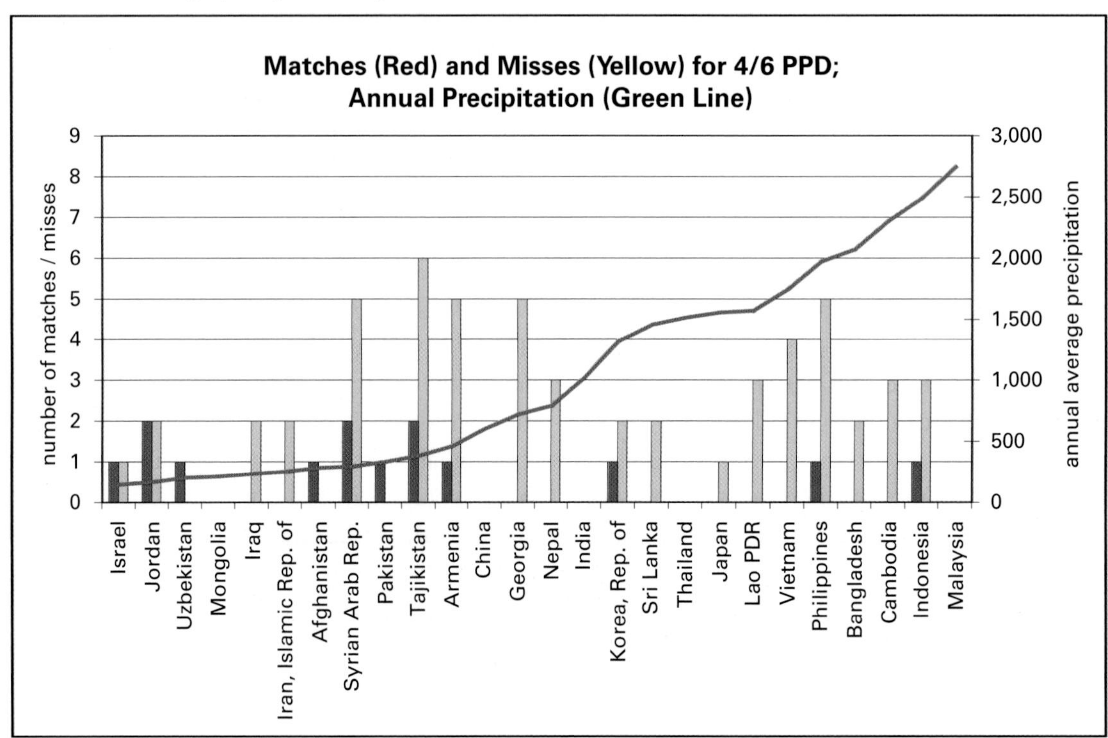

Figure 1.11. Match between drought disaster and climatic measure of drought (12-month average of Weighted Anomaly of Standardized Precipitation (WASP). Matches are in red, non-matches in yellow. Countries have been ordered left to right based on annual average precipitation (green line, in mm).

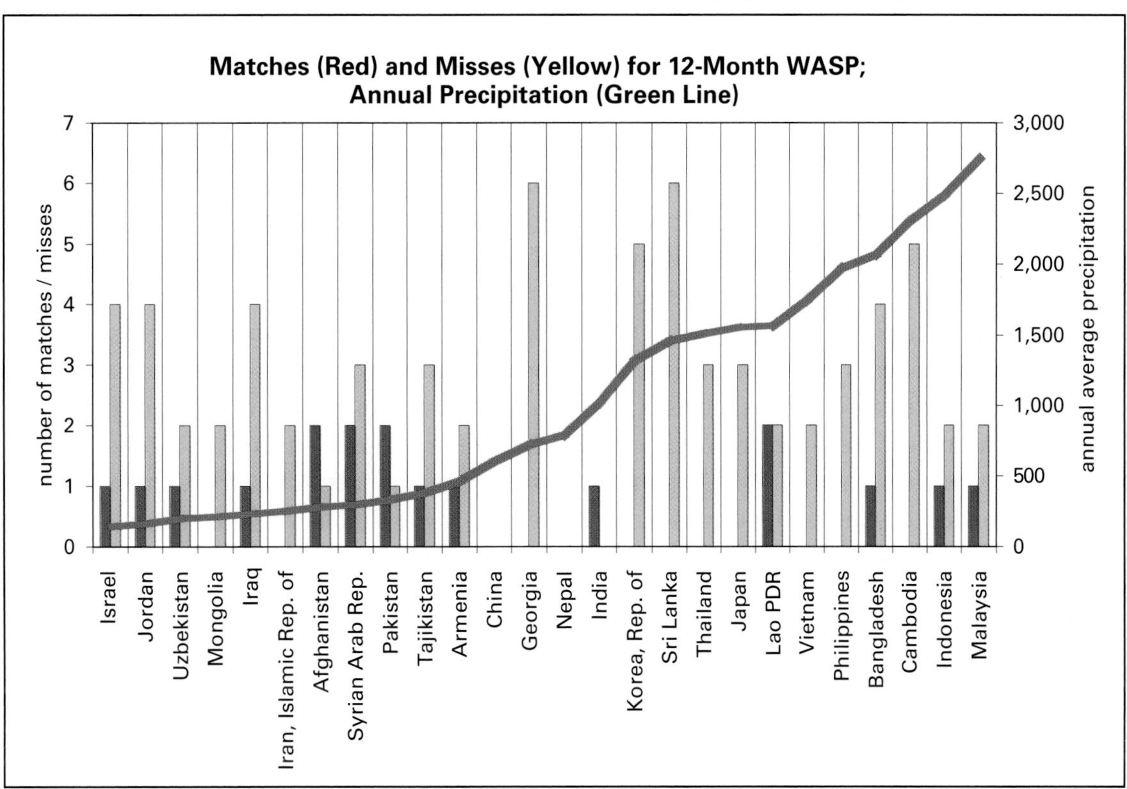

Figure 1.12. Number of matches for 12-month WASP compared to the total number of drought disaster reports (with monthly data). The scale is the same for both: Note that the 12-month WASP matches all 7 reported drought disasters for Israel, Afghanistan, Pakistan, Armenia, and Malaysia (with 10 non-matches for the same countries, cf. Figure 1.11).

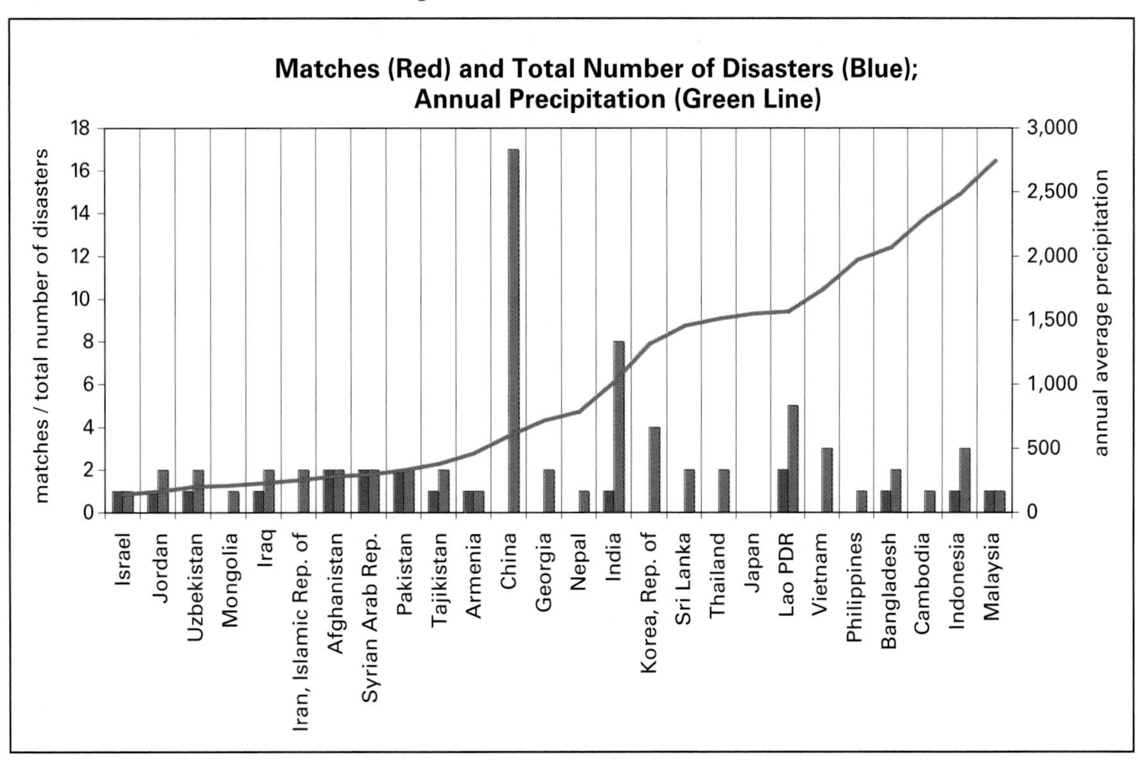

ity of multiple measures. Additionally, the behavior of the current estimates with different parameters (higher or lower thresholds, averaging periods) has not yet been explored.

The limitations of the precipitation data are also a concern. Here we have primarily used the Climate Prediction Center (CPC)'s Merged Analysis of Precipitation (CMAP) (Xie and Arkin 1996, 1997). To assess the effect of uncertainty in the precipitation data on the correspondence with the disaster, we have also calculated the 12-month WASP from the University of East Anglia's (UEA) 0.5x0.5 degree precipitation dataset (New et al. 2000) for the 1979–1995 period (the overlapping period with greatest underlying density of input stations in the UEA data). The correlation between the two WASP estimates is shown in figure 1.13. In the 1979–1995 period, the overall correspondence with disaster data is somewhat better with the CMAP-based data. However, the two data sources identify different disasters—the UEA-based data capture a disaster in both Nepal and Bangladesh, which the CMAP-based data do not. The chance of a random match for a given country is small but not insignificant, so such differences must be viewed with caution. It is possible that a careful analysis of the precipitation data, perhaps going back to the original station data, might provide a better drought estimate in data-scarce regions than any single gridded estimate.

Time Variations

To examine temporal variability more closely, the time series of the number of months the 12-month WASP exceeds the –1 threshold as well as the number of disaster reports is shown in figure 1.14 for the average over all Asian countries. In the climate data, both 1982–1983 and 1999–2000 are notable drought periods. There is a disaster maximum for both periods, but the latter is much larger. A vigorous El Niño (warm episode) dominated the global climate during the first period, while a vigorous La Niña (cold episode) strongly influenced the global climate during the later period, suggesting the possibility of large-scale patterns across the region for both periods. It should be noted that both El Niño and La Niña episodes deviated somewhat from their typical behavior, so extrapolation to future events is not straightforward. However, clear links between the Pacific climate and Asia precipitation have been documented for the La Niña event (Barlow et al. 2002; Hoerling and Kumar 2003; Tippett et al. 2003).

The 12-month WASP is shown in figure 1.15 for the two periods: in red for 1982–1983 and in blue for 1999–2000. As before, the countries are ranked based on average precipitation. In this region, average precipitation is closely related to latitude. A striking out-of-phase relationship is present between the two periods: in 1982–1983, the countries in the south and east of the region are dry, while the countries in the north and west are wet, and during 1999–2000 the reverse occurs. Although the climatic drought signal is large for both years, the disaster signal is less in 1982–1983, consistent with the weaker relationship between climatic drought and disaster incidence for the tropical countries. As a reminder, the current analysis is done with respect to the simple measure of incidence of drought disaster (whether a disaster is reported or not at the country level). In terms of population affected, for instance, the important events might be considerably different, depending to a large degree on what happens in only one or two countries, particularly in India.

Subregional Focus

We end with a brief consideration of specific countries. The Central-Southwest Asia countries are shown in figure 1.16 for both 12-month WASP (greens and browns) and the incidence of drought disasters (red bars). The large-scale, severe, persistent drought at the end of the record is clearly seen and has a good association with the disaster reports. While general drought analysis across multiple countries is important to identify appropriate monitoring and to forecast target variables, it should also be connected with much finer analysis. Uzbekistan, for instance, has a year of drought in 1986 that is similar in magnitude to the recent drought, yet is not associated with a disaster report. Is this due to a change in sociopolitical circumstances (independence from the former Soviet Union)? Problems in the precipitation data? Subcountry variations in the drought? Only one year of drought versus two? Lack of a drought this severe in neighboring countries affecting the regional economy? Consideration of this level of analysis in conjunction with the large-scale analysis would considerably improve both.

Figure 1.17 shows the same data for Laos and India. Both countries are particularly interesting as they show

Figure 1.13. Correlation between the 12-month WASP calculated from two different precipitation data sets: the University of East Anglia (UEA) precipitation data and the CPC's Merged Analysis of Precipitation (CMAP). The correlation is computed on the monthly data from Dec. 1979-Dec. 1995.

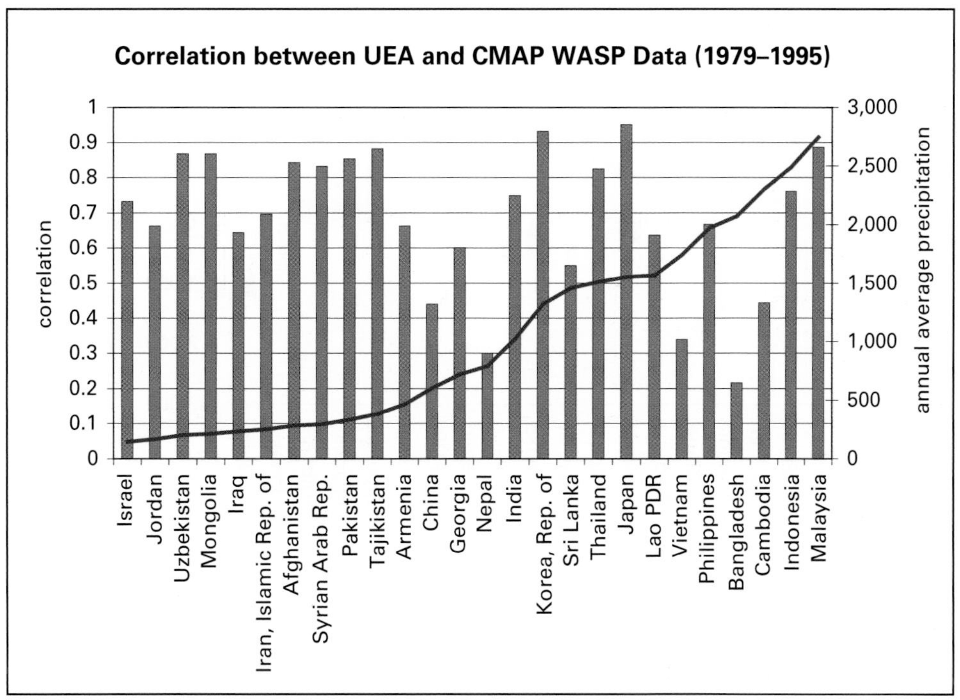

Figure 1.14. Time series of drought disasters and climatic drought events (based on 12-month WASP)

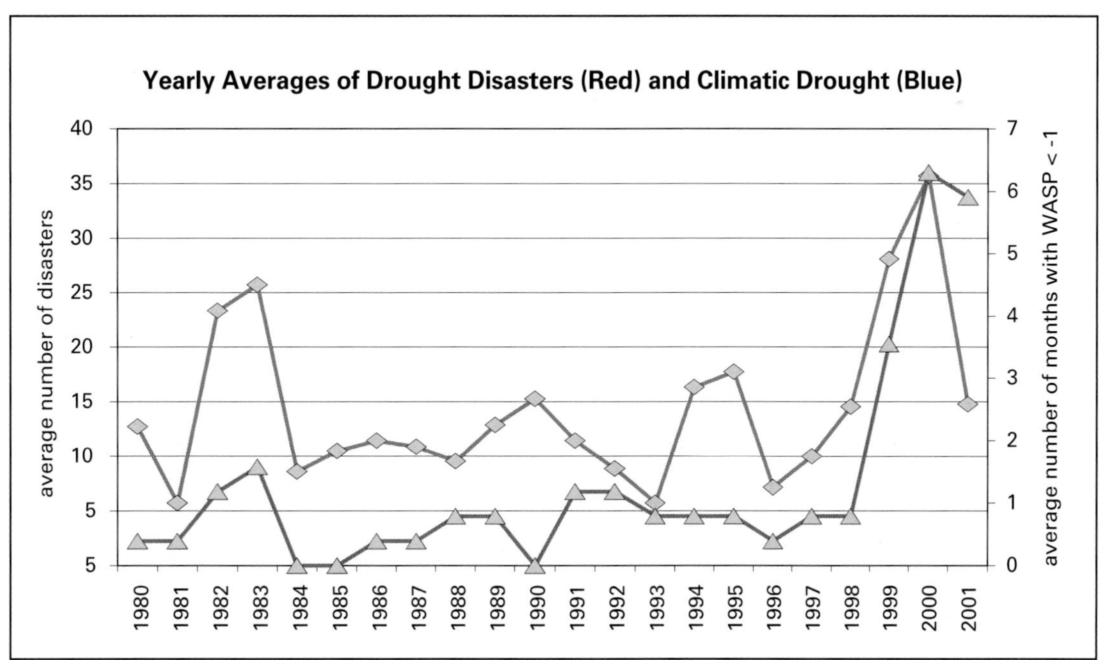

Figure 1.15. Climate anomalies (12-month WASP) for two periods: 1982-1983 (red) and 1999-2000 (blue)

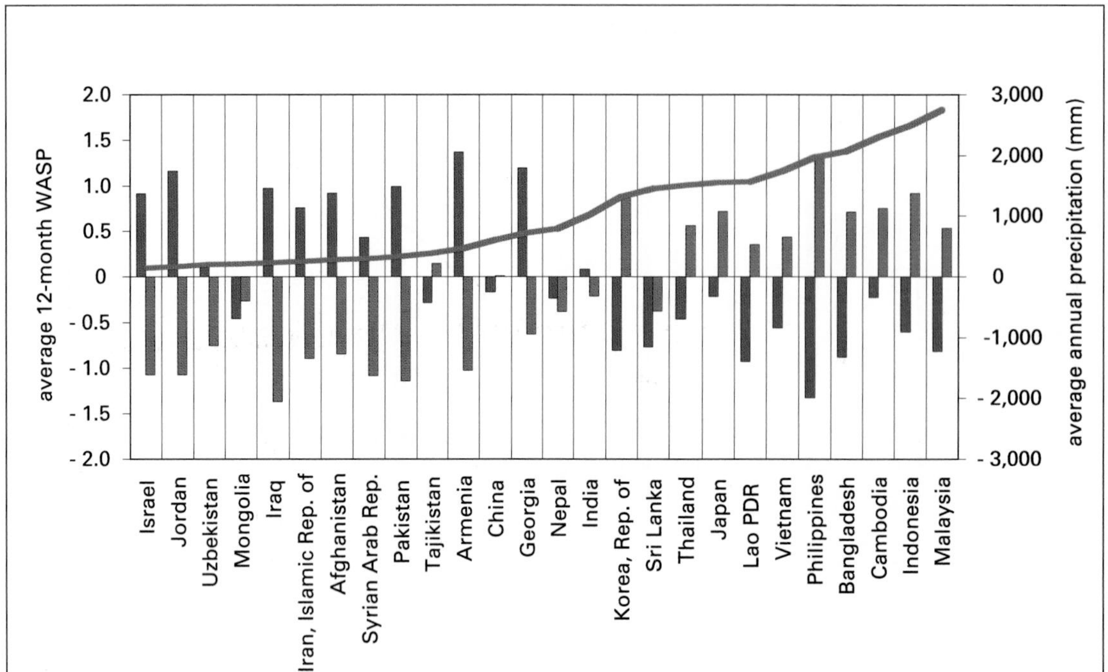

agreement between climatic drought and disaster incidence for several distinct events. India would benefit tremendously from higher resolution analysis—and, of course, there is a tremendous amount of information and analysis available for the country. Some province-level data are present in the EM-DAT data; for instance, Rajasthan is associated with several of the drought reports that show good agreement with the India-average WASP.

Developing a Drought Hazard Database

As noted in the introduction, a drought disaster is caused by the combination of both a climate hazard and a societal vulnerability. Using a climate-based estimate of drought that is shown to have a relationship with the occurrence of drought disasters, a collection of drought events based on the climate definition will constitute a database of drought hazard. As a preliminary step, such a database has been constructed from the results of the WASP analysis. For the countries that have a least one match between disaster report and WASP threshold, as described in the previous section, the starting and ending months for every period that meets the climate criteria are listed, along with a notation as to whether the climate drought event was associated with a disaster report. This database is intended only as a preliminary step, needs careful validation and an estimate of data error, and should be examined only with extreme caution.

As another preliminary step, climate data were added to the EM-DAT database for those drought disasters that could be identified as corresponding to the WASP-based drought estimate. A column was added that gives, for those cases, the largest value of the WASP estimate recorded over the current or previous three months to the disaster report. These data should also be considered only with extreme caution.

Common Features of Drought Disasters

Our preliminary results identify several recurring aspects of droughts associated with reported drought disasters:

- *Persistent and severe:* At the country level, precipitation deficits that are either less than 75 percent of

Figure 1.16. WASP estimate of climatic drought (shaded brown curve) and drought disaster declarations (red bars) for Central-Southwest Asia countries. Green shading indicates wet periods. The -1 threshold is shown as a black line.

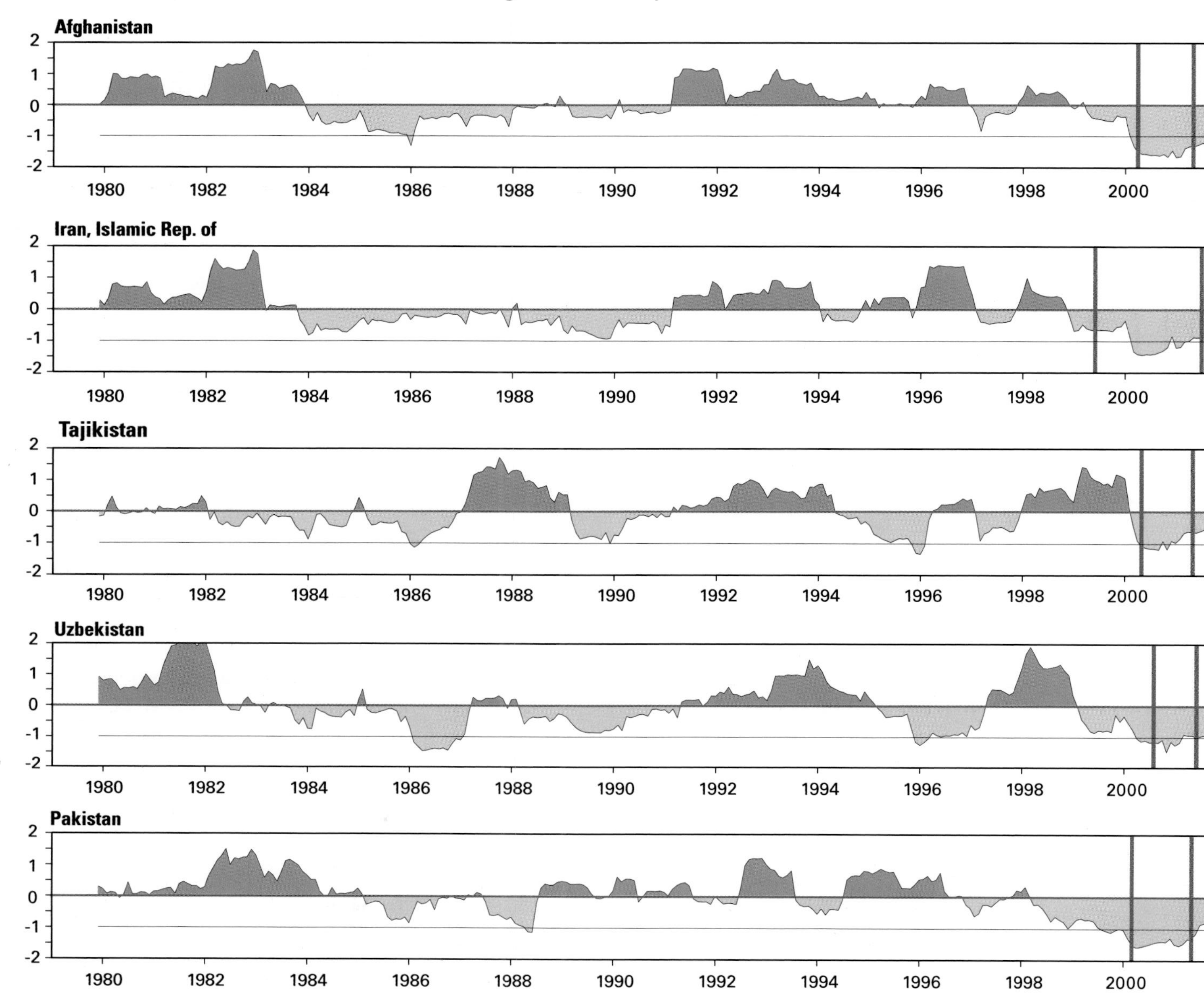

Figure 1.17. WASP estimate of climatic drought (shaded brown curve) and drought disaster declarations (red bars) for Laos and India. The -1 threshold is shown as a black line.

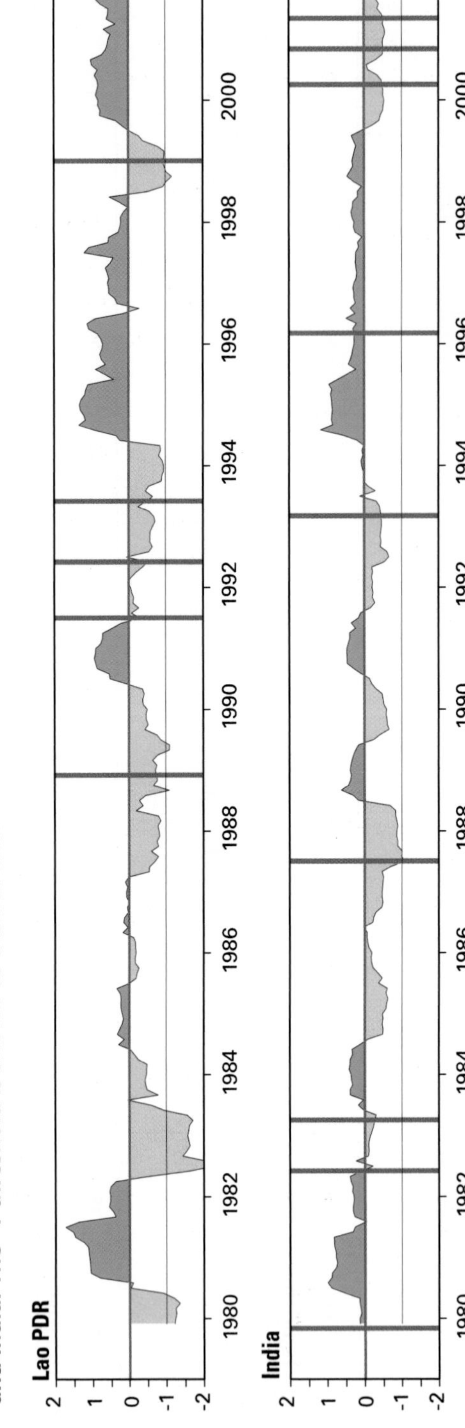

median for three consecutive months or have a WASP value of less than –1 in a 12-month average show a statistically significant association with the reported incidence of drought disaster.

- *Related to large-scale climate fluctuations:* The large number of drought disaster reports in 1999–2001 is closely related to widespread, severe climate anomalies.
- *Present in a range of climate regimes:* A normalized definition of climatic drought shows agreement with disaster reports across a wide geographic and climatic range (figure 1.11), from the semiarid mid-latitudes to the tropics, over a 15-fold range in mean annual precipitation (figure 1.1).
- *But apparently strongest in the semiarid countries:* The best association found in the current analysis is for countries with annual precipitation of less than 35 centimeters.

Although these features must be regarded as preliminary, particularly given the limitations of the data and the prominence of only two climate events, these features are not specific to Asia. The data from other regions of the world would provide an effective testing ground.

Summary

Drought disaster reports are compared with precipitation-based estimates of drought at the country level for the 27 countries listed in the Asia category in the EM-DAT database for the 1975–2001 period. The last three years of the record have, by far, the largest number of reports. This pronounced maximum appears not to be an artificial feature of EM-DAT reporting but rather physically linked to the exceptionally severe drought impacting Asia during that time.

An objective comparison was undertaken between the monthly disaster reports and two climate-based estimates of drought. Even at the country level, and with limited data, a relationship can be discerned between both climatic measures of drought and the incidence of drought disasters in the region. In fact, the climate drought estimate based on the 12-month WASP matches all reported drought disasters for Israel, Afghanistan, Syria, Pakistan, Armenia, and Malaysia, encompassing seven matches. Ten climatic droughts are also identified that do not have a corresponding disaster report (10 nonmatches). There is some suggestion that the relationship is stronger in the semiarid countries. The relationship is present in other climatic zones, however; Laos, for instance, shows a relationship over multiple events. This link between climatic drought and disaster reports is consistent through the two large climate events that affected the region during the period of analysis.

An understanding of the links between large-scale climate data and the incidence of disasters could enhance the utility of current climate monitoring and forecasting efforts. This pilot effort provides a preliminary identification of such links; further investigation is recommended, as outlined in the next section.

Recommendations

This preliminary analysis suggests a number of key extensions:

- *Subcountry analysis of Laos, Indonesia, Malaysia, and Bangladesh.* Based on the matches between climate disaster data, these countries are ideal targets for forging a link between large-scale analysis and local-scale data and expertise. The 1982–1983 El Niño event and seasonality are key issues.
- *Analysis of regions outside Asia.* These additional countries will allow further validation of the noted relationships, particularly in other semiarid countries and for the 1982–1983 versus 1999–2000 comparison. This is a natural extension of the current work, as the methodology, analysis tools, and datasets from the current analysis can be directly applied.
- *Investigation of other parameters in drought disaster reports.* Although this requires a large measure of caution, the other information (people killed, people affected, cost) should be assessed.
- *Assessment of the impacts of previous climatic droughts in Central-Southwest Asia.* Why are there no drought reports before the recent event in a region that comprises a wide range of sociopolitical situations?
- Consideration of other estimates of climatic drought

and precipitation station data. Other drought measures such as SPI, satellite-based vegetation indexes, and the PDSI should be included in the analysis. The parameter ranges of the estimates used here should also be explored more thoroughly. Comparing the results based on different precipitation datasets, particularly from station data only, rather than gridded data, would provide useful bounds on certainty in the climate data.

- *Consideration of supplementary impact data.* Crop failure is a frequent result of drought, and crop estimates, to the extent they are available, could provide a complementary set of data.
- *Regional vs. country-level analysis for China and India.* Given the often large discrepancy between the scale of a given country and that of climate variations (for example, drought) a closer examination of drought measures within specific, key regions of countries (for example, the North China Plain, Northwest India) would provide a necessary perspective on the country-level analysis.

References

Agrawala, S., et al. 2001. The Drought and Humanitarian Crisis in Central and Southwest Asia: A Climate Perspective. IRI Special Report 01-11:24.

Barlow, M., H. Cullen, and B. Lyon. 2002. Drought in Central and Southwest Asia: La Niña, the Warm Pool, and Indian Ocean Precipitation. *Journal of Climate* 15: 697–700.

Hoerling, M., and A. Kumar. 2003. The Perfect Ocean for Drought. *Science* 299: 691–94.

Lautze, S., et al. Qaht-e-Pool "A Cash Famine": Food Insecurity in Afghanistan, 1999–2002. Washington, DC: The United States Agency for International Development. Medford, MA: The Feinstein International Famine Center.

New, M., M. Hulme, and P. D. Jones. 2000. Representing Twentieth Century Space-Time Climate Variability. Part 2: Development of 1901–96 Monthly Grids of Terrestrial Surface Climate. *Journal of Climate* 13: 2217–38.

Tippett, M. K., M. Barlow, and B. Lyon. 2003. Statistical Correction of Central Southwest Asia Winter Precipitation Simulations. *International Journal of Climatology* 23: 1421–33.

Xie, P., and P. Arkin. 1996. Analyses of Global Monthly Precipitation Using Gauge Observations, Satellite Estimates, and

Figure 1.A.1. Persistent deficit of precipitation

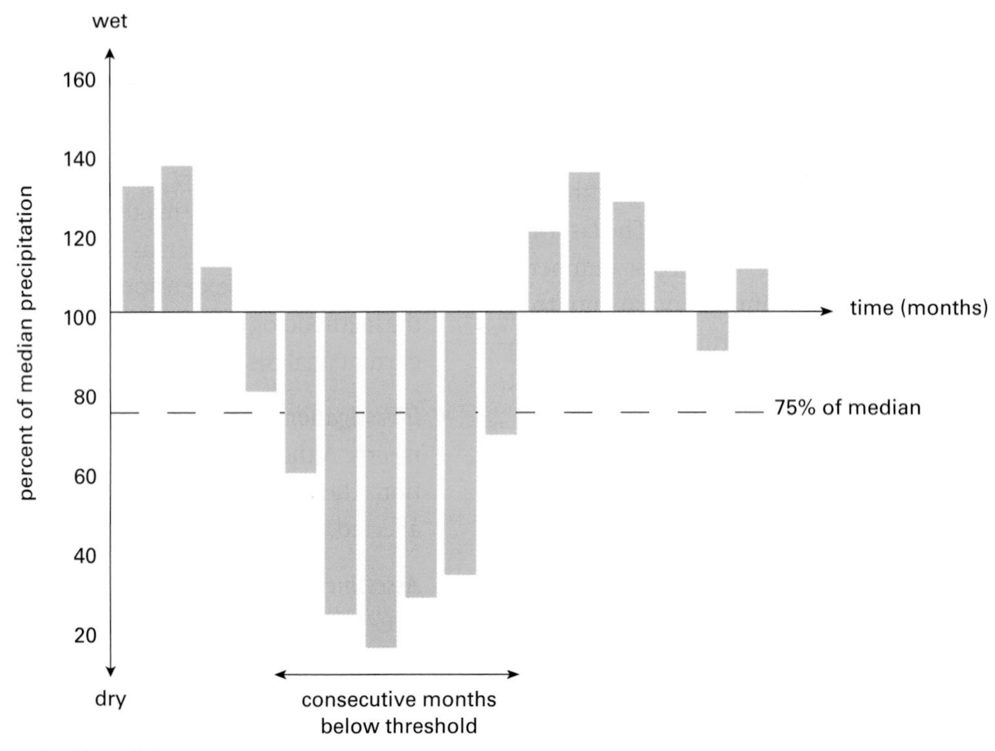

Source: Brad Lyon, IRI

Numerical Model Predictions. *Journal of Climate* 9: 840–58.

Xie, P., and P. Arkin. 1997. Global Precipitation: A 17-Year Monthly Analysis Based on Gauge Observations, Satellite Estimates and Numerical Model Outputs. *Bulletin of the American Meteorological Society* 78: 2539–58.

Annex 1.A

Description of climate-based measures of drought Persistent Deficit of Precipitation (PDP)

This index measures the persistence of monthly precipitation deficits for a given location. A deficit is defined to occur when the observed monthly-average precipitation falls below the long-term median value at a given location. Variations of this index measure the number of consecutive months that the observed precipitation falls below different thresholds (percent of median). For example, thresholds used in the study include 75 percent of median for 3 and 6 consecutive months and 75 percent of median for any 4 out of 6 consecutive months. A schematic of the method is shown below.

The Weighted Anomaly Standardized Precipitation Index (WASP)

This index was developed at the IRI as a simple, single-variable index to measure the relative surplus or deficit of precipitation on different time scales. The index is based solely on monthly precipitation but requires historical data (for at least a 25-year period) as well. The basic idea in standardizing (by the appropriate monthly standard deviation) the data is to compare regions with different precipitation climatologies on a single map (for example, a 25-mm monthly precipitation anomaly may be relatively small for some regions but quite large for others). The standardized precipitation anomalies are weighted according to the annual cycle of precipitation at a given location based on average monthly precipitation values. This weighting reduces the tendency for standardized precipitation measures to become artificially magnified at the start or end of the rainy season where there are distinct dry and wet seasons. The standardized, weighted anomalies are summed over different periods of interest; at the IRI, WASP analyses are routinely produced for the most recent 3-, 6-, 9-, and 12-month periods.

The mathematical definition of the version of the index used in the study is described below.

$$WASP_N = \frac{12}{\sigma_N} \cdot \sum_{i=1}^{N} \left(\frac{P_i - \overline{P}_i}{\sigma_i} \cdot \frac{\overline{P}_i}{\overline{P}_A} \right)$$

Where,

$WASP_N$ = the N-month WASP, where N is the number of months (here, 12) over which the standardized, weighted anomalies have been integrated;

σ_N = the standard deviation of the N-month WASP over the historical record for the last month in the integration;

P_i = the observed precipitation for month i;

$\overline{P}_i$ = the monthly climatological precipitation for month i;

σ_i = the monthly standard deviation in precipitation for month i; and

P_A = the average annual precipitation.

Chapter 2

Global Landslides Risk Case Study

Farrokh Nadim, Oddvar Kjekstad, Ulrik Domaas, Ramez Rafat, and Pascal Peduzzi

Background

The main objective of this study is to perform a data-based, first-order identification of geographic areas that form the global landslide risk disaster hotspots on an international scale, with the main emphasis on developing countries. This includes combining the identified hazard and vulnerability, for people and infrastructure, to determine risk. The probability of landslide occurrence is estimated from modeling of physical processes combined with statistics from past experience. The main input data for the assessment of landslide hazard are topography and slope angles, precipitation, seismic activity, soil type, hydrological condition, and vegetation. Vulnerability mainly depends on socioeconomic factors (population density, quality of infrastructure, collective organization) and the response capacity (prevention, capacity of aid intervention, and mitigation). The vulnerability evaluation was performed in close cooperation with United Nations Environment Programme (UNEP)/GRID-Geneva.

General Approach and Terminology

Definitions of hazard, vulnerability, and risk have evolved during the last few years. In this study, we use the terminology adopted by United Nations International Strategy for Disaster Reduction (UN/ISDR) (http://www.unisdr.org/eng/library/lib-terminology-eng%20home.htm).

Hazard	A potentially damaging physical event, phenomenon, and/or human activity that may cause the loss of life or injury, property damage, social and economic disruption, or environmental degradation. *Hazards can include latent conditions that may represent future threats and can have different origins: natural (geological, hydro-meteorological, and biological) and/or induced by human processes (environmental degradation and technological hazards). Hazards can be single, sequential, or combined in their origin and effects. Each hazard is characterized by its location, intensity, frequency, and probability.*
Geological hazard (geohazard)	Natural earth process or phenomenon that may cause the loss of life or injury, property damage, social and economic disruption, or environmental degradation. *Geological hazards include internal earth processes of tectonic origin, such as earthquakes, geological fault activity, tsunamis, volcanic activity and emissions, as well as external processes such as mass movements (landslides, rockslides, rockfalls or avalanches, surface collapses, and debris and mudflows).*
Hazard analysis	Identification, studies, and monitoring of any hazard to determine its potential, origin, characteristics, and behavior.

Hazard occurrence probability	Probability of occurrence of a specified natural hazard at a specified severity level in a specified future time period.
Risk	The probability of harmful consequences, or expected losses (deaths, injuries, property, livelihoods, economic activity disrupted, or environment damaged) resulting from interactions between natural or human-induced hazards and vulnerable conditions. Conventionally, risk is expressed by the notation Risk = Hazard x Vulnerability.
Elements at risk	Inventory of people, houses, roads or other infrastructure that are exposed to the hazard.
Risk assessment/ analysis	A process to determine the nature and extent of risk by analyzing potential hazards and evaluating existing conditions of vulnerability that could pose a potential threat or harm to people, property, livelihoods, and the environment on which they depend. *The process of conducting a risk assessment is based on a review of both of the following: the technical features of hazards such as their location, intensity, frequency, and probability; and an analysis of the physical, social, economic, and environmental dimensions of vulnerability. The risk assessment does so while taking into particular account the coping capabilities pertinent to the risk scenarios.*
Vulnerability	A set of conditions and processes resulting from physical, social, economic, and environmental factors that increase the susceptibility of a community to the impact of hazards. Also the degree of loss to an element at risk should a hazard of a given severity occur.

The present study focuses on rapid mass movements, like rockslides, debris flows, snow avalanches, and rainfall- and earthquake-induced slides.

The general approach adopted in the present study, for the evaluation of global landslide hazard-prone areas and risk hotspots, is depicted in figure 2.1.

General Approach for Landslide Hazard Evaluation

Landslide hazard level depends on a combination of trigger and susceptibility. In the first-pass estimate of landslide hazard, five parameters are used:

1. slope factor within a selected grid (S_r);
2. lithological (or geological) conditions (S_l);
3. soil moisture condition (S_h);
4. precipitation factor (T_p); and,
5. seismic conditions (T_s).

General Approach for Snow Avalanche Hazard Evaluation

The susceptibility to snow avalanche is derived from the combination of all avalanche formation parameters, namely, terrain slope, precipitation, and temperature. These parameters are integrated to form grid maps with pixel values through Geographical Information System (GIS) analyses. The corresponding probability of occurrence is found from statistical analyses of weather information for single grid cells, to obtain a return period of the events based on precipitation. The probability may then be extrapolated globally. The product of probability and susceptibility determines the hazard value for each grid cell. The initial prediction of the avalanche hazard uses three parameters:

1. slope within a selected grid (S_r);
2. precipitation values for four winter months (T_p); and,
3. temperature values (T_t).

The landslide/avalanche models were validated and refined on the basis of historical data, through selected

Figure 2.1. General approach for landslide hazard and risk evaluation

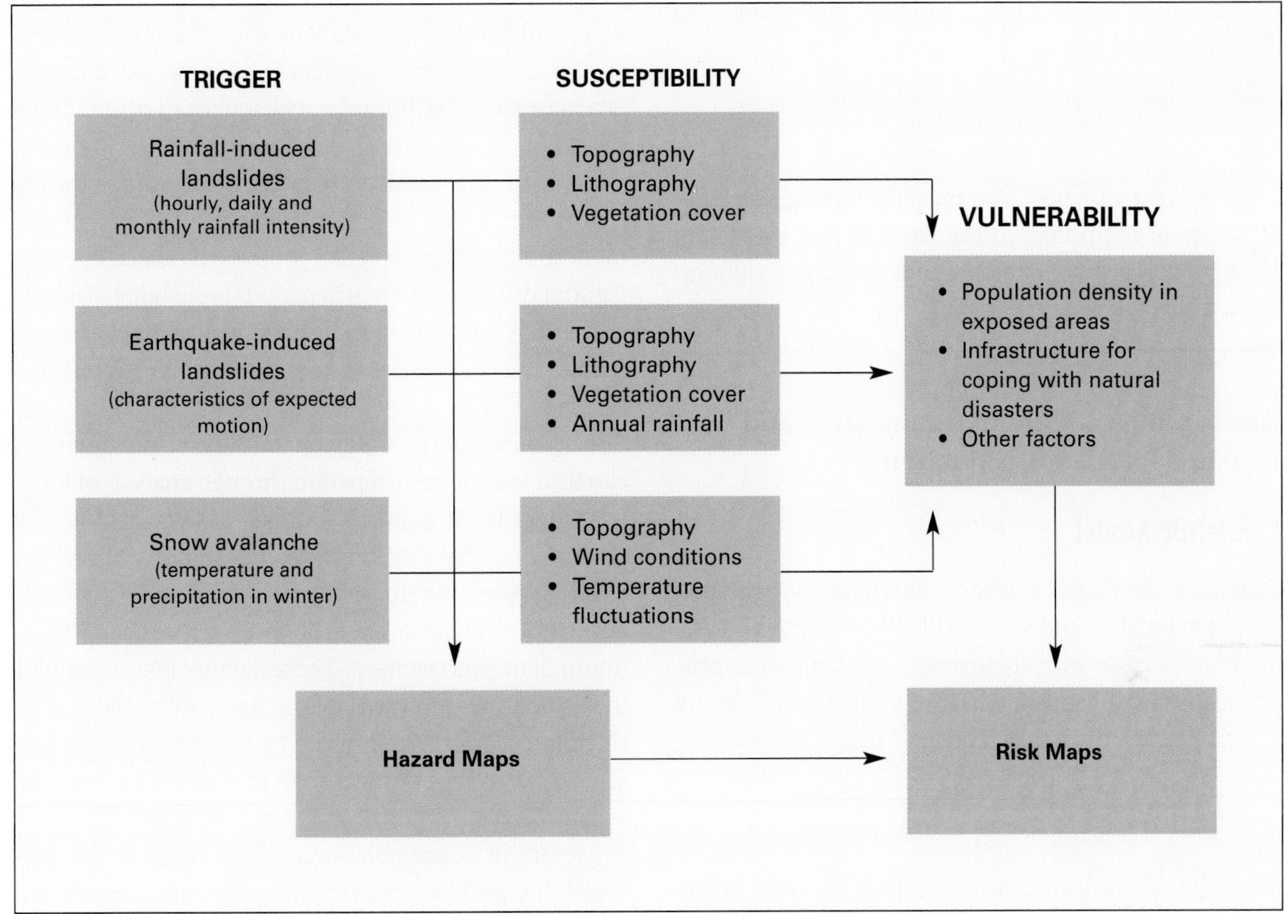

national case studies in Norway, Armenia, Nepal, Georgia, Sri Lanka, and Jamaica.

Approach for Vulnerability and Risk Assessment

The landslide vulnerability and risk assessment has been performed by UNEP/GRID in Geneva, following the approach of the recent UNDP World Vulnerability Report. Based on the UN definition (UN Disaster Relief Coordinator [UNDRO] 1979), risk is determined by three components: hazard occurrence probability, elements at risk, and vulnerability (see definitions above).

For risk estimation, the computation is based on human losses as recorded by various natural disaster impact databases. The estimation of expected losses is achieved by first combining frequency and population exposed, in order to provide the physical exposure, and then performing a regression analysis using different sets of uncorrelated socioeconomic parameters in order to identify the best indicators of human vulnerability for a selected hazard in a given country. According to the UNDRO definition, a formula for estimating the risk can then be derived as follows:

$$R = H \cdot Pop \cdot Vul$$

Where:

- R = Risk, that is, the number of expected human impacts (killed);
- H = Annual hazard occurrence probability;
- Pop = Population living in a given exposed area; and
- Vul = Vulnerability, depends on socio-politico-economic context.

Defining physical exposure (*PhExp*) as the annual frequency of a hazard with specified severity multiplied by the number of persons exposed ($PhExp = H \cdot Pop$), the risk can be evaluated by logarithmic regression using the following formula:

$$\ln(R) = \ln(PhExp) + \ln(Vul)$$

In the case of landslides, once the average physical exposure is computed on the basis of past events, an estimate of risk can be made using a proxy of vulnerability.

Description of Model for Landslide and Avalanche Hazard Evaluation

Landslide Model

The model developed for the study is based on a method proposed by Mora and Vahrson (1994). The method was modified for use with the datasets available for global application. The landslide hazard level H is defined by a combination of susceptibility and triggering factors:

$$H = SUSC * TRIG$$

where "SUSC" is the intrinsic susceptibility factor determined from a combination of slope factor "S_r," lithology (bedrock geology) factor "S_l" and relative soil moisture factor "S_h"; and "TRIG," which represents the triggering factor that initiates rapid movement and its probability of occurrence, is determined from a combination of seismic activity indicator "T_s" and precipitation (rainfall) indicator "T_p."

For each factor, an index of influence is determined by a reference value through a specific weighting (a weight of 1 for all factors was used in the first-pass analysis). Multiplying and summing these indexes determines the relative landslide hazard level $H_{landslide}$, given by:

$$H_{landslide} = (S_r * S_l * S_h) * (T_s + T_p)$$

The range for each parameter in the above equation is discussed in the section on "Sources of Data and Data Processing Procedures" below.

Model for Snow Avalanche Hazard

Any model for snow avalanche should include parameters describing the terrain and the snow. Steep terrain is a necessary condition for avalanches to occur. Snow cover conditions during the winter, snow precipitation, wind conditions, and temperature development during a storm can result in snow avalanches. The magnitude of these different parameters controls the avalanche size, run-out distance, and return period (probability of occurrence). It is difficult to produce a global avalanche hazard map based on all these factors, so simplifications must be made.

The probability of a given amount of precipitation can be related to return period through analysis of long-term data from weather stations. However, due to a paucity of global data from weather stations, this is not feasible. Available information is restricted to average annual precipitation, monthly precipitation, and maximum daily precipitation. These data are insufficient for the estimation of return periods and probabilities. The calculation of probability can be avoided through calibration of a susceptibility map in countries where the avalanche history has been known for many centuries. Therefore, it is possible to combine some of the susceptibility grid values to the known consequences and return periods. The estimated return periods for a number of locations in a country with long-standing records may then be used to estimate the probability for avalanches in other areas.

A specific weight was assigned to each factor in the avalanche model. Multiplying and summing these indexes determines a relative avalanche hazard level $H_{avalanche}$, given by:

$$H_{avalanche} = (S_r*0.4 + T_p*0.4 + T_t*0.2)*F$$

where "S_r" is the slope factor, "T_p" is a factor that depends on precipitation for four winter months, "Tt" is the temperature factor, and "F" is a factor that depends on the average temperature in winter months (F = 0 if average monthly temperature in winter months > 2.5°C; F = 1 otherwise).

Description of Model for Vulnerability and Risk Assessment

The vulnerability and risk model is based on a raster approach. Details of the model are provided in Annex 2.A. A raster file depicts the average frequency of landslides (resolution/frequency/area). In general terms, the spatial resolution (pixel size) should be as detailed as possible, taking into consideration the quality of input data.

The content of the pixel should represent either:

- The average frequency of occurrence and the average area of landslide in the pixel (if different from the pixel area). The unit of landslide area in this study is approximately 1 km^2; or
- A range of frequencies can be provided to reflect uncertainty. In this case, the average frequency is used in the Base Case calculation, and the difference between min. and max. frequencies is used for the computation of error margins.

Note that the probability of occurrence (such as 50 percent probability of occurrence in the next 100 years) is transformed into annual frequency by assuming that the hazard occurrence follows Poisson's law, and therefore:

$$E(x) = \lambda = -\ln(1 - P(x \geq 1))\geq$$

Where:

$E(x)$ = "Statistical expectance," that is the average number per year = λ; and

$P(x)$ = Probability of occurrence.

Information on class of severity, type of landslide (for example, avalanche, rockfall, mudflow, debris slide, and so on), potential intensity/magnitude could also be added to the content of the pixel, although it is not needed for purposes of analysis.

Identification of Vulnerability in Socioeconomic Context

Once the raster grid of frequencies is established, the resulting dataset is multiplied by the population dataset. The product is aggregated, at the national level, in order to obtain the average number of persons exposed per year. Historic records of casualties are then compared with this measure of physical exposure and with a series of national socioeconomic parameters that have been previously transformed and standardized. A logarithmic regression is then performed to identify which socioeconomic parameters are best linked with number of casualties. Coefficients (weights) are also associated with the different components of the expression:

$$K = C \cdot (PhExp_{landslides})^{a} \cdot V_1^{a_1} \cdot V_2^{a_2} \ldots \cdot V_p^{a_p}$$

Where:

K = Number of persons killed by a certain type of hazard;

C = Constant;

$PhExp$= Physical exposure (population living in exposed areas multiplied by the frequency of occurrence of the landslides);

V_i = Socioeconomic parameters; and

α_i = Exponent of V_i, which can be negative (for ratio).

This approach enables one to test the quality of the link between socioeconomic parameters and physical exposure as factors explaining casualties for a given hazard. It also provides useful information on what con-

Table 2.1. Description of variables

Information (values)	
X*:	Longitude of pixel center.
Y*:	Latitude of pixel center.
Area*:	Measure of area affected by landslide within the pixel (either in km^2 or in percentage of pixel surface).
Frequency*:	Average number of landslides per year.
Min. frequency:	Minimum value for the frequency range.
Max. frequency:	Maximum value for the frequency range.
Landslide type:	Numerical code for avalanche, mudflow, rockfall, and so on.
Severity class:	Numerical code for class of severity, otherwise anticipated magnitude or intensity.

* Required information for vulnerability analysis

ditions both increase the susceptibility and induce greater vulnerability in a society.

Computation of Vulnerability Proxy and Identification of Population at Risk

The approach described above is qualitative and should not be used as a predictive tool. A more quantitative approach involves computing a proxy of vulnerability. This proxy is based on the ratio between the number of people killed and the number of persons exposed, given by:

$$Vul^{a}_{proxy} = \frac{K^{\beta}}{PhExp^{\delta}}$$

Where:

Vul = Vulnerability proxy;
K = Past casualties as recorded in CRED; and
$PhExp$ = Physical exposure.

Once the vulnerability proxy is computed, it is multiplied by the physical exposure to produce a risk map on a pixel-by-pixel basis. This method is, however, a generalized approach that cannot take into account the significant vulnerability differences between a rural and urban population. This limitation can only be overcome through use of subnational datasets on socioeconomic features and on geo-referenced information on the number of casualties. Such an analysis would also require more records than would the analysis of average vulnerability derived from the national-level values.

Sources of Data and Data Processing Procedures

Landslides

As mentioned earlier, a simplified model, similar to that proposed by Mora and Vahrson (1994), was adopted for the study. In this model, the relative landslide hazard level $H_{landslide}$ is estimated through the following equation:

$$H_{landslide} = (S_r * S_l * S_h) * (T_s + T_p)$$

Considerations influencing the estimation of parameters are described below.

Estimation of slope factor S_r

The slope factor represents the natural landscape ruggedness within a grid unit.

Source: Global elevation dataset SRTM30 from ISciences.

Web site: http://www.isciences.com/

Description

In February 2000, NASA collected elevation data for much of the world using a radar instrument aboard the space shuttle that orbited the earth. Raw data have been processed over the past three years. NASA has now released a global elevation dataset called SRTM30, referring to the name of the mission and the resolution of the data, which is 30 arc-seconds, or approximately 1 km^2 per data sample near the equator. The SRTM30 dataset is NASA's latest achievement in improving the quality of digital elevation data available for public use. The data cover a range from 60 degrees south latitude to 60 degrees north latitude.

Classification

Slope data are reclassified on a geographical grid (WGS84). Cells are distributed in five different categories (0–4), as follows:

Table 2.2. Classification of slope factor "S_r" for evaluation of susceptibility

Range of slopes angle (unit: degrees)	*Classification*	S_r
00–01	Very low	0
01–08	Low	1
08–16	Moderate	2
16–32	Medium	3
32–75	High–very high	4

Note: S_r is set equal to zero for slope angles less than 1° (that is, for flat or nearly flat areas), because the resulting landslide hazard is null even if the other factors are favorable.

Estimation of lithology factor S_l

This is probably the most important factor and the most difficult to assess. Ideally, detailed geotechnical information should be used, but, at the global scale, only a general geological description is available. Rock strength and fracturing are the most important factors used to evaluate lithological characteristics. Since fracturing may occur in most rock types and is a local feature, the rock strength will be the most important factor on a global scale.

Source: Geological map of the World at 1/25,000,000 scale published by the Commission for the Geological Map of the World and UNESCO (2000). The map is available on a CD-ROM.

Description

This map is the first geological document compiled at a global scale showing the geology of the whole planet, including continents and oceans. In the map, three main types of formation are identified: sedimentary rocks, extrusive volcanic rocks, and endogenous rocks (plutonic or strongly metamorphosed).

Classification

Five susceptibility classes have been identified. Usually old rocks are stronger than young rocks. Plutonic rocks will usually be strong and represent low risk. Strength of metamorphic rocks is variable, but these rocks often have planar structures such as foliation and therefore may represent higher risk than plutonic rocks. Lava rocks will usually be strong, but may be associated with tuff (weak material). Therefore, areas with recent volcanism are classified as high risk. Sedimentary rocks are often very weak, especially young ones. The susceptibility classes are shown in table 2.3.

Estimation of soil moisture factor S_h

S_h is a soil moisture index, which indicates the mean humidity throughout the year and gives an indication of the state of the soil prior to heavy rainfall and possible destabilization.

Source: Data are extracted from Willmott and Feddema's Moisture Index Archive. They are produced and documented by Cort J. Willmott and Kenji Matsuura, at the Center for Climatic Research, Department of Geography, University of Delaware, Newark, USA.

Web site: http://climate.geog.udel.edu/~climate/html_pages/README.im2.html

Description

Data cover the standard meteorological period 1961–1990. Resolution of the grid is 0.5, 0.5 degrees. The gridded, mean monthly, total potential evapotranspiration (Eo) and unadjusted total precipitation (P) are taken from:

- Terrestrial Water Balance Data Archive: regridded monthly climatologies, and
- Terrestrial Air Temperature, monthly precipitation, and annual climatologies.

These data can be downloaded from the Web site. Estimates of the average-monthly moisture indexes for Eo and P are determined only for land-surface grid points. There are 85,794 points. Average-monthly mois-

Table 2.3. Classification of lithology factor "S_l" for evaluation of susceptibility

Lithology and stratigraphy	*Susceptibility*	*S_l*
• Extrusive volcanic rocks—Precambrian, Proterozoic, Paleozoic, Archean.	Low	1
• Endogenous rocks (plutonic and/or metamorphic)—Precambrian, Proterozoic, Paleozoic and Archean.		
• Old sedimentary rocks—Precambrian, Archean, Proterozoic, Paleozoic.	Moderate	2
• Extrusive volcanic rocks—Paleozoic, Mesozoic.		
• Endogenous rocks—Paleozoic, Mesozoic, Triassic, Jurassic, Cretaceous.		
• Sedimentary rocks—Paleozoic, Mesozoic, Triassic, Jurassic, Cretaceous.	Medium	3
• Extrusive volcanic rocks—Mesozoic, Triassic, Jurassic, Cretaceous.		
• Endogenous rocks—Meso-Cenozoic, Cenozoic.		
• Sedimentary rocks—Cenozoic, Quaternary.	High	4
• Extrusive volcanic rocks—Meso-Cenozoic.		
• Extrusive volcanic rocks—Cenozoic.	Very high	5

ture indexes are calculated according to Willmott and Feddema (1992) using the gridded average-monthly total Eo and P values, at the same resolution as the water-balance fields.

Classification

Five classes for soil moisture index are determined as shown in table 2.4.

Table 2.4. Classification of soil moisture factor "S_h" for evaluation of susceptibility

Soil moisture index (Willmott and Feddema 2002)	Susceptibility	S_h
-1.0 → -0.6	Low	1
-0.6 → -0.2	Moderate	2
-0.2 → +0.2	Medium	3
+0.2 → +0.6	High	4
+0.6 → +1.0	Very high	5

The map of the global soil moisture index is shown in figure 2.2.

Estimation of precipitation trigger factor T_p

Estimation of T_p is based on the 100-year extreme monthly rainfall.

Source: Monthly precipitation time series (1986–2003) from the Global Precipitation Climatology Centre (GPCC), run by Germany's National Meteorological Service (DWD).

Web site: http://www.seismo.ethz.ch/GSHAP
http://gpcc.dwd.de

Description

DWD is a German contribution to the World Climate Research Program and to the Global Climate Observing System. The data used are near real-time monitoring products based on the internationally exchanged meteorological data (GTS) with gauge observations from 7,000 stations worldwide. The products contain precipitation totals, anomalies, the number of gauges, and systematic error correction factors. The grid resolution is 1.0° × 1.0° latitude/longitude.

Classification

Monthly values are available for 17 years, from 1986 to 2002. The maximum registered values per annum were used to calculate the expected 100-year monthly precipitation for every grid point using a Gumbel distribution approach. The results were divided into five classes and show that the two highest classes (4 and 5) cover 5 percent of the accumulated precipitation. The susceptibility classes are shown in table 2.5.

Table 2.5. Classification of precipitation trigger indicator "T_p"

100-year extreme monthly rainfall (mm)	Susceptibility	T_p
0000–0330	Low	1
0331–0625	Moderate	2
0626–1000	Medium	3
1001–1500	High	4
> 1500	Very high	5

The map of the estimated 100-year extreme monthly rainfall in the world is shown in figure 2.3.

Estimation of seismic trigger factor T_s

Source: Peak Ground Acceleration (PGA) with a 475-year return period (10 percent probability of exceedance in 50 years) from the Global Seismic Hazard Program (GSHAP).

Web sites

http://www.gfz-potsdam.de/pb5/pb53/projects/en/gshap/menue_gshap_e.html
http://www.dwd.de/en/FundE/Klima/KLIS/int/GPCC/GPCC.htm

Description

GSHAP was launched in 1992 by the International Lithosphere Program (ILP) with the support of the International Council of Scientific Unions (ICSU) and in the framework of the United Nations International Decade for Natural Disaster Reduction (UN/IDNDR). The primary goal of GSHAP was to create a global seismic hazard map in a harmonized and regionally coordinated fashion, based on advanced methods in probabilistic seismic hazard assessments (PSHA). Modern PSHA are made of four basic elements: earthquake catalogue, earthquake source characterization, strong seismic ground motion, and computation of seismic hazard. For the purposes of this study, the PGA with a 475-year return period was used.

Classification

The GSHAP PGA_{475} data are distributed within 10 classes, as shown in table 2.6.

Figure 2.2. Global soil moisture index: 1961-1990

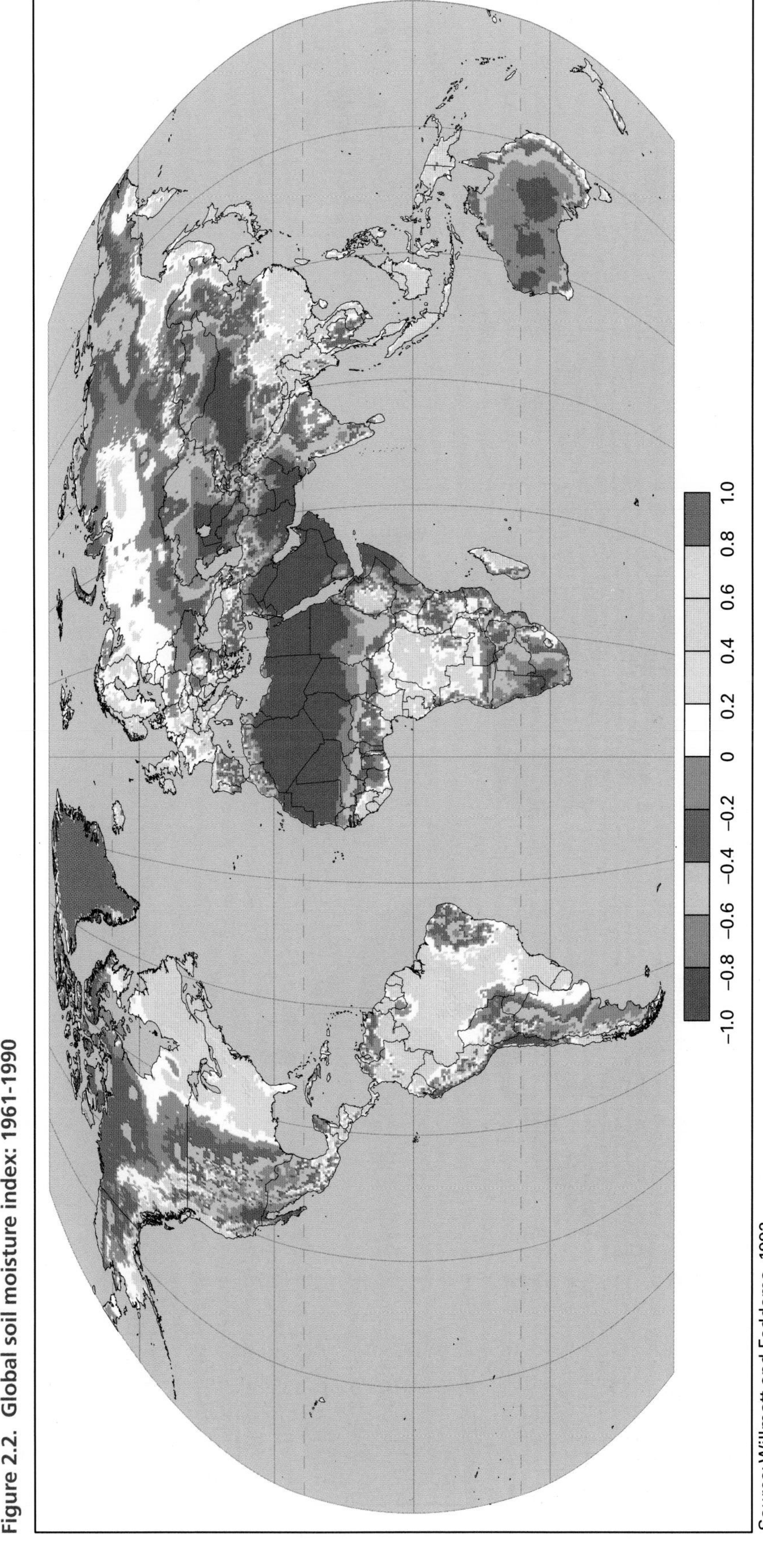

Source: Willmott and Feddema, 1992

Figure 2.3. Expected monthly extreme values for a 100-years event.

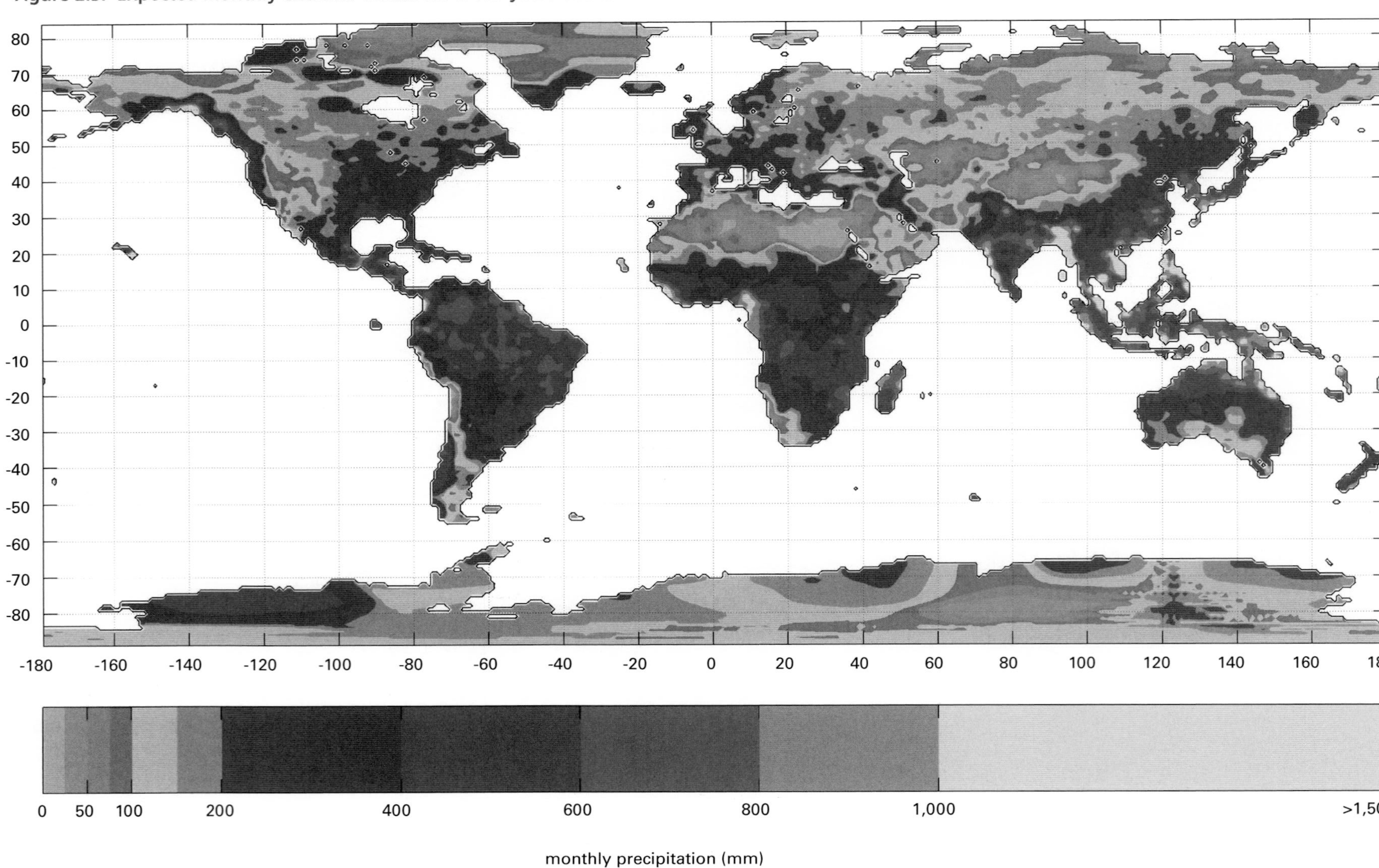

Source: http://www.dwd.de/en/FundE/Klima/KLIS/int/GPCC/GPCC.htm.

Table 2.6. Classification of seismicity trigger indicator "T_S"

PGA_{475} (m/s²)	*T_S*
0.00 – 0.50	1
0.51 – 1.00	2
1.01 – 1.50	3
1.51 – 2.00	4
2.01 – 2.50	5
2.51 – 3.00	6
3.01 – 3.50	7
3.51 – 4.00	8
4.01 – 4.50	9
> 4.50	10

Figure 2.4 shows the global map, developed in GSHAP, of the PGA with a return period of 475 years.

Classification of landslide hazard

The value of relative landslide hazard level $H_{landslide}$ obtained from the equation given in the "Landslide Model" section varies between 0 and 1500. In the original Mora and Vahrson (1994) model, the landslide hazard classification shown in table 2.7 is suggested. In this study, the classification shown in table 2.8 was used.

Table 2.7. Classification of landslide hazard potential based on the computed hazard index originally suggested by Mora and Vahrson (1994)

Values for $H_{landslide}$	*Class*	*Classification of landslide hazard potential*
< 6	1	Negligible
7–32	2	Low
33–162	3	Moderate
163–512	4	Medium
513–1250	5	High
> 1250	6	Very high

Table 2.8. Classification of landslide hazard potential based on the computed hazard index used in this study

Values for $H_{landslide}$	*Class*	*Classification of landslide hazard potential*
< 14	1	Negligible
15–50	2	Very low
51–100	3	Low
101–168	4	Low to moderate
169–256	5	Moderate
257–360	6	Medium
361–512	7	Medium to high
513–720	8	High
> 720	9	Very high

The annual frequencies of landslide events corresponding to these classes are given in table 2.13.

An example of how the different layers of input parameters interact to produce a landslide hazard map is shown in figures 2.5 to 2.9. Tajikistan and its neighboring regions are shown in the example.

Snow Avalanche

Susceptibility factors for snow avalanches are the slope factor (S_r), temperature (T_t), and precipitations (T_p). Relative avalanche hazard level is computed through the following equation:

$$H_{avalanche} = (S_r*0.4 + T_p*0.4 + T_t*0.2)*F$$

Estimation of slope factor S_r

Source: The data were derived from NASA's SRTM30 dataset (see description above for the reference source under the landslide hazard model).

Classification

In total, nine categories were defined, as shown in table 2.9. The most interesting categories for avalanches are categories 7, 8, and 9.

Table 2.9. Classification of slope factor "S_r" for snow avalanche susceptibility

Range of slopes angle (unit: degrees)	*Slope factor "S_r"*
0–1	1
1–2	2
2–4	3
4–6	4
6–9	5
9–12	6
12–17	7
17–25	8
> 25	9

Estimation of precipitation factor T_p

Source: Mean monthly precipitation data from the IIASA Climate Database (International Institute for Applied System Analyses, Austria).

Web site

http://www.grid.unep.ch/data/summary.php?dataid=GNV14&category=atmosphere&dataurl=http://www.grid.unep.ch/data/download/gnv14.tar.Z&browsen=

Figure 2.4. Expected PGA with a return period of 475 years

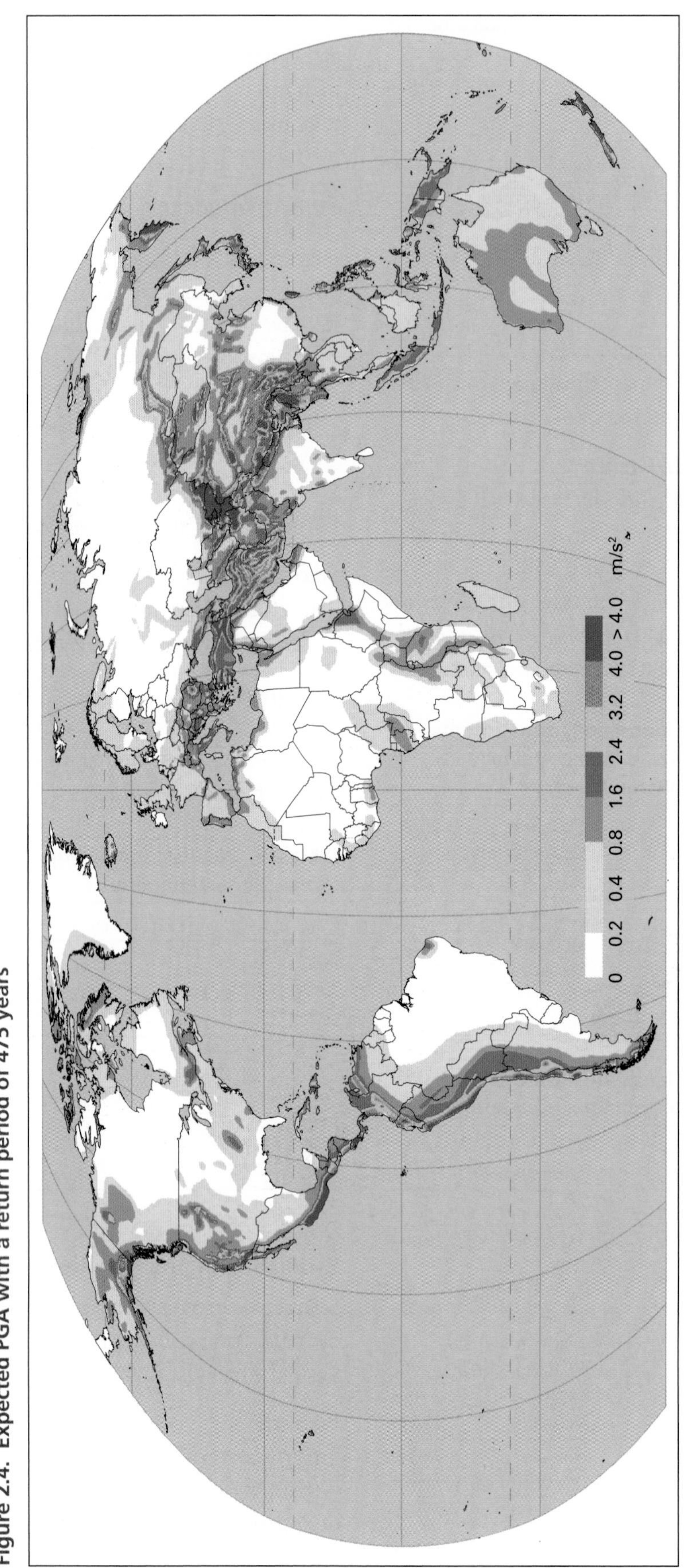

Figure 2.5. Variation of slope factor, S_r, in Tajikistan and its neighboring regions

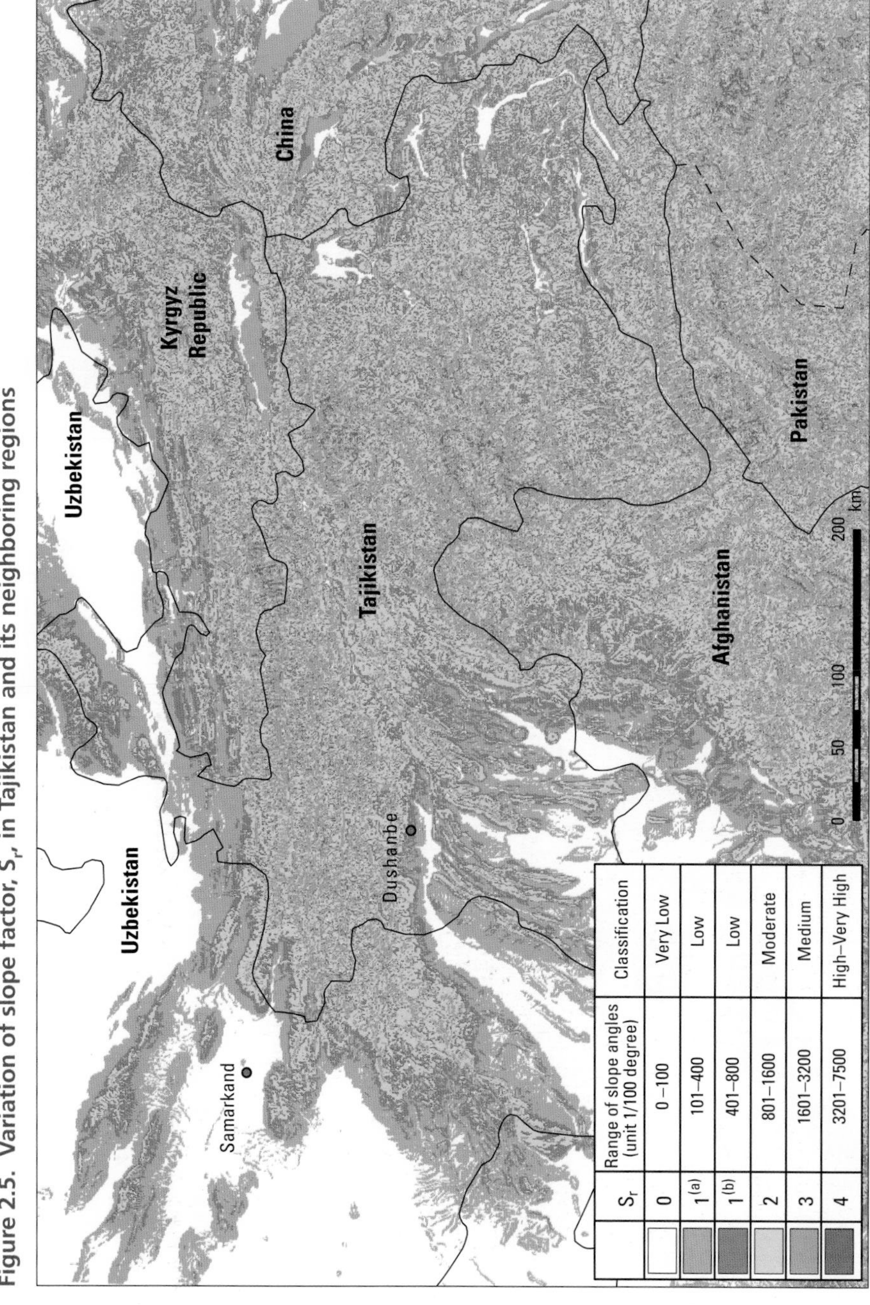

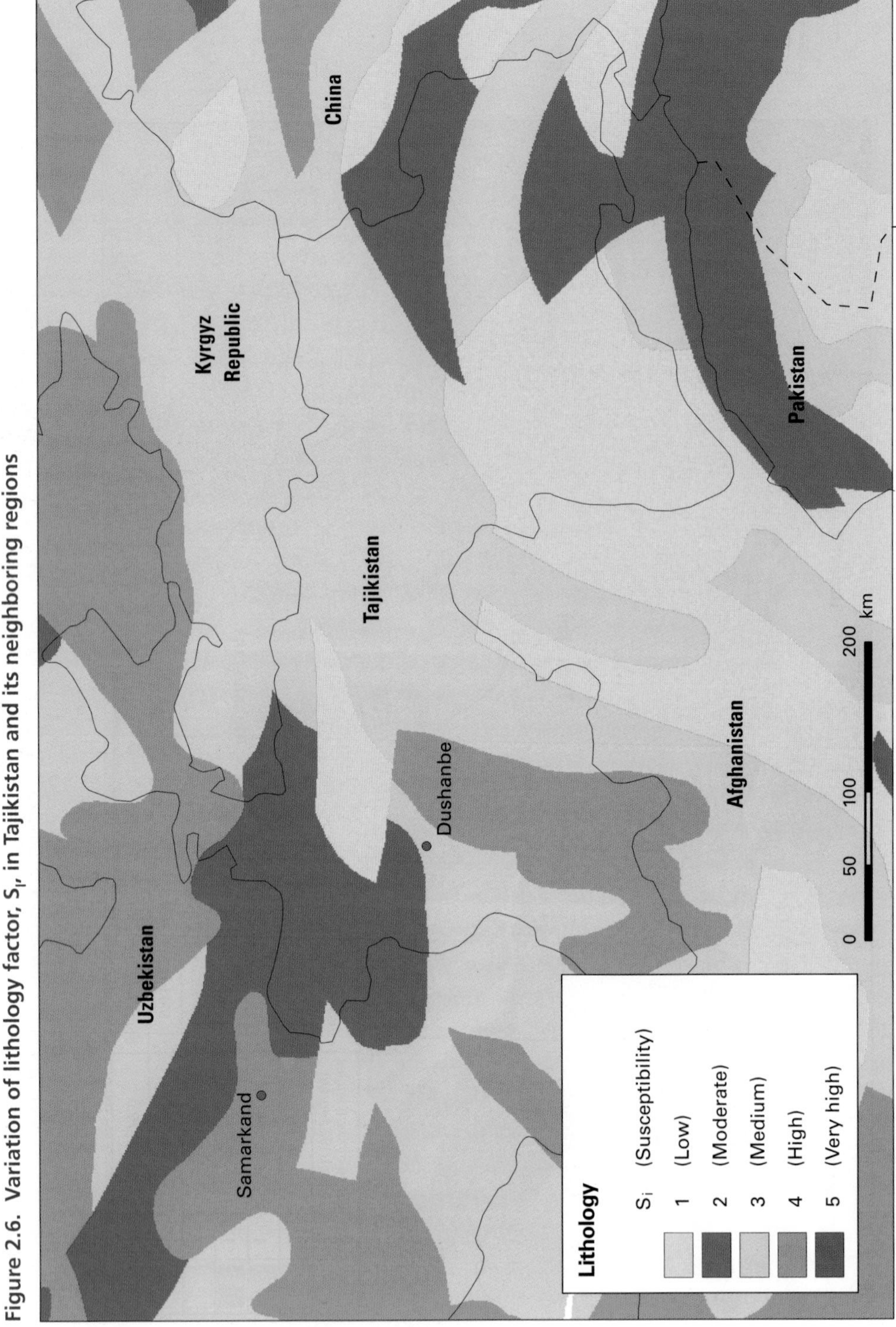

Figure 2.6. Variation of lithology factor, S_l, in Tajikistan and its neighboring regions

Figure 2.7. Variation of seismic trigger indicator, T_S, in Tajikistan and its neighboring regions

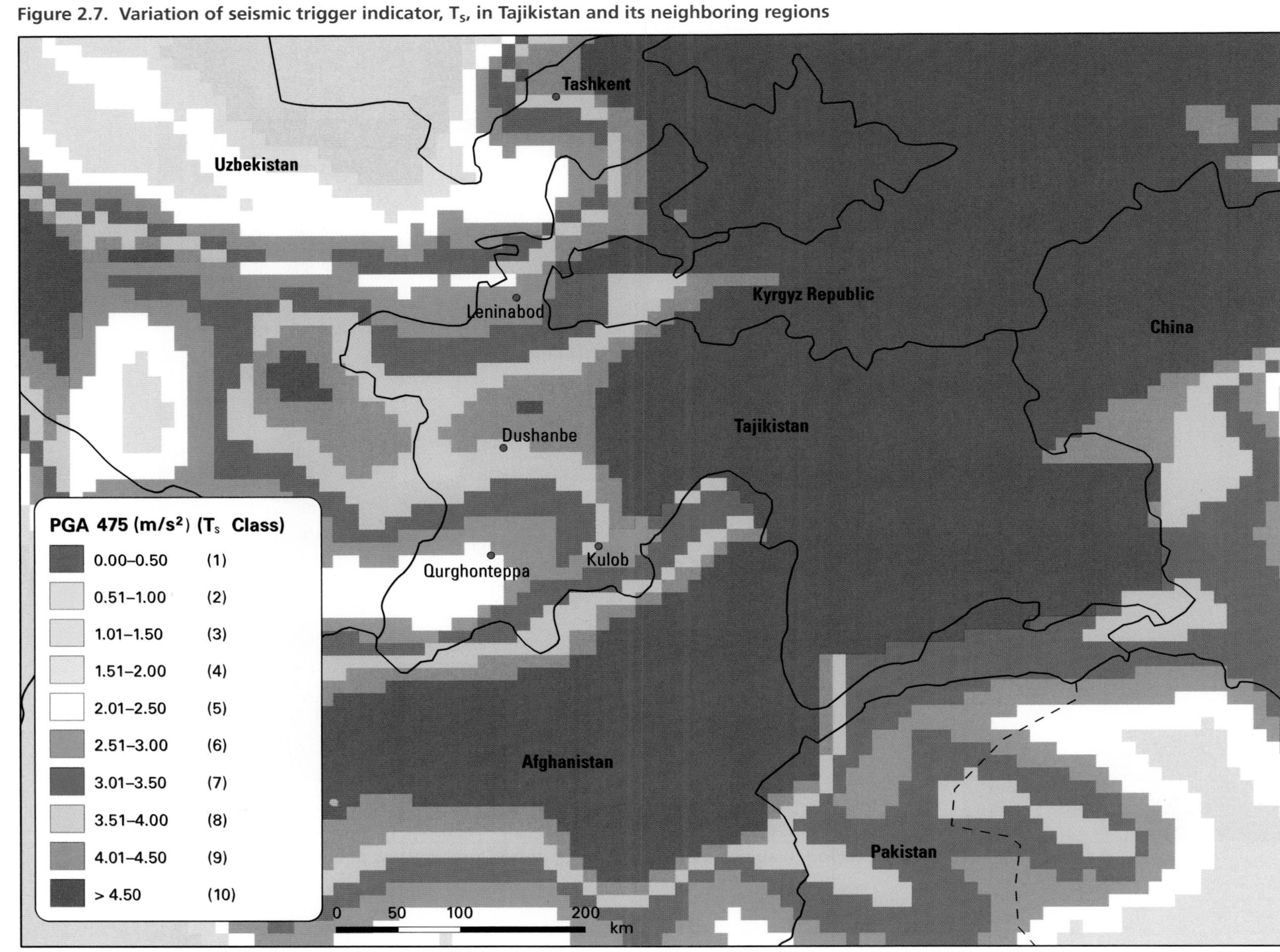

Figure 2.8. Variation of soil moisture factor, S_h, in Tajikistan and its neighboring regions

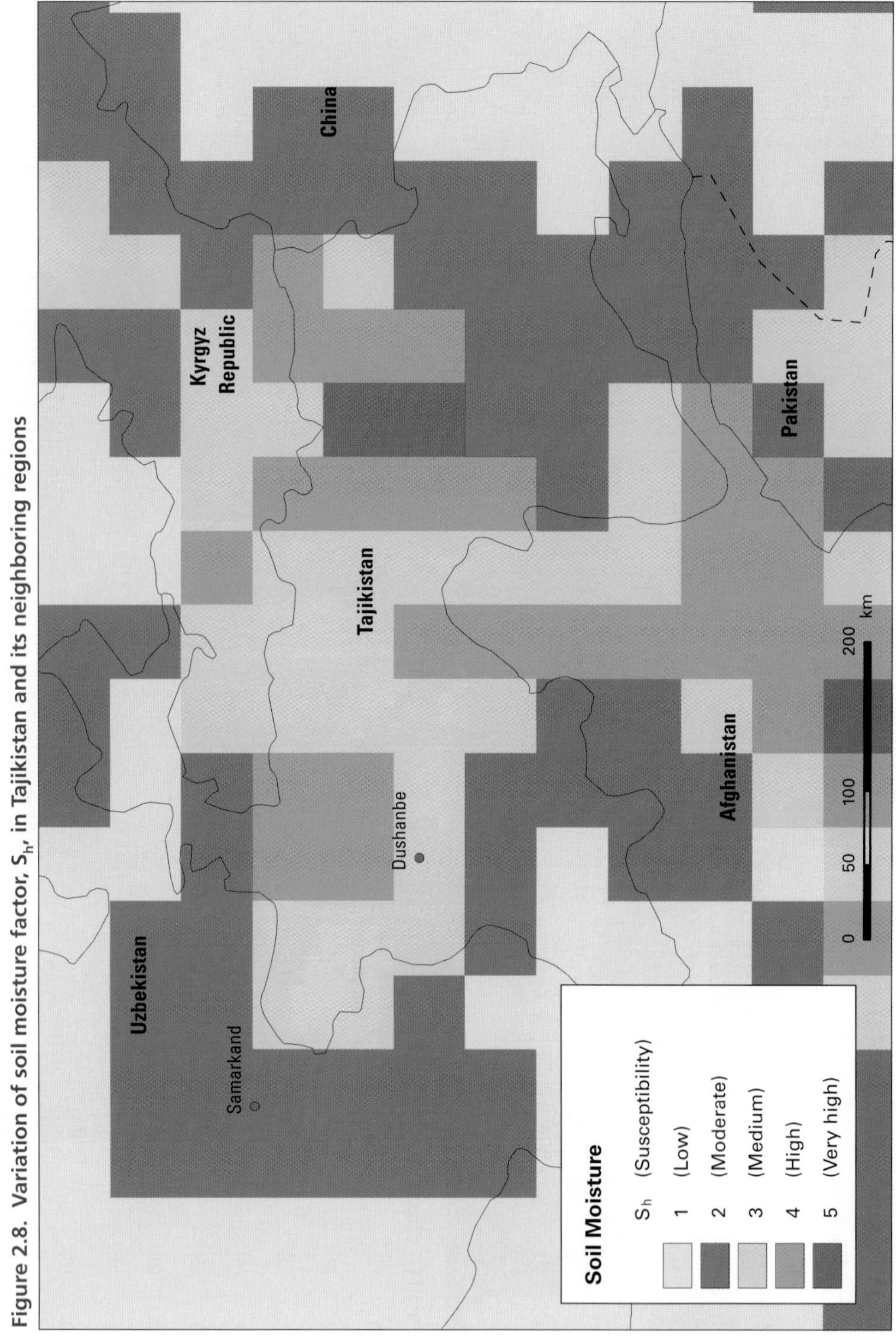

Figure 2.9. Landslide hazard zonation map obtained for Tajikistan and its neighboring regions

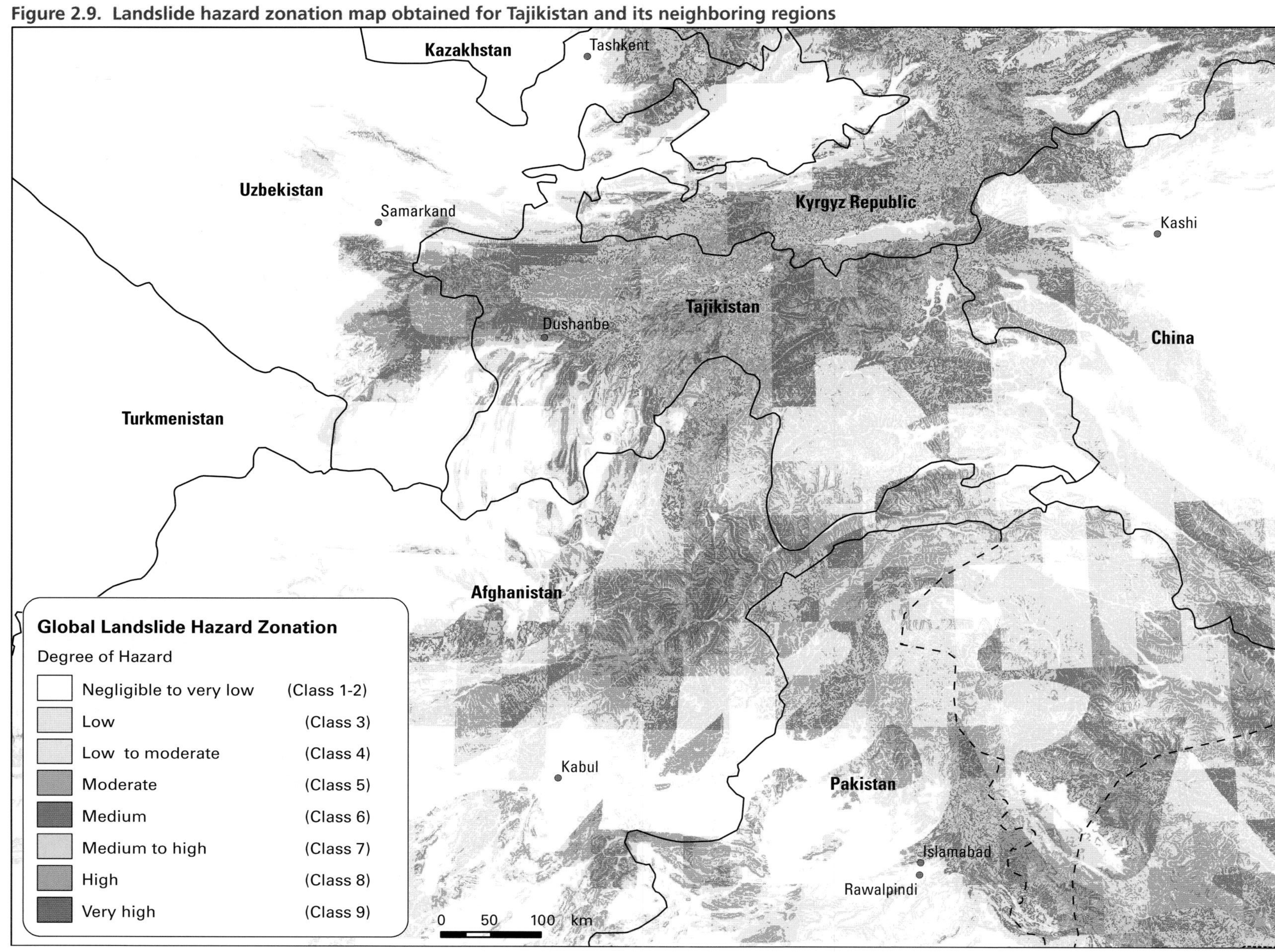

Description

Grid resolution is 0.5° × 0.5° latitude/longitude. The precipitation values for the four "winter months" in the northern and southern hemispheres have been added to the database. The amount of snow during the winter months greatly affects the number and size of the avalanches. Global differences in the expected winter snow are given by a global precipitation map for the winter months (December–March in the northern hemisphere and June–September in the southern hemisphere). This map does not show the best picture of the situation due to differences in the number of winter days. In reality, the more north the location of interest, the more it underestimates avalanche susceptibility.

Table 2.10. Classification of precipitation factor "T_p" for avalanche hazard evaluation

Winter Precipitation (mm/year)	*Precipitation factor "T_p"*
0–50	1
50–100	2
100–200	3
200–300	4
300–500	5
500–750	6
750–1000	7
1000–1500	8
> 1500	9

Estimation of temperature factor T_t

Source of the data Mean monthly temperature data from the IIASA Climate Database (International Institute for Applied System Analyses, Austria).

Web site

http://www.grid.unep.ch/data/summary.php?dataid=GNV15&category=atmosphere&dataurl=http://www.grid.unep.ch/data/download/gnv15.tar.Z&browsen=

Description

A global temperature map, with a resolution of 0.5° × 0.5° latitude/longitude, constrains the avalanche areas to colder regions. Areas with average temperature in at least one winter month (for example, January in the northern hemisphere) in the temperature range +5°C × to 0°C or colder were studied. In mountain areas above 1,000 m, precipitation occurs as snow when the temperature at sea level is less than +5°C. The model implies that the areas with longer cold periods have a greater potential to produce avalanches.

Table 2.11. Classification of temperature factor "T_t" for avalanche hazard analysis

Mean monthly temperature in winter months (°C)	*Temperature factor "T_t"*
2.5 → 30.5	0
1.5 → 2.5	1
0.5 → 1.5	2
0.0 → 0.5	3
-0.5 → 0.0	4
-1.0 → -0.5	5
-1.5 → -1.0	6
-2.0 → -1.5	7
-3.0 → -2.0	8
< -3.0	9

Classification of avalanche hazard

The value of avalanche hazard level $H_{avalanche}$ obtained from the equation given in the beginning of this section varies between 1 and 9.

Table 2.12. Classification of snow avalanche hazard potential

Values for $H_{avalanche}$	*Class*	*Classification of avalanche hazard potential*
4	1	-
4.1–4.5	2	-
4.6–5.0	3	-
5.1–5.5	4	Negligible
5.6–6.0	5	Low
6.0–7.0	6	Moderate
7.0–7.5	7	Moderate to high
7.5–8.2	8	High
8.3–9	9	Very high

Similar to the landslide hazard, the avalanche hazard is also divided into nine classes. The classes for avalanche hazard based on the computed value of $H_{avalanche}$ are shown in table 2.12. The annual frequencies of (major) avalanche events corresponding to these classes are given in table 2.13.

Global Landslide and Avalanche Hazard

The slide/avalanche hazard has been classified into nine classes; that is, each pixel is assigned a value varying from 1 to 9. The nine classes roughly correspond to the annual frequency of occurrence for a 1-km² pixel shown in table 2.13.

Table 2.13. Annual frequency of occurrence and typical return period (in years) for different classes of landslide and avalanche hazard

Class	*Annual frequency of occurrence (%)*	*Typical return period for serious events (in years)*
1	Virtually zero	Not relevant
2	Negligible	100,000–1,000,000
3	Very small	50,000–250,000
4	Small	20,000–10,000
5	0.0025–0.01%	10,000–40,000
6	0.0063–0.025%	4,000–16,000
7	0.0125–0.05%	2,000–8,000
8	0.025–0.1%	1,000–4,000
9	0.05–0.2%	500–2,000

Pixels in classes 1–4 have been ignored for the analyses. A serious slide event would involve 10 percent to 100 percent of a pixel area.

The combined annual frequency of landslide and avalanche events is approximately the sum of the frequencies for each event. The approximation is valid because the probability numbers are very small:

$$P[L \text{ or } A] = P[L] + P[A] - P[L] \cdot P[A] \approx P[L] + P[A]$$

where P[L] is the annual probability of a major landslide event and P[A] is the annual probability of a major avalanche event.

Comparisons of Model Predictions with Actual Slide Events

This section presents the results of some of the landslide, rockfall, and avalanche mapping analyses done in the study, with comparisons of observed hazards from Norway, Armenia, Nepal, Georgia, Sri Lanka, and Jamaica. These six countries were selected because relevant data for comparison of model predictions with actual slide events were available.

Examples of global hazard and risk maps obtained by the models developed in this study are shown in figures 2.10 and 2.11. Figure 2.10 gives a hazard map for Central American and Caribbean countries, and figure 2.11 shows a risk map for Central and South America.

Norway

Norway, a land with soft clay deposits, steep mountains, and deep fjords, regularly experiences landslides, mainly due to quick clays, rockfalls (if the rock masses fall into fjords, they can lead to potentially devastating tsunamis), and snow avalanches. Although Norway is by no means as much of a "hotspot" in terms of risk as many other Asian and Latin American countries, there are many observations of Norwegian slides that can be used to evaluate the reliability of the prediction model.

Landslides and Rockfalls

The prehistorical and historical maps of rock-avalanche events in figures 2.12 and 2.13 show that the highest rock-slide frequency—occurring in the high-risk areas in Western Norway—is concentrated in the inner fjords, and mainly at the bottoms of the fjords (the areas surrounding the innermost parts of the fjords). In a very few cases, slides were observed closer to the coast.

The results of the regional zonation carried out by the Geological Survey of Norway (NGU) and illustrated with red boundaries in figure 2.13 agree well with the observations close to the bottoms of the several fjords. A few of the large rockfalls/rock slides were, however, not predicted with the regional mapping, especially in the northeastern part of the area shown and midway between Molde and Aalesund.

Figure 2.14 presents the mapping predictions for landslide hazard (both landslides and rockfalls) in Western Norway, where the more hazardous areas are given a relative hazard value of 4 to 5 on a scale of 1 to 9 and are located close to the bottoms of fjords or the arms of fjords. Otherwise, the model predicts that most of Western Norway has a hazard value of 3, which represents a low hazard. The model is probably too simplified to be able to predict the type of rockfalls and landslides that occur in Norway.

Snow Avalanches

Figure 2.15 illustrates a snow avalanche hazard map obtained from the snow avalanche hazard model described earlier. Snow avalanches are frequent in Western Norway, especially in the mountains close to the fjords. Looking at the map in figure 2.15, there is a very good correlation between the predicted Avalanche Hazard Classes 7 (moderate to high) to 9 (very high)

Figure 2.10. Example landslide hazard map for Central American and Caribbean countries

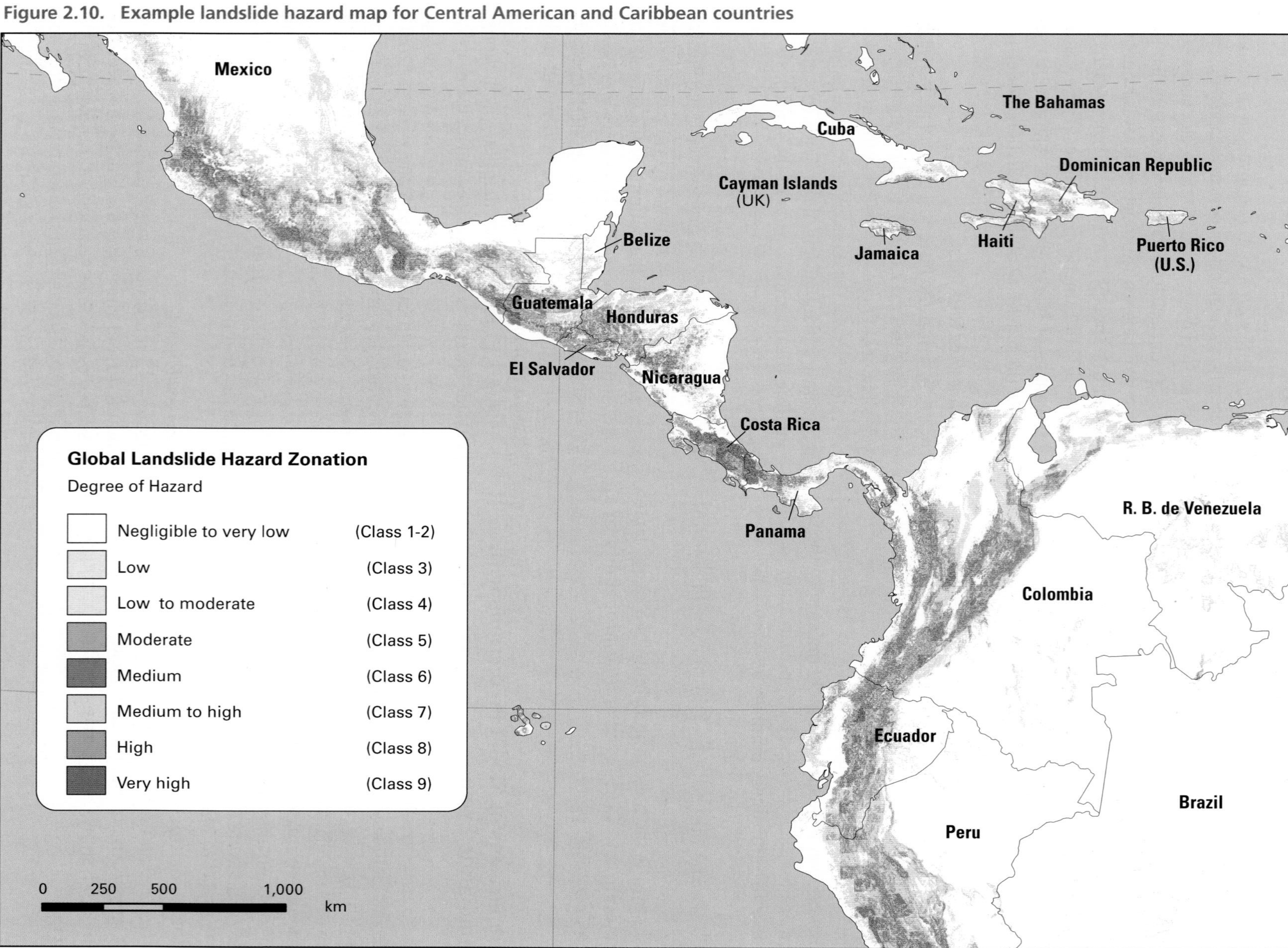

Figure 2.11. Example landslide risk map for parts of Central and South America

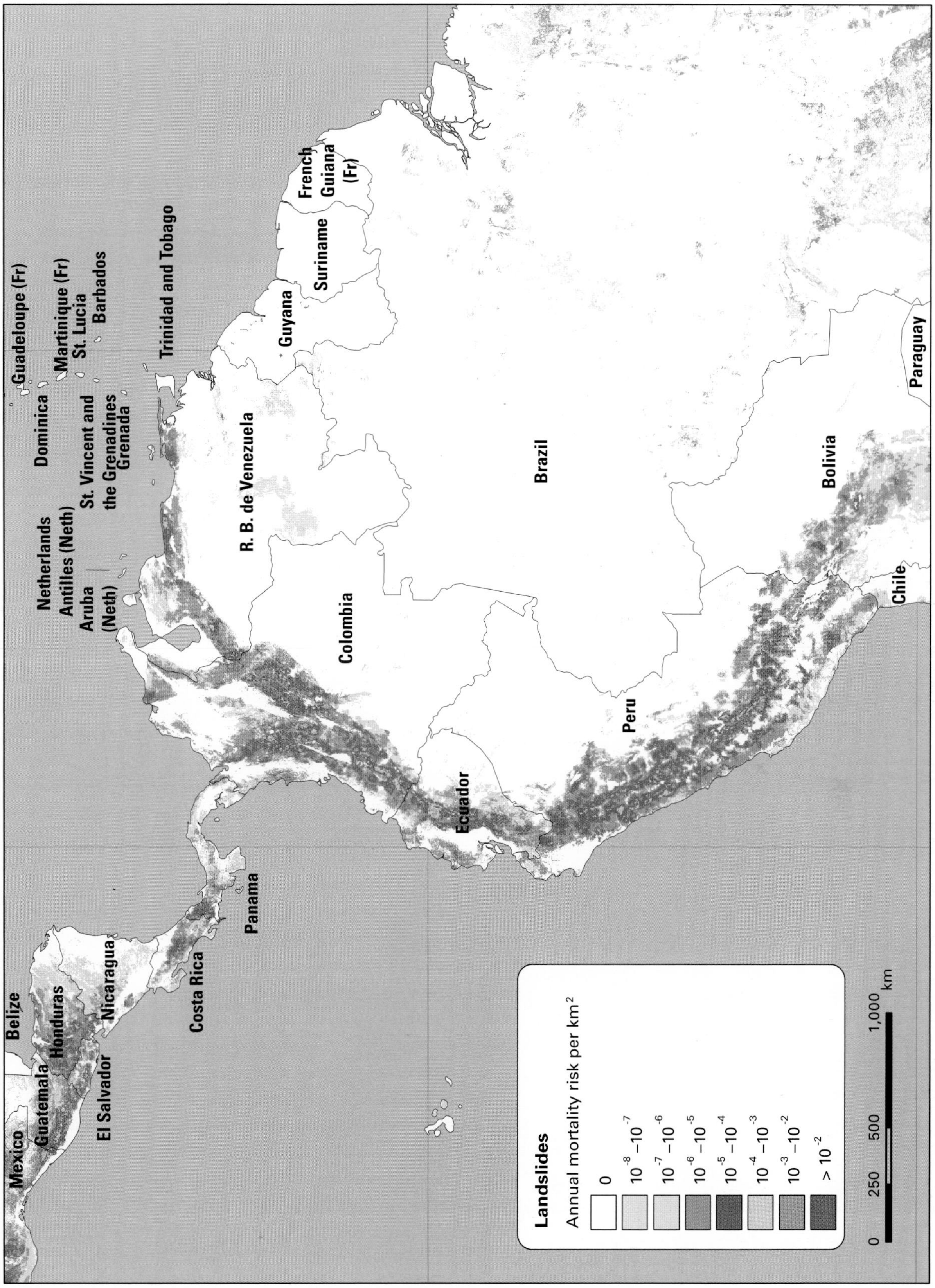

Mexico
Guatemala
Belize
Honduras
El Salvador
Nicaragua
Costa Rica
Panama
Aruba (Neth)
Netherlands Antilles (Neth)
St. Vincent and the Grenadines
Grenada
Dominica
Guadeloupe (Fr)
Martinique (Fr)
St. Lucia
Barbados
Trinidad and Tobago
R. B. de Venezuela
Guyana
Suriname
French Guiana (Fr)
Colombia
Ecuador
Peru
Brazil
Bolivia
Paraguay
Chile

Landslides
Annual mortality risk per km^2
0
10^{-8} – 10^{-7}
10^{-7} – 10^{-6}
10^{-6} – 10^{-5}
10^{-5} – 10^{-4}
10^{-4} – 10^{-3}
10^{-3} – 10^{-2}
$> 10^{-2}$

0 250 500 1,000 km

Figure 2.12. Historical rock avalanche events in Møre & Romsdal and Sogn & Fjordane Counties extracted from Norway's historical database (NGU/Astor Furseth)

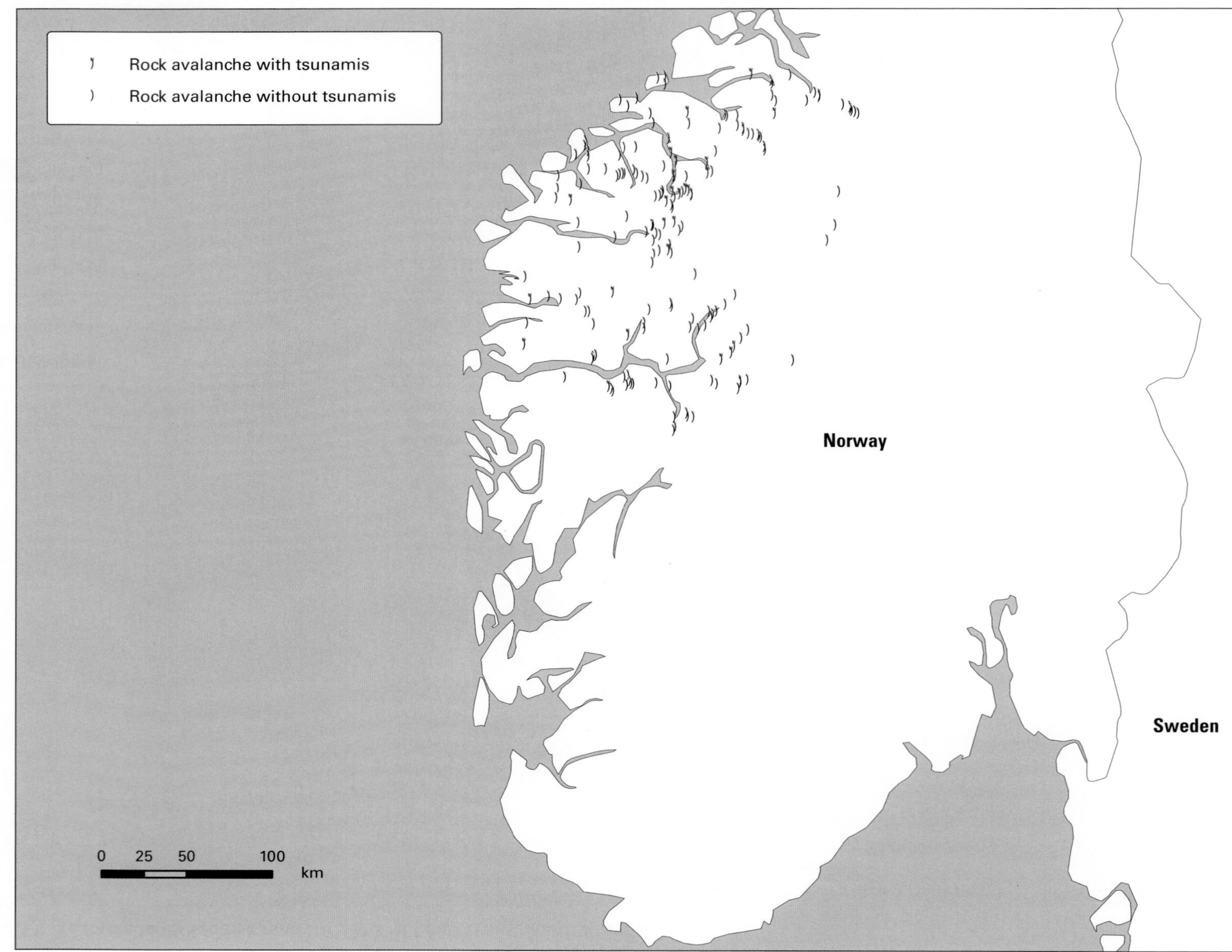

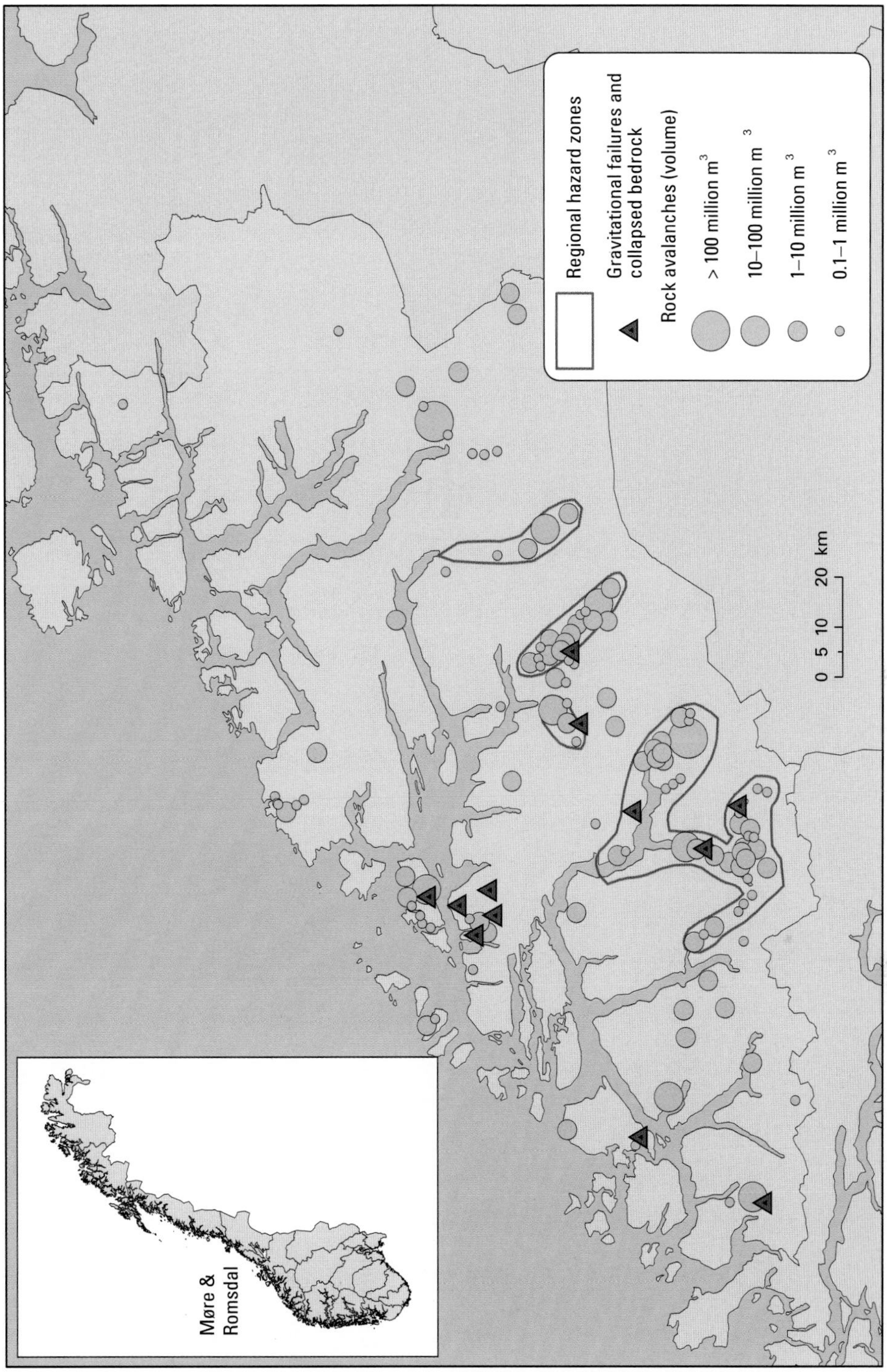

Figure 2.13. Regional hazard zonation in Møre & Romsdal County in western Norway. The hazard zones are characterized by the occurrence of a high number of both historical events and rock avalanche deposits.

Figure 2.14. Landslide hazard map (landslide and rock fall hazards) for the western part of Norway based on the simplified model

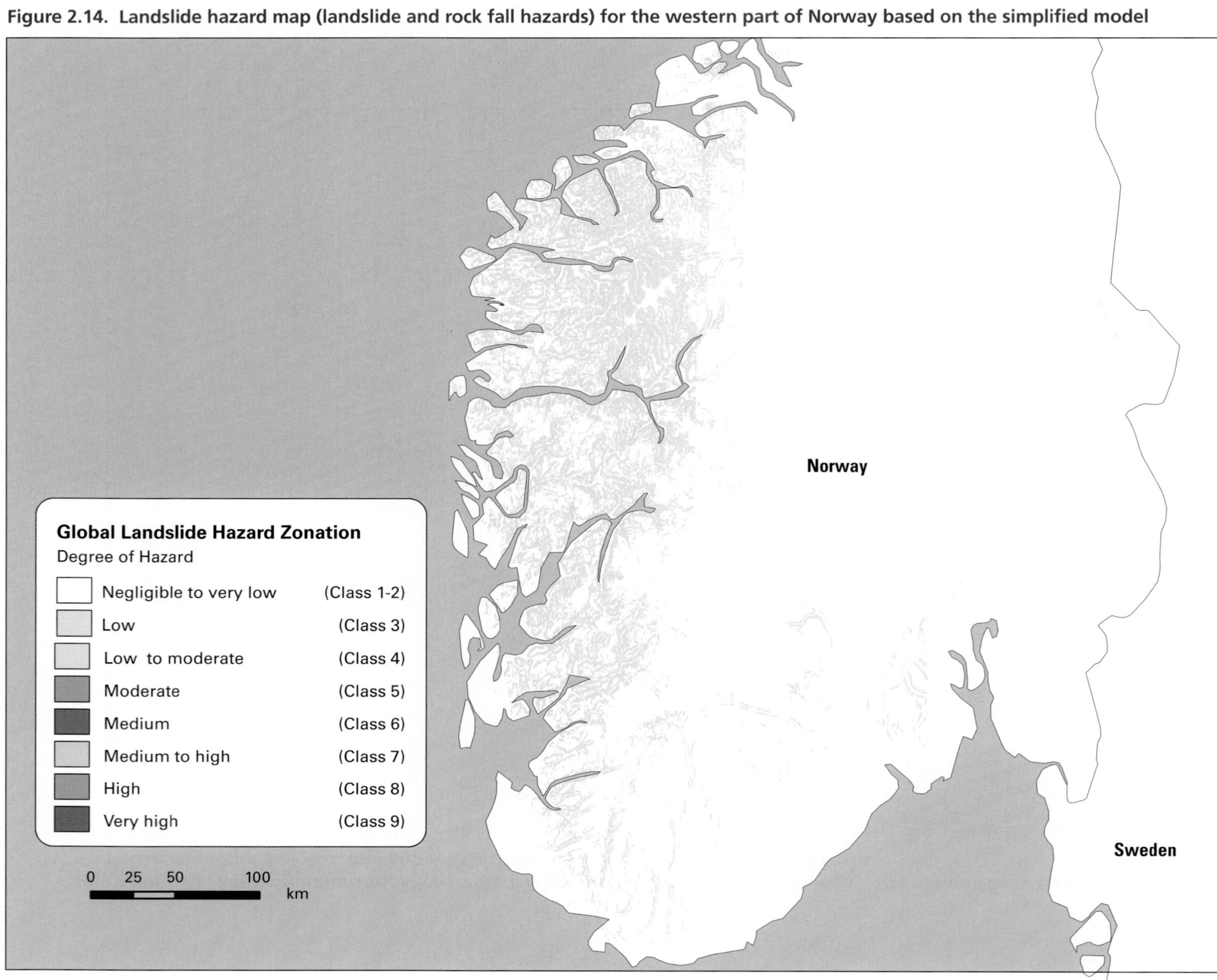

Figure 2.15. Snow avalanche hazard zones for Norway based on the avalanche hazard model

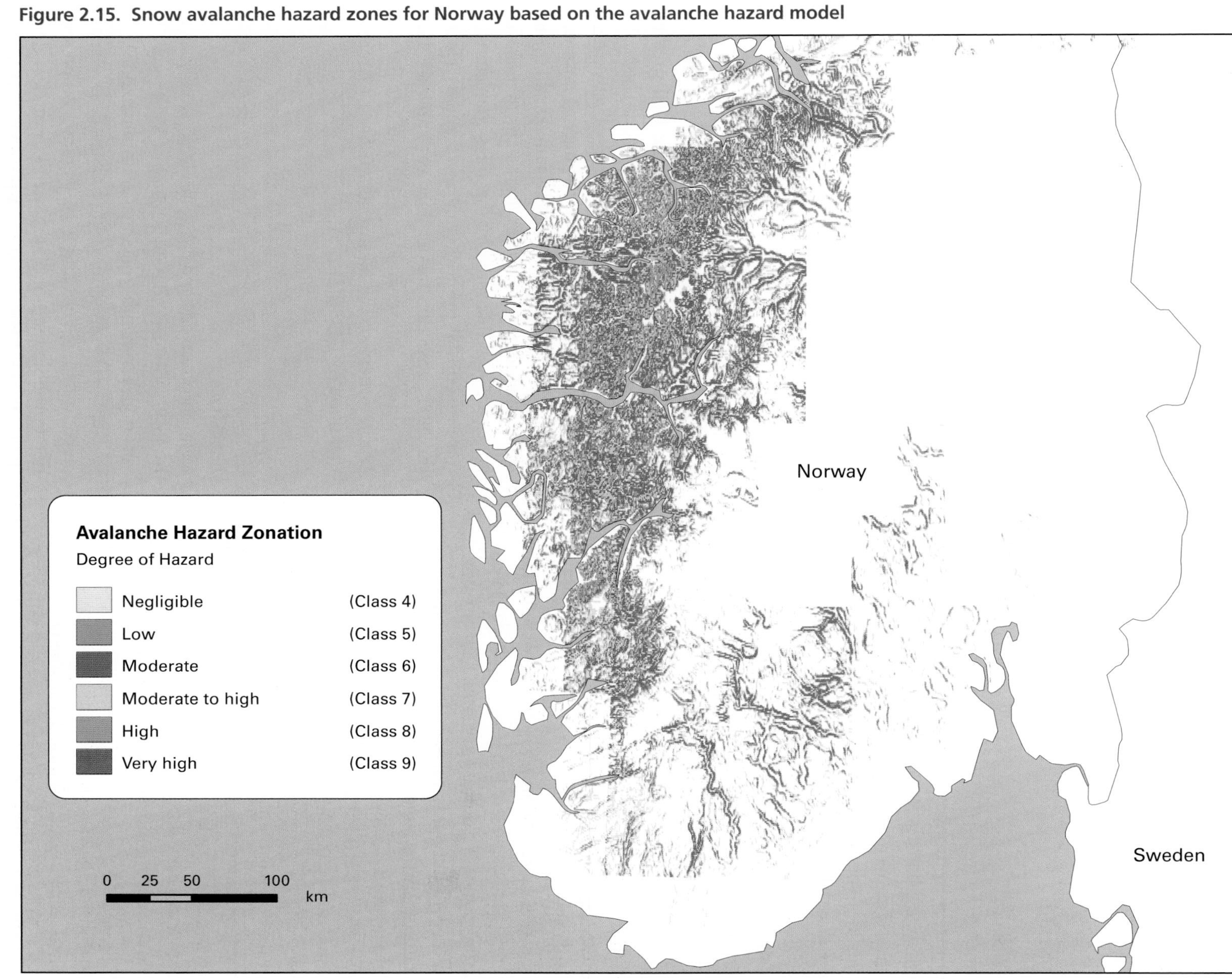

and the areas where frequent occurrence of snow avalanches in Norway is observed. There may be other areas with a high occurrence of snow avalanches, as not all of the territory is covered by observations; still, the agreement is very promising.

Armenia

Landslides

Armenia (figure 2.16) is one of the most disaster-prone countries in the world, as it features earthquakes, landslides, hailstorms, droughts, strong winds, and floods. The average value of direct damage caused by landslides approaches US$10 million per year, affecting the social and economic infrastructure (Stephanyan 2003).

More than 3,000 large landslides have been reported for Armenia, and one-third of the country is exposed to landslide hazards. Nearly 470,000 people are exposed, which represents about 15 percent of the total population. In five years, more than 2,000 families have been left homeless as a result of landslide activity. The potential for future catastrophic landslide events is very significant.

Several landslide areas or groups of landslides in Armenia are considered to be the most dangerous for the population: Vokhchaberd-Garni, Dilijan-Gosh, Agaiargan, Jermuk, Sunik (Sissian-Tolors), and Vanadzor. Nearly 300 of the largest landslides are in an active stage of development. They include an area of about 700 km^2, involving 100 settlements, where nearly 400,000 people live. About 1,500 km, of a total of 8,000 km of transport corridors in Armenia, are located in landslide-prone terrain. A typical huge landslide area covers a few km^2. In some instances, a village with a population from a few hundred to a few thousand inhabitants is situated in an active landslide area. A typical landslide exhibits a slow, creeping movement, with a thickness between 10 m and 100 m, and several, smaller, active creeping zones inside the area. The ground movements are horizontal, vertical, and rotational, causing tension cracks in the ground, settlements, and rotational-slip surfaces.

NGI previously produced a landslide hazard map for Armenia with support from the Armenian Scientific Research Company, GEORISK, and computations based on several datasets available on the Internet (Landsat7, Landscan 2001, Digital Chart of the World, and GLOBE data. See Annex 2A for more details). GEORISK provided NGI with the following information:

- Historical landslides;
- Landslide-prone zones: regions where landslide processes develop, regions of creep motion of the ground, regions of intense landslide processes, and regions of large seismic activity that involve the most hazardous landslides;
- Mudflows: Levels I, II, and III;
- Dams: high and low landslide hazard;
- Population density in a 5 × 5 km grid; and
- Population figures for cities, districts, and villages.

Figure 2.17 presents the superimposition of the GEORISK landslide inventory (blue curves) onto the global landslide hazard map obtained with the first-pass model in this study.

Especially for the areas in the center of the region mapped, the agreement between the NGI prediction and the GEORISK inventory is very good. The NGI prediction model assigns landslide values of between 4 and 6 (a scale of 1 to 6, where 6 is the highest hazard, was used in the previous study for Armenia) to all the landslide zones identified by GEORISK. The higher-hazard zones are well delimited by the areas characterized as most susceptible to slides (values of 5 and 6). However the NGI prediction model does not show the hazard area close to Yerevan, and can only indicate the southern periphery of the hazard zone close to Azerbaijan identified by GEORISK.

Nepal

Landslides

Data on observed landslides in Nepal were provided by Professor Narenda Raj Khanel of Tribhuwan University in Katmandu (personal communication).

The results of the mapping of hazards in Nepal are given in figures 2.18 and 2.19. Figure 2.20 presents a demographic map of Nepal with population density illustrated in different colors. A large proportion of the country has very low population density.

Figure 2.18 plots all of the observed landslides in Nepal between 1971 and 2000. Figure 2.19 presents the landslide hazard map predicted by the NGI model

Figure 2.16. Map of Armenia

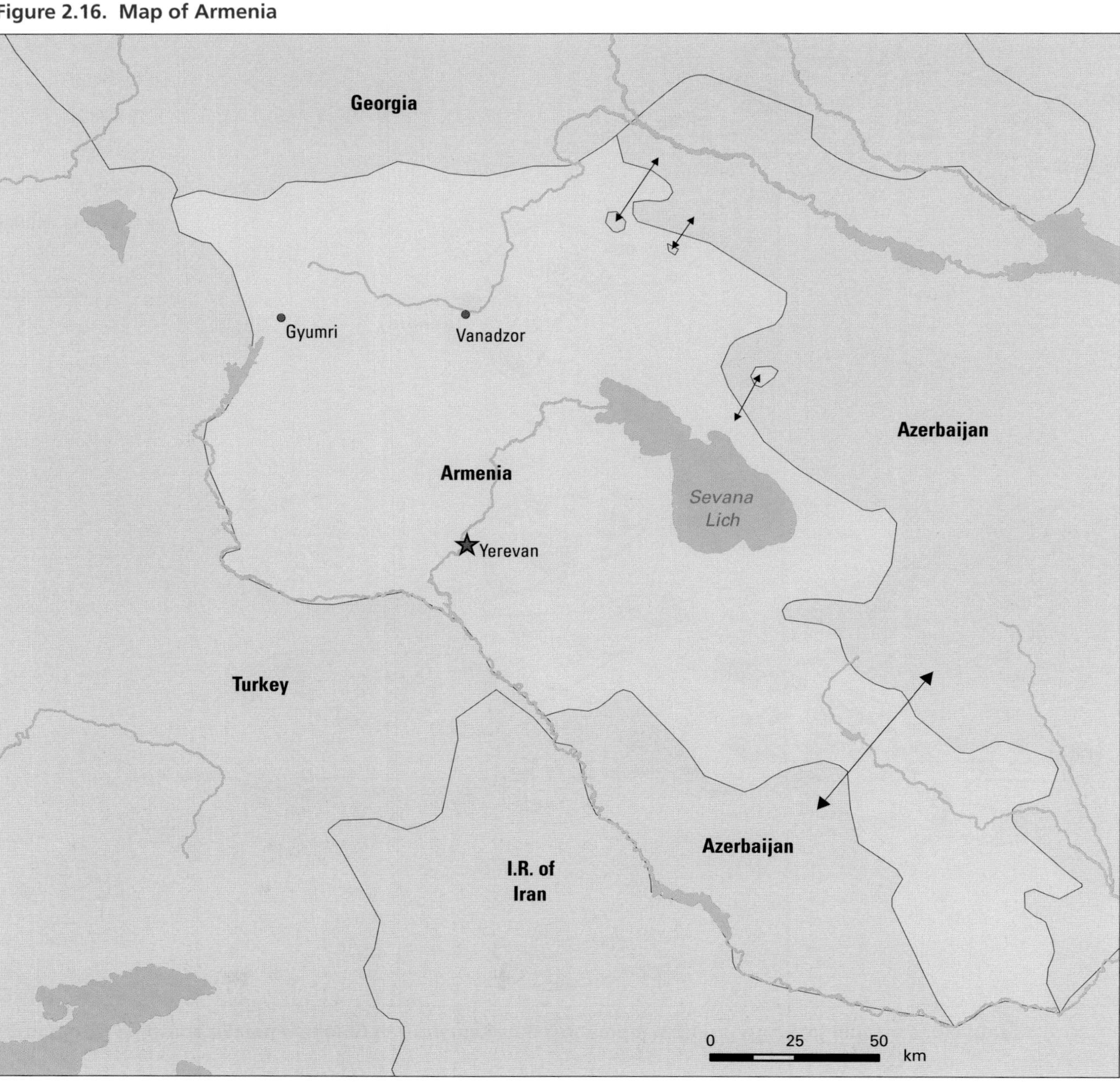

Figure 2.17. Comparison of global landslide hazard mapping in Armenia using NGI model with the GEORISK landslide inventory

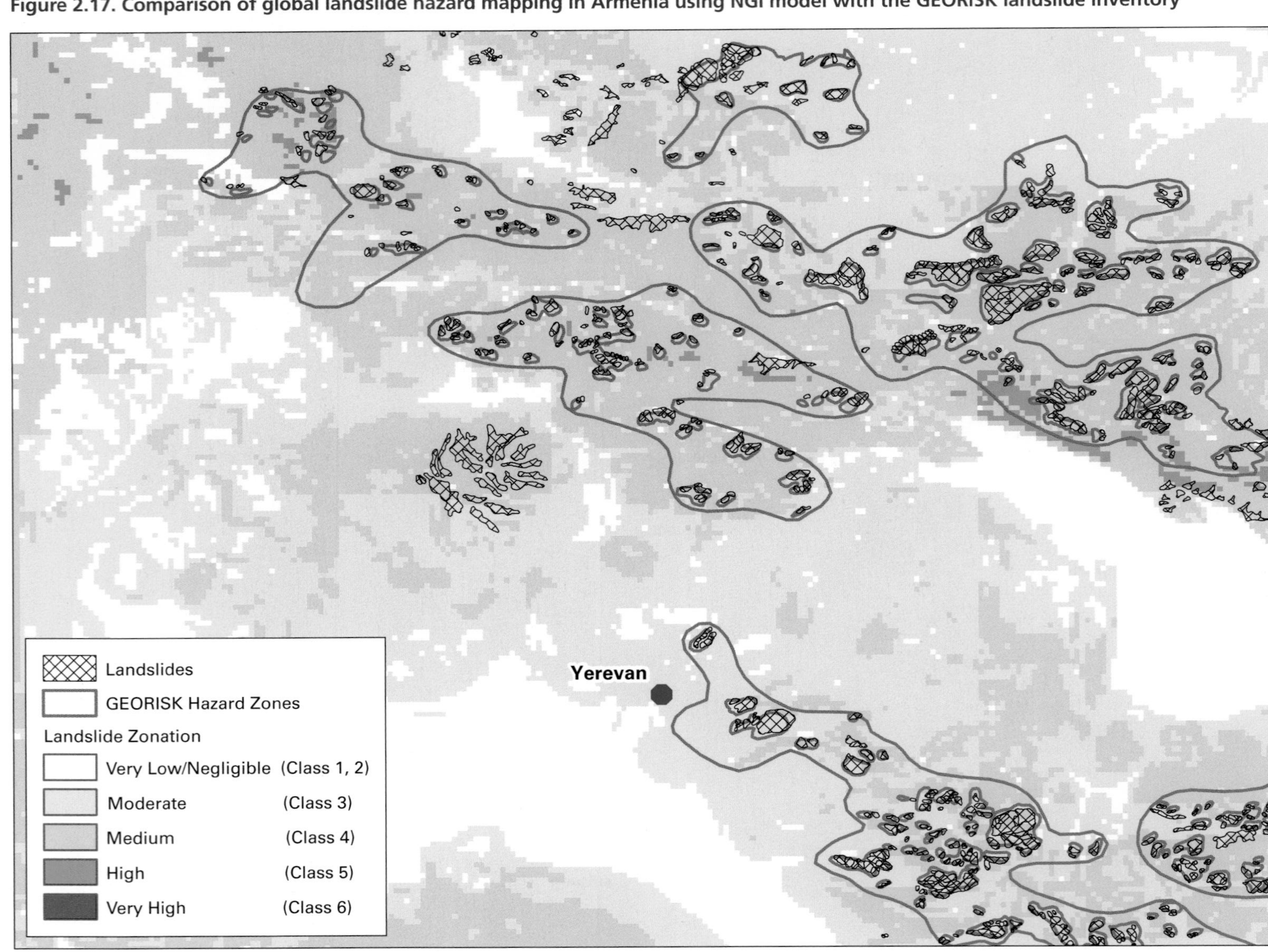

Figure 2.18. Major landslide events in Nepal during a 30-year time period (1971–2000)

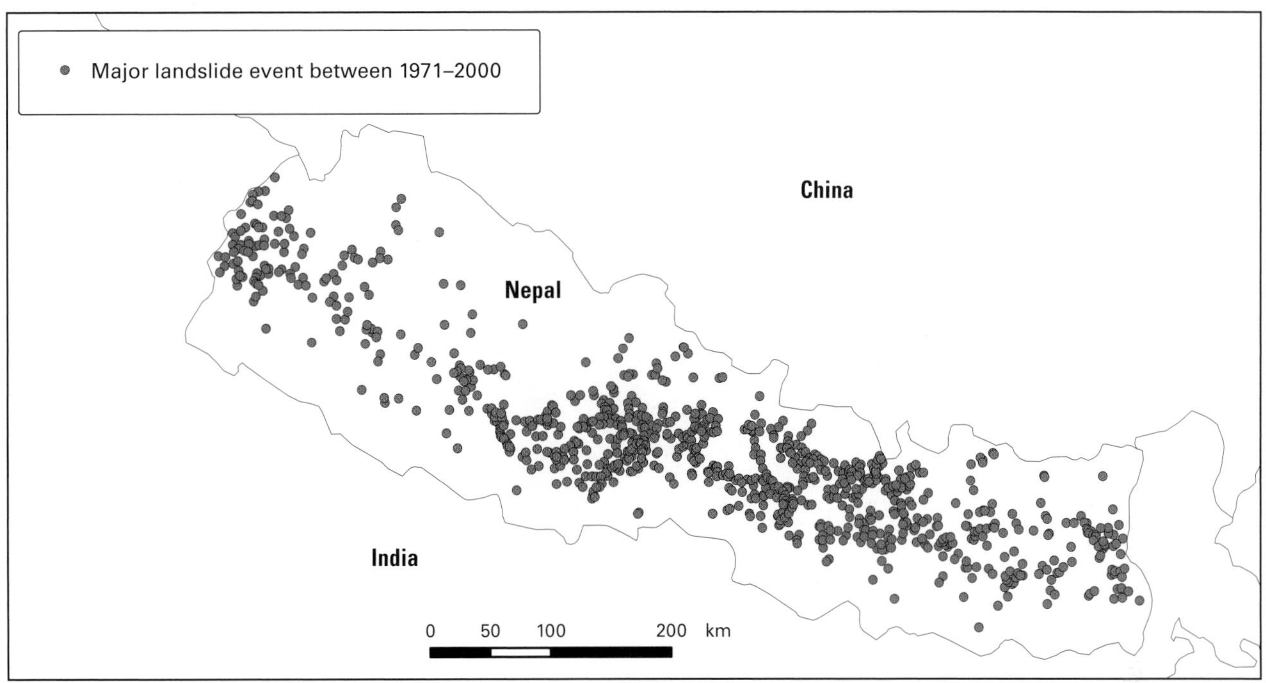

Source: Professor Narenda Raj Khanel.

Figure 2.19. Landslide hazard in Nepal predicted by the NGI model in this study

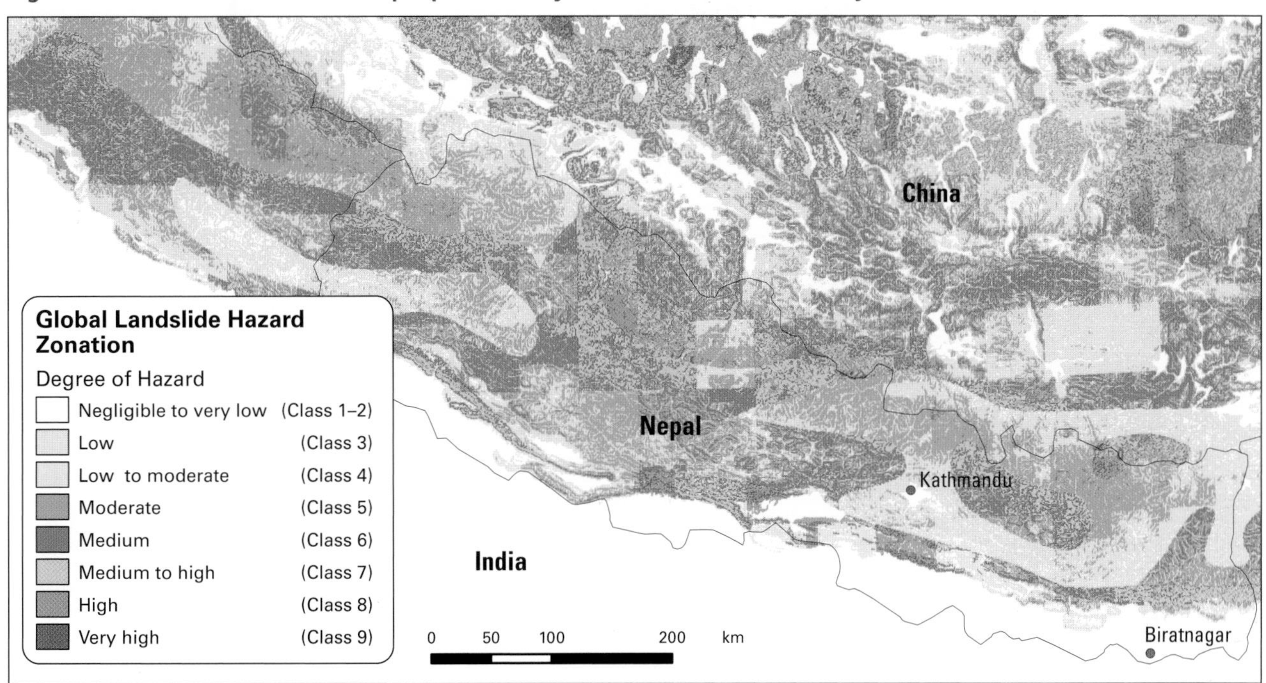

Figure 2.20. Population density map of Nepal in 1995. Numbers refer to population count in a 2.5' x 2.5' grid cell.

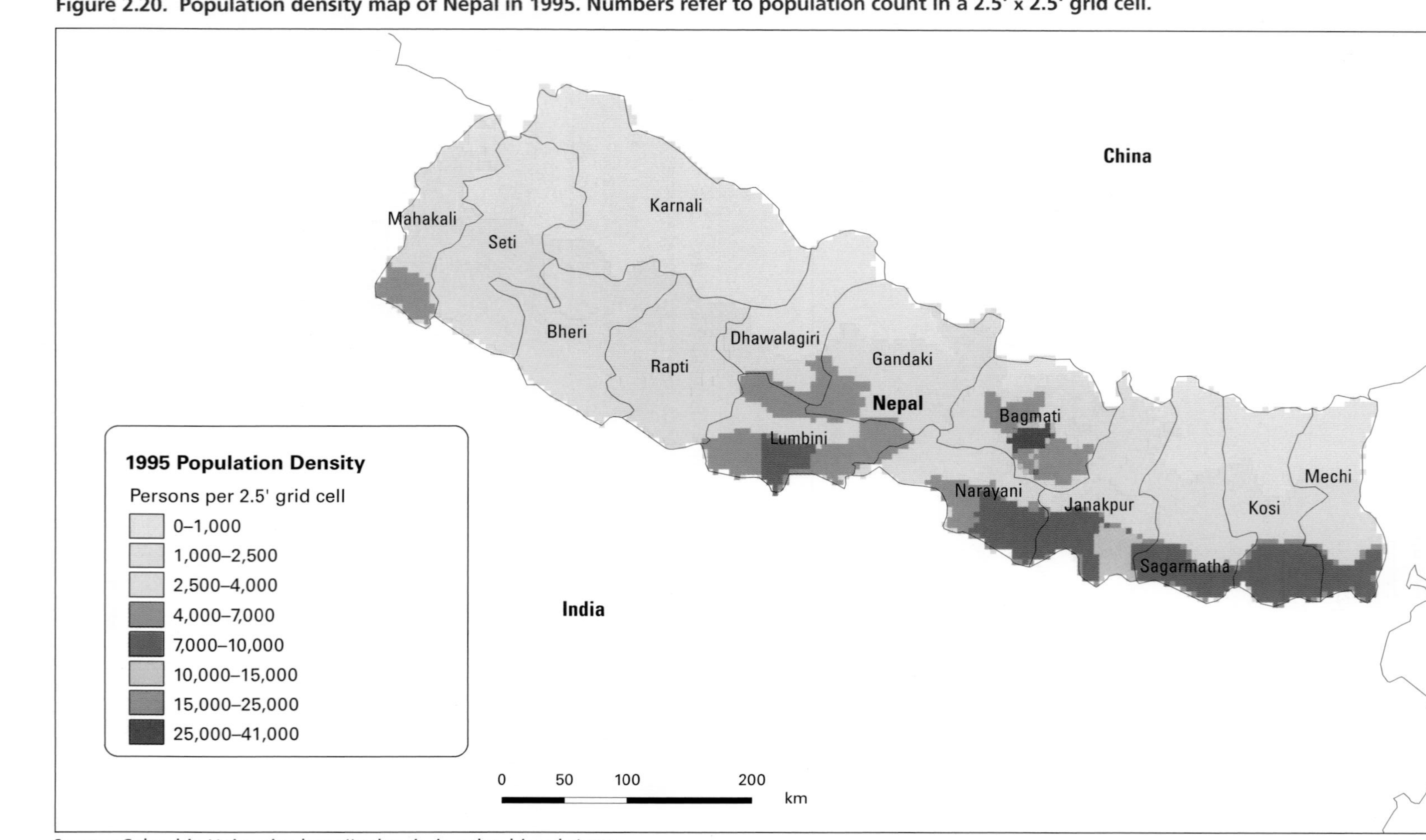

Source: Columbia University, http://sedac.ciesin.columbia.edu/gpw

developed in the present study. By superimposing the two maps, one can conclude the following:

- The model defines an approximate band featuring medium and medium-to-high hazard, which is generally consistent with observations of landslides.
- There is good agreement between the prediction map and the observations in defining a narrow band at the western end of Nepal with medium and medium-to-high hazard.
- The area with the highest density of landslides (the mid-section of the country) is only approximately identified by the prediction model.
- The model predicts a high hazard area in the north-northeastern part of the country, where few landslide events have been registered. This could be explained by the extremely low population density in that area, which implies that landslides occurring in that region would go unnoticed and unreported.

In summary, the prediction model yields a good first-pass approximation. Refinements would be needed to enable the model to produce hazard maps that can capture additional features of the landscape as well as geological and meteorological characteristics, and thus increase the model's ability to predict landslide susceptibility in a reliable manner.

Georgia

Information on landslide and snow avalanche hazards in Georgia was obtained from the Georgian Geophysical Society Web site (http://www.ggs.org.ge/others-natural.htm).

Landslides

As expected for a mountainous country, Georgia is prone to massive landslides, debris flows, and mudflows. There are some 10,000 potential landslide sites, 3,000 of which are very active. Most of the active landslide sites are located in Western Georgia, where the climate is humid.

Most landslides and debris flows in Georgia are triggered by heavy rainfall. The landslide activity increases when the accumulated annual precipitation exceeds the mean annual value by 200–400 mm. Statistical analyses show that 85 percent of debris flows originate after intense rain; a daily precipitation of 80–100 mm means there is a high probability of debris flow activation.

Figure 2.21 shows the landslide hazard predicted by the model developed in the present study.

The model in the present study can predict quite well the areas with "strong" and "high" landslide hazard susceptibility as suggested by the Georgian Geophysical Society, especially the general west-southeast trend and the highly susceptible areas in southwest Georgia. The model missed the "strong" hazard areas in the center of Georgia, and could not detect the "high" hazard area in southeastern Georgia.

On the other hand, the prediction model in this study suggests a higher landslide hazard in the center of Georgia, assigning "medium to high" and even "high" hazard labels, while the Georgian Geophysical Society characterizes the area as moderate to weak, with just a few indentations with high landslide hazard.

Snow Avalanches

Most of the avalanches (70 percent of them) in Georgia are triggered from January to March. The probability for avalanche occurrence is high if the snow cover thickness is 1 m or more. During the last 30 years, the danger of avalanches has increased due to uncontrolled forest harvesting activities in the Caucasian mountains. Increased avalanche activity was recorded in 1971, 1976–77, 1986–89, and 1996–97. The 1987 and 1989 winters were marked by extreme avalanche activity.

In January 1987, Western Georgia experienced a cyclone intrusion that covered the mountains in a thick layer of snow (up to 3–5 m in the Svanety region). This led to the triggering of some very large avalanches, resulting in dozens of fatalities, destruction of hundreds of buildings, and damage to infrastructure and lifelines.

Figures 2.22 shows the snow avalanche hazard predicted by the model developed in the present study.

W hereas the Georgian Geophysical Society mapping on its web site characterizes the northern part of Georgia as having a "moderate" to "high" snow avalanche hazard, the prediction model developed in this study characterizes the same area as "moderate" only, except the westernmost part of the country, which is categorized as having a "high" avalanche hazard. The trend showed by the two mappings is very similar.

Figure 2.21. Landslide hazard in Georgia predicted by the model developed in this study

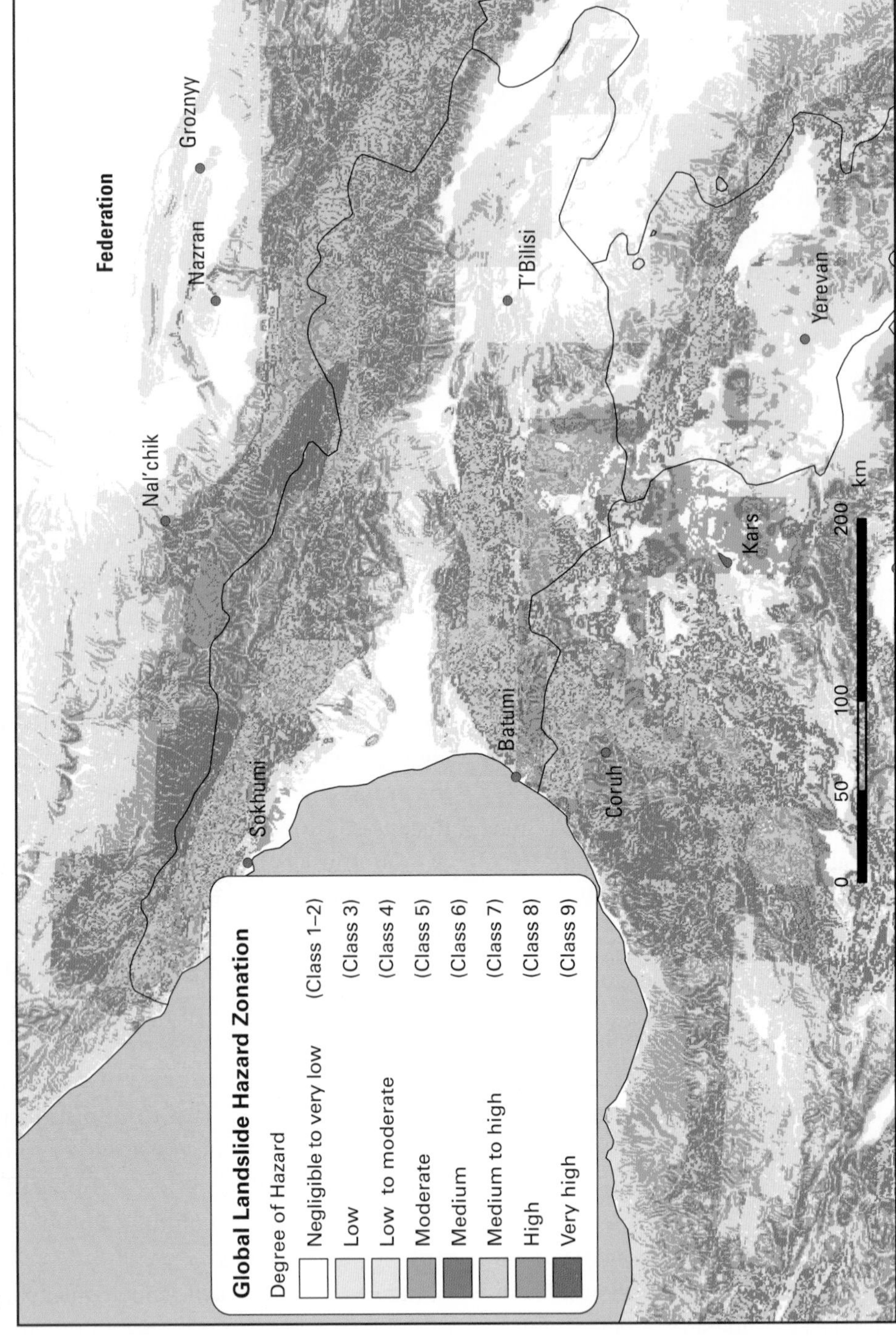

Figure 2.22. Snow avalanche hazard in Georgia predicted by the model developed in this study

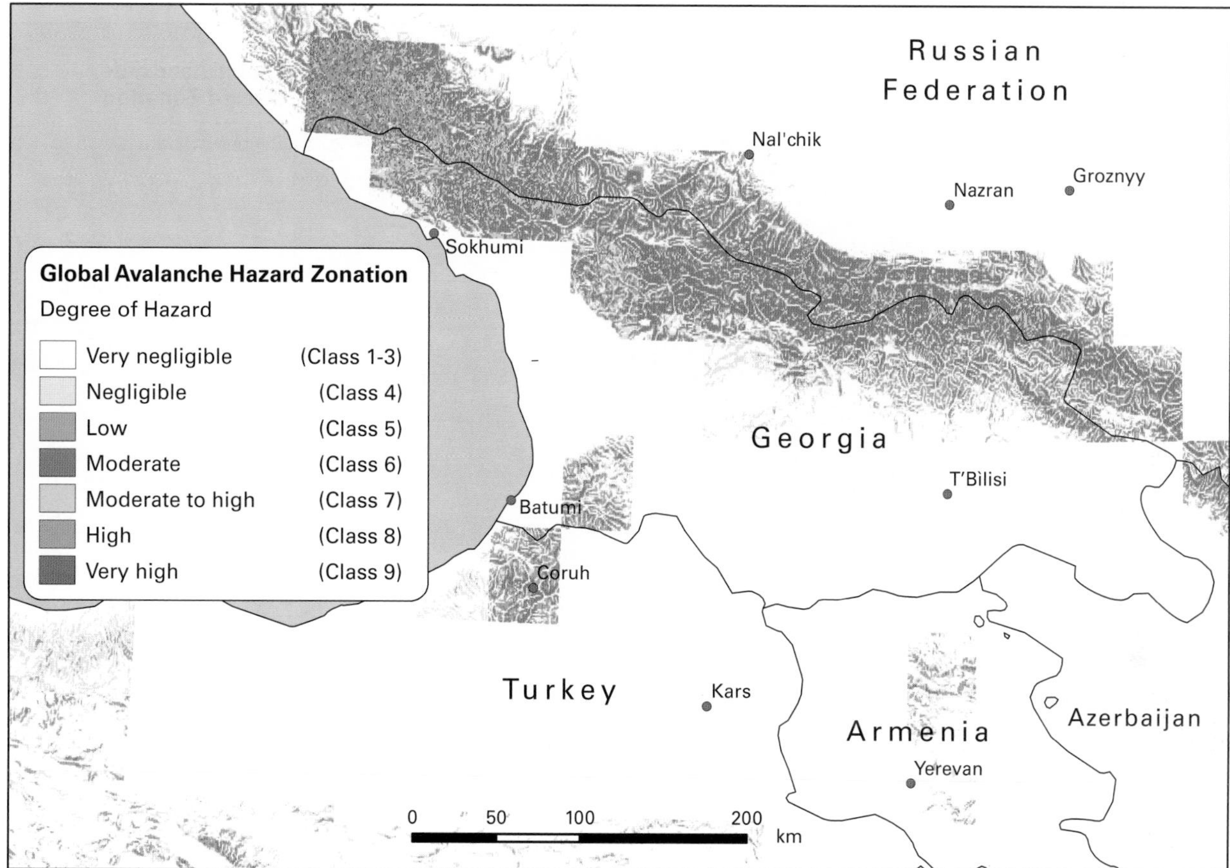

A limited extent of the southwest part qualified as "low to moderate," which is also well predicted by the new prediction model. The same remark also applies to the zones with a minimal snow avalanche hazard.

In summary, the model seems quite reliable for the mapping of both landslide and snow avalanche hazards in Georgia.

Sri Lanka

Landslides

Figure 2.23 presents a comparison between the observations of landslides in Sri Lanka over a 57-year period using NBRO data, with the landslide hazard map predicted by the model developed in this study. The landslides that have occurred are shown as punctual observations. The landslides group around the southern, central part of Sri Lanka.

Notwithstanding that the predicted hazard is low to negligible on a global basis, there is an excellent correlation between the location of the observed landslides and the "relative" hazard higher class predicted by the model at the same location. This example is a good application of the global model to a region that, on a global map, is not considered high risk. To make the results of mapping as meaningful as possible, the prediction in such regions would require local calibration and validation.

Jamaica

Landslides

Figures 2.24 and 2.25 compare historical landslide observations in Jamaica with the landslide hazard mapping predicted by the model developed in this study.

There is, in general, a good correlation between the locations of historical slides and the hazard classes predicted by the model. In particular, the model predicts well the large occurrence of landslides in eastern Jamaica and the extent of vertical hazard zones in the southern

Figure 2.23. Observed landslides in Sri Lanka between 1947 and 2003 (a) and prediction of landslide hazard in Sri Lanka by the model developed in this study (b).

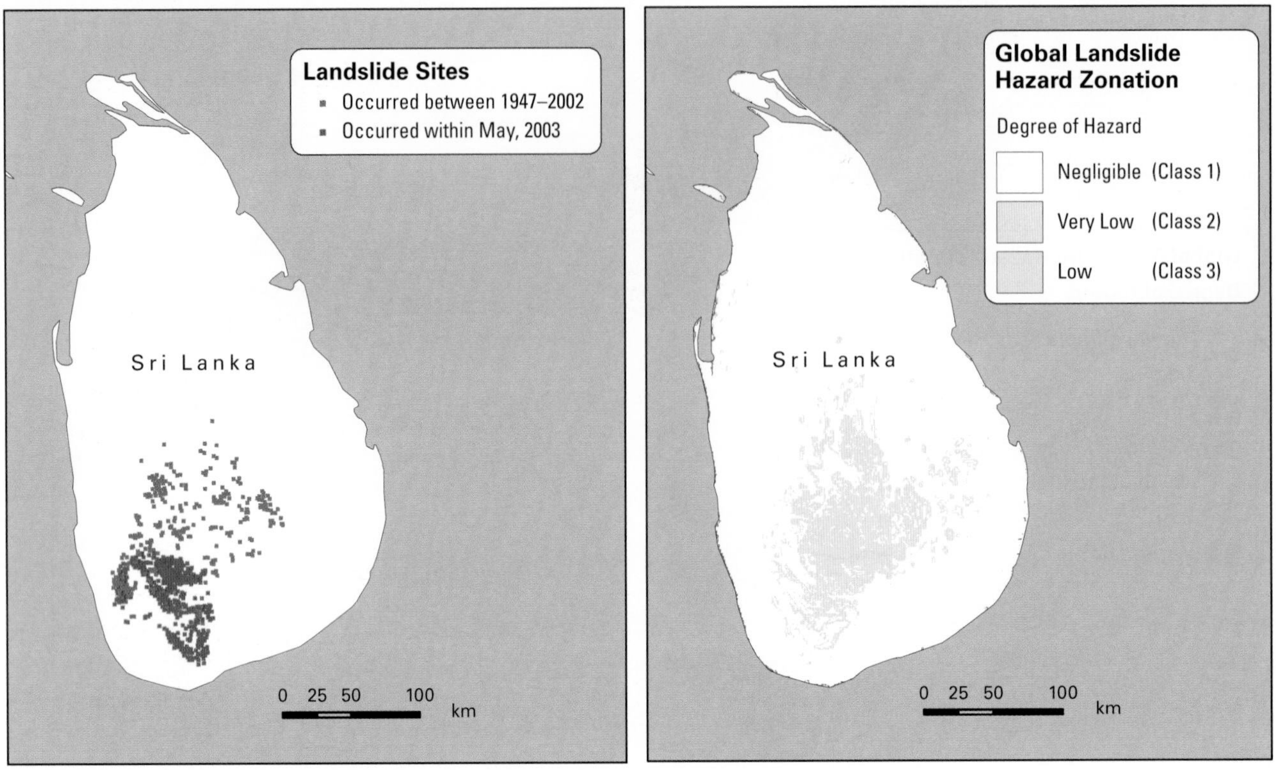

Source: Reprinted with permission from National Building Research Organization.

center of Jamaica. The model could not, however, detect the frequent landslides on the western part of Jamaica, nor in the center of the country.

Results of Global Analyses

Hotspots for Landslide Hazards

Landslides contribute to major disasters every year on a global scale, and the frequency of occurrence is on an upward trend. The increasing number of landslide disasters can be attributed in large part to the new reality of more extreme weather conditions combined with overexploitation of natural resources and deforestation, increased urbanization, and uncontrolled use of land. Recent examples are the mudflows of December 1999 in Venezuela, involving over 20,000 deaths, and the El Salvador earthquakes of 2001, which caused 600 deaths in just one landslide. Allocating resources for natural hazard risk management is a high priority among the development banks and international agencies working in developing countries.

Figures 2.26 to 2.28 illustrate the results obtained with the first-pass model for landslide hazard developed in this study.

In figure 2.26, the hotspots are identified on a world map. The regions are characterized by landslide hazards between negligible and very high (white to red). The main areas with moderate to very high landslide hazards include:

- Central America
- Northwestern South America
- Northwestern USA and Canada
- Hawaii
- Antilles
- The Caucasus region
- The Alborz and Zagros mountain ranges in Iran
- Turkey
- Ukraine

Figure 2.24. Historical landslide data in Jamaica (after Professor R. Ahmad)

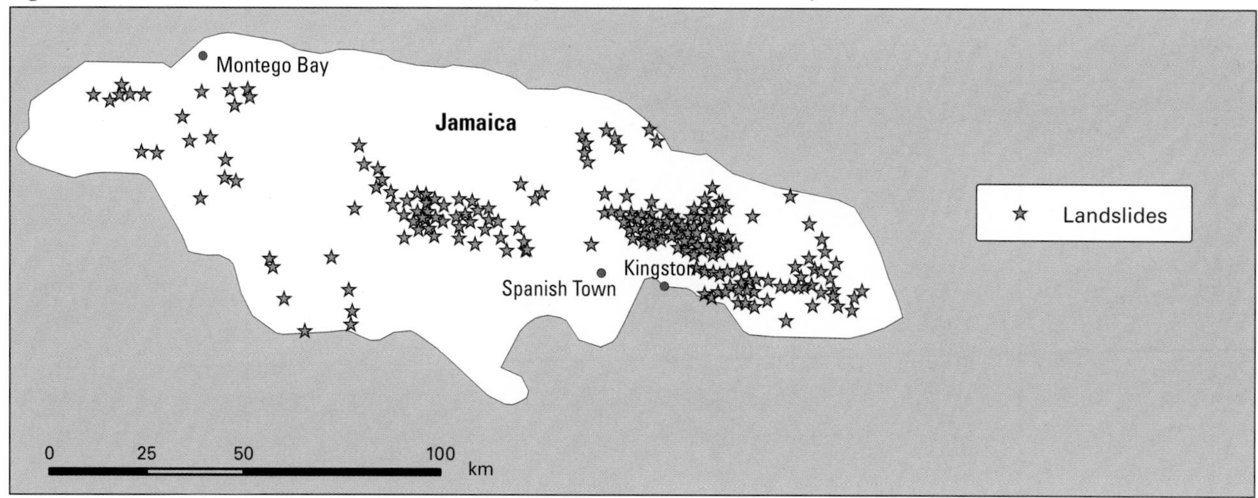

Source: Professor R. Ahmad

Figure 2.25. Prediction of landslide hazard in Jamaica with the model developed in this study

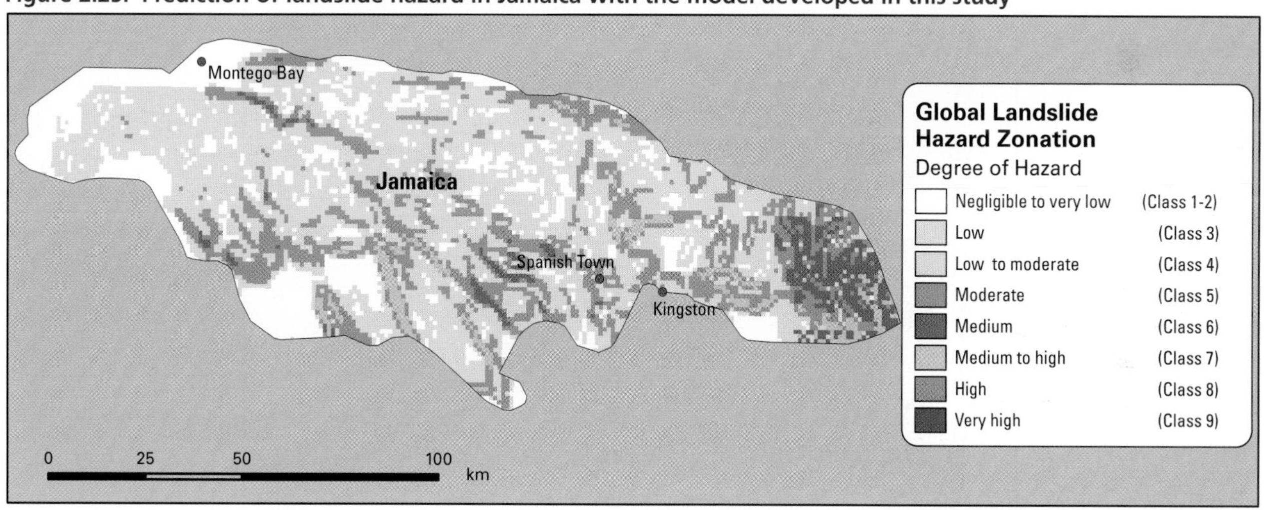

Figure 2.26. Global hotspot landslide hazard zonation for the world

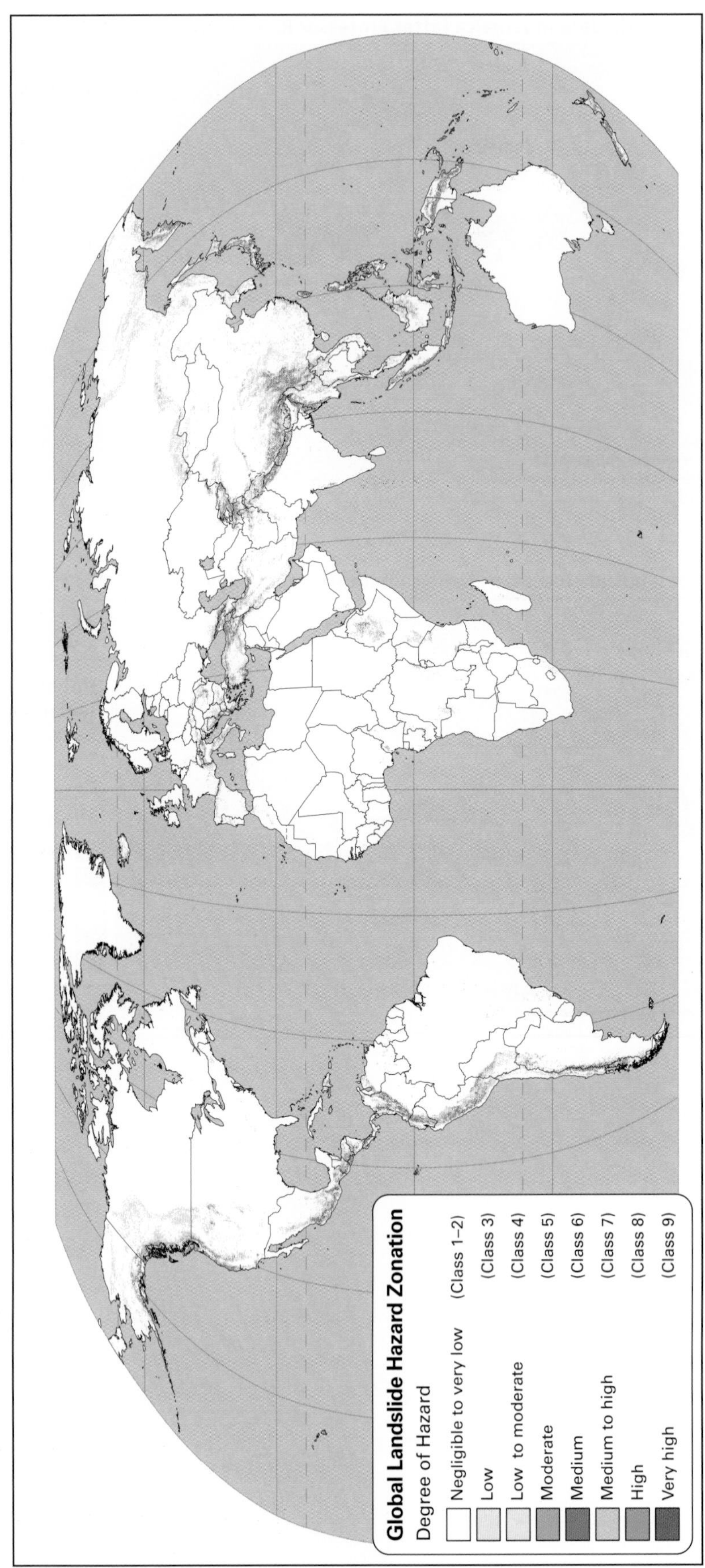

- The Himalayan belt
- Taiwan
- Philippines and Celebes
- Indonesia
- New Guinea
- New Zealand
- Italy
- Iceland
- Japan
- Kamtchatka

These areas are discussed further in the broader companion report, *Natural Disaster Hotspots: A Global Risk Analysis* (Dilley et al. 2005).

Figure 2.27 provides a more detailed mapping for Central Asia and the Middle East. Countries with "medium to high," "high," and "very high" landslide hazard scores include:

- Georgia
- Armenia
- Turkey
- Lebanon
- Iran
- A small part of southern Russia
- Tajikistan
- Kyrgyz Republic
- Afghanistan
- Nepal
- India
- Pakistan
- Southern China

Figure 2.30 presents the landslide hazard zonation for Central American and Caribbean countries, where the following countries are mapped with "medium to high," "high," and "very high" landslide hazard scores.

- Mexico
- Guatemala
- El Salvador
- Honduras
- Nicaragua
- Costa Rica
- Panama
- Colombia
- Ecuador
- Peru

Results of Risk Analysis

Hotspots for Landslide Risk

The model used for evaluation of landslide risk was described earlier. Details of the model are provided in Annex 2.A. The equation below provided the most stable correlation between number of expected fatalities due to landslides and socioeconomic parameters:

$$\ln(K) = 0.66\ln(PhExp\_all) + 0.70\ln(\overline{FC_{pc}}) + 0.36\ln(AR\_Land) - 2.44\ln(\overline{HDI}) - 14.98$$

Where:

K	=	The expected number of fatalities due to landslides;
PhExp_all	=	Physical exposure including all classes;
FCpc	=	The transformed percentage of forest in the country;
HDI	=	Transformed Human Development Index; and
Ar_Land	=	The percentage of arable land.

Although around 73 percent of the variation is explained by the regression, one has to keep in mind that this is not a predictive model, mostly because logarithmic regression prevents the use of "zero fatalities" in the analysis. However, the model can still be used to better understand the socioeconomic context of vulnerability and risk, and allows a differentiation of the classes of countries at risk.

Results of the analysis confirm the relevance of identification of physical exposure (landslide hazard model). Nearly 98 percent of the recorded landslide victims lived in countries affected by landslide classes 5 and higher. The process is validated by the good correlation observed between independent datasets such as reported casualties in CRED and frequencies of landslides as computed by the model described in the report, together with national socioeconomic parameters (such as HDI).

The risk evaluation study reveals that some countries with recorded casualties do not have a high physical exposure. Issues related to frequency in different climate regimes, and vegetation cover, might explain such discrepancies and could represent interesting topics for future studies.

Figure 2.27. Global hotspot landslide hazard zonation for Central Asia and the Middle East

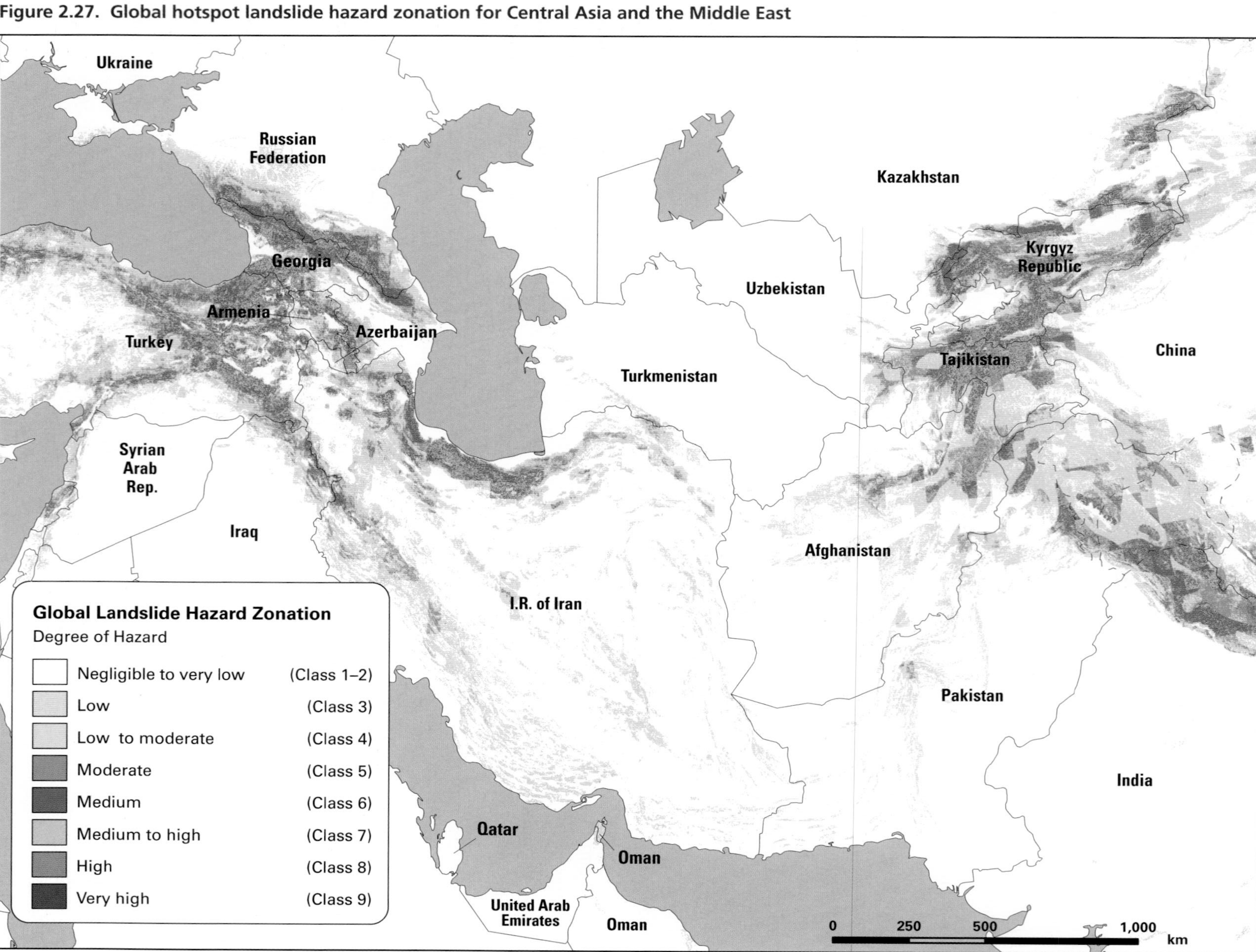

Figure 2.28. Global hotspot landslide hazard zonation for Central American and Caribbean countries

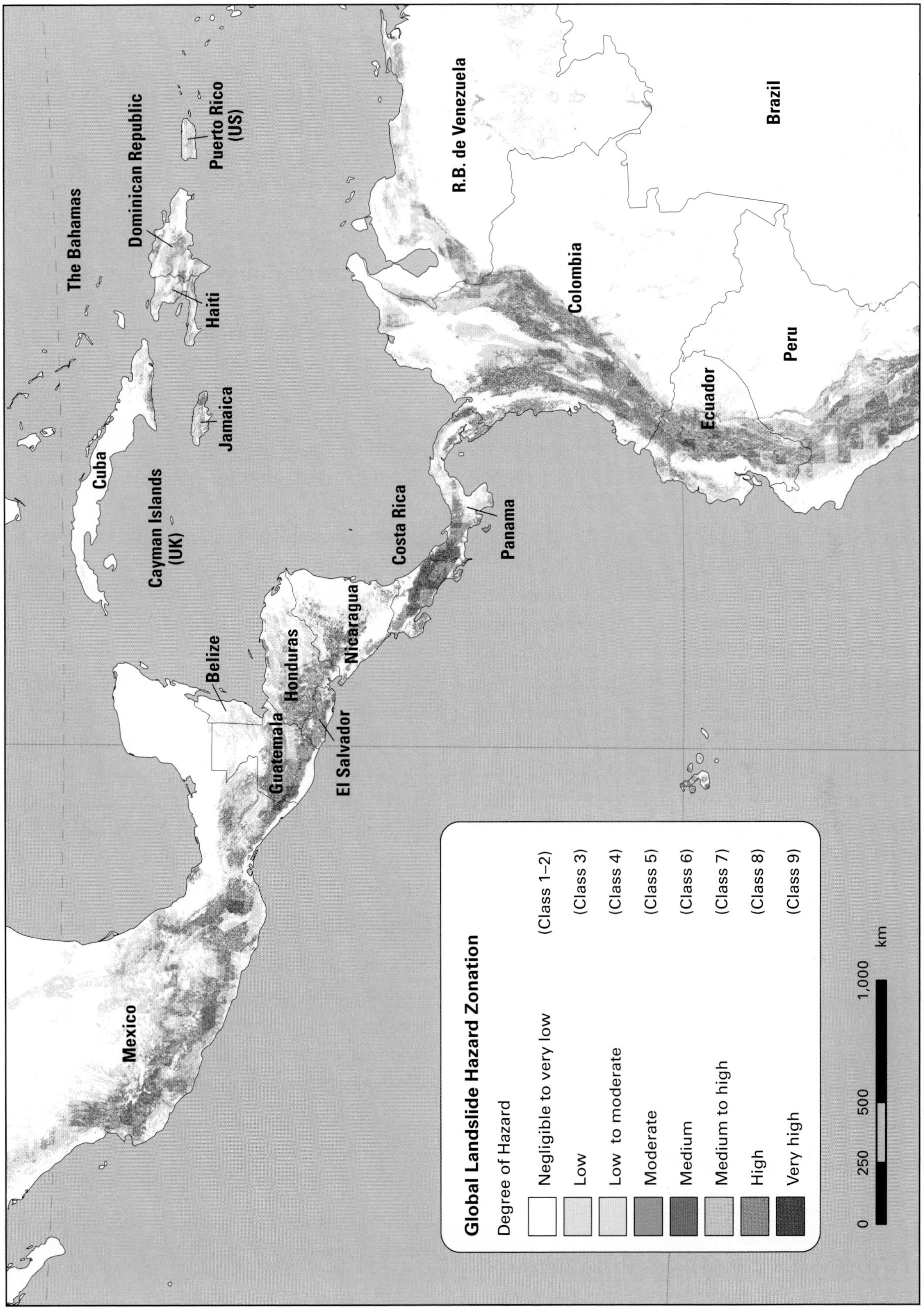

Conversely, countries with no recorded casualties over the 21-year period considered in this study cannot be evaluated using the method of vulnerability proxy. Data for a longer time period should be obtained.

The strong correlation between high physical exposure and low HDI, with high risk, is relatively straightforward to explain. However, the correlation between high percentage of forest and high landslide risk is more difficult to explain. This high correlation might be due to the effects of deforestation on susceptibility to landslides, which manifests itself indirectly through the "percentage of forest" parameter. Alternatively, countries with more forest coverage are likely to have more precipitation, and the effect of heavy precipitation is not adequately covered through the physical exposure parameter for these countries. The analyses demonstrate the need for data on deforestation, which might improve the model and further explain vulnerability.

Figures 2.29 and 2.30 illustrate some of the typical results obtained from the risk analyses.

Figure 2.29 presents a map of the landslide risk in Central America and Jamaica. One can observe that, with the model used, Colombia is the only country with greater than 10^{-2} risk of persons killed per year per square kilometer. Mexico, Guatemala, El Salvador, Honduras, Costa Rica, Panama, and Colombia show areas with risk between 10^{-2} and to 10^{-3}. Fairly large regions in nearly every country show rather large areas with landslide risk of 10^{-3} to 10^{-4}. The highest risk of persons killed per year per square kilometer in Jamaica is 10^{-3} to 10^{-4}.

Figure 2.30 presents a similar landslide risk map for Central Asia. In this case, Tajikistan, India, and Nepal show greater than 10^{-2} risk of persons killed per year per square kilometer. The same countries, plus Afghanistan and the Islamic Republic of Iran, show areas with risk between 10^{-2} and to 10^{-3}. Only a few other countries show areas with landslide risk of 10^{-3} to 10^{-4}.

Hotspots for Snow Avalanche Hazard

In the same manner, it is possible to develop global snow avalanche hazard maps. Figure 2.31 illustrates such global results obtained for Central Asia with the simple snow avalanche prediction model developed in this study.

The more susceptible countries (those with the highest avalanche hazard value) include the border of Georgia and Russia, Tajikistan, Afghanistan, and the Kyrgyz Republic. Each of these countries has areas with a "high" landslide hazard. The same countries, plus Turkey, the Islamic Republic of Iran, Pakistan, India, Uzbekistan, and Kazakhstan, are characterized as "moderate" snow avalanche hazard regions.

Recommendations for Further Studies

The study presented in this report was a first-pass analysis intended to identify global landslide hazard and landslide risk hotspots, with an emphasis on developing countries. The maps developed represent first-order identification of the geographic areas that constitute global landslide disaster hotspots. The probability of landslide occurrence was estimated from modeling physical processes and combining this information with historical observations and geological characteristics.

Rockslides, landslides, and snow avalanches were included in the study. The model was evaluated by comparing observations of the intensity and frequency of sliding events. The resulting landslide and avalanche hazard maps constitute the input to the global hotspots multihazard analysis in the companion report by Dilley et al. (2005).

The model developed and the methodology used in the study can be improved. The basic input data for the models could also be augmented and made more reliable. The following factors contributed to uncertainty in the results of the study:

- Scarcity of high-quality, high-resolution data on a global scale;
- Lack of a good-quality database and inventory of landslides for statistical analysis;
- Meaningful measure of terrain topography for a 1 km × 1 km grid cell; and,
- A reliance on proxies when desired information is rarely available. How good are these proxies?

Further studies are recommended on the following issues:

- Application of more sophisticated theoretical models for evaluation of landslide hazards;

Figure 2.29. Hotspot landslide risk zonation for Central America and Jamaica

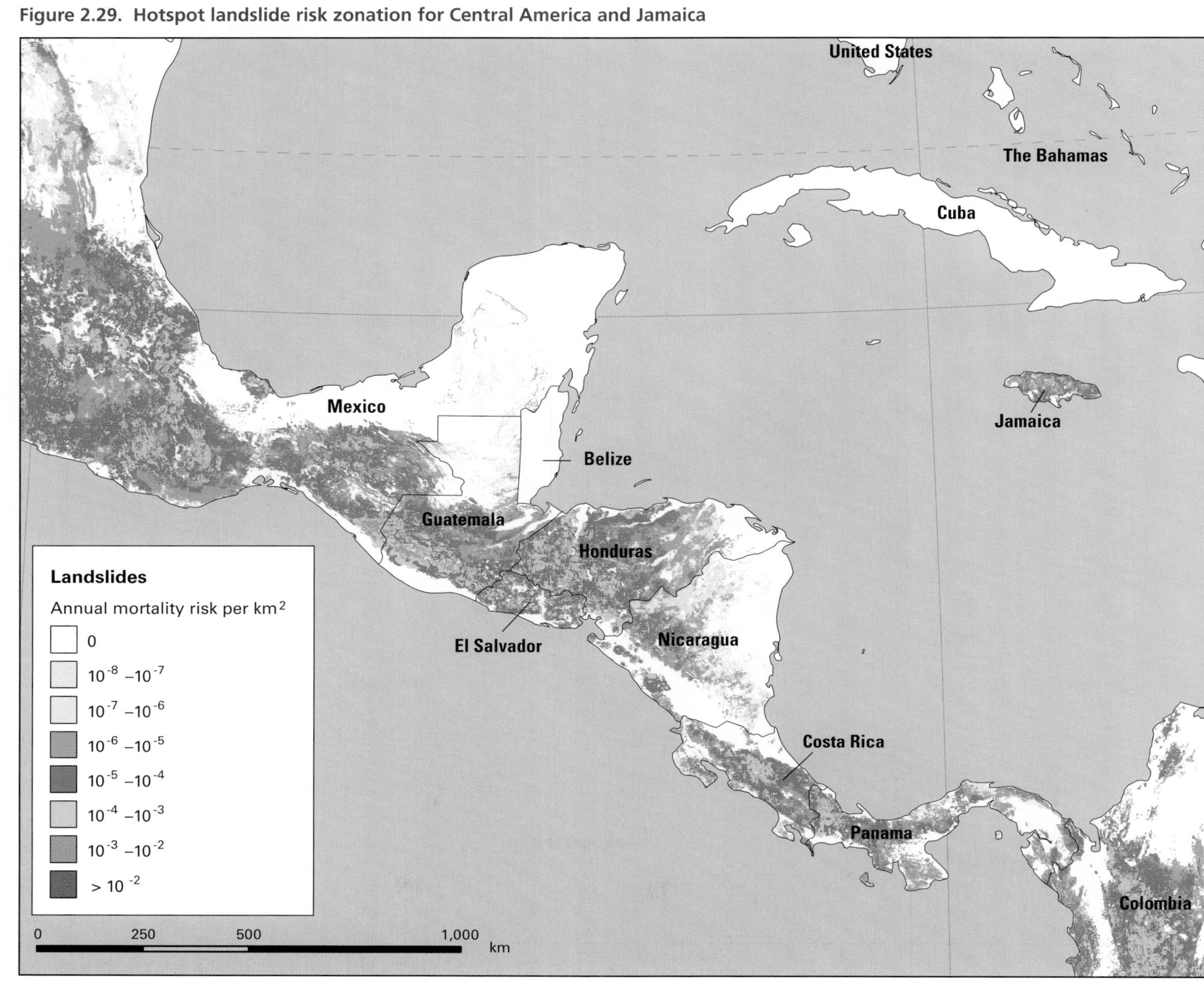

Figure 2.30. Hotspot landslide risk zonation for Central Asia

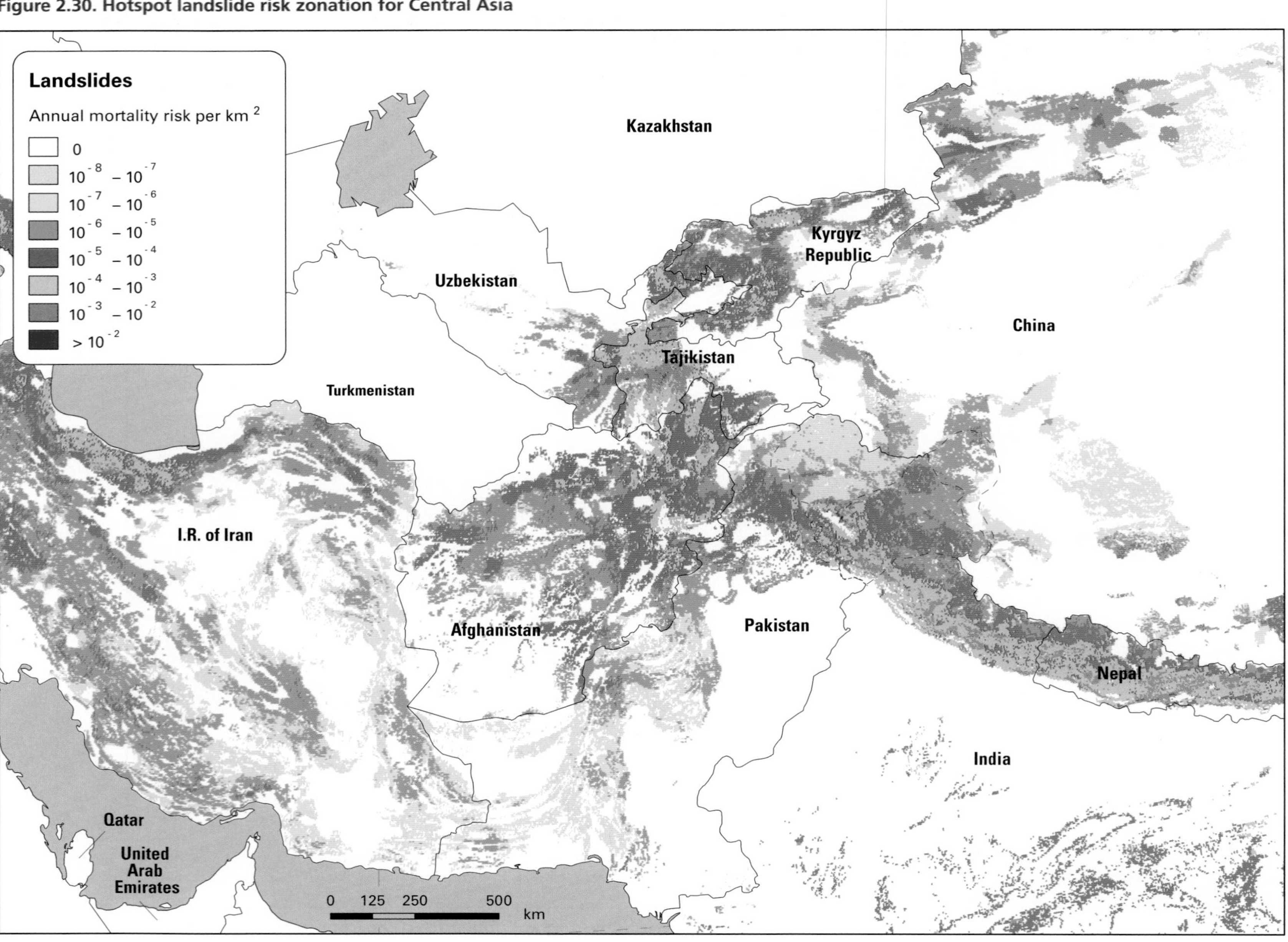

Figure 2.31. Global hotspot snow avalanche hazard zonation for Central Asia

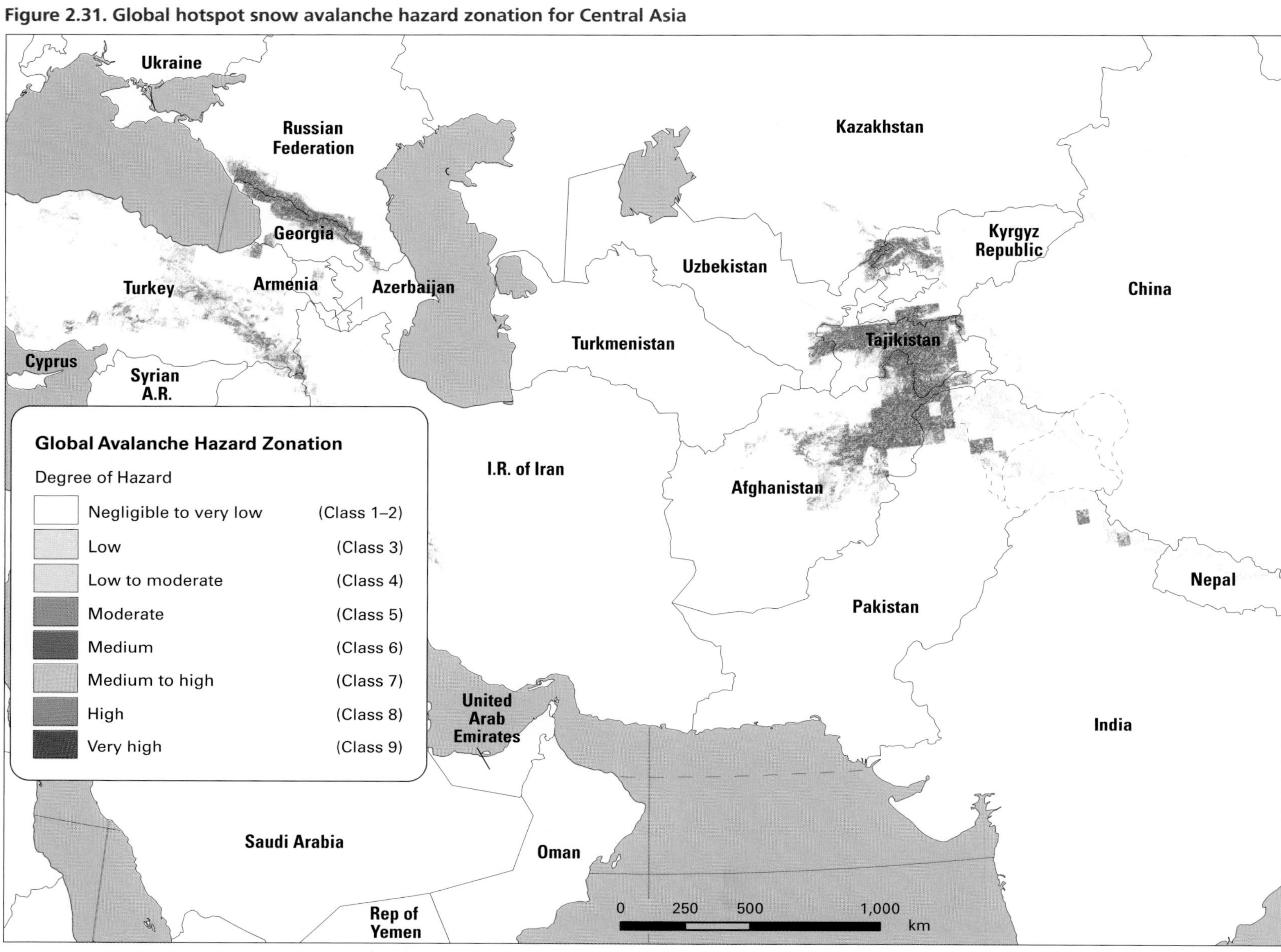

- More focused regional and international studies to calibrate and fine-tune the models for different regions of the world;
- Development of better databases of landslide inventory, fatalities caused by landslides, and economic consequences of landslides, at both the national and international levels.
- Direct evaluation of the economic risk associated with landslides and avalanches; and
- More detailed analysis of the effects of deforestation and vegetation cover on landslide hazard and vulnerability.

References

Blikra, L.H, A. Braathen, and E. Skurtveit. 2001. NGU Report 2962.01. 108. Hazard Evaluation of Rock Avalanches, the Baraldsnes Area. The Geological Survey of Norway, Trondheim. (1NGU, 2NGI).

Dilley, M., et al. 2005. Natural Disaster Hotspots: A Global Risk Analysis. Washington, DC: International Bank for Reconstruction and Development.

Leemans, R., and Wolfgang P. Cramer, 1991. The IIASA Database for Mean Monthly Values of Temperature, Precipitation and Cloudiness of a Global Terrestrial Grid. Laxenburg, Austria: IIASA, RR-91-18.

Mora, S., and W. Vahrson. 1994. Macrozonation Methodology for Landslide Hazard Determination. *Bulletin of the Association of Engineering Geologists* 31(1): 49–58.

Stephanyan, M., 2003. Regional Study. Managing Natural Disasters in Armenia. The World Bank Perspective. Country Risk Template.Yerevan, Armenia.

Willmott, C. J., C. M. Rowe, and Y. Mintz. 1985. Climatology of the Terrestrial Seasonal Water Cycle. *Journal of Climatology* 5: 589–606.

Willmott, C. J., and J. J. Feddema. 1992. A More Rational Climatic Moisture Index. *Professional Geographer* 44(1): 84–88.

Annex 2.A— Risk and Vulnerability Identification for Landslides

Results and Conclusions from Statistical Analysis

This appendix describes the method and results from the statistical analysis carried out to depict vulnerability and approach the risk of casualties caused by landslides. The research on landslide hazards was undertaken by the Norwegian Geotechnical Institute (NGI). The team from UNEP/DEWA/GRID-Europe first computed the physical exposure and then attempted to identify the socioeconomic context that leads to higher vulnerability. The research provides interesting results and clear connections between socioeconomic context and vulnerability. The method used in this study is based on the methodology developed during the project *Global Risk and Vulnerability Index Trend per Year* (GRAVITY). This project was described in the technical report (Peduzzi, Dao, Herold, Mouton (2002 and 2003)), which was made for the UNDP/BCPR and published in the report, *Reducing Disaster Risk: A Challenge for Development* (UNDP 2004).

Two different approaches were used for risk evaluation. The first method was based on observed casualties divided by physical exposure to map landslide risk distribution. Although this method allows for quantification of vulnerability, it doesn't explain why one population is more vulnerable than another. The second method used selected socioeconomic parameters through a statistical analysis in order to identify what particular socioeconomic parameters lead to higher vulnerability. The least developed and forested countries with high physical exposure were identified as being the most at risk. These first results are encouraging, but also demonstrate that further work is needed on the identification of frequencies for countries that include victims but were not selected in the physical exposure. This study also highlights the necessity to obtain accurate and relevant data on deforestation.

Working Definitions and Formulae

Hazards, Vulnerability, and Risk— Definitions and Concepts

The terminology used in this study is drawn from the UN and other experts. The definitions of the concepts are provided in the following paragraphs:

- **Risk:** *"The term risk refers to the expected losses from a particular hazard to a specified element at risk in a particular future time period. Loss may be estimated in terms of human lives, or buildings destroyed or in financial terms"* (UNDRO 1979; in Burton et al. 1993, p.34).

  Specificity in this research: The term "risk" is used to describe potential human losses (casualties) resulting from an expected future hazard.

- **Hazard:** *"The hazard can be defined as a potential threat to humans and their welfare"* (Smith 1996). The hazardous events vary in terms of magnitude as well as in *"frequency, duration, area extent, speed of onset, spatial dispersion, and temporal spacing"* (Burton et al. 1993, p.34).

  Specificity in this research: Only frequencies and area extent are considered in the model.

- **Physical Exposure:** *"Elements at risk, an inventory of those people or artifacts which are exposed to the hazard"* (Coburn et al. 1991, p. 49).

  Specificity in this research: Computation of average population annually exposed to landslides. In this research the element at risk is the population.

- **Vulnerability:** *"Reflects the range of potentially damaging events and their statistical variability at a particular location"* (Smith 1996). *"The degree of loss to each element should a hazard of a given severity occur"* (Coburn et al. 1991, p. 49).

  Specificity in this research: The discrepancies of casualties induced by different vulnerabilities are used to identify socioeconomic indicators reflecting such vulnerabilities.

By UN definition (UNDRO 1979), the risk is resulting from three components:

"***Hazard occurrence probability,*** *defined as the probability of occurrence of a specified natural hazard at a specified severity level in a specified future time period,* ***elements at risk,*** *an inventory of those people or artifacts which are exposed to the hazard and* ***vulnerability,*** *the degree of loss to each element should a hazard of a given severity occur*" (Coburn et al. 1991, p. 49).

Formula and Method for Estimating Risk and Vulnerability

The formula used for modeling risk combines the three components of the UNDRO definition (UNDRO 1979): the risk is a function of hazard occurrence probability, element at risk (population), and vulnerability. The following hypothesis was made for modeling the risk: the three factors explaining risk are multiplying each other.

$$R = H \cdot Pop \cdot Vul^{1}$$

Where:

- R = The risk, that is, the expected human impacts (expected number of killed people);
- H = The hazard, which depends on the frequency and strength of a given danger;
- Pop = The population living in a given exposed area;
- Vul = The vulnerability and depends on socio-politico-economic context of this population.

From the previous discussion, the physical exposure is defined as the *combination of both frequency and population exposed* to a given magnitude for a selected type of hazard. The hazard multiplied by the population can then be replaced by the physical exposure:

$$R = PhExp \cdot Vul$$

Where:

- $PhExp$ = The physical exposure, that is, the frequency and severity multiplied by exposed population.

One way of estimating the risk is to look at impacts from previous hazardous events. The physical exposure can be obtained by modeling the area extent affected by one event. Using the area affected, the figure representing exposed population can be extracted using a Geographical Information System (GIS); the population affected multiplied by the frequency provides the physical exposure. The identification of parameters leading to higher vulnerability can then be carried out by replacing the risk in the equation by casualties reported in EM-DAT from CRED and running a statistical analysis for highlighting links between socioeconomic parameters, physical exposure, and observed casualties.

Computation of Physical Exposure

General Description

In broad terms, the physical exposure was estimated by multiplying the hazard frequency by the population living in the exposed area. The frequency of hazard was derived for different strengths of events, and the physical exposure was computed according to the equation below:

$$\mathrm{PhExp}_{nat} = \sum F_i \cdot Pop_i$$

Where:

- $PhExp_{nat}$ = The physical exposure at the national level;
- F_i = The annual frequency of a specific magnitude event in one spatial unit as provided by NGI; and
- Pop_i = The total population living in the spatial unit (divided by 10, following NGI's recommendations).

The frequencies used were the ones of classes 2 and higher as described in table 2.A.1.

Table 2.A.1. Classes of frequencies

Class	*Annual frequency of occurrence (in %)*	*Typical return period for serious events (year)*
9	0.05–0.2	500–2,000
8	0.025–0.1	1,000–4,000
7	0.0125–0.05	2,000–8,000
6	0.0063–0.025	4,000–16,000
5	0.0025–0.01	10,000–40,000
4	0.001–0.005	20,000–100,000
3	0.0004–0.002	50,000–250,000
2	0.0001–0.001	100,000–1,000,000

[1] The model uses a logorithmic regression; the equation is similar but with an exponent for each of the parameters.

The total population annually exposed is slightly higher than 4,350. This feature is very similar to the average number of people killed per year worldwide (1,727). This is a good sign for the quality of physical exposure. Ninety-eight percent of the recorded victims are within the countries affected by landslides of class 5 and over. The remaining 2 percent of casualties happen in countries affected only by classes 2 to 4.

Extraction of population was based on the CIESIN, IFPRI, and WRI Gridded Population of the World (GPW, Version 2) at a resolution of 2.5'[2] (equivalent to 5 × 5 km at the equator). This layer was further completed by the Human Population and Administrative Boundaries Database for Asia (UNEP) for Taiwan and the CIESIN Global Population of the World Version 2 (country-level data) for the former Yugoslavia. These datasets reflect the estimated population distribution for 1995. Since population growth is sometimes very high in the 1980–2000 period, a correction factor using country totals was applied in order to estimate current physical exposures for each year as follows:

$$PhExp_i = \frac{Pop_i}{Pop_{1995}} \cdot PhExp_{1995}$$

Where:

$PhExp_i$ = The physical exposure of the current year;

Pop_i = The population of the country at the current year;

Pop_{1995} = The population of the country in 1995; and

$PhExp_{1995}$ = The physical exposure computed with population in 1995.

To take into account the increase of population (hence, the increase of physical exposure), an average physical exposure using the number of casualties is then computed to better reflect the situation at the time the events occurred. The formula is similar to the one used to transform socioeconomic values.

[2] GPW2 was preferred to the ONRL Landscan population dataset, despite its five-times-lower spatial resolution (2.5' against 30"), because the original information on administrative boundaries and population counts is almost two times more precise (127,093 administrative units against 69,350 units). Furthermore the Landscan dataset is the result of a complex model that is not explained thoroughly and that is based, among other variables, on environmental data (land-cover), making it difficult to use for further comparison with environmental factors (circularity).

$$PhExp_{av} = \sum \frac{K_{ic} \cdot PhExp_{ic}}{K_{tot}}$$

Where:

$PhExp_{av}$ = Average physical exposure pondered by the casualties;

K_{ic} = Killed from landslides for the year "i" and the country "c";

$PhExp_{ic}$ = Physical exposure for the year "i" and the country "c"; and

K_{tot} = Total number killed from landslides for the selected country.

Identification of Risk to Landslide

Risk Distribution Using Vulnerability Proxy

A quantitative approach can be used by computing a proxy of vulnerability. This proxy is based on the ratio between the number of people killed and the number of people exposed (see equation below).

$$Vul^{a}_{proxy} = \frac{K^{\beta}}{PhExp^{\delta}}$$

Where:

Vul = Vulnerability proxy;

K = Past casualties as recorded in CRED; and

$PhExp$ = Physical exposure: population living in exposed areas multiplied by the frequency of occurrence of the landslides.

All three parameters can be at a certain power.

Once the vulnerability proxy is computed, it can be multiplied by the physical exposure to produce a risk map at the pixel level. This method is, however, a generalized approach that cannot take into account the significant vulnerability differences between rural and urban populations. This limitation can only be overcome by the use of subnational datasets on socioeconomic features and on geo-referenced information on the number of casualties. Such analysis would also require more records than would the analysis of average vulnerability derived from the national-level values. The data for the number of victims from the two most extreme events (Venezuela, 1999, and Colombia, 1985) were removed because the events' magnitudes were deemed incompatible with the other events.

Note: The limitation of such a method is that countries without reported casualties are not represented in the risk analysis. Physical exposure involving all the classes had to be taken into account in order to have some measure of physical exposure in countries where casualties are reported.

Examples of Distributions

Identification of Vulnerability in the Socioeconomic Context

Once the raster grid of frequencies is established, this dataset is multiplied by a dataset of population. The result is aggregated at the national level in order to obtain the average number of persons exposed per year. The figures from past casualties are then compared with physical exposure and with a series of national socioeconomic parameters that have been transformed and standardized. A logarithmic regression is then performed to identify which socioeconomic parameters are best linked with the casualties. Coefficients (weights) are also associated with the different components of the expression (see equation below):

$$K = C \cdot (PhExp_{landslides})^{a} \cdot V_1^{a_1} \cdot V_2^{a_2} \ldots \cdot V_p^{a_p}$$

Where:

K	=	The number of persons killed by a certain type of hazard;
C	=	The multiplicative constant;
$PhExp$	=	The physical exposure: population living in exposed areas multiplied by the frequency of occurrence of the landslide;
V_i	=	The socioeconomic parameters; and
α_i	=	The exponent of V_i, which can be negative (for ratio).

This will enable a test of the quality of the link between the socioeconomic contextual parameters and physical exposure, both of which are features that help to explain casualties. It also provides useful information on what conditions increase societal susceptibility to landslides. Table 2.A.2., vulnerability indicators, provides a list of socioeconomic parameters that were used in the analysis.

The factors considered for the analysis were selected according to the following criterion:

- Relevance: vulnerability factors (outputs-orientated), resulting from the observed status of the population, not based on mitigation factors (inputs, action taken). Example: school enrollment rather than education budget.

Data quality and availability: data should cover the 1980–2000 period and most of the 249 countries and territories. Situations in territories were separated from those in countries; for example, the situation in Martinique is valid only for this island and is not taken into account for computing socioeconomic average at the national level (France).

Statistical Analysis: Methods and Results

Defining a Multiplicative Model

The statistical analysis is based on two major hypotheses. First, that the risk can be approached by the number of victims of past hazardous events. Second, that the equation of risk follows a multiplicative model:

$$K = C \cdot (PhExp)^{a} \cdot V_1^{a_1} \cdot V_2^{a_2} \ldots \cdot V_p^{a_p}$$

Where:

K	=	The number of persons killed by a certain type of hazard;
C	=	The multiplicitive constant;
$PhExp$	=	The physical exposure: population living in exposed areas multiplied by the frequency of occurrence of the hazard;
V_i	=	The socioeconomic parameters; and
α_i	=	The exponent of Vi , which can be negative (for ratio).

Using the logarithmic properties, the equation could be written as follows:

$$\ln(K) = \ln(C) + \alpha \ln(PhExp) + \alpha_1 \ln(V_1) + \alpha_2 \ln(V_2) + \ldots \alpha_p \ln(V_p)$$

This equation provides a linear relation between logarithmic sets of values. Significant socioeconomic parameters V_i (with transformations when appropriate) and exponents α_i could be determined using linear regressions.

Figure 2.A.1. Distribution of risk utilizing a vulnerability proxy in Central America

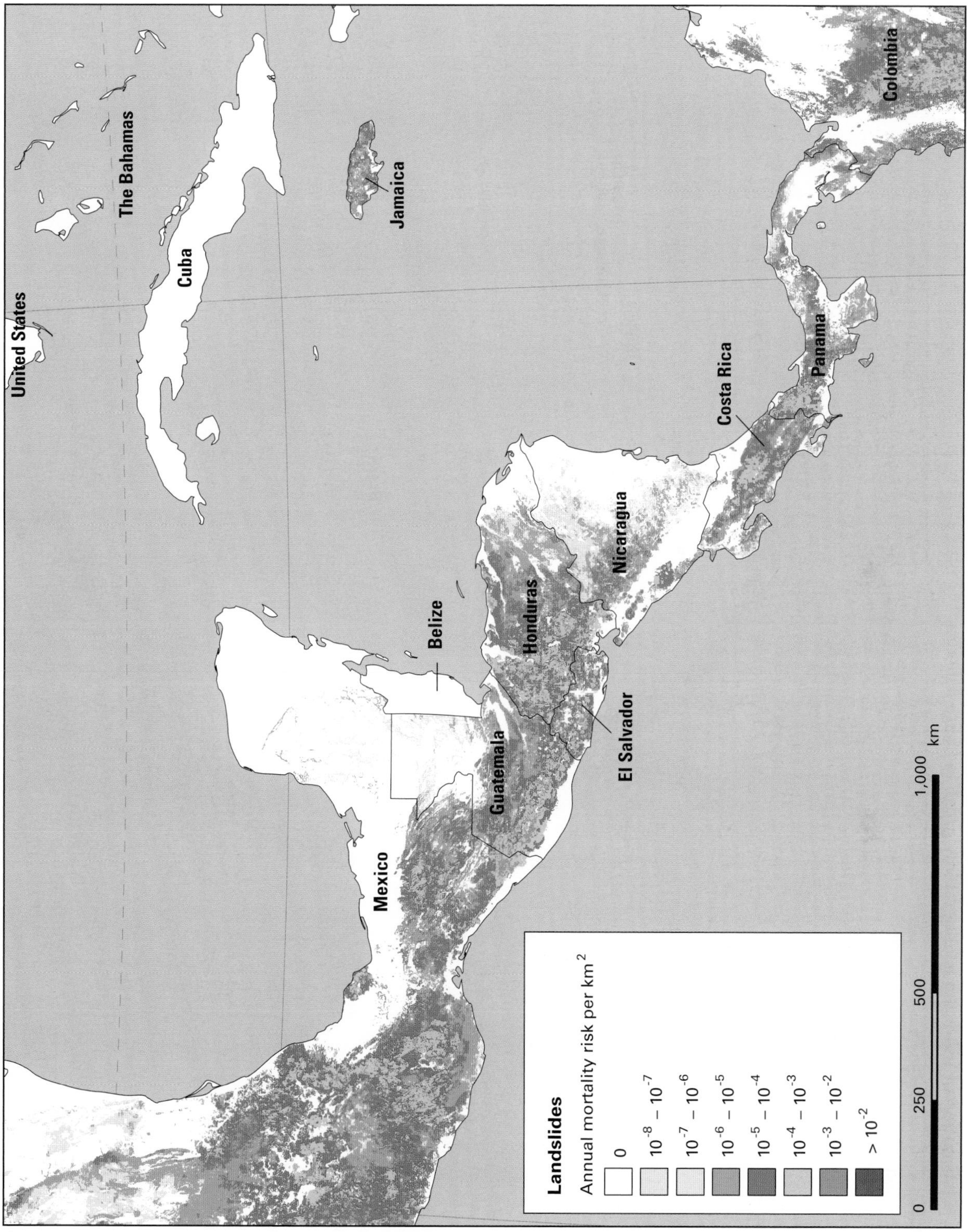

Figure 2.A.2. Distribution of risk using a vulnerability proxy in South America

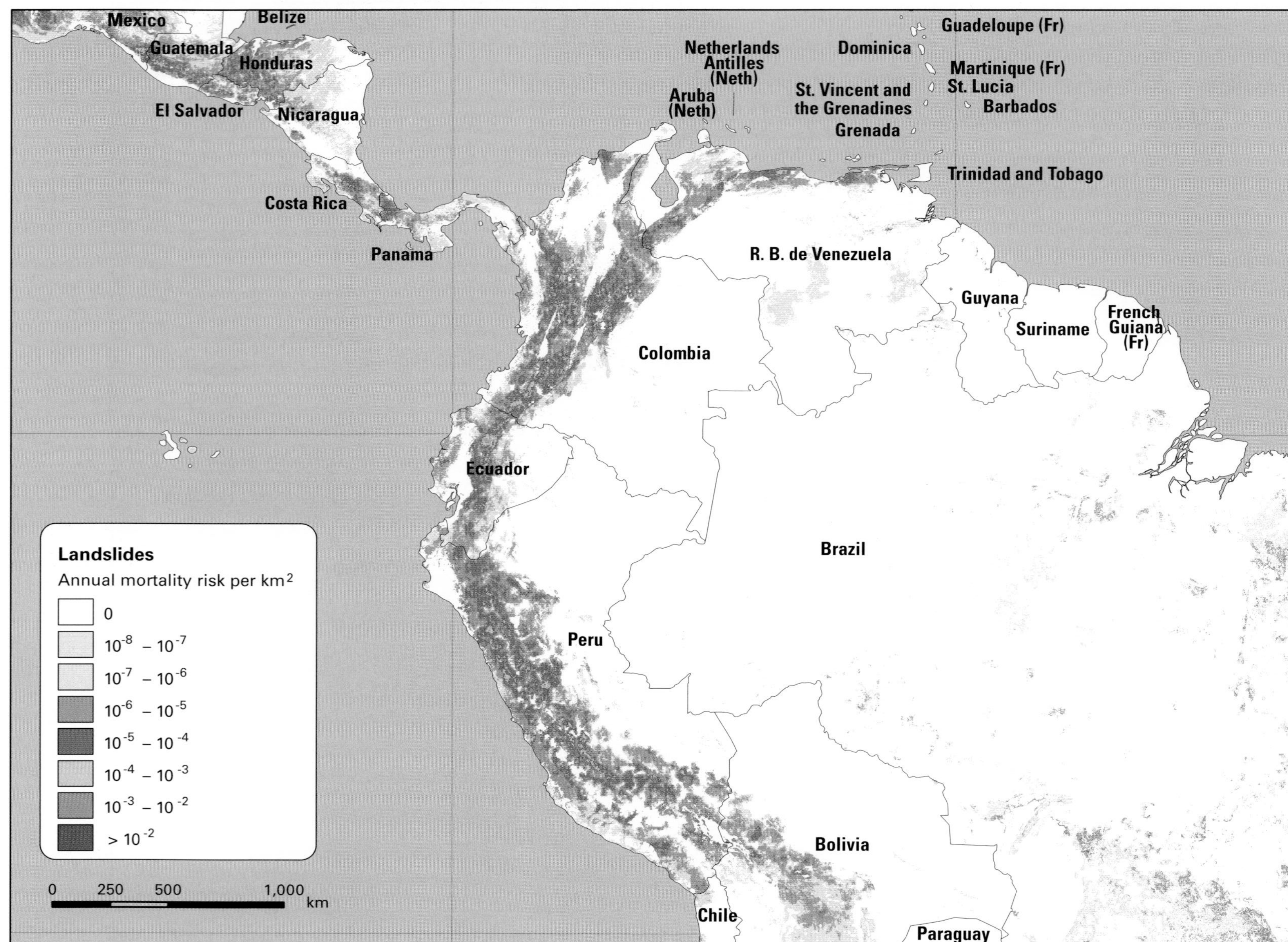

Figure 2.A.3. Distribution of risk utilizing a vulnerability proxy in Central Asia

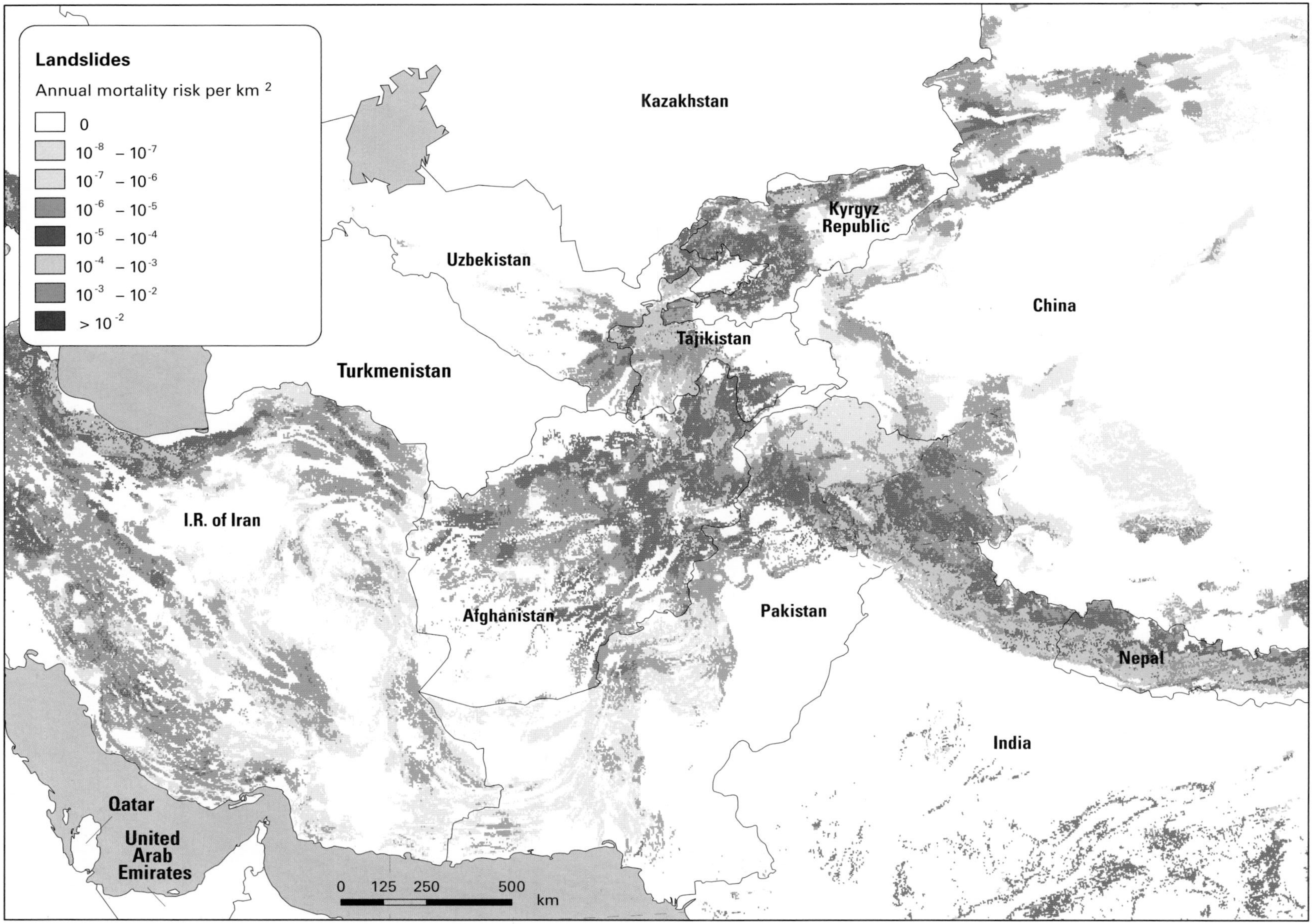

Table 2.A.2. Vulnerability indicators

Categories of vulnerability	*Indicators*	*Source*[1]
Economic	Gross Domestic Product per inhabitant at purchasing power parity Human Poverty Index (HPI) Total debt service (% of the exports of goods and services), Inflation, food prices (annual %), Unemployment, total (% of total labor force)	WB UNDP WB ILO
Type of economical activities	Percentage of arable land Percentage of urban population Percentage of agriculture's dependency for GDP Percentage of labor force in agricultural sector	FAO UNPOP WB FAO
Dependency and quality of the environment.	Forests and woodland (in percentage of land area), Percentage of irrigated land Human Induced Soil Degradation (GLASOD)	FAO FAO UNEP
Demography	Population growth, Urban growth, Population density, Age dependency ratio,	UNPOP GRID[2] GRID[3] WB
Health and sanitation	Average calorie supply per capita, Percentage of people with access to adequate sanitation, Percentage of people with access to safe water (total, urban, rural) Number of physicians (per 1,000 inh.), Number hospital beds Life expectancy at birth for both sexes Under five years old mortality rate	FAO WHO/ UNICEF WHO/ UNICEF WB WB UNPOP UNPOP
Politic	Index of Corruption	WB
Early warning capacity	Number of Radios (per 1,000 inh.)	WB
Education	Illiteracy Rate, School enrolment, Secondary (% gross), Labor force with primary, secondary or tertiary education	WB UNESCO UNESCO WB
Development	Human Development Index (HDI)	UNDP
Risk	Victims (killed by landslides)	CRED

[1] FAOSTAT (Food and Agriculture Organisation, FAO) / GRID: UNEP/Global Resource Information Database / WB: World Development Indicators (World Bank) / UNDP: Human Development Report (UNDP) / ILO: International Labour Office / UNPOP: UN Dep. Of Economic and Social Affairs/Population Division. Most of the data were reprocessed by the UNEP Global Environment Outlook team. Figures are available at the GEO Data Portal (UNEP), http://geodata.grid.unep.ch, CRED: Université Catholique de Louvain (as of 2002), EM-DAT: The OFDA/CRED International Disaster Database, http://www.cred.be/

[2] calculated from UNPOP data

[3] calculated from UNEP/GRID spatial modelling based on CIESIN population data.

Detailed Process

Data on Victims. The number of killed was derived from the CRED database and computed as the average number of killed per year over the 1980–2000 period.

Filtering the Data. The statistical models for each disaster type were based on subsets of countries, which excluded:

- Countries with no physical exposure or no victims reported (zero or null values).
- Countries without all the selected socioeconomic variables.
- Eccentric values, when exceptional events or other factors would clearly show abnormal levels of victims, for example, the landslides in Caracas (Venezuela, 1999) and in Armero (Colombia, 1985).

Transformation of Variables. The average of socioeconomic parameters was computed for the 21-year period. The average of the socioeconomic parameters was reached by using the number of victims to better reflect the situation at the time the events occurred.

$$V_{p}\_a_{v} = \sum \frac{K_{ic} \cdot V_{ic}}{K_{tot}}$$

Where:

V_{p_av} = Socioeconomic value reached by number of people killed for a selected country;

K_{ic} = Killed from landslides for the year "i" and the country "c";

V_{ic} = Socioeconomic value for the year "i" and the country "c"; and

K_{tot} = Total number killed in landslides for the selected country.

For some of the indicators, the logarithm was computed directly; for other parameters expressed in percentage form, a transformation was applied so that all variables would range between -∞ and +∞. This appeared to be relevant as some of the transformed variables were proved to be significant in the final result. For others, no logarithmic transformation was needed; for instance, the population growth already behaves in a cumulative way.

$$V'_{i} = \frac{V_{i}}{(1-V_{i})}$$

Where:

V'_i = The transformed variable (ranging from -∞ to + ∞), and

V_i = The socioeconomic variable (ranging from 0 to 1).

Figure 2.A.3. Transformation for variables ranging between 0 and 1

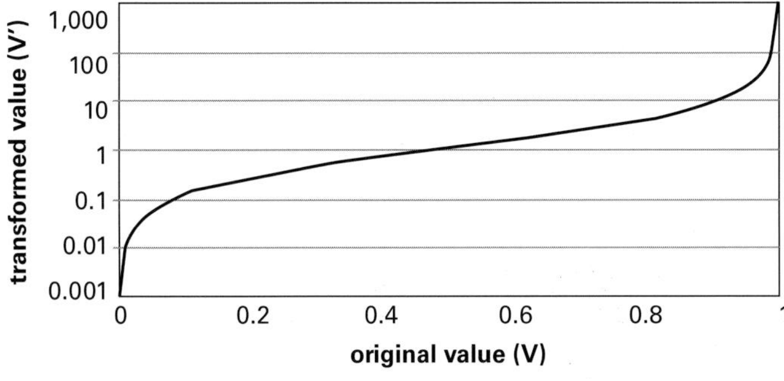

Choice Between Variables. One important condition when computing regressions is that the variables included in a model should be independent; that is, the correlation between two sets of variables should be low. This is clearly not the case with HDI and GDP per capita expressed in purchasing power parity (hereafter referred to as GDP_{ppp}), which are highly correlated. In order to keep the sample as complete as possible, a choice of available variables had to be made. This choice has been performed by the use of both matrix-plots and correlation-matrixes (using low correlation and visualization of scatter plot as selection criteria).

The Stepwise Approach. The validation of regression was carried out using R^2, variance analysis and detailed residual analysis.

Once the model was derived, the link between the estimated number of people killed and number of killed observed was provided by both graphical plots and computation of Pearson correlation coefficients in order to ease the visualization of the efficiency by the readers.

This model allows the identification of parameters leading to higher/lower risk, but should not be used as a predictive model, because small differences in logarithm scale induce large ones in the number of killed.

Results

The results following this method are relevant, especially considering the independence of the data sources (no auto-correlation suspected).

During a multiple regression analysis, it is not possible to test variables that are correlated together. Such variables have to be separated into five different groups of analysis.

The equation below depicts the steadiest correlation found. The other variables showing relevant (although inferior) correlation are also provided.

$$\ln(K) = 0.66\ln(PhExp\_{all}) + 0.70\ln(\overline{FC_{pc}}) + 0.36\ln(AR\_Land) - 2.44\ln(HDI) - 14.98$$

Where:

K = The number killed in landslides;

$PhExp\_{all}$ = Physical exposure, including all the classes;

FC_{pc} = The transformed percentage of forest in the country;

HDI = The transformed Human Development Index; and

Ar_Land = The percentage of arable land (AR).

Table 2.A.4. Exponent and p-value for landslide multiple regression

R=0.852,	R^2=0.727 adjusted R^2= 0.703	
Countries=53	B	p-level[3]
Intercept	–14.979	0.000011
PHEX_all	0.6616	0.000000
% forest	0.7026	0.000002
% AR_Land	0.3649	0.000168
HDI	-2.4406	0.000104

Figure 2.A.5. Predicted killed versus observed for landslide

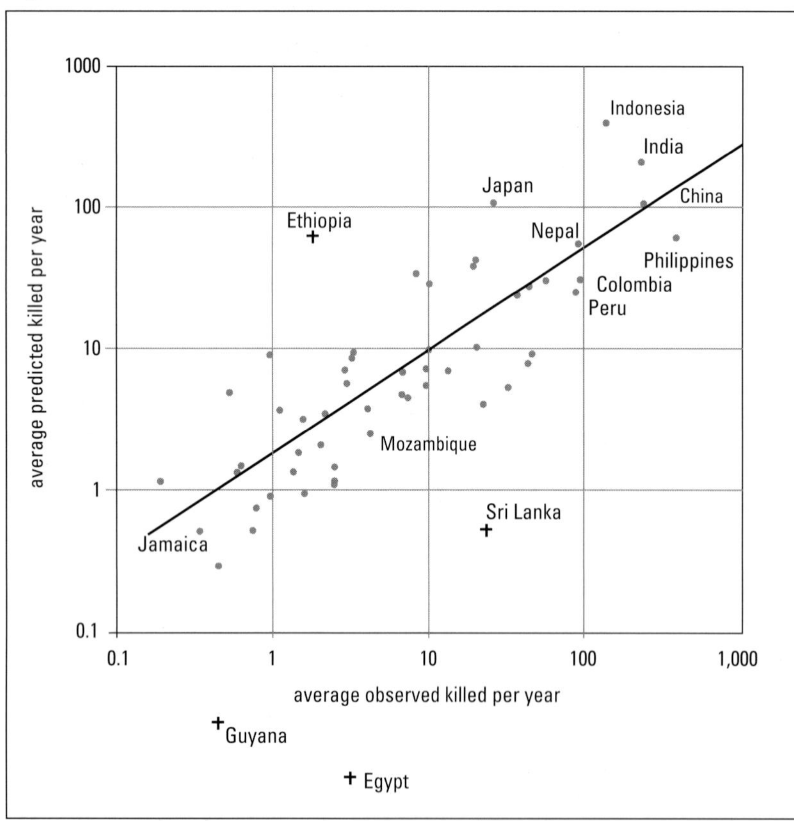

[3] In broad terms, a p-value smaller than 0.05, shows the significance of the selected indicator, however this should not be used blindly.

Some countries were removed from the analysis, as they obviously didn't fit in with the rest: Egypt, Ethiopia, Guyana, and Sri Lanka. Aside from Ethiopia, all the others have low frequencies, ranging anywhere between 1 and 4. Ethiopia and Egypt do not fit into the model, perhaps because of their low levels of forestation.

Comments and Discussion

First, these results demonstrate that the work conducted on identifying physical exposure was relevant (p-value $< 10^{-6}$). Although most of the countries affected by landslides of classes 5 and higher include 98 percent of their recorded victims, some of the countries were missing, such as: Sri Lanka, Mozambique, Republic of Moldova, Liberia, Guyana, Egypt, and Angola.

To avoid exclusion of these countries in our statistical analysis, we first used frequencies of classes 2 and over to compute physical exposure. Further analysis with physical exposure involving only classes 5 and over or 6 and over shows less correlation. The physical exposure of classes 2 and over produced the best results, although we had to exclude some of the countries with low hazard levels. This can be explained by the fact that some countries (for example, Brazil, the Republic of Korea) with quite a large amount of casualties have a very large percentage of their hazard area in the lower classes (2–4). When including only high classes (5–9), these countries are not totally excluded like some others (for example, Sri Lanka, Mozambique). But, their physical-exposure levels are much smaller than their recorded-casualty levels, a circumstance that caused problems while doing the statistical analysis.

In the end, four of them were rejected by the model (see list above), although Mozambique, Republic of Moldova, Liberia, and Angola were still included.

Although at first sight, the results suggest that more forested countries are at greater risk, this is probably due to the fact that forested countries are subject to deforestation. For obvious reasons, countries without forests cannot suffer from deforestation. In the absence of relevant data on deforestation, it is crucial that appropriate data on deforestation be included in the model. Yet another explanation for landslide risk may stem from the link between hazard level and forestation level: large forests are usually in wet areas, thus increasing the risk of landslides triggered by precipitation. This is still an open question that needs further evaluation.

The variable "arable land" seems to indicate that rural populations are more vulnerable to landslides. The variable also could be reflecting the types of activities in addition to the type of habitat.

More obviously, countries with a lower HDI are more vulnerable to landslides. In developing countries—featuring less-resilient infrastructure and lower levels of education—land planning is left to local authorities or even to individuals. In such cases, due to either ignorance or lack of choice, populations are settling in risk-prone areas. However, just because less-developed countries are more vulnerable, it does not necessarily mean that improving their development levels will drastically decrease the number of casualties. Indeed, the results in the UNDP report (UNDP/BCPR 2004) state that overly rapid development can lead to higher risk.

In terms of landslides, one can easily understand that development based on exportation of timber can lead to a higher risk of landslides in forested areas. The tragedy of Caracas (Venezuela) in 1999 is sadly explicit. Rapid and inappropriate urban growth from new workers coming into the capital city led to devastating flood-triggered landslides.

As explained before, variables with auto-correlation cannot be analyzed together. For this reason, groups of noncorrelated variables were made and statistical analyses were performed several times. In the tables provided hereafter, other socioeconomic contexts leading to higher risk are shown: parameters such as corruption, habitation on highly degraded soil (GLASOD_34), and GDP purchasing power parity. These parameters have been selected using the relevant p-values. Habitation on highly degraded soil was always associated with densely forested countries. This calls for a further analysis of deforestation.

Because of missing data, the model was not applicable to the following countries: Afghanistan, Bosnia, Democratic Peoples Republic of Korea, Georgia, Kyrgyz Republic, Lebanon, Liberia, Puerto Rico, Taiwan, Tajikistan, and Vanuatu. For these areas, another model should be developed.

Further research is needed to differentiate between areas where earthquakes are the main trigger versus where precipitation is the main trigger. Areas that are more arid and humid might have a different level of vulnerability.

Other Results

Other interesting results were found but disregarded as they were either less significant (higher p-value, lower R^2), included fewer countries, or were less meaningful in terms of interpretation. They are provided in the tables below.

Table 2.A.4. Other exponents and p-values for landslide multiple regression

37 countries	B	*p-value*
Intercept	-6.82	0.011
Pop_loc	0.79	0.000
Percentage forest	0.48	0.006
Corruption	-0.75	0.040

R= 0.71, R^2 = 0.50, adjusted R^2 = 0.45

55 countries	B	*p-value*
Intercept	-7.392	0.0626
Ln_nbEvent	1.081	0.000000
Pop_loc	0.307	0.041
Percentage forest	0.293	0.037
HDI	-1.273	0.013

R= 0.87[4], R^2 = 0.75, adjusted R^2 = 0.73

32 countries	B	*p-value*
Intercept	-7.26	0.000751
PhExp_6+	0.727	0.000004
Percentage forest	0.545	0.001605
GDPppp	0.280	0.013075
GLASOD_34	-0.827	0.006

R=0.86, R2=0.747, Adj R2=0.70

55 countries	B	*p-value*
Intercept	-14.225	0.00000
PhExp_cred	0.635	0.00000
Percentage forest	0.485	0.000137
HDI	-1.477	0.005955

R= 0.85, R^2 = 0.72, adjusted R^2 = 0.71

[4] Highest correlation, but auto-correlation suspected between number of events and Pop_loc, intercept p-value > 0,05.

Conclusions

The results from this analysis confirm that identification of physical exposure was relevant. The process is validated by the good correlation between national socioeconomic parameters (such as HDI) and independent datasets such as reported casualties in CRED and frequency of landslides (as computed by the model described in the main report using slopes, lithology, level of precipitation, seismicity, and so on).

Although around 73 percent of the variation is explained by the regression, one has to keep in mind that this is not a predictive model, mostly because logarithmic regression prevents the use of "0" in the analysis and minimizes the differences. However, classes of countries at risk can be established. The model can be used to better understand socioeconomic context, and, eventually, classes of countries at risk can be derived.

The study revealed that some countries with recorded casualties did not have appropriate physical exposure. The question of frequencies in different climates and at different vegetation levels might be the source of such discrepancies and could constitute interesting future developments.

Conversely, countries with no recorded casualties over the 21-year period cannot be considered using the method of vulnerability proxy. Data for a longer period should be obtained.

Explanations for how high physical exposure and low HDI lead to high risk are quite straightforward. The selection of countries with high percentages of forestation is less easy to explain. Could this be because of deforestation (which occurs more often in densely, as opposed to sparsely forested countries)? Could this be an indirect way of measuring traditional activities in a country? In any case, the model failed to explain risk for nine countries, demonstrating the need for data on deforestation in order to improve the model and further explain vulnerability. This was highlighted by the selection of variables such as forested countries associated with degraded soils.

References

Anand, S., and A. Sen. 2000. The Income Component of the Human Development Index. *Journal of Human Development* 1(1).

Blaikie, P., et al. 1996. *At Risk: Natural Hazards, Peoples Vulnerability and Disasters.* London and New York: Routledge.

Bolt, B.A., et al. 1975. *Geological Hazards.* New York: Springer-Verlag Berlin-Heidelberg.

Burton, I., R. W. Kates, and G. F. White. 1993: *The Environment as Hazard,* Second Edition. New York/London: Guilford Press, 31–47.

Carter, N. 1991. *Disaster Management, a Disaster Manager's Handbook.* Manila: Asian Development Bank.

Coburn, A. W., R. J. S. Spence, and A. Pomonis. 1991. *Vulnerability and Risk Assessment.* UNDP Disaster Management Training Program, 57.

Dao, H., and P. Peduzzi. 2004. *Global Evaluation of Human Risk and Vulnerability to Natural Hazards,* Enviro-info 2004. Sh@ring, Editions du Tricorne, Genève, Vol. I, 435–446.

Dao, H., and P. Peduzzi. 2003. *Global Risk and Vulnerability Index Trends per Year (GRAVITY), Phase IV: Multiple Risk Integration.* Scientific report. Geneva, Switzerland: UNDP/BCPR.

Peduzzi, P., H. Dao, and C. Herold. 2005. Mapping Disastrous Natural Hazards Using Global Datasets, *Natural Hazards,* Vol. 35, Issue 2, 265–289.

Peduzzi, P., H. Dao, and C. Herold. 2002. *Global Risk and Vulnerability Index Trends per Year (GRAVITY), Phase II: Development, Analysis and Results.* Scientific report. Geneva, Switzerland: UNDP/BCPR.

Peduzzi, P., et al. 2001. *Feasibility Study Report on Global Risk and Vulnerability Index Trends per Year (GRAVITY).* Scientific report. Geneva, Switzerland: UNDP/BCPR.

Peduzzi, P., et al. 2003. *Global Risk and Vulnerability Index Trends per Year (GRAVITY), Phase IIIa: Drought Analysis.* Scientific report. Geneva, Switzerland: UNDP/BCPR.

Smith, K. 1996. *Environmental Hazards, Assessing Risk and Reducing Disaster.* London and New York: Routledge.

Tobin, G. A., and B.E. Montz. 1997. *Natural Hazards, Explanation and Integration.* New York and London: The Guilford Press.

UNDRO (United Nations Disaster Relief Coordinator). 1979. *Natural Disasters and Vulnerability Analysis in Report of Expert Group Meeting* (July 9–12, 1979). Geneva: UNDRO, 49.

UNEP (United Nations Environment Programme). 2002. *GEO: Global Environment Outlook 3: Past, Present and Future* Perspectives. 446 pp.

UNDP/BCPR (United Nations Development Programme/Bureau for Crisis Prevention and Recovery). 2004. *Reducing Disaster Risk: A Challenge for Development.* New York. 146 pp.

Internet References

CIESIN, IFPRI, WRI. 2000. *Gridded Population of the World* (GPW), Version 2. http://sedac.ciesin.org/plue/gpw/

Deichmann, Uwe. 1996. GNV197—*Human Population and Administrative Boundaries Database for Asia.* Geneva, Switzerland: UNEP/GRID. http://www.grid.unep.ch/data/grid/gnv197.php

International Decade for Natural Disaster Reduction. http://www.unisdr.org/unisdr/indexidndr.html

ISRIC, UNEP. 1990. *Global Assessment of Human Induced Soil Degradation (GLASOD).* http://www.grid.unep.ch/data/grid/gnv18.php

OFDA/CRED (Office of U.S. Foreign Disaster Assistance/ Center for Research on the Epidemiology of Disasters). 2001. EM-DAT: The OFDA/CRED International Disaster Database. http://www.cred.be/emdat

Peduzzi, P. 2000. I*nsight of Common Key Indicators for Global Vulnerability Mapping.* Presentation for the Expert Meeting on Vulnerability and Risk Analysis and Indexing, September 11–12, 2000. Geneva, Switzerland: UNEP/DEWA/GRID-Geneva. http://www.grid.unep.ch/activities/earlywarning/preview/appl/reports/ reports.htm

Peduzzi, P. 2001. Project of Risk Evaluation, Vulnerability Indexing and Early Warning (PREVIEW). Geneva: Switzerland: UNEP/DEWA/GRID-Geneva. http://www.grid.unep.ch/activities/earlywarning/preview/index.htm

UNDP. 2004. Reducing Disaster Risk: A Challenge for Development. http://www.undp.org/bcpr/disred/rdr.htm

UNDP. 2002. Human Development Indicators. http://www.undp.org/

UNEP, CGIAR, NCGIA. 1996. Human Population and Administrative Boundaries Database for Asia.http://www.grid.unep.ch/data/grid/human.php

UNEP/GRID (as of 2002). GEO-3 Data portal. http://geodata.grid.unep.ch/

Chapter 3

Storm Surges in Coastal Areas

Robert J. Nicholls

Flooding of low-lying coastal areas can occur for a host of reasons, such as tsunamis, intense local precipitation, high river flows, and storm surges (Penning-Rowsell and Fordham 1994; Smith and Ward 1998; Parker 2000). Some of these flood mechanisms may interact with each other, as well as with other hazards such as human-induced subsidence. Coastal areas are characterized by growing concentrations of human population and socioeconomic activity (Sachs et al. 2001; Small and Nicholls 2003), which means such floods can have severe impacts, including significant loss of life in certain situations. Widespread efforts to mitigate coastal flood hazards are already apparent, and this need is likely to intensify throughout the 21st century due to the above trends, as well as to a general increase in risks due to climate change.

This paper focuses on storm surges as a coastal hazard, including identifying regions where the impacts of storm surges are potentially of particular significance and locating potential "hotspots" within these regions (as much as the available data allow). Storm surges are generated by tropical and extra-tropical storms. The low barometric pressure and wind set-up combine to produce large temporary rises in sea level that have the capacity to cause extensive flooding of coastal lowlands. They are usually associated with strong winds and large onshore waves, which increase the damage potential relative to the potential damage caused by surge-induced high water levels alone. The largest surges are produced by hurricane landfalls, but extra-tropical storms can also produce large surges in appropriate settings. Flooding by surges contributes to the damage and disruption causes by coastal storms. It also threatens human life—drowning by surges is generally the biggest killer during coastal storms.

The paper examines the controls and occurrence of storm surges, including the following issues:

- The characteristics and magnitudes of surges around the world;
- Regional exposure and risk of flooding from storm surges, both now and further into the 21st century;
- Damages, and especially fatalities, due to flooding by storm surges (this issue is based on historical experience, which has already identified some "hotspots"); and
- Detailed case studies of selected surge-prone areas.

It is important to recognize that the global datasets on these issues are incomplete and that expert judgment has been critical to developing the paper. Therefore, global analyses of flooding due to storm surges, such as the analysis developed by Nicholls (2004), have been important in the analysis. These regional analyses cannot identify storm surge hotspots per se, but they do indicate the regions where they are more likely to occur now and in the future under a range of scenarios. When this broad-scale analysis is combined with historical information on storm surge disasters, hotspots can be defined, and hence appropriate case studies can be selected.

What Is a Storm Surge?

Surges are changes in sea level (either positive or negative) resulting from variations in atmospheric pressure and associated winds. They occur on top of normal tides, and when positive surges are added to high tides they can cause extreme water levels and flooding (flooding is most severe when a surge coincides with spring tides). Surges are most commonly produced by the passage of atmospheric tropical or extra-tropical depressions.[5] Surges can occur in the open ocean, where the surge occupies only part of the area (for example, a hurricane landfall on ocean coasts), as well as in enclosed basins such as the Baltic, where the surge event will influence most, or all, of the basin.

The magnitude of the surge is controlled partly by the storm track and intensity, and partly by the configuration of the coastline and seabed. Onshore winds serve to pile water against the coast and to generate surface currents and waves, which add to the maximum sea surface elevation. A depression also reduces the atmospheric pressure, resulting in a rise in sea level (the inverted barometer effect). As a rule of thumb, an atmospheric change of 1 mb results in a sea level change of 1 cm. Hence a deep depression with a central pressure of 960 mb will cause the sea level to rise about 0.5 m above what it would have been had the atmospheric pressure been at the average value of 1,013 mb. Coastlines fronted by a wide, shallow continental shelf experience larger surges than do coastal areas with steeper slopes and greater water depths. Coastal configuration is also important. The southern North Sea, for example, is open to the north and nearly closed to the south, thus amplifying the potential for surges. Given appropriate conditions, surges due to extra-tropical storms can reach 2 to 3 m in the southern North Sea, as happened in the storm surge of January 31–February 1, 1953, and even more in the German Bight, as happened in the 1962 surge. In 1953, over 300 people lost their lives in the United Kingdom (Kelman 2002), and nearly 2,000 people were killed in the Netherlands (figure 3.1) (Smith and Ward 1998). In 1962, about 300 people were killed in Germany (Ascher 1991). Indicative surge magnitudes for hurricane landfall are given in table 3.1, showing that surges of 6 m or more are possible. In the 1971 cyclone in Bangladesh, the maximum surge reached 3.8 m (12.5 feet) above the predicted high tide, resulting in water depths exceeding 4.9 m (16 feet) (figure 3.2). The highest-ever recorded surge was in 1899 in Bathhurst Bay, Australia, when a surge reached 13 m (http://www.ns.ec.gc.ca/weather/hurricane).

The strong winds that contribute to surge events also produce large storm waves. The offshore wave height is dependent upon the fetch, the wind strength, and the length of time the wind has been acting upon the sea surface. Waves increase sea levels and have significant potential to cause damage and exacerbate flooding. In particular, wave action can cause considerable erosion to protective backshore landforms (for example, barrier islands, dune ridges), and damage artificial structural defenses. In the extreme, they can cause breaching of these defenses, enabling tidal waters to flood onto coastal lowlands in the lee of these defenses. Hence, surges and the associated wave action need to be considered together as part of the storm surge hazard.

The areal cover and depth of flooding due to storm surge depends upon a range of parameters, including surge height and duration, defense standards, and land elevation. In "natural" situations with little or no coastal defenses apart from natural dunes, such as those found on the U.S. east coast, a storm surge typically diminishes 0.2 to 0.4 m per km inland. Therefore, an extreme 6-m storm surge might reach 11 to 16 km inland if elevations are low (only 1 to 2 meters), as is often the case (Pielke and Pielke 1997). However, steeper slopes will curb inland penetration. In areas where land elevations are at or below sea level, surges could potentially create bigger flood problems. In the Netherlands, over half the country is threatened by flooding from surges and rivers, but the flood defenses are built to a high standard (nominally up to a 1 in 10,000 year event) (Peerbolte 1994). Many coastal areas that are threatened by surges have characteristics similar to those of the Netherlands, with extensive low-lying areas of land claim,[6] protected by flood defenses. This has increased both the size of the flood plain and the threatened population (for example, Germany and Bangladesh). Thus, the existing situation has co-evolved into a potentially more vul-

5. Tropical and extra-tropical storms are examples of weather systems that circulate in a counterclockwise direction in the Northern Hemisphere and a clockwise direction in the Southern Hemisphere. Extra-tropical storms form over land or the ocean as the result of the temperature contrast between the colder air at higher latitudes and the warmer air closer to the equator. Tropical cyclones form over the ocean waters of the tropics, and are termed "hurricanes" when sustained surface winds are 33 m/s or greater. In the eastern Pacific, hurricanes are termed typhoons, while in the Indian Ocean they are termed cyclones.

6. While the term reclamation is often used to describe land claim, this term is incorrect, as the process is usually the claiming of intertidal and wetland areas, or even subtidal areas—that is, land claim (French 1997).

Figure 3.1. Areas in the southwest Netherlands flooded by the 1953 storm surge, February 1, 1953 (from Edwards 1953)

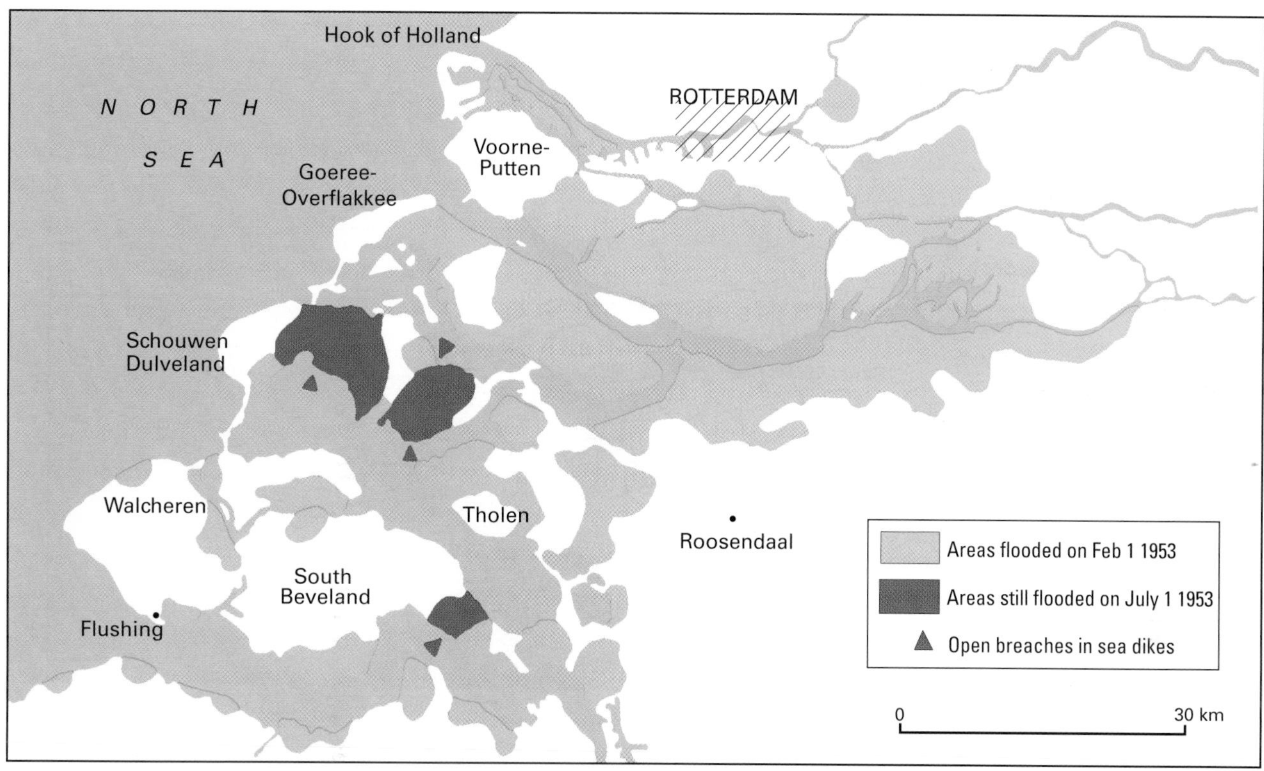

Reproduced with permission from "VII-The Storm Floods in The Netherlands," W.E Boerman. *Geography,* 38, p 184. The Geographical Association, Sheffield, UK. www.geography.org.UK.

Table 3.1. Hurricane characteristics and indicative surge magnitudes based on the Saffir-Simpson scale

Scale Number	*Central Pressure (hPa)*	*Wind Speed (km/hr)*	*Surge magnitude (m)*
1	>980	120–149	1.2–1.6
2	979–965	150–179	1.7–2.5
3	964–945	180–209	2.6–3.8
4	944–920	210–249	3.9–5.5
5	<920	>249	>5.5

Source: Smith and Ward 1998.

nerable situation, compared to the natural situation. Human-induced subsidence has also increased the number of people potentially exposed to flooding by storm surges. Table 3.2 lists some major coastal cities that have experienced significant human-induced flooding due to groundwater withdrawal, and, hence, flooding due to surges has potentially been exacerbated. In Japan, 2 million people live below the normal high water level due to subsidence and depend on flood defenses every day to stop floods, with a much larger population threatened by flooding due to surges (and other flood hazards, such as tsunamis) (Mimura et al. 1994). Figure 3.3 shows some of the threatened areas in Tokyo with and without sea-level rise.

Flooding due to surges has a range of impacts, including property damage and destruction, human distress and health effects, and, in the worst case, fatalities. Most of the world's coasts experience relatively small surges, and impacts might be quite localized with limited flood areas and shallow flood depths. However, even under relatively mild surge regimes (< 1 m), significant property damage can occur, as happens in the well-known flooding of the historic city of Venice (Penning-Rowsell 2000; Harleman et al. 2000). However, deep

Figure 3.2. A simplified reconstruction of the November 1970 storm surge in Bangladesh. Circled data indicate the height by which astronomical high tide was exceeded; isolines show the depth of water above the ground surface.

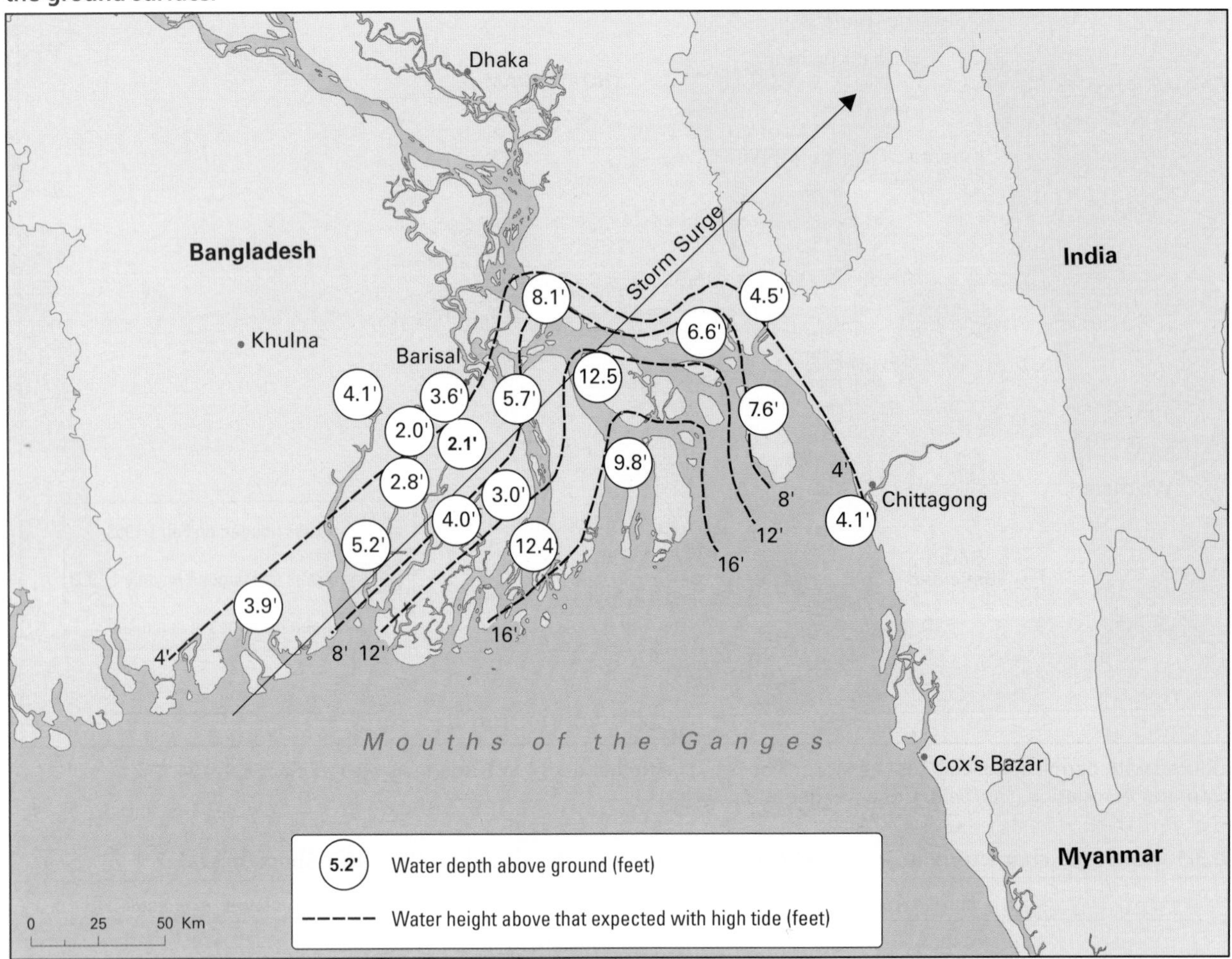

Reproduced with permission of the publisher from K. Smith and R. Ward, Floods: *Physical Processes and Human Impacts.* ©1998 by John Wiley & Sons, Limited.

Table 3.2. Some major coastal cities and human-induced subsidence during the 20th century

Megacity	*Maximum Subsidence (m)*	*Date Human-Induced Subsidence Commenced*	*Surge Potential*
Shanghai	2.80	1921	Tropical Storms
Tokyo	5.00	1930s	Tropical Storms and Extra-Tropical Storms
Osaka	2.80	1935	Tropical Storms and Extra-Tropical Storms
Bangkok	1.60	1950s	Tropical Storms
Tianjin	2.63	1959	Tropical Storms and Extra-Tropical Storms
Jakarta	0.90	1978	Limited
Metro Manila	0.40	1960	Tropical Storms

Source: Adapted from Nicholls 1995.

Figure 3.3. Areas in Tokyo that are below normal high-water and surge levels with and without a 1-m rise in sea level. These low-lying areas have been largely created by human-induced subsidence.

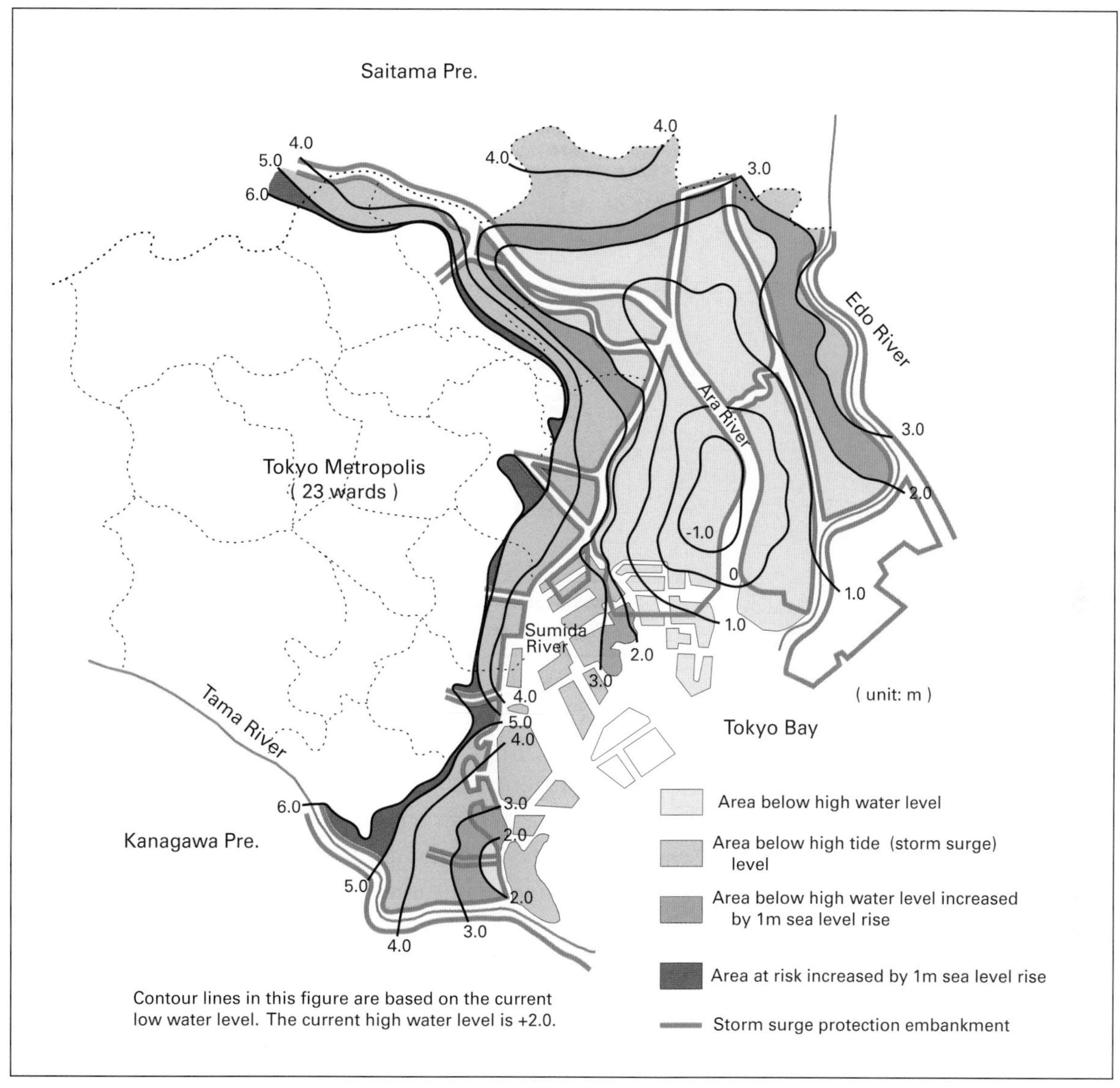

Source: Reproduced with permission from N. Mimura, M. Isobe, and Y. Hosakawa, "Impacts on sea level rise on Japanese coast zones and response strategies." In Global Climate Change and the Rising Challenge of the Sea. Proceedings of the Third IPCC CZMS Workshop, Margarita Island, Venezuela, R.B de, March 1992.

surges and fast-moving water can lead to death by drowning. It is noteworthy that millions of people have drowned due to storm surges around the world, with regular recurrence in some notable hotspots around the North Sea, the Bay of Bengal, and East Asia (see the sections covering the definition of storm surge hotspots and the case studies). Figure 3.4 indicates those areas of the world's coasts that are affected by tropical cyclones and, thus, prone to significant surges. These areas include the Caribbean and North America; parts of East Africa; much of south, Southeast, and East Asia; and much of the Pacific, including Papua New Guinea and Australia. Extra-tropical storms affect mid- and high-latitude coastal areas, with noteworthy surge potential in the North Sea, the Baltic Sea, and in the Rio de la Plata (between Argentina and Uruguay), to name just three locations. Parts of North America and East Asia are subject to both tropical and extra-tropical storms, and, hence, surges can result from more than one causal mechanism (for example, Zhang et al. 2000).

Figure 3.4. Coasts affected by tropical cyclones

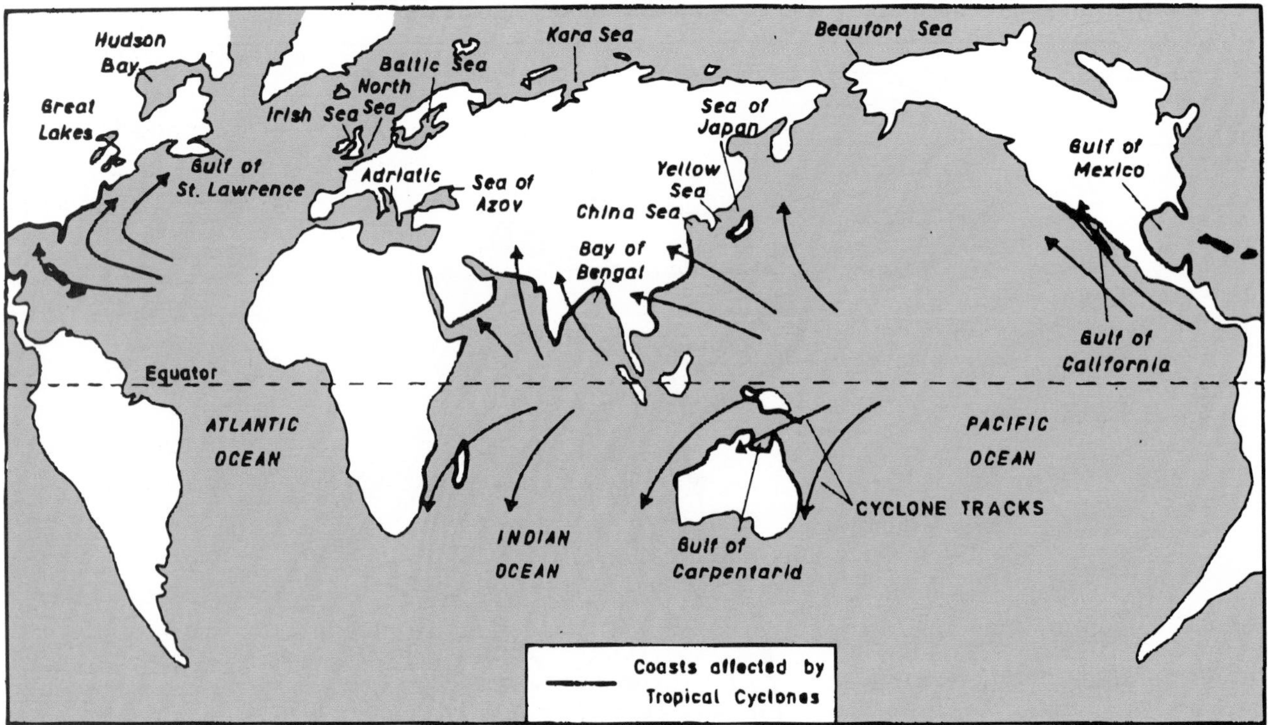

Source: Reprinted from *Coastal Environments: an introduction to the physical, ecological, and cultural systems of coastlines,* R.W.G. Carter, p228, ©1988, with permission from Elsevier.

It is important to note that extra-tropical and tropical storms can produce a range of hazards in addition to surges and waves, particularly intense precipitation, wind damage, and even tornadoes and water spouts. It is sometimes difficult to separate the impacts of these different hazards, and the overall impacts of the storm event are "integrated" into a composite set of impacts that does not distinguish between the contributions of the different hazards (Pielke and Pielke 1997). For instance, Hurricane Andrew produced a 4-meter surge in Biscayne Bay, southern Florida, but the major damage in Florida was due to the hurricane-force winds. Similarly, Hurricane Mitch in Central America in 1998 produced a significant surge that damaged and destroyed coastal homes and drowned many people on the coast. However, the main impact of the event was the intense precipitation and run-off further inland, which caused most of the damage and loss of life (UNEP 2002). Surges may also interact with other types of flood mechanism, as appears to happen in the Philippines (Perez et al. 1999). As a result of this, databases such as the EM-DAT Disaster Database (http://www.cred.be/emdat/) have been found to be of limited value to this study, as the surge component of different disasters is simply not recorded, except for those limited number of events where the surge impacts were dominant. When defining surge impacts, the most robust statistic is usually the number of fatalities, as other damages are integrated across all the hazards produced by the storm event, as noted above.

Responding to Storm Surges

While human processes such as land claim may have increased the areas threatened by storm surges, humans also have responded to this threat in various ways, and, hence, reduced the vulnerability of coastal populations to such flooding. There is a range of possible strategies for dealing with weather-induced hazards such as surges, as summarized in table 3.3. These strategies can be described as follows. Choosing change means accepting the hazard and changing land use, or even relocating exposed populations. Reducing losses includes trying to reduce the occurrence of the hazardous event or, more commonly, reducing the impacts of a hazardous event when it occurs. Both flood-protec-

Table 3.3. Generic approaches to hazard reduction based on purposeful adjustment

Purposeful adjustment	Option
Choose change	Change location Change use
Reduce losses	Prevent effects Modify event
Accept losses	Share loss Bear loss

Source: Burton et al. 1993.

tion and flood-warning systems are approaches to reduce losses. Accepting losses includes bearing the loss, possibly by exploiting reserves, or sharing the loss through mechanisms such as insurance. Hence the ability to recover from the disaster is of the utmost importance if losses are accepted. Note that these strategies are not mutually exclusive, and hazard reduction might include elements of all three approaches. These approaches can also be applied at various levels, from the individual up to communities and beyond (for example, large cities or even nations).

Over time, technology is increasing the options that are available for hazard risk reduction, particularly those strategies that reduce losses (Klein et al. 2000). In areas with large populations and strong economies, there is usually a bias toward loss reduction, and it can be argued that many of the populated coastal areas threatened by storm surges would not have evolved in the way that we see today without the availability of these hazard risk reduction strategies. Examples of these approaches include warning systems, defense works, and resistant infrastructure. This approach is most developed in urban areas around the North Sea, other parts of Europe, China, and Japan, where flooding by surges claimed many lives up to the middle of the 20th century (see the section on defining storm surge hotspots). A particular problem is that while strategies to reduce losses (for example, flood defense) only reduce, rather than remove, the risk, the measures are sometimes seen as invulnerable and, hence, encourage further development in what remain potentially hazardous areas (for example, Parker 2000). Therefore strategies to respond to surges need to analyze the response to the full range of risk, including any residual risk. This might mean combining a flood warning system with flood protection such as dikes and flood walls—the flood forecast and warning system comes into public action only if the flood protection is at risk of failure, and its primary goal is to preserve life via evacuation.

Climate change and sea-level rise represent an additional challenge around the world's coastal zones. Article 3.3 of the UNFCCC suggests that proactive adaptation (as well as mitigation to reduce greenhouse gas emissions) deserves particular attention from the international climate change community given the threat of human-induced climate change:

> The Parties should take precautionary measures to anticipate, prevent or minimize the causes of climate change and mitigate its adverse effects. Where there are threats of serious or irreversible damage, lack of full scientific certainty should not be used as a reason for postponing such measures, taking into account that policies and measures to deal with climate change should be cost-effective so as to ensure global benefits at the lowest possible cost....

The threat of climate change is extending the scope of reduction strategies for weather-related hazards such as surges and focusing attention on the coming decades. The Intergovernmental Panel on Climate Change (IPCC), Third Assessment Report (TAR) included a dedicated chapter on adaptation for the first time (Smit et al. 2001). Coastal zones constitute an area where there has been particular interest in adaptation given the inevitability of global-mean sea-level rise (Klein et al. 2000, 2001; Tol et al. forthcoming). Some coastal countries such as the United Kingdom and Japan are at the forefront of planning for climate change, with the major emphasis being on the implications for flooding of coastal areas, as sea-level rise will increase the risk of flooding due to surges and other flood mechanisms.

In general, proactive adaptation is aimed at reducing a system's vulnerability by either minimizing risk or maximizing adaptive capacity. Five generic objectives of anticipatory adaptation can be identified (Klein and Tol 1997):

- *Increasing the robustness of infrastructural designs and long-term investments*—for example, by extending the range of extreme water levels and wave loading that a system can withstand without failure and changing a system's tolerance of loss or failure (for example, by increasing economic reserves or insurance);

- *Increasing the flexibility of vulnerable managed systems*—for example, by allowing mid-term adjustments (including change of activities or location) and reducing economic lifetimes (including increasing depreciation);
- *Enhancing the adaptability of vulnerable natural systems*—for example, by reducing other (non-climatic) stresses and removing barriers to migration (such as managed realignment);
- *Reversing trends that increase vulnerability ("maladaptation")*—for example, by introducing setbacks for new development or relocation of existing development in vulnerable areas such as coastal flood plains;
- *Improving societal awareness and preparedness*—for example, by informing the public of the risks and possible consequences of flooding by surge and by setting up early-warning systems.

As with the approaches listed in table 3.4, these approaches are not mutually exclusive.

Each of these five objectives of adaptation is relevant for hazard reduction to surges. However, for coastal zones, another classification of adaptation options is often used, one that distinguishes between the following three basic hazard management strategies (IPCC CZMS 1990):

- *Protect*—to reduce the risk of coastal hazards by decreasing their probability of occurrence;
- *Retreat*—to reduce the risk of coastal hazards by limiting their potential effects;
- *Accommodate*—to increase society's ability to cope with the effects of coastal hazards.

Klein et al. (2001) discuss these three strategies in detail and provide examples of technologies for implementing each of them. While the main hazard that is considered is sea-level rise, aspects of the approaches that are discussed are relevant to all weather-related hazards in coastal areas, including surges.

These strategies are applicable both for adaptation to climatic variations such as surges, and climate change and sea-level rise. Protecting coastal zones would involve increasing the robustness of infrastructural designs, and making long-term investments in construction of seawalls and other coastal infrastructure. Efficient management of beach and coastal sediments is also an important strategy to maintain and enhance soft defenses, which can also sustain recreational and other functions. A retreat strategy would serve to avoid placing vulnerable infrastructure and populations in the present and future flood plain. A strategy to accommodate could include increasing the flexibility or coping capacity of managed systems. Examples include implementing flood-warning systems, raising buildings above flood levels to minimize flood damage (as is already practiced in the United States as part of the National Flood Insurance Program), and sharing losses via insurance mechanisms. While protection has dominated the response to hazards in urban areas, proactive adaptation needs to consider the opportunities to retreat or accommodate in less-developed and developing coastal areas.

A key point about the effective implementation of hazard reduction strategies is that they involve more than implementing a set of technical measures. They need to be thought of as an ongoing process, including planning, design, implementation, and monitoring (Klein et al. 1999, 2001; Willows and Cornel 2002). The case studies support this point.

Hence, there is a range of hazard reduction strategies available for responding to the flood threat of surges. While continued technology development may further increase the detailed options that are available, new problems and issues will continue to emerge: climate change is only one example of how future conditions can be expected to change. Reducing losses/protection has been the main response in the past, and this seems likely to continue. However, the implementation of proactive adaptation and the utilization of adaptive management principles raise opportunities to use other approaches in areas with lower levels of development and in areas that are developing or redeveloping, including recovery from disaster. This stresses that hazard reduction is an ongoing process rather than a simple set of technical measures, and it needs to be implemented on this basis. Lastly, hazard risk reduction strategies need to be implemented in the wider coastal context; thus, they comprise one issue within the broader goal of integrated coastal zone management.

Table 3.4. Regional contributions to coastal flooding in 1990 and the 2020s based on the analysis of Nicholls (2004). Only population change is considered. PHZ—people in the hazard zone (that is, the potentially exposed population). PAR—People at risk, or the number of people potentially flooded per year. Analysis uses the A1 scenario for the 2020s, but all the SRES population scenarios are similar in the 2020s.

	1990				*2020s*			
	PHZ		*PAR*		*PHZ*		*PAR*	
Region	*Millions*	*%*	*Thousands*	*%*	*Millions*	*%*	*Thouands*	*%*
1. North America	13.2	6.7	13	0.1	18.1	6.2	18	0.1
2. Central America	0.8	0.4	18	0.2	1.6	0.6	39	0.2
3. South America Atlantic Coast	4.6	2.3	33	0.3	6.7	2.3	36	0.2
4. South American Pacific Coast	1.4	0.7	13	0.1	2.3	0.8	21	0.1
5. Caribbean	1.2	0.6	10	0.1	1.5	0.5	13	0.1
6. Atlantic Small Islands	0.0	0.0	0	0.0	0.0	0.0	0	0.0
7. North and West Europe	19.0	9.6	19	0.2	21.6	7.4	22	0.1
8. Baltic	1.4	0.7	15	0.1	1.5	0.5	16	0.1
9. North Mediterranean	4.1	2.1	5	0.1	4.3	1.5	6	0.0
10. South Mediterranean	5.6	2.8	229	2.2	10.5	3.6	436	2.7
11. Africa Atlantic Coast	6.9	3.5	342	3.3	16.0	5.5	822	5.0
12. Africa Indian Ocean Coast	7.0	3.6	562	5.4	14.0	4.8	1,165	7.1
13. Gulf States	0.4	0.2	2	0.0	0.9	0.3	4	0.0
14. South Asia	52.3	26.5	4,292	41.6	90.8	31.0	7,461	45.5
15. Indian Ocean Small Islands	0.1	0.1	2	0.0	0.3	0.1	5	0.0
16. South-East Asia	26.5	13.5	1,874	18.2	39.3	13.4	2,742	16.7
17. East Asia	44.1	22.4	2,869	27.8	54.5	18.6	3,565	21.8
18. Pacific Large Islands	0.5	0.3	2	0.0	0.9	0.3	4	0.0
19. Pacific Small Islands	0.1	0.1	3	0.0	0.2	0.1	5	0.0
20. Former USSR	7.8	3.9	8	0.1	8.3	2.8	8	0.1
TOTAL (millions)	197		10.3		293		16.4	

Source: Nakicenovic et al. 2000; Arnell et al. 2004.

Regional Exposure to Storm Surges: 1990 to the 2080s

Given the lack of consistent data on the flood impacts of storm surges, regional analyses are utilized to identify the regions where flooding due to surges is most common. These regions are likely to contain most of the storm surge "hotspots."

The Global Vulnerability Analysis was developed to examine the impacts of sea-level rise at both regional[7] and global scales (Hoozemans et al. 1993; Nicholls et al. 1999; Nicholls 2004). It includes estimates of the coastal flood plain at risk from storm surges, flood plain population, and return period of different events. Validation suggests that the results are of the right order of magnitude. While significant uncertainties remain (Small et al. 2000; Small and Nicholls 2003), these data and the analysis provide a broad "snap-shot" of the regional exposure and frequency of flooding due to storm surges in 1990, and how they might change under a range of scenarios leading into the 2080s. The results of this analysis are expressed in terms of number of people exposed or impacted by flooding due to surges. Two of these parameters are considered here:

- *People in the hazard zone:* the number of people exposed to flooding by storm surges, ignoring sea defenses. This is defined as the people living below the 1,000-year storm surge elevation and is a measure of exposure.
- *People at risk (or Average Annual People Flooded):* an estimate of the average number of people who experience flooding caused by storm surges each year, including the benefits of protection from sea defenses.

7. The 20 regions listed in table 3.4 represent the smallest scale at which it is meaningful to report these results.

Figure 3.5. People at risk (that is, people potentially flooded) versus people in the flood hazard zone in 1990 for 20 global regions.

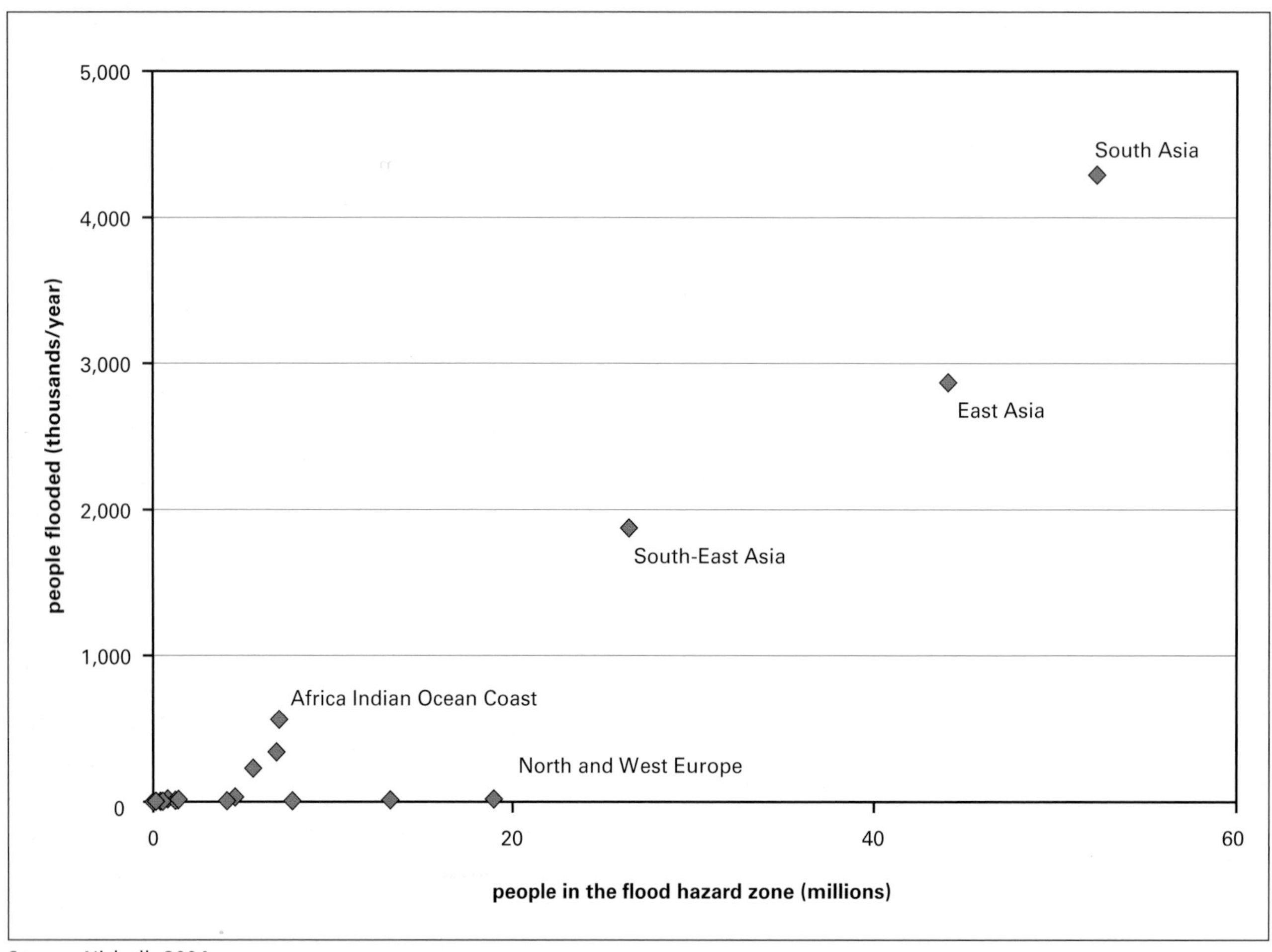

Source: Nicholls 2004.

Table 3.5. The range of scenarios used by Nicholls (2004)

	Environmental Changes	*Socioeconomic Developments*
Climate-Induced	Global-mean sea level	GDP/capita (which controls the upgrade of flood defenses to climate variability—no allowance for the effects of sea-level rise is made)
Not Climate-Induced	Vertical land movement	Population

Table 3.6. Estimates of the global exposure and incidence of flooding under the four SRES scenarios in the 2080s, plus 1990 estimates as a reference

SRES Scenario	*People in the Flood Plain (millions)*	*People at Risk (millions/year)*
1990s	197	10
A1FI	314	7
A2	562	47
B1	304	3
B2	399	19

Source: Nicholls 2004.

This is estimated as the number of people in the hazard zone multiplied by the risk of being flooded and, hence, measures the likelihood of flooding actually occurring.

It should be noted that this analysis does not consider the depth of flooding, due to the inadequacies of the available data. Flood depth is an important parameter when considering the storm surge hotspots.

Considering the base year (1990), it is estimated that, globally, a total of about 200 million people were living in areas vulnerable to flooding caused by storm surges. Further, it is estimated that about 10 million people potentially experience flooding from storm surge each year, which is about 5 percent of the exposed population. There are also important regional differences, which are summarized in table 3.5 and figure 3.5. Collectively, the south, east, and south-east regions of Asia contained about 60 percent of the exposed population and nearly 90 percent of the people who experience flooding. Other regions, such as North America and north and western Europe, contain a large exposed population (13 million and 19 million people, respectively), but due to higher defense standards vis-a-vis Asia, the incidence of floods due to surges is small. However, despite the protection, the residual risk of flooding due to surges still needs to be considered. Note that, in practice, there are important differences between Europe and North America that the methods used do not explicitly address. In Europe, floods are mainly managed using hard defenses such as dikes and sea walls, with beach nourishment increasingly being utilized in conjunction with the hard defenses. In contrast, the United States follows an approach based on accommodation of the surge hazard—all new buildings are raised above the 1-in-100-year surge elevation.

The data in table 3.8 also show how both the exposure and incidence of flooding are dynamic due to the rapid increase in global and, hence, coastal populations. By the 2020s, the number of people living in areas vulnerable to flooding caused by storm surges could be about 290 million people, or nearly a 50 percent increase over 1990 values. This increase assumes uniform changes across countries and, hence, does not consider the potential for coastward migration to increase exposure. More rapid population growth in coastal areas is widely reported (Bijlsma et al. 1996; WCC'93 1994), but more quantification is required. It also shows a relative increase in the population exposed to flooding by storm surges within the developing world, as these are the areas that are expected to experience the largest increases in population. Lastly, climate change and sea-level rise may exacerbate these flood risks as discussed below.

The frequency, magnitude, and impacts of storm surges will change through the 21st century due to a combination of (1) sea-level rise and climate change, (2) increasing direct human modifications to coastal areas (for example, further land claim around estuaries), and (3) socioeconomic changes (Warrick et al. 2000). Concern about increasing hurricane intensity was first raised by Emanuel (1988), who hypothesized that in a globally warmed world, deeper depressions would be possible, thus potentially producing stronger maximum winds, waves, and, hence, surges. Debate about the likely changes to hurricane intensity continues (for example, Henderson-Sellers et al. 1998; Knutson et al. 1998). An intensification of extra-tropical storms has also been suggested in some climate models under global warming (for example, Carnell and Senior 1998). However, the IPCC TAR came to no firm conclusions on these changes (Houghton et al. 2001) and both increases and decreases remain possible, with regional variability in the patterns of change very likely. Further, it is likely that long-term changes in surge frequency will be difficult to distinguish from the large inter-annual and inter-decadal variations in storm frequency, intensity, and duration that the limited data show (for example, WASA Group 1998; Alexandersson et al. 2000; Zhang et al. 2000; Araujo et al. 2002). Hence, by far the most certain aspect of climate change that will influence surge characteristics is global-mean sea-level rise (Church 2001).

An analysis based on the SRES scenarios was performed using (1) increases in relative sea level, (2) changes in coastal population, and (3) improving defense standards (see table 3.5) (Nicholls 2004). The sea-level rise scenarios are derived from the Hadley Centre (see Johns et al. 2003) (table 3.6). The global SRES socioeconomic scenarios are shown in table 3.7. The SRES regional scenarios were downscaled by the Center for International Earth Science Information Network (CIESIN), and made available on the IPCC Data Distribution Centre (DDC) blue pages (http://ipcc-ddc.cru.

uea.ac.uk) (see Arnell et al. 2004). The overall flood analysis simply assumed that rising relative sea level raises the surge uniformly, with no other physical changes.

The results show quite dramatic changes to the 2080s as illustrated in figure 3.6 and table 3.8. The number of people who are potentially exposed to surges increases by about 50 percent to 150 percent above 1990 values. The incidence of flooding shows greater divergence, with the A1FI and B1 worlds having a lower incidence of flooding due to surges compared to 1990 in terms of people affected, while the A2 and B2 worlds have a greater incidence of flooding. In terms of regional effects, six regions are apparent in figure 3.6 to varying degrees: (1) South Asia (which is the most consistently threatened region), (2) South-East Asia, (3) East Asia, (4) Africa Atlantic Coast, (5) Africa Indian Ocean Coast, and (6) the Southern Mediterranean. As will be discussed in the following section, these Asian regions already contain important surge "hotspots," but Africa does not. Hence, this analysis is suggesting that new problems with surge hazards might emerge around the continent of Africa through the 21st century. While not apparent in the data presented here, small island regions (the Caribbean, Indian Ocean islands, and Pacific small islands) also appear especially vulnerable to increased flooding in relative terms (Nicholls 2004).

These differences between the SRES worlds are only partly related to the magnitude of sea-level rise. In particular, the A2 world appears to be inherently more vulnerable to flooding caused by surges within the full range of potential scenarios analyzable by this method (Nicholls 2004). However, it is important to note that these results cover only a range of possible futures (Arnell et al. 2004; Nicholls 2004); thus, worlds with greater and lesser flood problems due to surges can be envisaged.[8] The overall conclusion is that the surge hazard will evolve significantly throughout the 21st century, and new problems may emerge in areas where present problems are relatively minor. These issues are further developed in the two following sections.

Defining Storm Surge "Hotspots"

The previous section defined broad regions where storm surge flooding might be an important issue, both now and throughout the 21st century. However, flooding and its impacts are more localized than the regions considered in the previous section. This reflects both the occurrence of particular areas with significant surges and high exposure to such events as flooding. Furthermore, the implications of flooding need to be evaluated in terms of flood depths, property damage, and human health implications, including fatalities.[9]

In terms of the impacts of surge events, fatalities provide some of the most certain information, which in some cases extends back almost 1,000 years (Lamb 1995). Lists of major surge events that caused substantial numbers of fatalities are widely published (for example, Ali 1999), but none appears to be comprehensive. Therefore, the author developed a synthesis of a number of sources that

Table 3.7. Global-mean sea-level rise scenarios (cm) used by Nicholls (2004) (referenced to 1990), including the IS92a GGa1 scenario as a reference

Year	*IS92a*	*SRES*				*SRES scenario range*
	GGa1	*A1FI*	*A2*	*B1*	*B2*	
2020s	9	5	5	5	6	1
2050s	21	16	14	13	14	3
2080s	37	34	28	22	25	13

Source: Nicholls 2004.

Table 3.8. The SRES Socioeconomic Scenarios for the 2080s: A Global Summary

Year and Scenario		*Population (billions)*	*GDP (trillion US 1990 $)*	*GDP/capita (thousands US 1990 $)*
1990	5.3	20.1	3.8	
2080s	A1	7.9	416	52.6
	A2	14.2	185	13.0
	B1	7.9	289	36.6
	B2	10.2	204	20.0

Source: Nakicenovic et al. 2000.

8. Factors that control vulnerability include attitudes and implementation of environmental management, level of economic wealth, and population size. Greater global inequities could also be explored, such as a scenario where development in Africa follows the observations of the last 30 to 50 years, which would lead to a much more vulnerable situation than exists in any of the SRES scenarios (Nicholls 2003).

9. Flood damages are strongly linked to flood depth (for example, Penning-Rowsell et al. 2003).

Figure 3.6. People at risk (that is, people potentially flooded) versus people in the flood hazard zone in the 2080s for 20 global regions. These estimates consider four SRES futures: A1FI, A2, B1, and B2, plotted on the same scale for ease of comparison. The results assume that population change in the flood plain equals national change in population, and that protection standards are directly related to GDP/capita, with a 30-year delay.

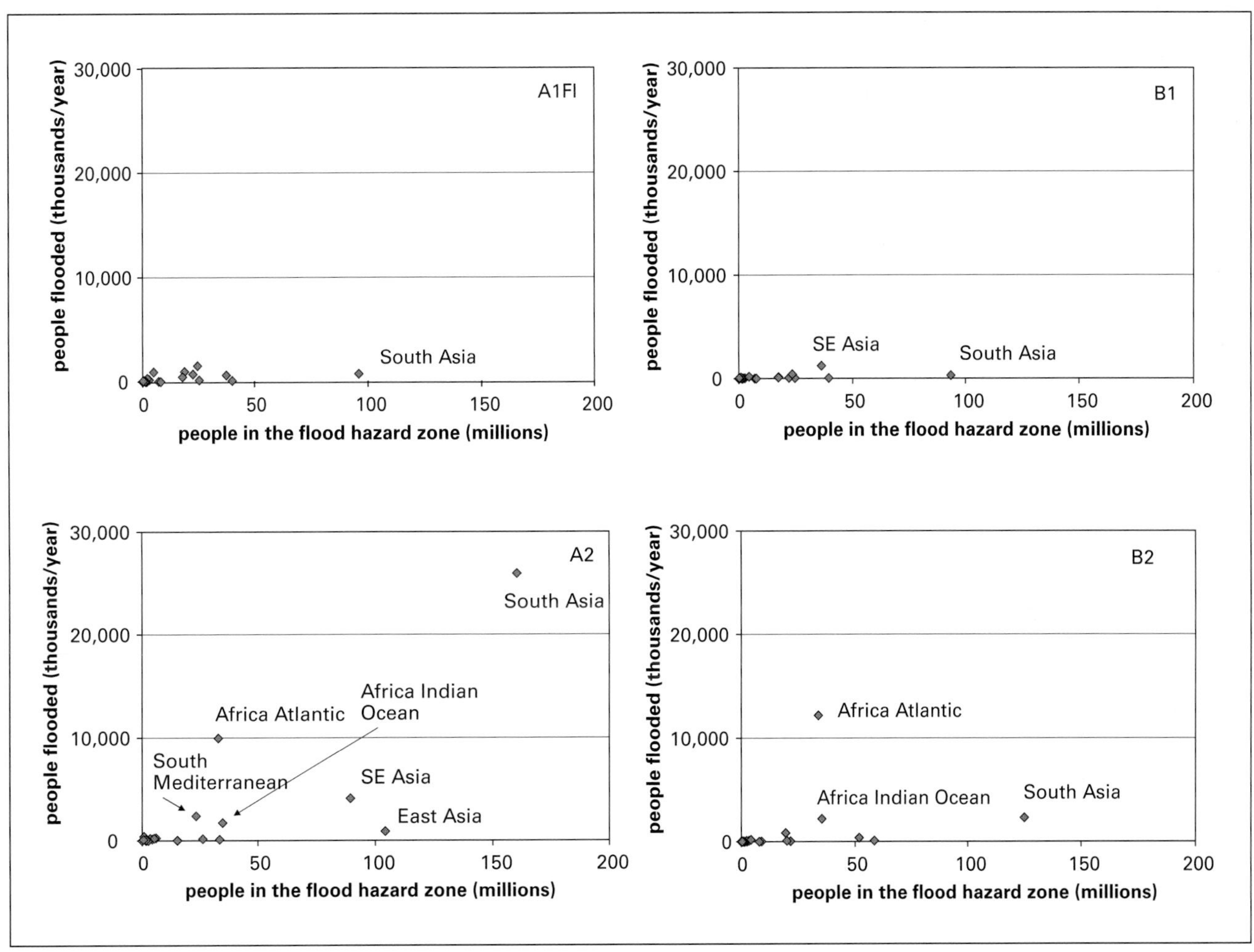

Source: Nicholls, 2004.

are all clearly indicated. Table 3.9 lists those surge events over the last 300 years in which >1,000 people died and in which storm surge was a major or the major contribution to these deaths, mainly by drowning.[10] Known exceptions where other factors contributed to most deaths—such as the hurricane flood around Lake Okeechobee, Florida, in 1928 (Pielke and Pielke 1997) and Hurricane Mitch (UNEP 2002)—are indicated. Note that table 3.9 is not considered fully comprehensive, and undoubtedly surge events have been omitted due to the limited access to sources.[11] Equally important, it is likely that some events will have been poorly documented and effectively "forgotten." A region where this seems particularly likely encompasses the Pacific islands. It is also noteworthy that the precise geographic location of many of the events is not well defined, with the impacted area being reported only to the level of country. While this gives a better idea of the hotspot locations than did the indication in the previous section, follow-up research would probably be able

10. In the United States, 90 percent of deaths in hurricanes were due to storm surge; while this cannot simply be applied to other areas, it gives an indication of the important role of surges in causing fatalities in low-lying coastal areas during storms.

11. Data for North America and Bangladesh appear to be more comprehensive than data for China and Japan.

Table 3.9. Deaths associated with major hurricanes, cyclones, and typhoons (MC) and extra-tropical storm (ETS) disasters (>1,000 deaths) since 1700. Events where surge is known to be only a minor cause of deaths are indicated. Note that there is a 1717 event in table 3.10 that is not included here as it is too imprecise in terms of number of deaths.

Year	Location	Event Type	Deaths	Sources
1970	Bangladesh	MC	300,000–500,000	1,3,4
1737	India	MC	300,000	1,3
1881	China	MC	300,000	1,3,4
1923	Japan	MC	250,000	1,3,4
1584	Bangladesh	MC	200,000	4
1897	Bangladesh	MC	175,000	1,3,4
1991	Bangladesh	MC	138,000–140,000	1,3,4
1694	Shanghai, China	MC	100,000	10
1876	Bangladesh	MC	100,000	1,3,4
1862	Zhujiang Delta, China	MC	80,000	10
1847	India	MC	75,000	1
1724	Jiangsu Province, China	MC	70,000	10
1922	Santao, Guangdong, China	MC	60,000–70,000	10, 12
1854	India	MC	50,000	4
1912	China	MC	50,000	12
1864	India	MC	50,000	1,3,4
1833	India	MC	33,000–50,000	1,3,4
1822	Bangladesh	MC	40,000	1,3,4
1912	Bangladesh	MC	40,000	4
1919	Bangladesh	MC	40,000	4
1942	India	MC	40,000	4
1780	Barbados, Martinique and St. Eustatius, Caribbean	MC	20,000–22,000	1,3,4,9, 11
1839	India	MC	20,000	1,3,4
1789 (uncertain)	India	MC	20,000	1,3,4
1989	India	MC	20,000	4
1965 (May 11)	Bangladesh	MC	19,279	1,3,4
1998*	Honduras and Nicaragua (Hurricane Mitch)	MC	10,000 –17,000	5, 11
1965 (May 31)	Bangladesh	MC	12,000	4
1963	Bangladesh	MC	11,500	1,3,4
1961	Bangladesh	MC	11,468	4
1937	Hong Kong	MC	11,000	4
1985	Bangladesh	MC	11,000	3,4
1876	Bangladesh	MC	10,000	1
1906	Hong Kong	MC	10,000	4
1971	India	MC	10,000	4
1999	Orissa, India	MC	10,000	5
1974	Honduras	MC	8,000–10,000	9, 11
1900	Galveston, Texas (U.S.)	MC	8,000 (6,000–12,000)	6,9
1977	Krishna Delta, India	MC	8,547–10,000	1,4,8
1930	Santo Domingo, Dominican Republic	MC	8,000	9, 11
1941	Bangladesh	MC	7500	4
1963	Cuba-Haiti	MC	7,196–8,000	1,4,9
1991*	Leyete, Philippines	MC	6,000	12
1776	Guadeloupe	MC	6,000	9
1988	Bangladesh	MC	5,708	4
1960 (Oct 9)	Bangladesh	MC	5,149	1,4
1895	India	MC	5,000	4
1959	Isle Bay, Japan	MC	4,697	2
1775##	Newfoundland Banks	MC	4,000	9
1899	Puerto Rico & Carolinas (U.S.)	MC	3,433	9
1928	Puerto Rico, Florida (U.S.) and Caribbean	MC	3,411	9
1932	Cuba, Jamaica and Cayman Islands (U.K.)	MC	3,107	9

Table 3.9. continued

Year	*Location*	*Event Type*	*Deaths*	*Sources*
1960 (Oct 30)	Bangladesh	MC	3,000	4
1934	El Salvador, Honduras	MC	3,000	11
1934	Osaka Bay, Japan	MC	2,702	2
1953	East Coast, UK and Delta Region, the Netherlands	ETS	2,100 (1,800–2,300)	3, 7
1945	Southern Kyushu, Japan	MC	2,076	2
1893	Louisiana (U.S.)	MC	2,000	6
1924	Leningrad (St. Petersburg), Russian Federation	ETS	2,000	3
1893	South Carolina/Georgia (U.S.)	MC	1,000–2,000	6
1928#	Florida (U.S.), Puerto Rico, Guadelope	MC	3,370	6, 11
1994	Fujian Province, China	MC	1,216	10
1917	Tokyo Bay, Japan	uncertain	1,127	2
1969	India	MC	1,000	1
TOTAL (based on best/median estimate)			2.9 million fatalities	

Sources

1. Nicholls et al. (1995)
2. Mimura et al. (1994)
3. Smith and Ward (1998)
4. Ali (1999)
5. UNEP (2002)
6. Pielke and Pielke (1997)
7. Kelman (2002)
8. Winchester (2000)
9. Elsner and Kara (1999)
10. Li et al. (2000)
11. Environment Canada Web Site www.ns.ec.gc.ca/weather/hurricane
12. http://www.noaa.news.noaa.gov/stories/s334b.htm
13. * Deaths were mainly due to nonsurge effects, particularly high precipitation and runoff
14. # Deaths in Florida (1,836 people) were mainly due to flooding around Lake Okeechobee, rather than ocean storm surge.
15. ## Assumed that deaths mainly due to shipwrecks.

to better define the precise areas that were impacted in each case, and, hence, improve the capability to map them.

The data in table 3.9 show that at least 2.9 million people have died from storm surges since 1584[12], with at least 2.6 million deaths since 1700. Surges due to tropical storms are by far the major cause, with only two extra-tropical storms being included in table 3.9 (and one event in table 3.10). The time series shows that there has been a number of surge events with significant fatalities throughout the last 300 years (figure 3.7). Smaller events are much better represented in the data after 1850, possibly indicating an increase in the number of surge events causing fatalities, or, more likely, that more-comprehensive information is available for this more-recent period. This is shown in figure 3.8, where the number of events is presented for 50-year

Table 3.10. Deaths in storm surges around the North Sea from the 11th to the 18th centuries. All surges were due to extra-tropical storms.

Year	*Deaths*
1200s	>100,000
1200s	>100,000
1200s	>100,000
1200s	306,000
1446	>100,000
1421	>100,000
1570	400,000
1634	"some thousands"
1671	"some thousands"
1682	"some thousands"
1686	"some thousands"
1717	"some thousands"
TOTAL	>1.2 million

Source: Lamb, 1995.

12. Adding the data in table 3.10 would increase this number to nearly 4 million deaths since the 1200s.

Figure 3.7. Deaths by major hurricanes, cyclones, and typhoons (MC) and extra-tropical storms (ETS) from 1700 to 2000. Data taken from Table 3.9, excluding those cases where storm surge was not the main cause of death.

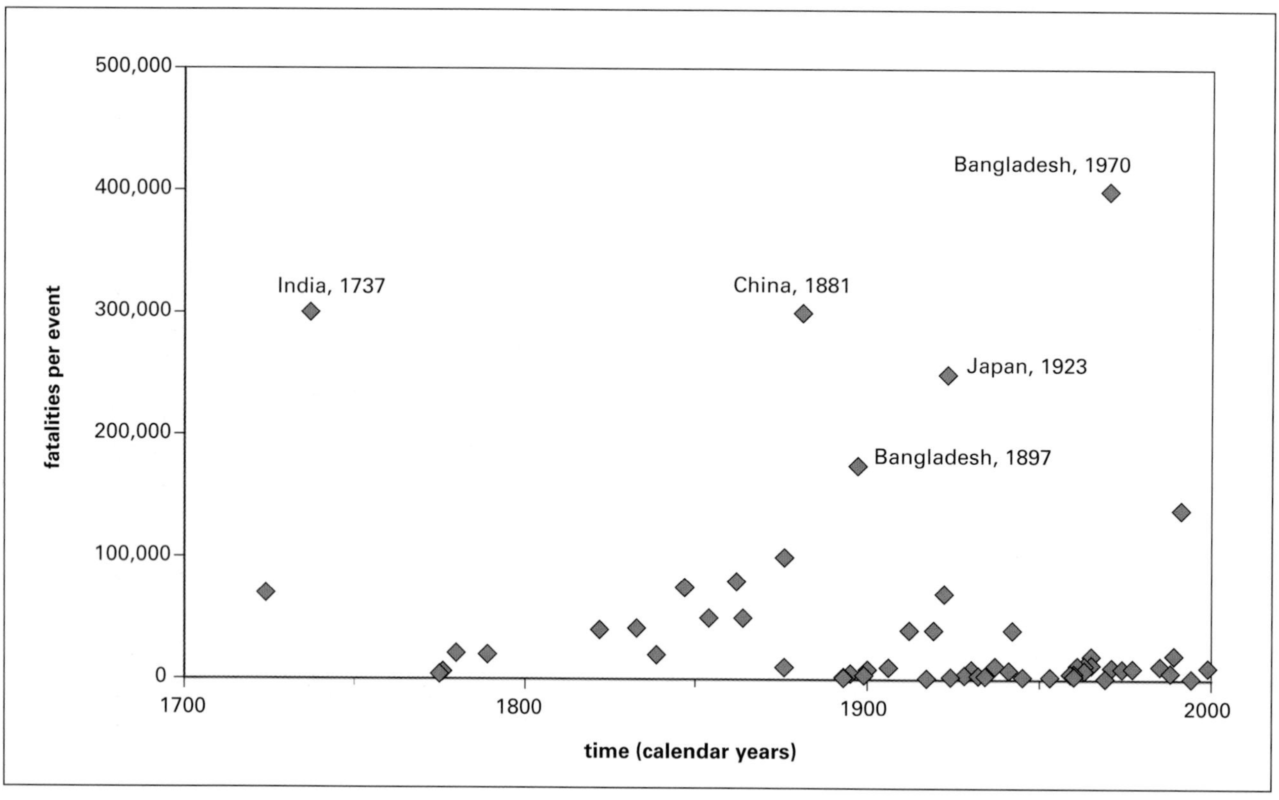

Figure 3.8. Number of "significant" events based on two thresholds of deaths: > 50,000 deaths, and > 20,000 deaths, as well as all events (>1,000 deaths)

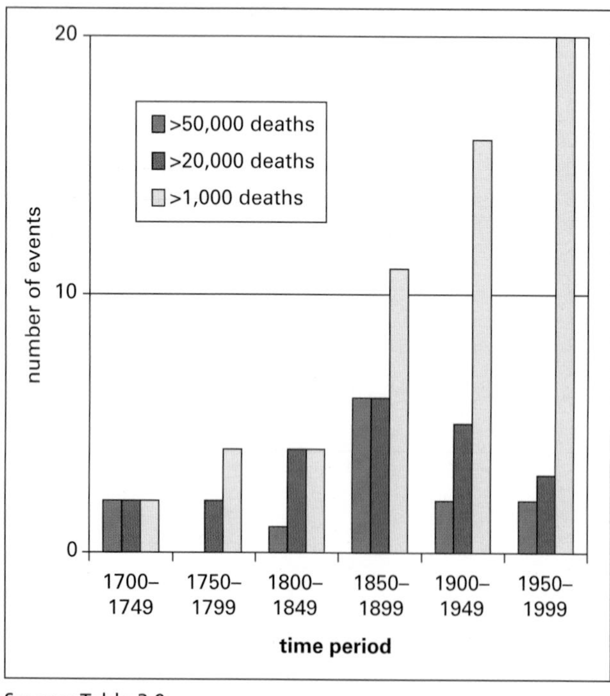

Source: Table 3.9.

time periods based on different thresholds to define "significant" events. If all the surge events in table 3.9 are considered, the number of events increases substantially as we approach the present. This trend is not apparent if a higher threshold is considered; this circumstance would suggest that the number of "major" events peaked in the last 50 years of the 19th century and that the occurrence of "major" surges (in terms of fatalities) has declined subsequently. Figure 3.9 shows the average number of fatalities per year averaged over 50-year periods. Since 1850, the long-term average is 10,000 to 15,000 deaths per year due to storm surges, although this method of presentation disguises the contribution of a few big events such as the 1970 cyclone in Bangladesh (figure 3.7).

Only a few regions are represented in table 3.9, and these regions have some correspondence to those regions indicated in the previous section. Some impacts are apparent in the Caribbean and North America as well as in Europe. However, most fatalities have occurred in Asia, with the major hotspot for fatalities due to surges

Figure 3.9. Annual deaths due to surges, averaged over 50-year periods using the data in Table 3.8

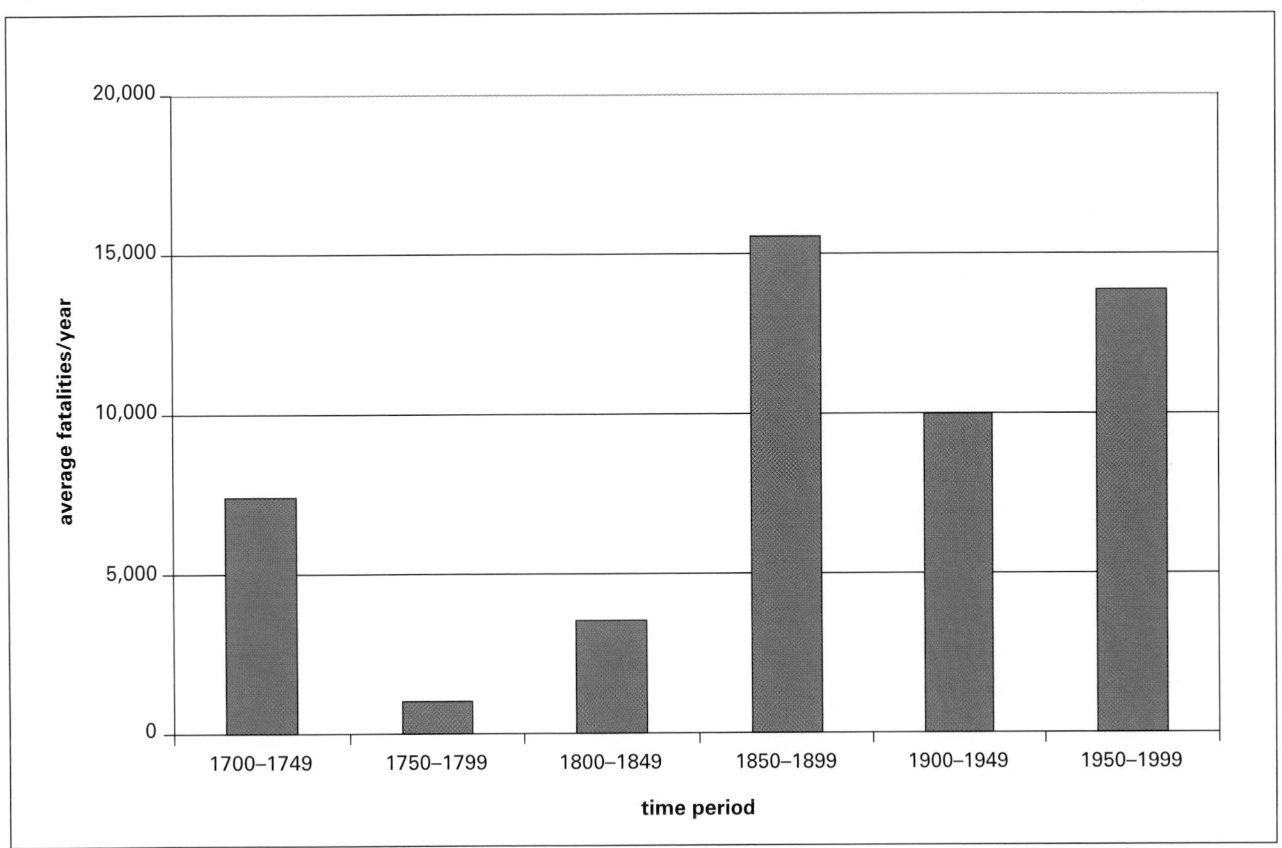

is the Bay of Bengal.[13] While the data quality is limited, it is estimated that over the last 300 years about 1.7 million people have been killed during cyclones, with the majority having drowned due to storm surges; this figure translates into 65 percent of the global total of surge deaths for that period. The most major event was the 1970 cyclone in which as many as 500,000 people may have been killed in a single event (Burton et al. 1993). The super-cyclone in Orissa, India, in 1999 that involved 10,000 fatalities serves as the most recent major event (UNEP 2002).[14] In East Asia (Japan and China), there have been at least 800,000 deaths due to surges over the last 300 years, comprising about 30 percent of the global total. While the death toll has been significant in some events, it is noteworthy that over the last 50 years, the number of deaths has been quite small in contrast to the number at the Bay of Bengal, where a significant number of deaths has continued to occur.[15] Thus, table 3.9 identifies the Bay of Bengal, and especially Bangladesh, as the number-one surge "hotspot" at the present time.

It is worth noting that the high incidence of death due to surges around the Bay of Bengal is not unique in human history. There was similar loss of life due to storm surges around the North Sea in the late Middle Ages (table 3.10). More recently, improved defenses have greatly reduced the death toll, but as demonstrated in the 1953 storm surge (about 300 deaths in the United Kingdom and about 1,800 deaths in the Netherlands) and the 1962 storm surge (about 300 deaths in Germany), these areas remain threatened. Defenses have subsequently been improved to 1 in 1,000 standards or higher (making failure very unlikely), and operational flood warning systems have been established, so

13. All the fatalities in Bangladesh and most of those in India have occurred on the coast of the Bay of Bengal, as there is a much lower frequency of cyclones (1:4) and less extensive coastal lowlands on the west coast of India.

14. Bangladesh is considered in more detail in the case studies section.

15. However, subsidence has been a major problem, as illustrated by Shanghai in the case studies section.

Figure 3.10. Deaths per event for hurricanes making landfall in the United States

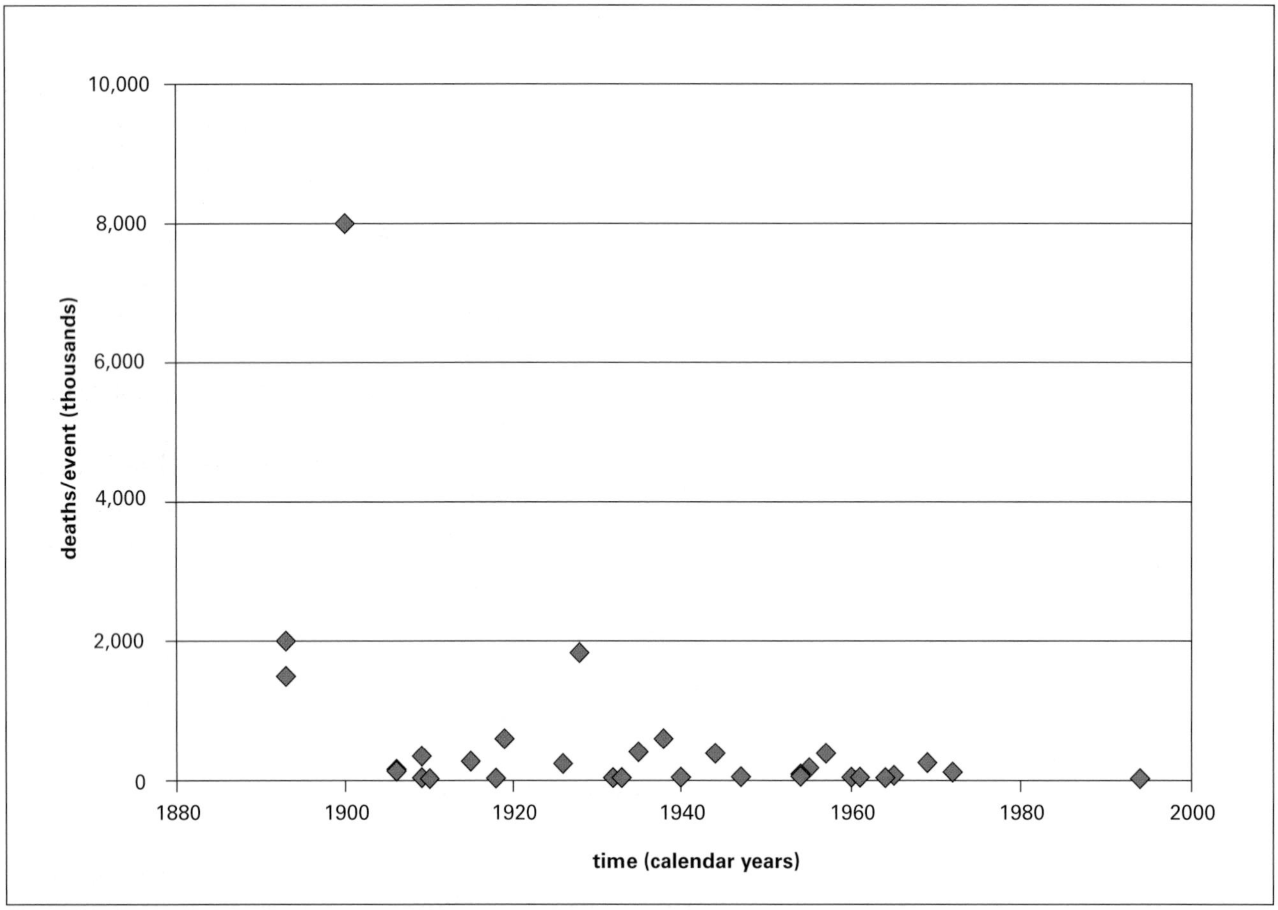

Source: Pielke and Pielke, 1997

the future death toll is likely to remain low. However, the populations and investments in the flood-prone areas are large and increasing (see the next section) (Nicholls and Branson 1998). It is probably no coincidence that the United Kingdom, Germany, and the Netherlands are preparing for sea-level rises with more purpose than are most other coastal countries (Tol et al. forthcoming).

The death toll from hurricanes has also declined on the U.S. coast over the 20th century (figure 3.10). In terms of response, this mainly reflects improved forecasts, warnings, and evacuation systems rather than increased levels of protection. However, the decreased death toll may also represent an element of luck, as there has been a lack of hurricane strikes on the most vulnerable areas (Pielke and Pielke 1997). One concern is a potential direct hit on New Orleans, where much of the land lies below sea level and potential flood depths are substantial. It is estimated that 25 percent of Florida's population lives in areas that would be seriously impacted by storm surges during a category 3 or stronger hurricane; the estimate increases to 90 percent of the population in south-western Florida (Elsner and Kara 1999). In the absence of hard defenses, evacuation is essential, but could be problematic in some areas such as the Florida Keys. New York City has been struck by a number of surges produced by extra-tropical storms (so-called "northeasters"), including the December 1992 flood that came within 30 to 60 cm of causing widespread flooding of the rail and tunnel infrastructure—this would have had severe impacts, including significant loss of life (Rosenzweig and Solecki 2001).[16]

Several regions might be omitted by this analysis. In particular, impacts on many of the small Pacific Islands may not be adequately captured, although the death

16. Surges on the U.S. east coast are considered in more detail in the case studies section.

toll appears uncertain. Major hurricanes can occur in this region, as illustrated recently by Hurricane Zoe in December 2002, which impacted Tikopia and Anuta in the Solomon Islands with 148-mph (238 km/hr) winds and an 18-ft (5.5 m) storm surge, plus waves. Fortunately, this did not result in a large loss of life, but the damage to the islands' economies is immense, and it is unclear how rapidly they will recover. From 1965 to 1995, tropical cyclones in Fiji caused significant economic damage, but most of this can be attributed to the non-surge impacts of the cyclone (Olsthoorn et al. 1999). The death toll was about 50 people, with surges being only a minor contributor. Equally noteworthy is that cyclone landfalls on the Indian Ocean islands (for example, Mauritius) and on the East African coast do not appear to have produced significant numbers of fatalities to date. This probably reflects the limited exposure to flooding at the present time. However, this exposure might change, as might the frequency and magnitude of surge events (see the previous section).

We now consider other types of damage due to surges. Significant damage due to hurricanes and tropical cyclones has occurred in all of the areas defined in figure 3.1. Damage due to surges produced by extra-tropical storms has occurred on the Atlantic coast of Europe, the North Sea, the Baltic Sea, the Mediterranean, Northern China, Republic of Korea, Japan, and the eastern seaboard of the United States. This damage can take many forms, including direct damage to property, agriculture, and industry (especially coastally focused industries such as petrochemicals). Indirect damage due to disruption and dislocation also occurs. Lastly, there are the intangible impacts that are difficult, if not impossible, to measure in economic terms, such as health effects and psychological well-being. The insurance industry has concerns about the financial damages, especially in developed countries where insurance coverage is high.

However, as already noted, these impacts are related to a range of hazards, including storm surges that the tropical or extra-tropical storm generates. Therefore, it is more difficult to link these damages to surges. Of the $30 billion or more in damages caused by Hurricane Andrew, only about $100 million (or <3 percent) were directly linked to flooding due by surges (see table 7.3 in Pielke and Pielke 1997). In general, as the wind speeds associated with a storm event increase, so the damage due to surges is expected to fall relative to other related hazards (although this is a heuristic rather than a quantified concept at the present time).

Based on these observations, table 3.11 attempts to summarize the available information on surge hotspots around the world. It distinguishes events that produce fatalities from those events that produce other damages. For the same regions, table 3.12 identifies geographic areas where the impacts from surge events could be particularly significant. This judgment is based primarily on land elevation, population density, and historical experience, with some consideration of possible future conditions.

In terms of information about the distribution of storm surge hazard, tables 3.11 and 3.12 represent the most precise global view that has been possible to develop in the time available to prepare this paper. The detailed case studies in the following section are designed to illustrate the nature of storm surge hazard in a number of the more vulnerable regions.

Case Studies

Four case study areas have been selected based on the preceding discussion. They serve to illustrate the nature of the surge hazard in four of the more vulnerable regions identified in tables 3.11 and 3.12. Two of the areas are developed-world areas, reflecting the greater availability of information and the issues of high exposure and potential flood risk: (1) southern North Sea (United Kingdom, Netherlands, Germany), and (2) U.S. East Coast. There are two developing-country areas: (3) Bangladesh, and (4) Shanghai (China).

Southern North Sea

This region experiences significant surges due to extra-tropical storms, and the locations susceptible to flooding feature large populations and substantial investments. Most of the flood-prone areas around the region are former wetlands that have been subject to land claim, which started in some areas 2,000 years ago under the Romans. Land claim created habitable areas that attracted larger populations to the coast. However, surges caused regular flooding and loss of life as illustrated in

Table 3.11. An expert synthesis of storm surge hotspots around the world. Under fatalities, high indicates the potential for more than 1,000 deaths in a surge event. Other damage estimates are based on the expert judgment of the author.

Surge-Prone Regions	*Hotspots*		*Commentary*	*Mentioned in Table 3.9*
	*Fatalities**	*Other Damage*		
Bay of Bengal (Bangladesh and Eastern India)	High	High	Improved flood warnings may reduce fatalities.	uncertain
Western India/Pakistan	? Unclear	? Unclear	Cyclones less frequent than Bay of Bengal (1:4) and less exposure.	uncertain
China/Japan	Potentially high	Potentially high	Ongoing flood damage reported in China	uncertain
Rep. of Korea	Low	Low	Lacks large low-lying coastal areas, but this is changing due to extensive land claim.	yes
Thailand, Vietnam, Philippines	Potentially high in deltas	Medium to high	Frequently impacted by typhoons, and population of low-lying areas is growing rapidly, but not mentioned in Table 3.9, except for an event where surge was a minor cause of fatalities (hence, yes).	yes
Pacific Islands	Probably high	High	Limited historical information.	yes
Australia and New Zealand	Low	Low	Limited habitation in low-lying coastal areas	yes
Indian Ocean Islands	Low	Low	Limited habitation in low-lying coastal areas	yes
Eastern Africa and Oman	Low	Low	Habitation in low-lying coastal areas is not significant, but there is a potential to increase.	yes
Rio de la Plata (Argentina and Uruguay)	Low	Low	Difficult to assess due to limited literature—may suggest limited impacts to date.	yes
Caribbean	Potentially high	Medium to high	Human activity is concentrated around the islands, and hence exposed to surge—however, the role of surge relative to other hurricane impacts is less clear.	uncertain
Central America and Mexico	Potentially high in local areas	Medium to high	Human activity is often concentrated away from the coast, which is untypical globally. Hence, other hurricane impacts appear relatively more important than in other regions (for example, Hurricane Mitch), although there are localized hotspots.	uncertain
U.S. Gulf and East Coasts	Potentially high	High	Effective evacuation has reduced fatalities, but potential hotspots remain.	uncertain
Europe—Atlantic coast	Potentially high	Potentially high	Hard defenses and improved flood predictions and warnings appear to have been effective in reducing this hazard.	yes
Europe—Mediterranean coast	Locally high	Medium to high	Surges are not large, so deaths are unlikely, except in areas of land claim where flood depths could be substantial. However, significant damage and disruption can occur.	yes
Europe—North Sea coast	Potentially high	Potentially high	Hard defenses and improved flood predictions and warnings appear to have been effective in reducing this hazard.	uncertain
Europe—Baltic Sea coast	Locally high	Medium to high	Hard defenses and improved flood predictions and warnings appear to have been effective in reducing this hazard.	uncertain

*Note: Under fatalities, high indicates the potential for more than 1,000 deaths in a surge event. Other damage estimates are based on the expert judgment of the author.

Table 3.12. Potential and actual hotspots vulnerable to flooding by the storm surge. This information is indicative; it is not an exhaustive list of all potential and actual hotspots.

Surge-Prone Regions	*Potential and Actual Hotspots*
Bay of Bengal (Bangladesh and Eastern India)	Ganges-Brahmaputra mouth (Figure 3.2), (Bangladesh and West Bengal), Mahandi Delta (Orissa) and the Krishna and Godavari Deltas (Andhra Pradesh)
Western India/Pakistan	Indus Delta and Karachi (Pakistan), Mumbai (India)
China/Japan	Lower Liaohe River Plain (China), North China Plain (China), East China Plain and Shanghai (China), Hanjiang River Deltaic Plain (China), Pearl River Deltaic Plain Guangzhou and Hong Kong (China), Guangxi Coastal Plain (China), North Hainan Plain (China), Taiwan Coastal Plain and Taipei (Taiwan), Metropolitan Toyko (Japan), Metropolitan Osaka (Japan)
Republic of Korea	inconclusive
Thailand, Vietnam, Philippines	Red River delta (Vietnam), Mekong delta (Vietnam), Metro Manila (Philippines), Chaophraya delta and Bangkok (Thailand)
Pacific Islands	Most capital cities which are all on the coast, and all atoll islands
Australia and New Zealand	inconclusive
Indian Ocean Islands	inconclusive
Eastern Africa and Oman	inconclusive
Rio de la Plata (Argentina and Uruguay)	Buenos Aires (Argentina) and Montevideo (Uruguay) (assumed)
Caribbean	Most capital cities which are on the coast
Central America and Mexico	inconclusive
U.S. Gulf and East Coasts	New York City, Florida, particularly southern Florida and the Keys, New Orleans
Europe—Atlantic coast	inconclusive
Europe—Mediterranean coast	Areas of land claim and high subsidence on the Northern Adriatic Coastal Plain in Italy (Nicholls and Hoozemans, 1996).
Europe—North Sea coast	London and Kingston-upon-Hull (U.K.), the western Netherlands, Hamburg, and Bremen Germany
Europe—Baltic Sea coast	Main hotspot is St Petersburg (Russian Fed.) with potential hotspots such as Helsinki, (Finland) and Copenhagen (Denmark).

table 3.10. As technology improved, so did defenses. The catastrophic losses described in table 3.10 ceased in the 18th century, helped to some degree by a decline in the frequency of major coastal storms (Lamb 1995). However, major floods continued up to the middle of the 20th century:

- The East Coast (United Kingdom) and the delta region of the Netherlands (figures 3.11 and 3.1) were last flooded in 1953.
- Germany, including Hamburg, was last flooded in 1962.

The response to these events was further massive investment in flood-defense infrastructure, as illustrated by the mobile storm surge barriers on the Thames in Greenwich, London, and across the Western Scheldt in the Netherlands. Many of these defenses are built to a 1-in-1,000-year standard or higher, and up to a 1-in-10,000-year standard for some defenses in the Netherlands.[17] Equally important, an effective storm tide warning service has been developed that provides up to 36-hours warning of a potential flood event. Collectively, these new measures have been effective for the last 20 years[18], and there has been no flooding around the southern North Sea, even though the extreme water levels of the 1953 event have been repeated and even exceeded in some locations. However, the human and infrastructural exposure remains substantial, potentially approaching 15 million people[19] today, and there

17. The only other place in the world where so many defenses are built to a similar standard is Japan.
18. The new defenses were not completed until the early 1980s, suggesting that a 30-year time lag in response to flooding via major structural measures should always be assumed.
19. The population living beneath the 1-in-1,000-year storm surge elevation.

Figure 3.11. Flooding of the East Coast of England during the 1953 storm surge

Source: Reproduced with permission of the publisher from Steers, J.A., "The East Coast Floods, January 31–February 1, 1953," *Geographic Journal,* 119, pp280-298. Oxford: Blackwell Publishing.

is rapid development occurring in these flood-prone areas. These areas also are subject to increasing risks due to sea-level rise and climate change (Flather and Smith 1998; Lowe and Gregory 1998).

London, a city whose location was selected by the Romans 2,000 years ago, illustrates many of these issues. One million Londoners, or about 12 percent of the city's population, are potentially exposed to flooding caused by storm surges. They are defended by a complex system involving fixed flood defenses of varying standards along the entire length of the tidal Thames, the mobile Thames Barrier at Greenwich (which is closed before a surge arrives), and a suite of warning systems that are used to decide when to close the Barrier (Gilbert and Horner 1984). While the possibility of a barrier was discussed earlier in the 20th century, the decision to build the present defenses was made in direct response to the 1953 storm surge. While there were a few deaths within London proper and while the city was largely spared on this occasion, the high vulnerability of London was apparent to all, and it galvanized collective action. The new defenses became fully operational when the Barrier was completed in 1983—that is, 30 years after the decision to build was made. Parallel developments in storm surge warning were fundamental to the operation of the Barrier. Since the Barrier was completed, London's derelict docklands have been regenerated with new transport links, homes, and businesses, including the important new financial district around Canary Wharf. Significant future development is planned alongside the Thames, with 200,000 new homes proposed in the next 15 years alone (termed the Thames Gateway proposal). This will extend London eastward toward the North Sea, and many of the proposed sites for building are potentially flood prone.

The design life of the Barrier extends to 2030, when rising flood levels due to a combination of global sea-level rise and more local changes will reduce the residual flood risk to below a 1-in-1,000-year standard. Given the long lead-time to upgrade the defenses, planning of the upgrade of the flood defenses to the end of the 21st century is already in its early stages. Substantial raising of the fixed flood defenses will be required, although it is hoped the Barrier can continue to operate until 2100 with only marginal investment. The Thames Gateway proposal reinforces the need for this upgrade, and it will be interesting to see if the design standard (that is, the acceptable level of risk) is maintained at the 1-in-1,000 level, or if it is increased further toward the levels seen in the Netherlands. The new flood strategy includes consideration for the first time of inland realignment of the flood defense line (that is, a planned retreat policy [Klein et al. 2001]) as a complimentary strategy to raising defenses. This reverses a long-term trend of encroachment and land claim into the tidal Thames (Shih 2002).

It is noteworthy that it is not widely appreciated that there is and always will be a residual flood risk for London. The operational flood management authority is the (England and Wales) Environment Agency. It is trying to communicate this point to Londoners and to begin education about what might happen in the highly unlikely event of a flood. However, this is a difficult issue that requires much more work— emergency planning needs to be interwoven much more with the post-2030 plans for flood management. In terms of flood damages, all insured properties in London receive flood coverage as part of a standard home insurance policy. Therefore, losses would be shared in the unlikely event of a flood event. However, it is worth noting that the U.K. insurance industry is concerned about its exposure to flooding, as this is seen as one of the biggest potential losses that U.K. insurers face. Flood insurance is being selectively withdrawn in areas outside London: this is a situation that would arguably reduce the resilience of England in the face of major flood events (Clark 1998).

In conclusion, the surge hazard co-evolved with human development of the coastal zone, and this continues today. Land claim created the conditions that attracted high populations to the flood-prone areas and, hence, raised the exposure in a region where large (and, thus, potentially) killer surges can occur. The coastal populations adapted to these threats, but it is only in the last 50 years that the threat has really been reduced, primarily due to protection and warning measures. However, as the long history of this region shows, complacency could be fatal, and flood management will need to keep developing to manage the changing risks of surge flooding.

Bangladesh, Bay of Bengal

In terms of fatalities, Bangladesh is presently the dominant storm surge hotspot globally, as already discussed. This concentration of fatalities reflects several interacting factors that have a lot in common with the issues raised in section on the southern North Sea. These factors include (1) a high and rapidly growing coastal population, with little alternative land, (2) extensive coastal lowland areas that are close to sea level, (3) significant and frequent landfall of tropical cyclones, and (4) shallow coastal areas that exacerbate the surge potential of the cyclones. Coastal Bangladesh is also an active delta (of the Ganges-Brahmaputra), and net accretion of land is occurring (Nicholls et al. 1995). With the pressure for land and the need for food, this has led to extensive land claim of these emerging areas and active promotion of accretion (for example, Koch 1986). However, these new land areas were not well protected from surge events, and the new population was highly vulnerable to coastal flooding (Burton et al. 1993). This is best illustrated in the 1970 cyclone event, in which between 300,000 and 500,000 people drowned in coastal Bangladesh.

Figure 3.12 shows the death toll during cyclones from the years 1800 to 2000. The 1970 event stands out as the most significant event in terms of fatalities and would seem to be part of a rising trend in deaths due to surges.[20] It can be argued that land claim has been one factor exacerbating vulnerability to surges in Bangladesh. The 1970 event caused a reassessment of preparations for surge flooding in coastal Bangladesh. There was the building of robust shelters for people and their animals, as well as improvements in the forecast and warning systems, with an emphasis on how to disseminate warnings

20. The 1876 cyclone in Bangladesh may have had a death toll of up to 400,000, although the uncertainties are great.

Figure 3.12. Deaths per surge event in Bangladesh from 1800 to 2000 using the data in Table 3.9.

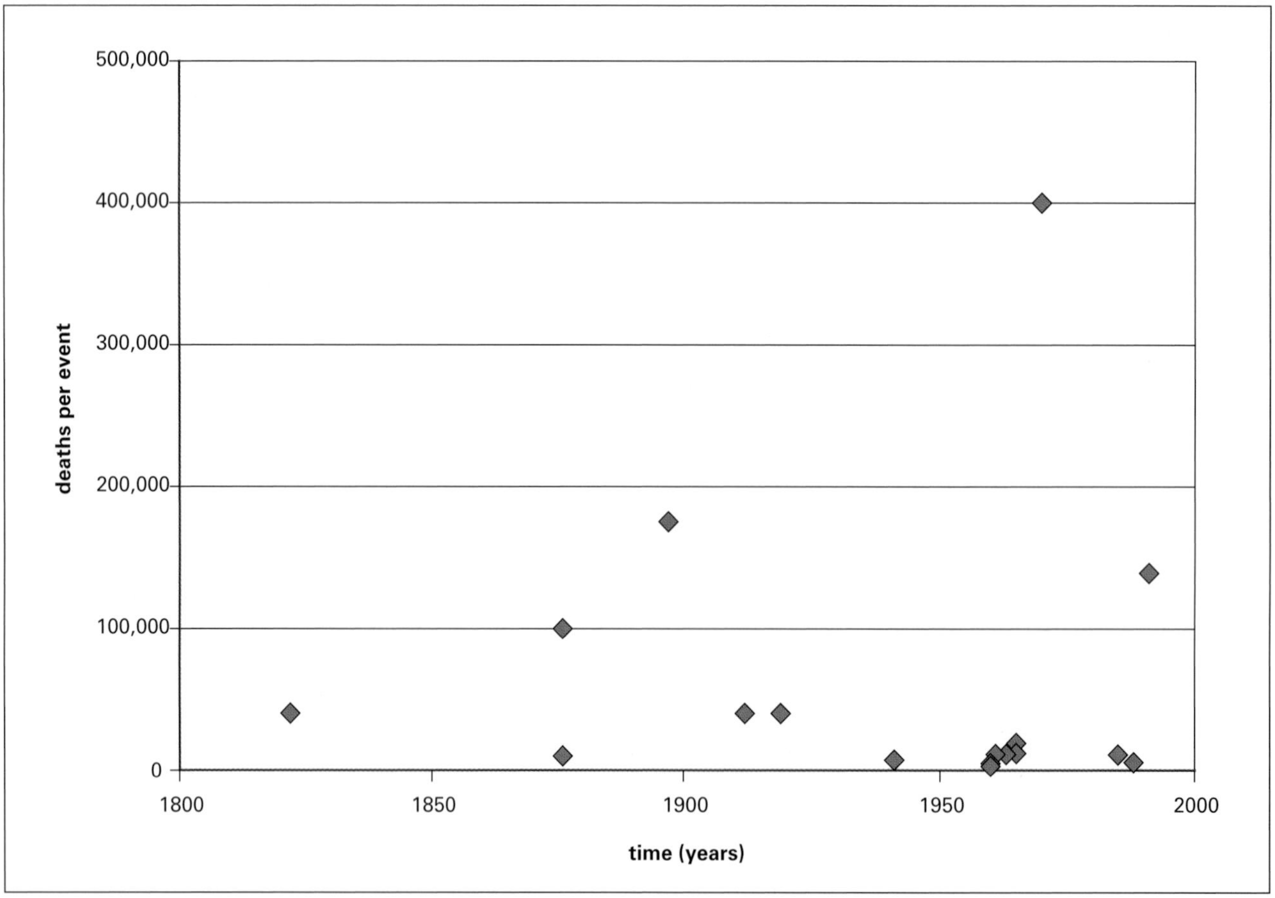

from Dhaka (which is inland) to the threatened people along the coast. While the loss of life in the 1991 event was again significant, it was substantially lower than in 1970, despite the event being comparable in terms of the surge characteristics (Kausher et al. 1996). Efforts to improve warnings have continued through the 1990s, and it is suggested rather anecdotally that they are becoming more effective (White 2000). However, as the death toll falls, there is concern that the lessons learned from the avoided floods are not being considered. The underlying pressures remain, and without substantial and continuing efforts, it is likely that significant deaths due to surges will recur, although probably not on the scale of the 1970 and 1991 events.

While the death toll appears to be declining, other surge-related damages are likely to remain significant, although, not surprisingly, most of the literature focuses on the large number of deaths. Further efforts are likely to be necessary to mitigate flood damage and disruption. Hence, it would seem that the surge hazard in Bangladesh will continue to co-evolve with human use of the coastal zone throughout the 21st century.

U.S. East Coast

The U.S. East Coast faces surges from hurricanes (in summer and autumn) and extra-tropical storms (so-called northeasters) in the autumn to spring months. The analysis of Zhang et al. (2000) shows that the relative importance of these two types of surges changes as you move northward: north of Hampton Road, Virginia, northeasters dominate, while to the south tropical storms and hurricanes are apparent. Figure 3.13 (a) shows the potential for surges on the Gulf and East Coasts, while figure 3.13 (b) shows the surge that occurred during the hurricane of September 14–15, 1944.[21] A major surge due to a northeaster occurred during the Ash Wednesday

21. The smaller surges after the main surge are called the resurgences (Smith and Ward 1998).

Figure 3.13. Surges on the U.S. Gulf and East Coast. Relative storm-surge potential (a), and surge graphs for six Atlantic coast locations (b), the hurricane of September 14–15, 1944.

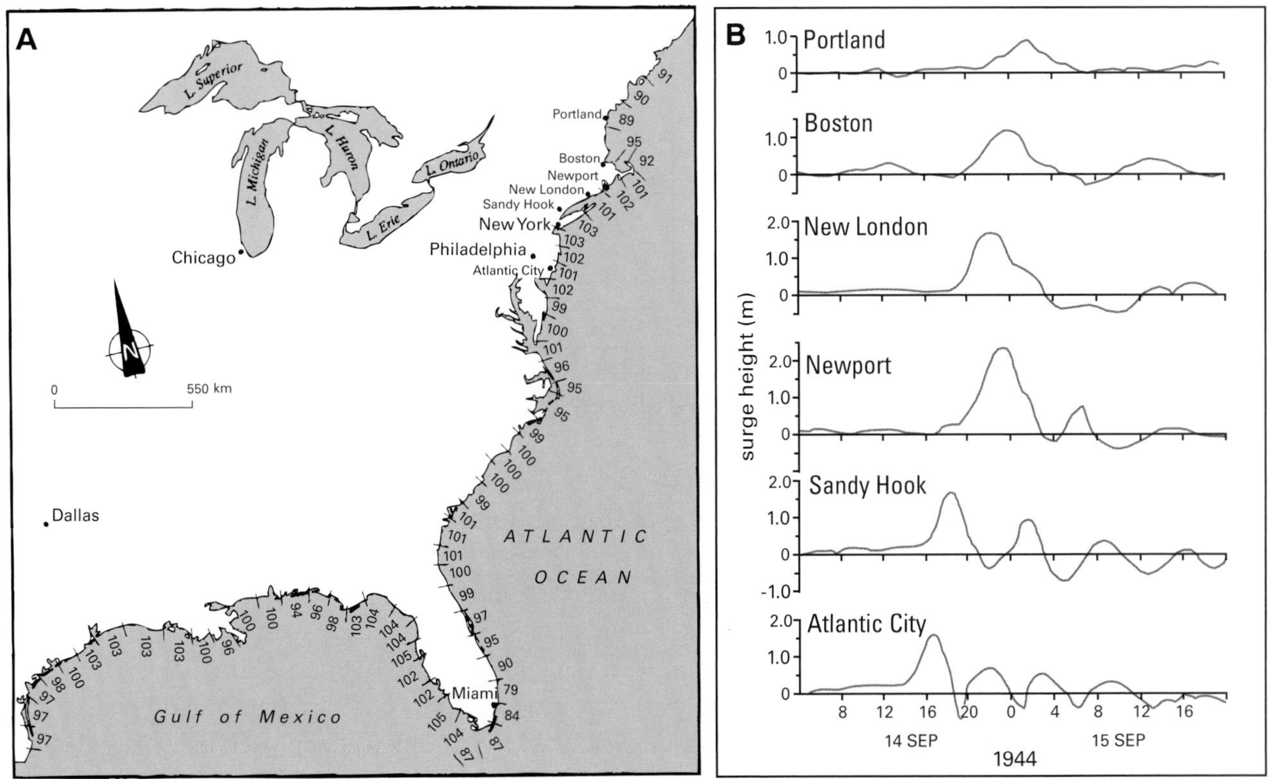

Source: Reproduced with permission of the publisher from K. Smith and R. Ward, *Floods: Physical Processes and Human Impacts.* ©1998 by John Wiley & Sons, Limited.

Figure 3.14. Subsidence from the 1920s to the 1990s in Shanghai, China

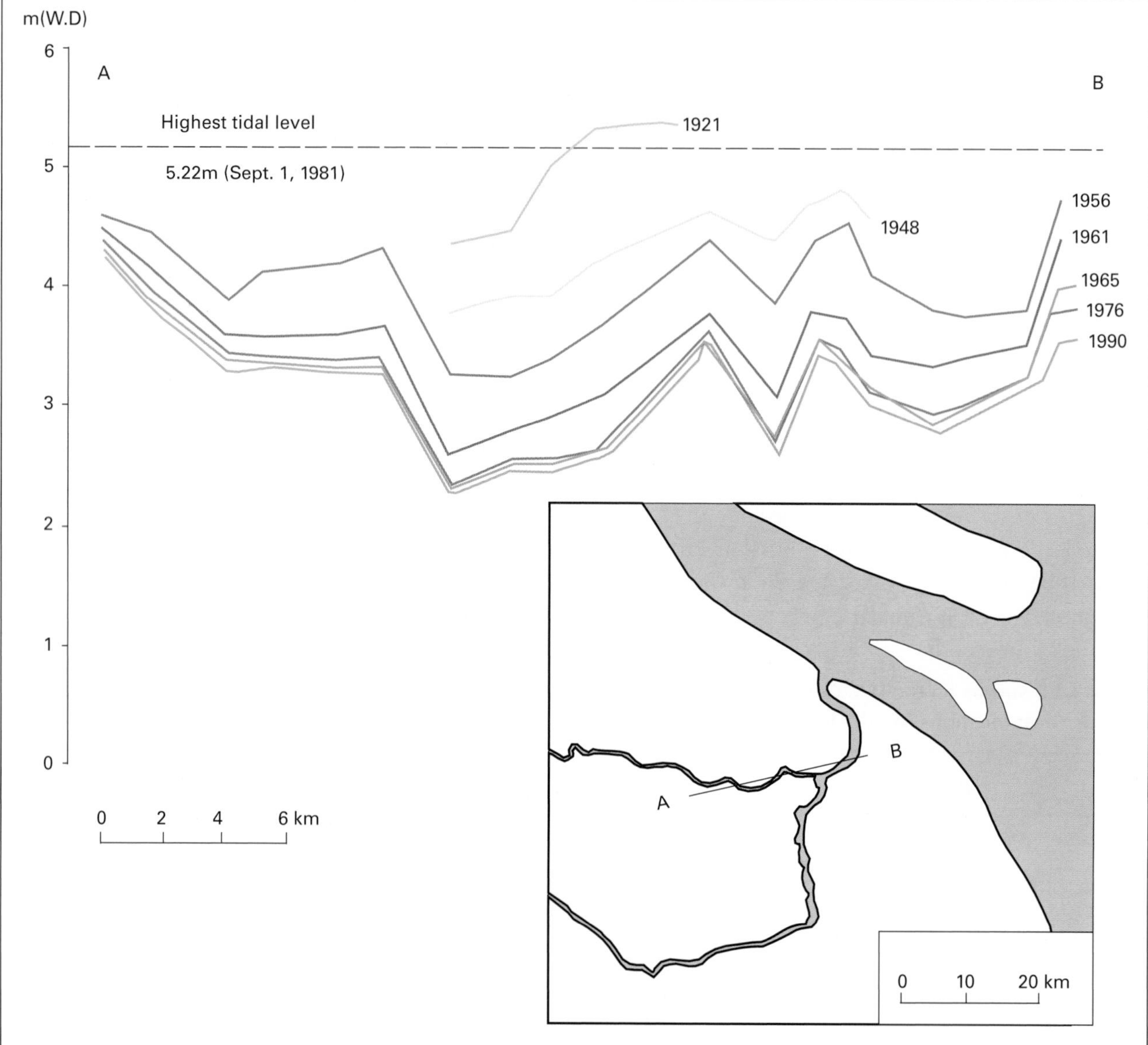

Source: Reproduced with permission from "Potential impacts of sea-level rise on the Shanghai area," B. Wang, S. Chen, K. Zhang, and J. Shen. Journal of Coastal Research, 1998, special issue 14, pp151–166.

storm of 1962. The surge was up to 2 meters high and persisted for 5 high tides, resulting in major coastal erosion along a large length of the U.S. east coast. More recently, the December 1992 northeaster produced substantial floods around New York City, including flooding some important parts of the transportation infrastructure, and coming close to flooding much more critical parts of the underground transportation infrastructure (Rosenzweig and Solecki 2001).

Apart from areas such as New York City, Miami, and New Orleans, the U.S. coastal population density is lower than the population density around the North Sea and in Bangladesh. Hence, the death toll during surge events has been relatively small and has diminished over time, as shown for the East and Gulf Coasts in figure 3.10. On the East Coast, the largest death toll in the 20th century occurred during the 1938 hurricane in which 600 people died (Pielke and Pielke 1997). This has led to a different approach to management of the surge hazard. Instead of the large investment in dikes and surge barriers seen around the North Sea, there has been a focus on:

(1) effective warning systems and evacuation plans, and
(2) flood-proofing and raising of new buildings above the 1-in-100-year flood elevation.

This has reduced the death toll in storm events, but storm damages continue to be significant (Pielke and Pielke 1997). An underlying driver of increased damage is a coastward relocation of the expanding national population. This trend seems set to continue, and, hence, exposure to storms will inevitably continue to increase. When combined with widespread erosional trends and also rapid relative sea-level rises during the 20th century, this suggests that the impacts due to flooding during surges will inevitably increase. While the United States has the resources to respond to these challenges, it will be interesting to see how rapidly the country moves to increase protection along the U.S. East Coast. The expansion of the use of beach nourishment might be seen as a first step in this direction (Neumann et al. 2001). More focused management is required where critical infrastructure is threatened (as in New York City), as these areas are potential hotspots where major surge-related losses could occur (Rosenzweig and Solecki 2001).

Shanghai, China

Shanghai is a good example of a sinking coastal city (table 3.2). It is built on geologically young deposits of the Changjiang (Yangtze) delta, and it subsided as much as 2.8 m during the 20th century (figure 3.14) due to shallow, unregulated groundwater withdrawal (Han et al. 1995; Wang et al. 1998). The groundwater withdrawals were triggered by the growing city and economy in the 1920s, and subsidence continued until the 1960s when groundwater withdrawal was regulated and subsidence rates were reduced to 3 to 4 mm per year—rates of subsidence one would expect in a deltaic setting. Therefore, while human action triggered the subsidence problem, this also made it possible to greatly reduce the subsidence by managing the groundwater withdrawal.

Shanghai was always flood prone due to both high river flows and typhoons. Table 3.9 includes 100,000 deaths due to flooding during a typhoon in 1694. However, the subsidence promoted a substantial increase in the incidence of flooding, the actual flood depths, and the area affected (Guo 1991).[22] A range of new flood protection measures was implemented, including a lot of small-scale measures such as flood barriers and sand bags for individual buildings. This culminated in large new flood walls, built in the early 1990s, that protect the main city to a 1-in-1,000-year standard. However, future subsidence problems remain possible. Anecdotal reports suggest that illegal groundwater withdrawal has increased in Shanghai over the last 10 years, and the rate of subsidence has increased again. This illustrates the ongoing nature of managing surge-induced flooding, as is apparent in all the case studies.

This experience will have commonalities with many other large subsiding cities, all of which are in Asia (table 3.2). There are several other cities that might start to experience subsidence as they develop and, hence, become more exposed to surges. Hanoi and Ho Chi Minh City (Saigon) in Vietnam, and Yangon in Myanmar are potential examples, with Hanoi known to be actively subsiding (Tom et al. 1996).

Conclusions

This document represents a first attempt to draw together the information related to storm surge "hotspots." The relevant information is widely scattered and often not in a form that can be readily synthesized and compared across regions. Therefore, it should be considered as a work in progress rather than as a definitive statement on storm surge hazard. It is also apparent that only the broad regions that are vulnerable to surges can be mapped with the present level of knowledge (see tables 3.11 and 3.12), which points to the need to continue this type of analysis so that comparative studies of hazards can be improved and developed. This provides an improved basis for sharing experiences and is fundamental to many international efforts that need objective methods to prioritize and target the limited resources for hazard mitigation.

Nonetheless, a number of important conclusions can be drawn that are of relevance to the "hotspot" analysis:

22. The subsidence has a range of other impacts, including damage to buildings (Nicholls 1995).

- Surges are a major issue in only a few global regions, with the Bay of Bengal being the most affected region, and Bangladesh being the main "hotspot" for surge impacts.
- While surges are only one aspect of the impacts of a storm, they are the main killer, and surges have led to several million deaths over the last two centuries, mainly in Asia and particularly in Bangladesh.
- High death rates due to surges appear to be linked to land claim and substantial coastal modification, which have encouraged growth in vulnerable coastal populations without appropriate consideration of the potential for surges (for example, southern North Sea and Bangladesh).
- The death toll in surge events appears to have fallen substantially around the world as protection measures and forecasts/warnings are improved, including most recently in Bangladesh.
- However, there is no room for complacency, and the surge hazard will continue to evolve throughout the 21st century due to changing socioeconomic conditions, coastal land use, and climatic risks.
- Damages and disruptions due to surges are more difficult to define as they are one aspect of the storm and as these impacts are often aggregated with other damages, such as damages caused by tornados and other types of wind storms.

Therefore, while it is useful to analyze surge by itself, it is also important to analyze the integrated impacts of coastal storms, as these are what coastal communities experience. In the future, a mixture of analyses is required—one that considers each storm hazard, as well as the integrated impacts.

References

Alexandersson, H., H. Tuomenvirta, T. Schmith, and K. Iden. 2000. Trends of Storms in NW Europe Derived from an Updated Pressure Dataset. *Climate Research* 14: 71–73.

Ali, A. 1999. Climate Change Impacts and Adaptation Assessment in Bangladesh. *Climate Research* 12: 109–116.

Araujo, I., D. Pugh, and M. Collins. 2002. Trends in Components of Sea Level around the English Channel. *Proceedings of Littoral* 2002 EUROCOAST 107–114.

Arnell, N. W., et al. 2004. Climate and Socioeconomic Scenarios for Climate Change Impacts Assessments: Characterising the SRES Storylines. *Global Environmental Change* 14(1): 3–20.

Ascher, G. 1991. The Case of Hamburg. In: *Impact of Sea Level Rise on Cities and Regionsm,* R. Frasetto (ed.). Proceedings of the First International Meeting "Cities on Water," Venice, December 1989. Marsilio Editori, Venice, 75–80.

Bijlsma, L., et al. 1996. Coastal Zones and Small Islands. In: *Impacts, Adaptations and Mitigation of Climate Change: Scientific-Technical Analyses,* R. T. Watson, M. C. Zinyowera, and R. H. Moss (eds.), Contribution of Working Group II to the Second Assessment Report of the Intergovernmental Panel on Climate Change. Cambridge, UK: Cambridge University Press, 289–324.

Burton, I., R. W. Kates, and G. F. White. 1993. 2nd edition. New York: The Guildford Press, 290.

Carnell, M. G. R., and C. A. Senior. 1998. Changes in Mid-Latitude Variability due to Increasing Greenhouse Gases and Aerosols. *Climate Dynamics* 14: 369-383.

Carter, R. W. G. 1988. *Coastal Environments.* Academic Press, 617.

Church, J.A. 2001. Changes in sea level. In: *Climate Change 2001: The Scientific Basis,* J. T. Houghton, et al. (eds.), Contribution of Working Group I to the Third Assessment Report of the Intergovernmental Panel on Climate Change. Cambridge, UK: Cambridge University Press, 639–693.

Clark, M. 1998. Flood Insurance as a Management Strategy for UK Coastal Resilience. *The Geographical Journal* 164(3): 333–343.

Edwards, K. C. 1953. The storm floods of 1st February 1953: VIII. The Netherlands Floods: Some Further Aspects and Consequences. *Geography* 38: 182–187.

Elsner, J. B., and A. B. Kara. 1999. *Hurricanes of the North Atlantic: Climate and Society.* New York and Oxford: Oxford University Press, 488.

Emanuel, K. A. 1988. The Dependency of Hurricane Intensity on Climate. *Nature* 326: 483–485.

Flather, R., and J. Smith. 1998. First Estimates of Changes in Extreme Storm Surge Elevations due to the Doubling of CO2. *The Global Atmosphere and Ocean System* 6: 193–208.

French, P. W. 1997. *Coastal and Estuarine Management.* London: Routledge, 251.

Gilbert, S., and R. Horner. 1984. *The Thames Barrier.* London: Thomas Telford, 182.

Guo, H. 1991. Causes and the Performance of the Construction Work for Flood Tide Prevention in Shanghai. In: *Impact of Sea-Level Rise on Cities and Regions,* R. Frassetto (ed.). Proceedings of the First International Meeting "Cities on Water" (Venice, December 11–13, 1989), Marsilo Editori, Venice, 150–168.

Han, M., J. Hou, and L. Wu. 1995. Potential Impacts of Sea-Level Rise on China's Coastal Environment and Cities: A National Assessment. *Journal of Coastal Research,* Special Issue No. 14: 79–95.

Harleman, D. R. F., et al. 2000. Blocking the Tide. *Civil Engineering,* October 2000: 52–57.

Henderson-Sellers, A., et al. 1998. Tropical Cyclones and Global Climate Change: A Post-IPCC Assessment. *Bulletin of the American Meteorological Society* 79: 19–38.

Hoozemans, F. M. J., M. Marchand, and H. A. Pennekamp. 1993. *A Global Vulnerability Analysis: Vulnerability Assessment for Population, Coastal Wetlands and Rice Production on a Global Scale,* 2nd edition. The Netherlands: Delft Hydraulics.

Houghton, J. Y., et al. (eds.). 2001. Contribution of Working Group I to the Third Assessment Report of the Intergovernmental Panel on Climate Change. Cambridge, UK: Cambridge University Press.

IPCC CZMS. 1990. *Strategies for Adaptation to Sea Level Rise.* Report of the Coastal Zone Management Subgroup, Response Strategies Working Group of the Intergovernmental Panel on Climate Change, Ministry of Transport, Public Works and Water Management. The Hague, 122.

Johns, T. C., et al. 2003. Anthropogenic Climate Change from 1860 to 2100 Simulated with the HadCM3 Model under Updated Emissions Scenarios. *Climate Dynamics,* submitted in revision.

Kausher, A., et al. 1996. Climate Change and Sea-Level Rise: The Case of the Coast. In: *The Implications of Climate and Sea-Level Change for Bangladesh,* R.A. Warrick and Q. K. Ahmad (eds.). Kluwer, Dordrecht, 335–405.

Kelman, I. 2002. CURBE Fact Sheet 3: U.K. Deaths from the 1953 Storm Surge. Version 2, January 11, 2003. Downloaded from http://www.ilankelman.org/disasterdeaths/1953 DeathsUK.doc

Klein, R. J. T., and R. S. J. Tol. 1997. Adaptation to Climate Change: Options and Technologies—An Overview Paper. Technical Paper FCCC/TP/1997/3, United Nations Framework Convention on Climate Change Secretariat. Bonn, Germany, 33.

Klein, R. J. T., R. J. Nicholls, and N. Mimura. 1999. Coastal Adaptation to Climate Change: Can the IPCC Technical Guidelines be Applied? *Mitigation and Adaptation Strategies for Global Change* 4: 51–64.

Klein, R. J. T., et al. 2000. Coastal-Adaptation Technologies. In: *IPCC Special Report on Methodological and Technological Issues in Technology Transfer,* B. Metz, et al. (eds.). Cambridge, UK: Cambridge University Press, 349–372.

Klein, R. J. T., et al. 2001. Technological Options for Adaptation to Climate Change in Coastal Zones. *Journal of Coastal Research* 17(3): 531–543.

Koch, F. H. 1986. Land Development in the Ganges-Brahmaputra Estuary in Bangladesh. Presented at Symposium on Low Land Development, Indonesia, August 1986. In: *Sea-Level Rise: A Selective Retrospective,* P. C. Schroder (ed.). Delft: Delft Hydraulics, 14.

Knutson, T. R., R. E. Tuleya, and Y. Kurihara. 1998. Simulated Increase in Hurricane Intensities in a CO2-Warmed Climate. *Science* 279: 1018–1020.

Lamb, H. H. 1995. *Climate, History and the Modern World,* 2nd edition. London: Routledge, 433.

Li, C. X., et al. 2000. Some Problems of Vulnerability Assessment in the Coastal Zone of China. In: *Global Change and Asia-Pacific Coasts,* N. Mimura and H. Yokoki (eds.). Proceedings of APN/SURVAS/LOICZ Joint Conference on Coastal Impacts of Climate Change and Adaptation in the Asia-Pacific Region, Kobe, Japan. November 14–16, 2000. Asian-Pacific Network for Global Change Research, Kobe and the Center for Water Environment Studies, Ibaraki University, 49–56. (Downloadable at www.survas.mdx.ac.uk)

Lowe, J., and J. Gregory. 1998. A Preliminary Report on Changes in the Occurrence of Storm Surges around the United Kingdom under a Future Climate Scenario. Hadley Centre for Climate Prediction and Research (unpublished).

Mimura, N., M. Isobe, and Y. Hosakawa. 1994. Impacts of Sea Level Rise on Japanese Coastal Zones and Response Strategies. In: *Global Climate Change and the Rising Challenge of the Sea,* J. O'Callaghan (ed.). Proceedings of the Third IPCC CZMS Workshop, Margarita Island, Venezuela, March 9–13, 1992, National Oceanic and Atmospheric Administration, Silver Spring, MD, USA, 329–349.

Murty, T. S. 1984. Storm Surges—Meteorological Ocean Tides. *Canadian Journal of Fisheries and Aquatic Sciences* (Bulletin 12): 897.

Nakicenovic, N., et al. 2000. Special Report on Emissions Scenarios: A Special Report of Working Group III of the Intergovernmental Panel on Climate Change. Cambridge: Cambridge University Press, 599.

Neumann, J. E., et al. 2001. Sea Level Rise and its Effects on Global Resources. In: *Climate Change: Science, Strategies and Solutions,* E. Claussen (ed.). Boston: Brill, 43–62.

Nicholls, R. J. 1995. Coastal Megacities and Climate Change. *Geojournal* 37(3): 369–379.

Nicholls, R. J. 2004. Coastal Flooding and Wetland Loss in the 21st century: Changes under the SRES Climate and Socioeconomic Scenarios. *Global Environmental Change* 14, 69–86.

Nicholls, R. J., and J. Branson. 1998. Coastal Resilience and Planning for Uncertainty: An Introduction. *Geographical Journal* 164: 255–258.

Nicholls, R. J., and F. M. J. Hoozemans. 1996. The Mediterranean: Vulnerability to Coastal Implications of Climate Change. *Ocean and Coastal Management* 31: 105–132.

Nicholls, R. J., F. M. J. Hoozemans, and M. Marchand. 1999. Increasing Flood Risk and Wetland Losses due to Global Sea-Level Rise: Regional and Global Analyses. *Global Environmental Change* 9: S69–S87.

Nicholls, R. J., N. Mimura, and J. C. Topping. 1995. Climate Change in South and South-East Asia: Some Implications for Coastal Areas. *Journal of Global Environmental Engineering* 1: 137–154.

Olsthoorn, A. A., W. J. Maunder, and R. S. J. Tol. 1999. Tropical Cyclones on the Southwest Pacific: Impacts on Pacific Island Countries with Particular Reference to Fiji. In: *Climate, Change and Risk,* T. E. Downing, A. J. Olsthoorn, and R. S. J. Tol. (eds.). London: Routledge, 221–224.

Parker, D. J. (ed.). 2000. *Floods,* 2 volumes. London: Routledge, 431 and 317.

Peerbolte, B. 1994. Hazard Appraisal: Modelling Sea-Level Rise and Safety Standards. In: *Floods Across Europe,* E. Penning-Rowsell, and M. Fordham (eds.). London: Middlesex University Press, 107–134.

Penning-Rowsell, E. C. 2000. Has Venice Crossed the Rubicon? In: *Floods,* Volume 1, D. J. Parker (ed.). London: Routledge, 277–287.

Penning-Rowsell, E. C., and M. Fordham (eds.). 1994. *Floods Across Europe.* London: Middlesex University Press, 214.

Penning-Rowsell, E., et al. 2003. *The Benefits of Flood and Coastal Defence: Techniques and Data for 2003.* Flood Hazard Research Centre, Middlesex University, 322.

Perez, R. T., L. A. Amadore, and R. B. Feir. 1999. Climate Change Impacts and Responses in the Philippines Coastal Sector. *Climate Research* 12: 97–107.

Pielke, R. A. and R. A. Pielke. 1997. *Hurricanes: Their Nature and Impacts on Society.* New York: Wiley, 279.

Rosenzweig, C., and W. D. Solecki (eds.). 2001. Climate Change and a Global City: The Potential Consequences of Climate Variability and Change—Metro East Coast. Report for the US Global Change Research Program, National Assessment of the Potential Consequences of Climate Variability and Change for the United States. New York: Columbia Earth Institute, 224.

Sachs, J. D., A. D. Mellinger, and J. L. Gallup. 2001. The Geography of Poverty and Wealth. *Scientific America* 284(3, March): 70–75.

Shih, S. 2002. A Framework for Analysis of Managed Realignment for the Thames Estuary. MSc Thesis. Enfield, London, UK: Middlesex University, 88.

Small, C., V. Gornitz, and J. E. Cohen. 2000. Coastal Hazards and the Global Distribution of Human Population. *Environmental Geosciences* 7: 3–12.

Small, C., and R. J. Nicholls. 2003. A Global Analysis of Human Settlement in Coastal Zones. *Journal of Coastal Research* 19(3): 584–599.

Smit, B., et al. 2001. Adaptation to Climate Change in the Context of Sustainable Development and Equity. In: *Climate Change 2001: Impacts, Adaptation and Vulnerability,* J. J. McCarthy, O. F. Canziano, and N. Leary (eds.). Contribution of Working Group II to the Third Assessment Report of the Intergovernmental Panel on Climate Change. Cambridge, UK: Cambridge University Press, 877–912.

Smith, K., and R. Ward. 1998. *Floods: Physical Processes and Human Impacts.* Chichester: Wiley, 382.

Steers, J. A. 1953. The East Coast Floods, January 31–February 1, 1953. *Geographical Journal* 119: 280–298.

Tol, R. S. J., R. J. T. Klein, and R. J. Nicholls. Forthcoming. Towards Successful Adaptation to Sea Level Rise along Europe's Coasts. *Journal of Coastal Research.*

Toms, G., et al. 1996. Coast Zone: Vulnerability Assessment. First Steps Towards Integrated Coastal Zone Management. Final Report. Government of the Socialist Republic of Vietnam and Government of the Netherlands, UNEP, 2002. *Global Environment Outlook* 3. London, UK: Earthscan, 446.

United Nations Environment Programme (UNEP). 2002. *GEO: Global Environment Outlook 3: Past, Present and Future Perspectives.* pp446.

Wang, B., et al. 1998. Potential Impacts of Sea-Level Rise on the Shanghai Area. *Journal of Coastal Research,* Special Issue No. 14: 151–166.

Warrick, R. A., and Q. K. Ahmad (eds.). 1996. *The Implications of Climate and Sea-Level Change for Bangladesh.* Kluwer, Dordrecht, 415.

Warrick, R. A., et al. 2000. Climate Change, Severe Storms and Sea Level: Implications for the Coast. In: *Floods,* Volume 2, D. J. Parker (ed.). London: Routledge, 130–145.

WASA Group. 1998. Changing Waves and Storms in the Northeast Atlantic. *Bulletin of the American Meteorological Society* 79: 741–760.

WCC'93. 1994. Preparing to Meet the Coastal Challenges of the 21st century. Report of the World Coast Conference, Noordwijk, The Netherlands, November 1–5, 1993. Ministry of Transport, Public Works and Water Management. The Hague, 49 + apps.

White, G. F. 2000. Lessons for Flood Hazard and Disaster Management from the International Decade–and Future Challenges. In: *Floods,* Volume 1, D. J. Parker (ed.). London: Routledge, 271–275.

Willows, R., and R. Connell (eds.). 2002. Climate Adaptation: Risk, Uncertainty and Decision-Making. UKCIP Technical Report. (www.ukcip.org.uk).

Winchester, P. 2000. The Political Economy of Riverine and Coastal Floods in South India. In: *Floods,* Volume 1, D. J. Parker (ed.). London: Routledge, 56–68.

Zhang, K., B. C. Douglas, and S. P. Leatherman. 2000. Twentieth-century Storm Activity along the U.S. East Coast. *Journal of Climate* 13: 1748–1761.

Chapter 4

Natural Disaster Risks in Sri Lanka: Mapping Hazards and Risk Hotspots

Lareef Zubair and Vidhura Ralapanawe, Upamala Tennakoon, Zeenas Yahiya, and Ruvini Perera

Introduction

The goals for this case study of natural disasters in Sri Lanka were (1) to examine the methodologies needed for subnational assessments of hazard, vulnerability, and hotspots; (2) to assess the interplay among hazards and vulnerability; and (3) to assess the consequence of combinations of multiple hazards and vulnerability factors. In the terminology used here, a "natural disaster" occurs when the impact of a hazard is borne by "elements at risk" that may be vulnerable to the hazard. The elements considered in this study are simplified into categories of people, infrastructure, and economic activities.

Sri Lanka has an area of 65,000 square kilometers and a population of 18.7 million (Department of Census and Statistics 2001).The principal topographic feature is an anchor-shaped mountain massif in the south-central part of the island (figure 4.1). The topography and differences in regional climate (figures 4.2 a and b) are underlying causes of the contrasts in many facets of the island.

The most frequent natural hazards that affect Sri Lanka are droughts, floods, landslides, cyclones, vector-borne epidemics (malaria and dengue), and coastal erosion (Tissera 1997). Tsunamis are infrequent but have caused severe damage. Recent understanding of the tectonics of the Indian Ocean region points to an increasing risk of earthquakes. The risk of volcanoes is small. Here, we have addressed only those hazards related to droughts, floods, landslides, and cyclones. We are mapping spatial risks of epidemics in a separate project to develop an early warning system.

Drought is the most significant hazard in terms of people affected and relief provided. The relief disbursements for drought between 1950 and 1985 were SL Rs 89 million (approximately US$1 million), whereas floods accounted for only SL Rs 7.5 million.

The prevalence of drought may be surprising given that Sri Lanka receives an average of 1,800 mm of rainfall annually. However, it is distributed unevenly both spatially (figure 4.2.a) and temporally (figure 4.2.b). A large part of the island is drought prone from February to April and, if the subsidiary rainy season from May to June is deficient, drought may continue into September. In our analysis, we use a regionalization of Sri Lankan climate into four climatologically homogeneous regions (Puvaneswaran and Smithson 1993)—western and eastern slopes and northern and southern plains—as shown in figure 4.2.a.

During the time frame of the study, disaster management has been carried out in Sri Lanka by the Department of Social Services under the Ministry of Social Services. Relief work for disasters is the responsibility of the parent body, the Ministry of Social Welfare. The Government of Sri Lanka is currently revising its organizational structure for dealing with and planning for natural and manmade disasters.

Our analysis is carried out in the context of civil wars that, together, extended from 1983 to 2002. During this period, natural disasters accounted for 1,483 fatalities, while civil wars accounted for more than 65,000. War has devastated infrastructure and communities' ability to deal with hazards, reduced incomes, weakened safety nets, and undermined capacity to recover from hazard events. For example, there has been a severe toll on hospital availability. Although there has been peace since 2002, longer-term consequences such as unexploded landmines, war orphans, and the war-disabled continue. The availability of data on hazards and vulnerability is restricted in the war zones. The vulnerability analysis

Figure 4.1. The district boundaries of Sri Lanka are shown over the topography

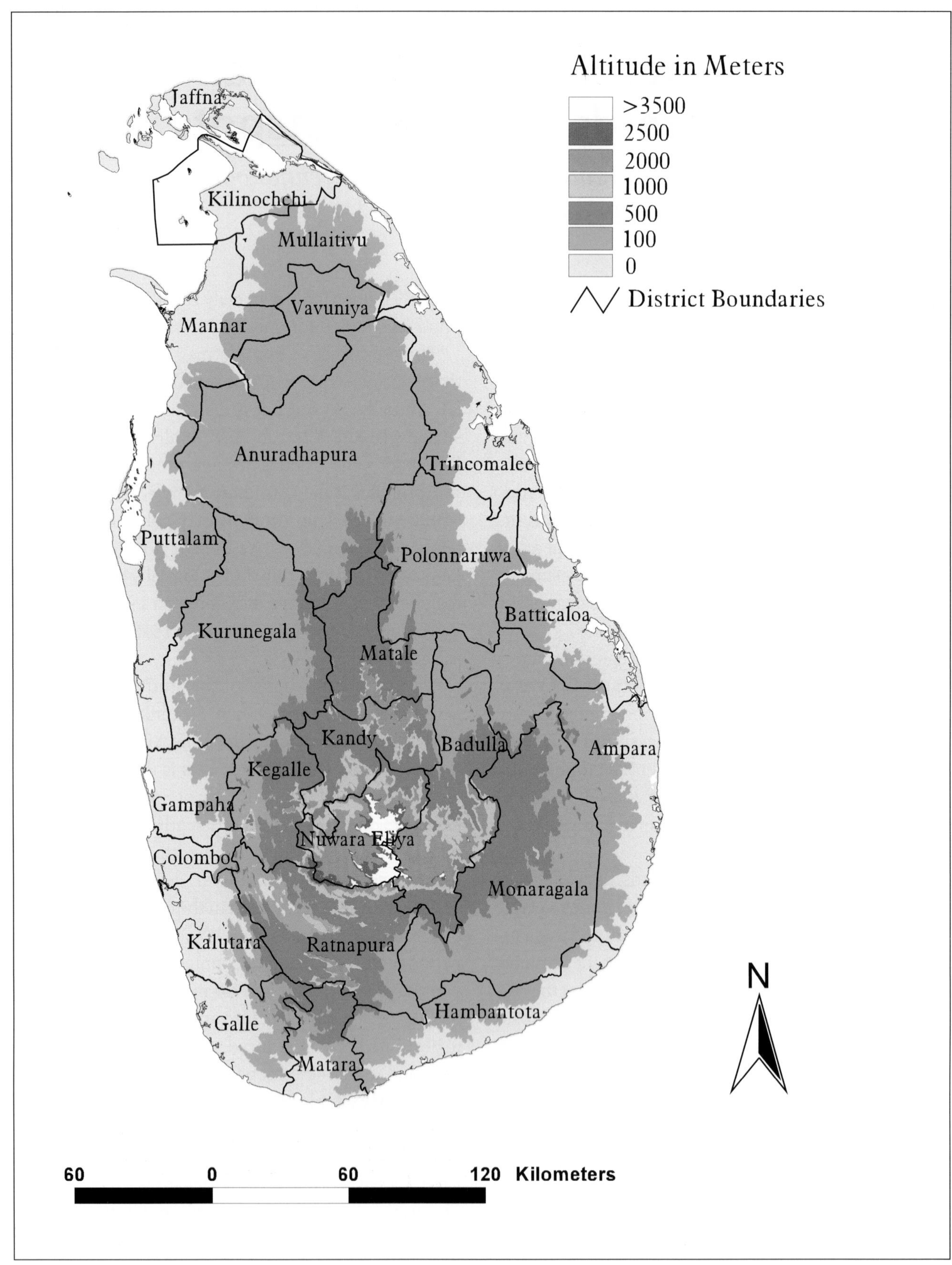

Figure 4.2.a. The average annual rainfall climatology estimated based on data from 284 stations in the period between 1960 and 1990. Homogenous climatological regions as proposed by Puvaneswaran and Smithson (1993) are overlaid.

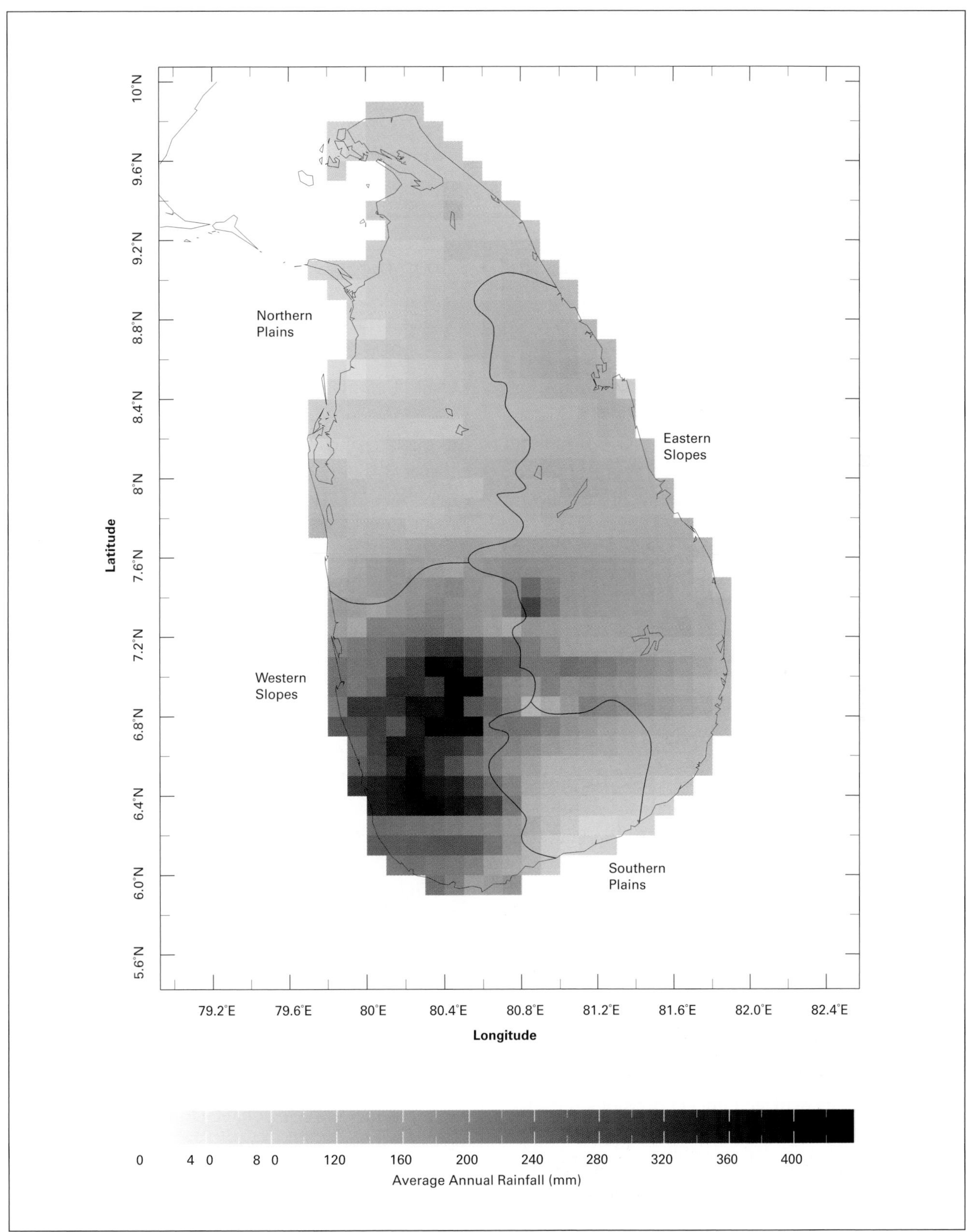

Figure 4.2.b. The average monthly rainfall between 1869 and 1998 for Sri Lanka

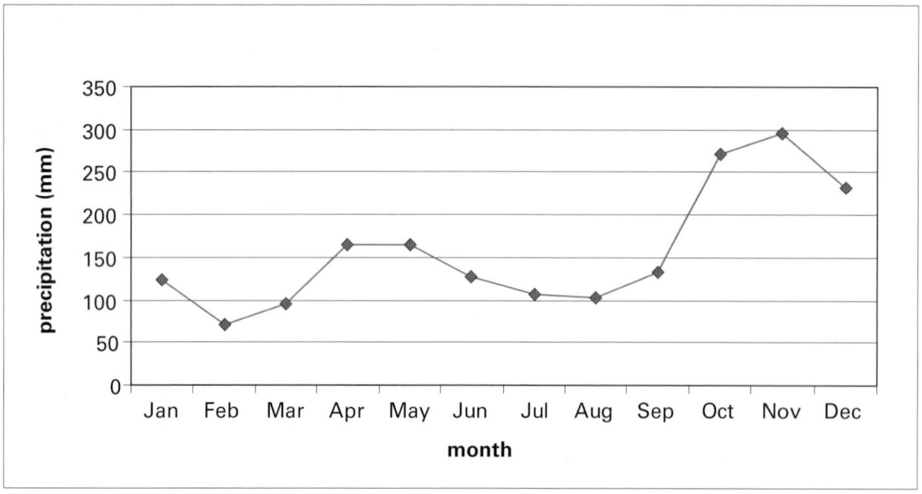

is complicated by the two-decade-long war. While the precision of our analysis may be affected by the history of war, vulnerabilities created by the war make efforts to reduce disaster risks all the more important.

The specific objectives for this study are as follows:

- To undertake a subnational analysis of droughts, floods, cyclones, and landslides;
- To assess vulnerability to these hazards at the subnational level;
- To assess multihazard risks and hazard hotspots at the subnational level; and
- To assess methodologies for incorporating climatic information into hazard analysis.

We shall describe the data that were used, the methodologies used for hazard and vulnerability assessment, and the analysis of multihazard risk in the following sections.

Data

In-Country Data

The administrative divisions in Sri Lanka are provinces, districts, divisional secretariat divisions (DSDs), and Grama Niladhari (Village Officer) divisions (GNDs). There are 9 provinces, 25 districts, 323 DSDs, and 14,113 GNDs, organized hierarchically.

Disaster-Related Data: The sources of data were the Sri Lanka Department of Social Services, Sri Lanka Department of Census and Statistics, and the Central Bank of Sri Lanka. These data were of varying resolutions, ranging in scope from the district level (droughts, floods, and cyclones) to the DSD level (later instances of flood) to the GND level (landslides). Most disaster incidence data also contained relief expenditures.

Climate Data: Data were obtained from the Sri Lanka Department of Meteorology and secondary sources. Although the country has around 400 functioning rainfall stations, only a subset of these possesses uninterrupted records. The records in the Northern Province were limited over the last two decades because of war. We used data from 284 rainfall stations from 1960 to 2000 to construct gridded data at a resolution of 10 km. Using 1960 to 1990 as the base period, monthly climatologies were calculated. Monthly anomalies were calculated by deducting the climatology from observed values (figure 4.2.a).

Hydrological Data: Data were obtained from the Sri Lanka Department of Irrigation and through secondary sources for monthly river flow measurements at 140 gauging stations. These data had numerous gaps.

Landslide Hazard–Related Data: Data were obtained through the National Building Research Organization of Sri Lanka.

Population, Social, Economic, and Infrastructure Data: The Department of Census and Statistics provided population data. Data at the DSD level were selected for comparison and analysis. Gross domestic product (GDP) measures, including regional GDP, were obtained from the Central Bank of Sri Lanka.

Food Security Data: An assessment of food security in Sri Lanka was conducted under the Vulnerability Assessment and Mapping Program of the World Food Programme (WFP), Sri Lanka office. The identification of DSDs with three levels of food insecurity was obtained from their maps.

Hazards and disaster records had good identification of where these occurred, but often only the year when these occurred was available. The temporal resolution was improved by interrogation of multiple data sources and by consulting government officials.

Global Data Sources

Hazard Data—Floods: Dartmouth Flood Observatory carries an archive of large flood events from 1985 onward. This database contains specific dates of the floods, severity class, and affected area. However, the spatial resolution is coarse, as the data have been derived from the district level.

Climate Data: The data available at the International Research Institute for Climate and Society (IRI) Data Library with long coverage for Sri Lanka is lower in resolution (250 km grid).

Exposure Data—Population, Social, Economic, and Infrastructure Data: Center for International Earth Science Information Network's (CIESIN's) Gridded Population of the World (GPW2) dataset contains population data on a 5 km grid. The gridding methodology of GPW2 utilizes district-level population data. "Landscan 2001" contains gridded population data on a 1 km grid calculated using population, roads, slope, land cover, and nighttime lights.

Vulnerability Data: The United Nations Development Programme (UNDP) Human Development Reports provide a number of key indicators at the national level. The UNDP Human Development Report for Sri Lanka provides most of these indicators at the district level.

Disaster Data—EM-DAT: The Office of U.S. Foreign Disaster Assistance/Center for Research on the Epidemiology of Disasters (OFDA/CRED) International Disaster Database has recorded 48 natural disasters in Sri Lanka during the period from 1975 to 2001, including four instances of epidemics. EM-DAT identifies 9 droughts, 2 landslides, 3 cyclones and storms, and 33 flood events (including floods caused by the cyclones). The dataset contains dates and affected areas and people. The United Nations Environment Programme/GRID (UNEP/GRID) datasets include global cyclone tracks for the period from 1980 to 2000.

Exposure and Vulnerability

Exposure and vulnerability may be assessed for the three categories of elements at risk—people, economic activity, and infrastructure.

People

Population: The population of Sri Lanka was 19.2 million in 1998 (293 persons per km^2) with an uneven distribution (figure 4.3). Fifty-five percent of the population is concentrated in 20 percent of the land area (Department of Census and Statistics 2001). Thirty percent of the population resides in urban areas. The least-populated districts (covering 40 percent of the island) host 10 percent of the population. In these districts, population density ranges from 35 to 100 people per km^2, which is still high by global standards (De Silva 1997). The highest population is in the Colombo, Gampaha, and Kalutara districts of the Western Province. There is a secondary population center in the Kandy District in the Central Province and in the Galle District along the southern coast. The high density of people in the wet parts of the island increases the number of people who are vulnerable to floods and landslides.

Impoverishment and mortality are direct consequences of, as well as contributors to, natural disasters. In this context, food security measures a community's resilience to the hazards and often its exposure. Food security calculated by the WFP Sri Lanka office in 2002 was based on the availability of food, access to food, and utilization of food (figure 4.4). Based on this study, 93 DSDs out of 323 were categorized as "Most Vulnerable," 82 as "Less Vulnerable," and 148 as "Least/Not Vulnerable" (World Food Programme 2002). The spatial variability of the Least/Not Vulnerable category shows two contiguous regions and some scattered areas. One con-

Figure 4.3. The density of population in each of the 323 Divisional Secretarial Divisions based on data from the census of 2001

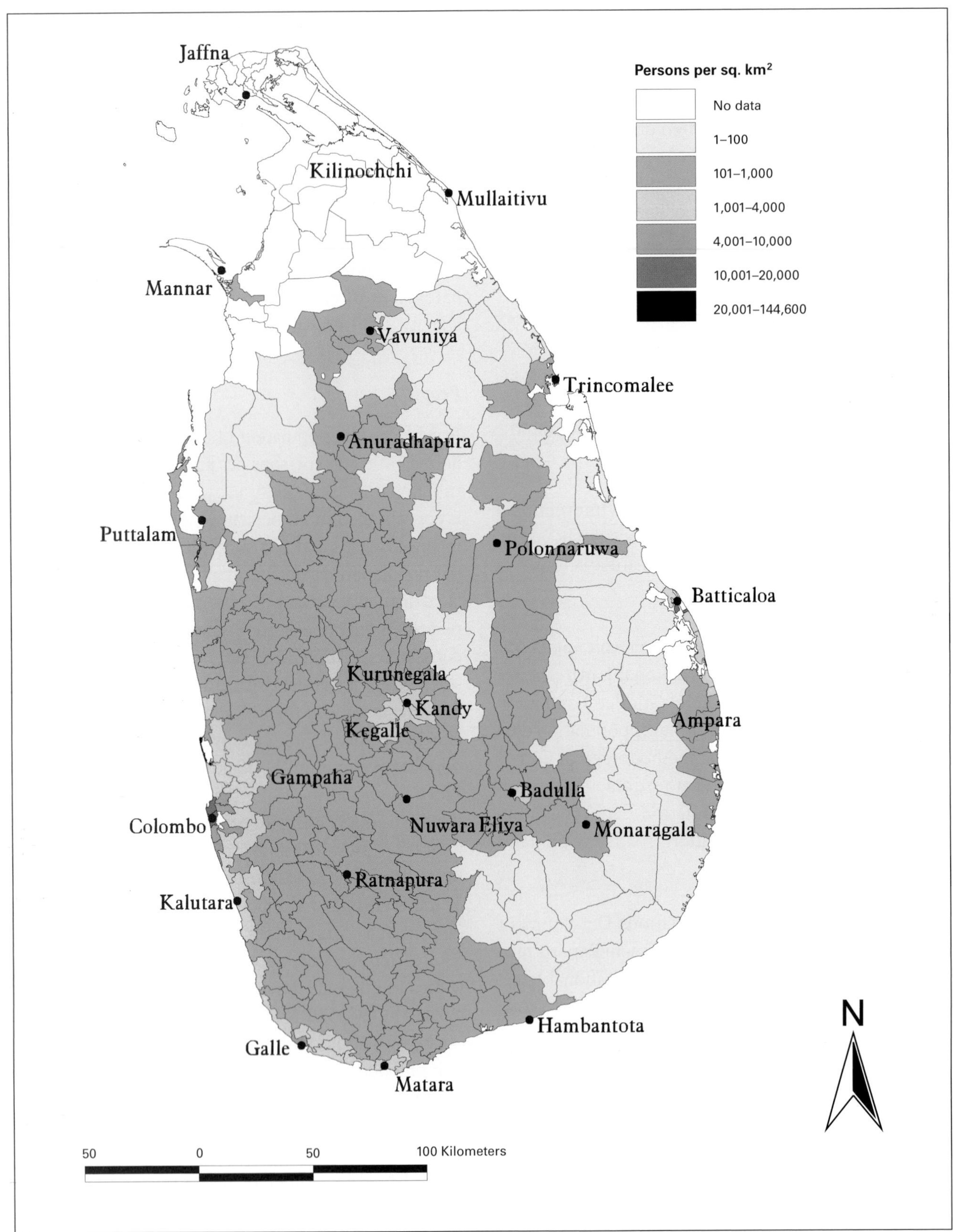

Figure 4.4. The food insecurity index of Divisional Secretariat Divisions (DSDs) as estimated by the World Food Programme

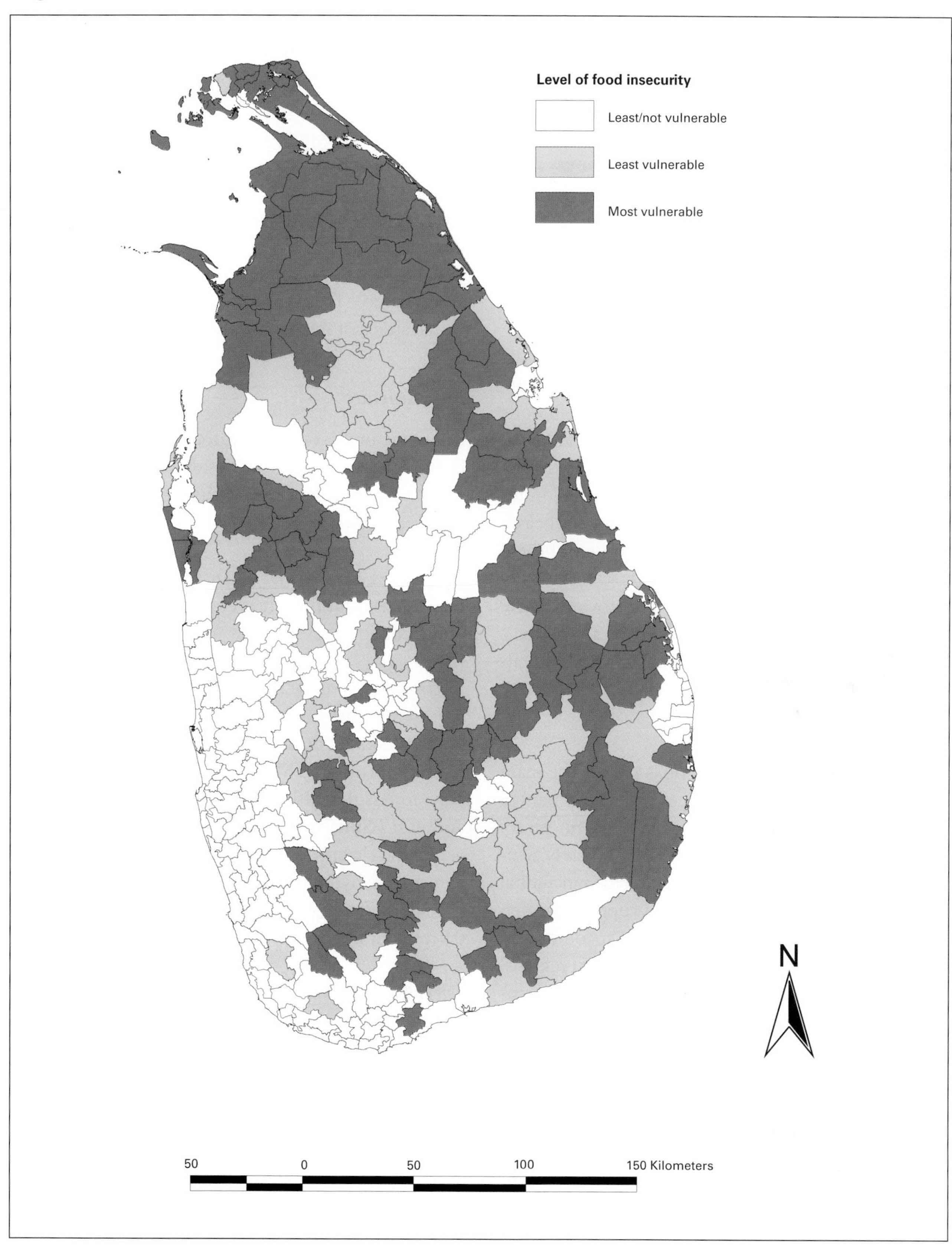

tiguous region is the western coastal region, which has higher rainfall, better infrastructure facilities, and industry. A second contiguous region with high food security is the area around Kandy which also has higher rainfall and better infrastructure facilities. A third contiguous areas is the region around Anurhadhapura, which has improved infrastructure, increased irrigation and lower population density. The higher food insecurity in the northern and eastern areas is due to a combination of war and dry climatic conditions punctuated by cyclones and heavy rainfall.

Economic activity

Industrial and infrastructure sectors account for the bulk of the national GDP (figure 4.5.a). Agriculture, animal husbandry, and fisheries provide livelihoods for one-third of the employed (figure 4.5.b), followed by employment in industries, infrastructure, and services. The disruption in agriculture, industry, and infrastructure caused by natural disasters is addressed below, along with descriptions of the salient features of these elements in relation hazards.

The Western Province had the largest provincial GDP (figure 4.6) with SL Rs 180 billion (US$3.4 billion); the Central Province came in second with SL Rs 46 billion (US$0.88 billion) at constant 1990 prices (UNDP 1998).

Agriculture: The primary food crop is paddy. The main *Maha* cropping season commences with heavy rainfall starting in late September and ends in March. A secondary season, *Yala,* extends from May to early September, and during this season only half of the agricultural land is cultivated because of limited supply of water. The major cash crops are tea, rubber, coconut, and spices; and their cultivation is largely in the wet regions. The agrarian economy is thus susceptible to disruption through droughts and floods. Our previous work has shown a link between rainfall variations and agricultural production (Zubair 2002). Note that there is an extensive irrigation network that modulates the spatial distribution of vulnerability.

Industry: The major industries are textile and apparel, food and beverage processing, chemical and rubber, and mining and minerals. Industries are heavily concentrated in Colombo, Gampaha, and Kalutara in the Western Province. In the last two decades, industrial production has shifted from heavy industries for domestic consumption to export-oriented textile and other processing.

Industries are concentrated in a few regions in western Sri Lanka (figure 4.7) that are particularly prone to flooding. Drought in the Central Highlands can affect industry drastically through deficits in hydropower production. A quarter of the manufactured products are from the processing of agricultural products (tea, rubber, and tobacco). Thus, these industries could be affected by hazards that impact agricultural production.

Infrastructure

Infrastructure development, too, reflects a pattern of heavy development in the Western Province with subsidiary development in the metropolitan districts of Kandy and Galle.

Roads: Sri Lanka has an extensive road network with better density and coverage compared with most developing countries.

Electricity Generation and Distribution: As of 1995, 53 percent of households had access to electricity. However, the spatial distribution of electricity availability ranges from more than 90 percent in Colombo and Gampaha to less than 40 percent for districts in the north and east (Gunaratne 2002). Of the total nationally generated electrical energy, approximately 60 percent comes from hydropower, putting it at high risk during drought periods. The droughts in 1995-96 and 2000-01 resulted in blackouts for the whole country.

Telephones: The density of telephones is low with 41 landlines and 23 cellular phones per 1,000 persons in 2000 (UNDP 1998). The spatial distribution of access indicates that Colombo has more than 50 percent of the landlines.

Separate indexes for roads, electricity, and telephone densities were analyzed to develop an infrastructure density index. The road index was constructed by nor-

Figure 4.5.a. Sectoral breakdown of the GDP for 2001

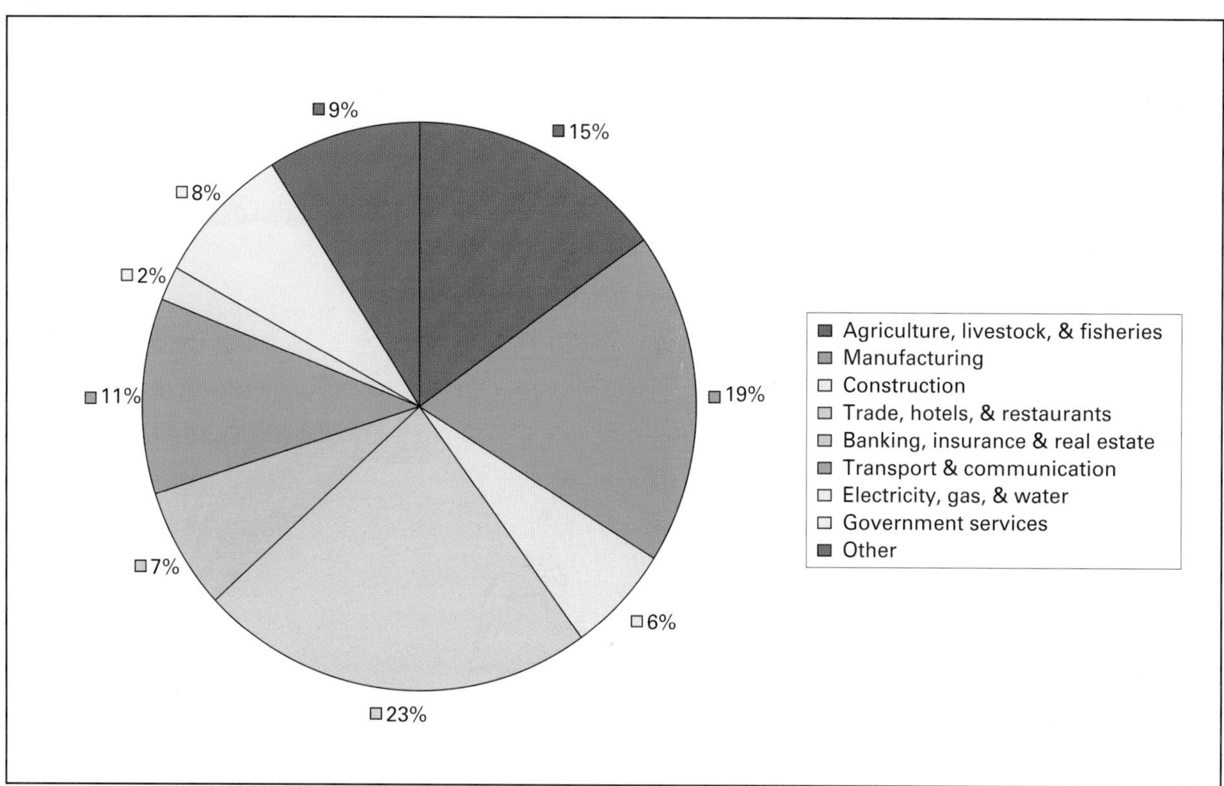

Source: Department of Census and Statistics 2001

Figure 4.5.b. Sectoral breakdown of the labor force for 2001

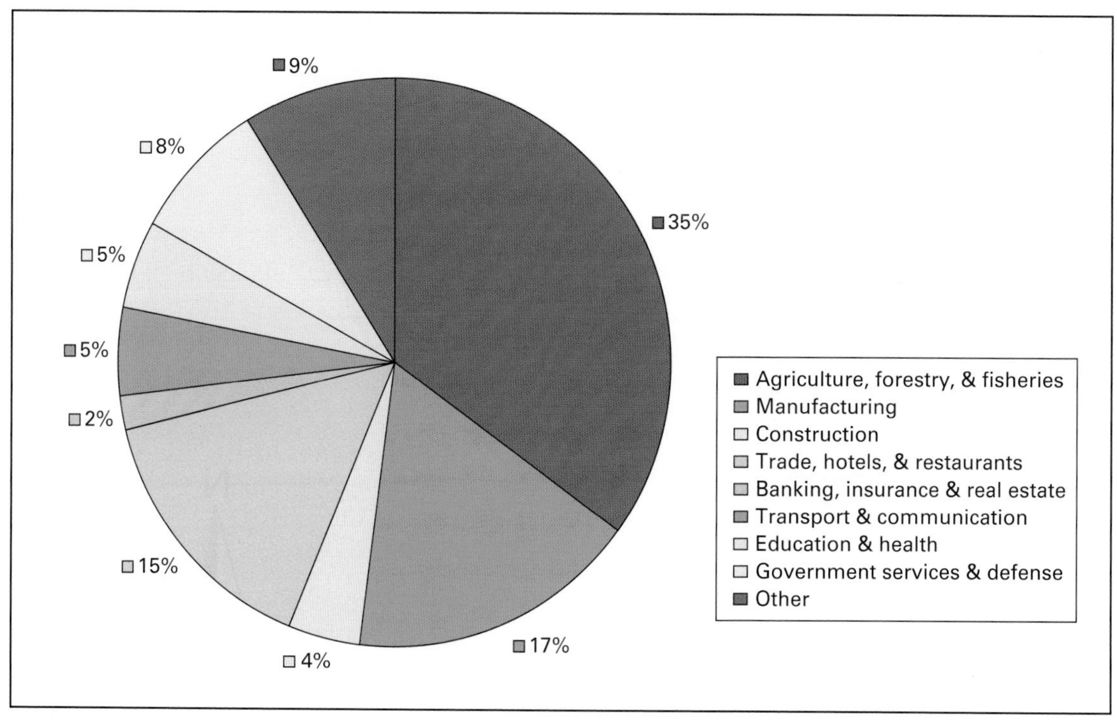

Source: Department of Census and Statistics 2001

Figure 4.6. The gross domestic product (GDP) by province for 1995

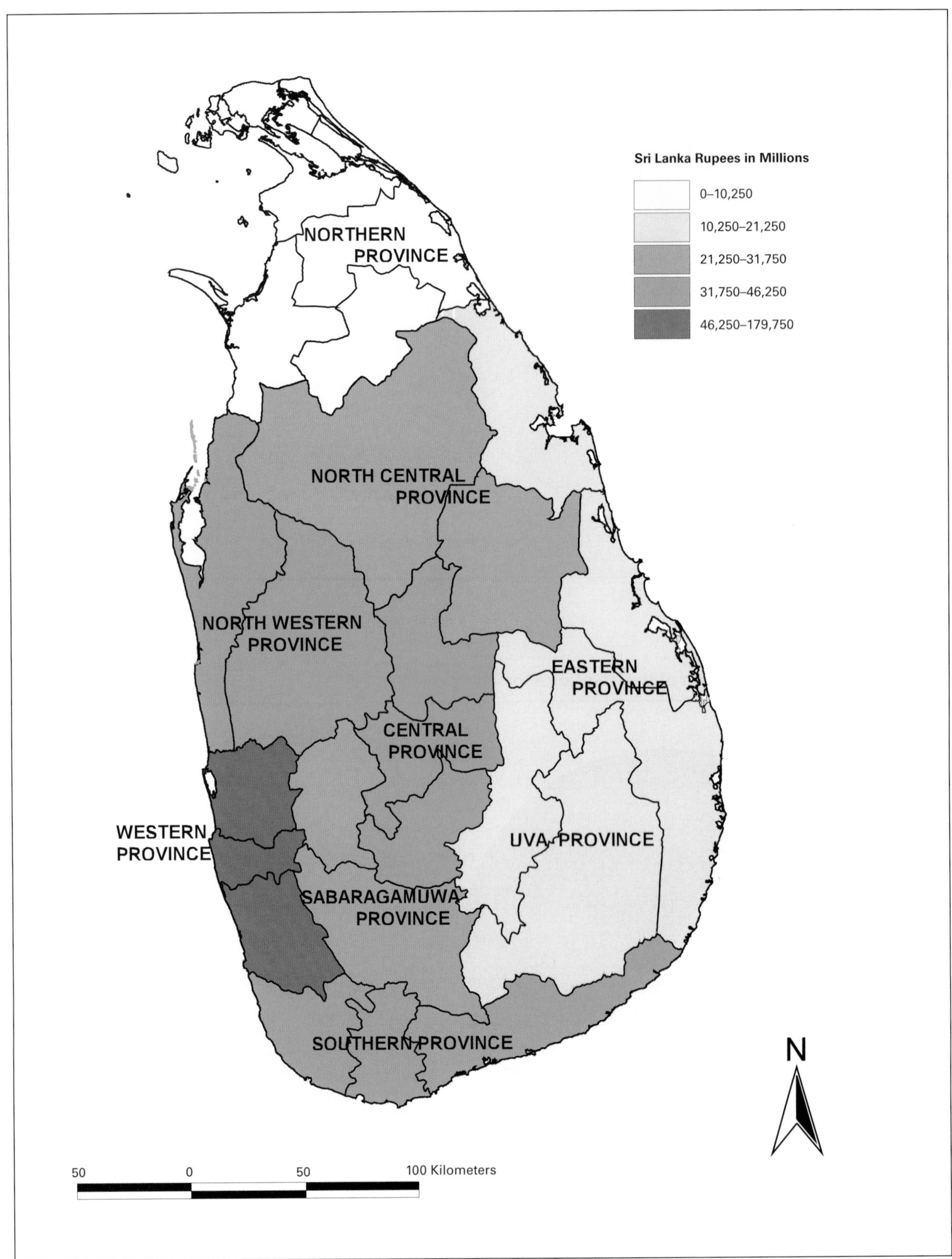

Figure 4.7. The estimate of industrial output in the districts in 1995

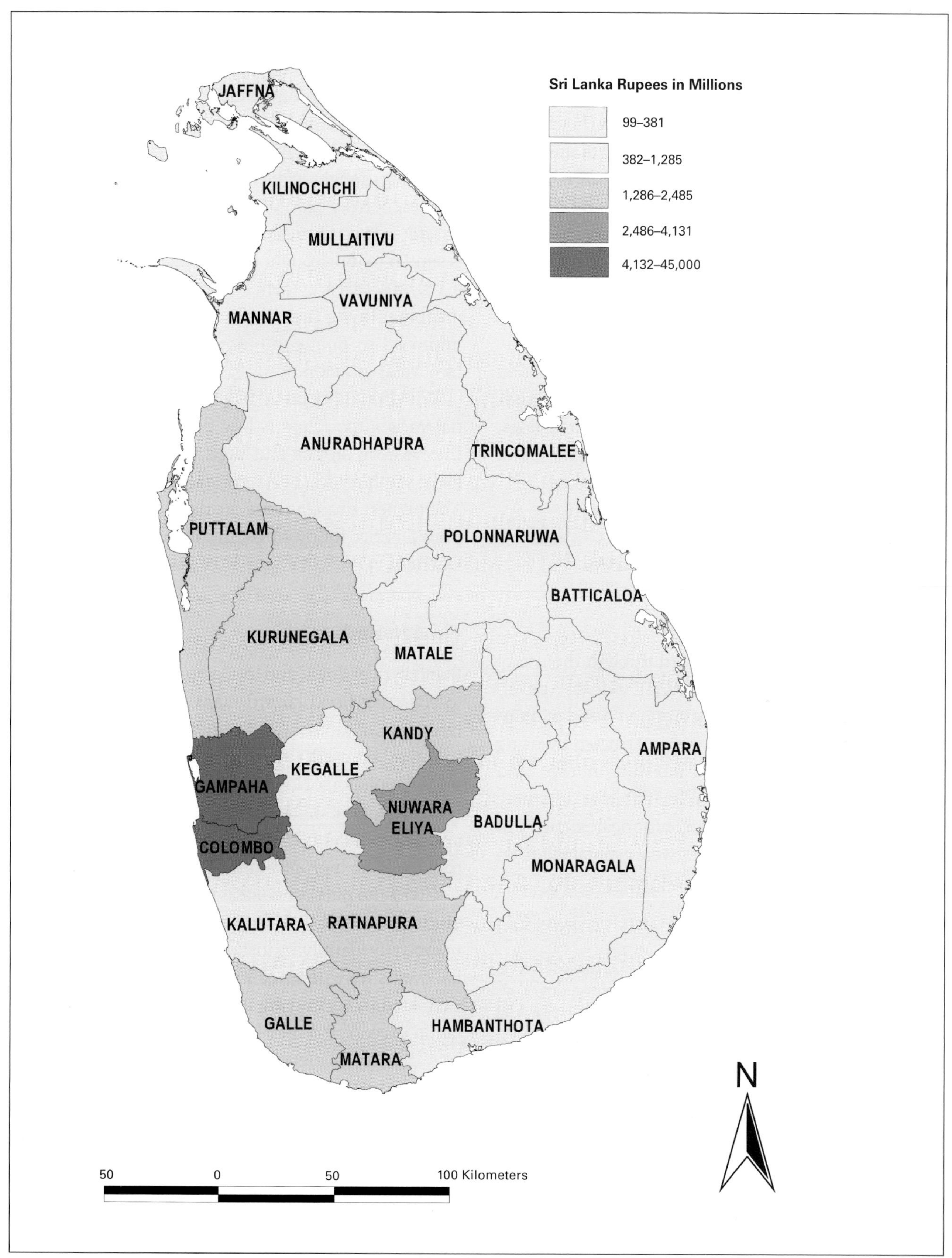

malizing the length of different categories of roads (classes A, B, and C) per district. The telephone and electricity indexes were constructed as the number of households that have access to these facilities in each district. These three indexes were evenly normalized and aggregated to create an infrastructure index (figure 4.8).

There is a high concentration of infrastructure facilities in Colombo. This skewed distribution is largely due to the heavy concentration of telecommunication facilities. Electricity and telephone facilities have been severely disrupted in the Northern Province because of the war, and there are no estimates of recent conditions. Thus, interpretation of the infrastructure index for these areas needs to be tempered with caution.

Infrastructure elements that are at risk from natural hazards include the road network (floods and landslides), electrical distribution system (floods, landslides, and cyclones), electricity generation (droughts), and telephones (floods, landslides, and cyclones).

Analysis of Individual Hazard Risks

Drought Hazard

Drought hazards can be estimated through the use of several methods. However the WASP indexes[23] developed by Lyon (2004) are the best option based on rainfall alone. Other indexes may be constructed by using stream flow, vegetation or soil moisture indexes, and so on, but these data are not available at adequate levels of resolution, reliability, and historical extent. Both 6- and 12-month WASP indexes were estimated for Sri Lanka (figure 4.9).

There is a stronger tendency toward drought in the southeastern district of Hambantota and the northwestern region, which includes the Mannar and Puttalam districts. The drought tendency is markedly less pronounced in the southwest corner of Sri Lanka where there is heavy rainfall.

A drought disaster risk map was constructed by weighting drought incidences for severity of the drought *in terms of relief expenditure (figure 4.10)*. The drought hazard map constructed from rainfall data (figure 4.9) is similar to the drought disaster incidence map (figure 4.10), and this is evidence of the plausibility of hazard mapping. In the future, the drought mapping may be improved by taking into account factors such as surface water availability.

The drought disaster risk map shows marked spatial variability. There is low drought disaster risk in the western slopes and high drought disaster risk in the southeastern, northern, and northwestern regions. The highest drought disaster risk is in the Anuradhapura District followed by the Badulla and Batticaloa Districts.

Flood Hazard

Rainfall, river flows, and topographical data can be used to construct flood hazard maps. Such an effort needs hydrological modelling. An archive of satellite images, too, may be used to identify flood-prone areas with higher resolutions. However, the stream-flow data needed for hydrological modeling and satellite archives are not available with required consistency, resolution, and history to create high-resolution maps.

Given the purposes of this study and the 10 km resolution to which it is limited, flood hazards may be mapped by identifying instances in which extreme rainfall events were detected in the past. Flood hazard was estimated by identifying instances of monthly precipitation exceeding a threshold of 600 mm (figure 4.11).

A disaster incidence map of floods incurring losses was constructed by using the number of major floods in the last 50 years at district level using data from the Social Services Department and Dartmouth Flood Observatory (figure 4.12). The frequency was normalized over area and scaled from 1 to 100. There are similarities between the essential features of the flood hazard esti-

23. WASP is an acronym for the Weighted Anomaly Standardized Precipitation index. This index gives an estimate of the relative deficit or surplus of precipitation for different time intervals ranging from 1 to 12 months. In this case, analysis is based on 6-month and 12-month indexes. To compute the index, monthly precipitation departures from the long-term average are obtained and then standardized by dividing by the standard deviation of monthly precipitation. The standardized monthly anomalies are then weighted by multiplying by the fraction of the average annual precipitation for the given month. These weighted anomalies are then summed over varying time periods—here, 6 and 12 months. On the plots, the value of the given WASP index has itself been standardized. Regions with an annual average precipitation of less than 0.2 mm/day have been "masked" from the plot.

Figure 4.8. Infrastructure density index estimated for each district, as described in the text

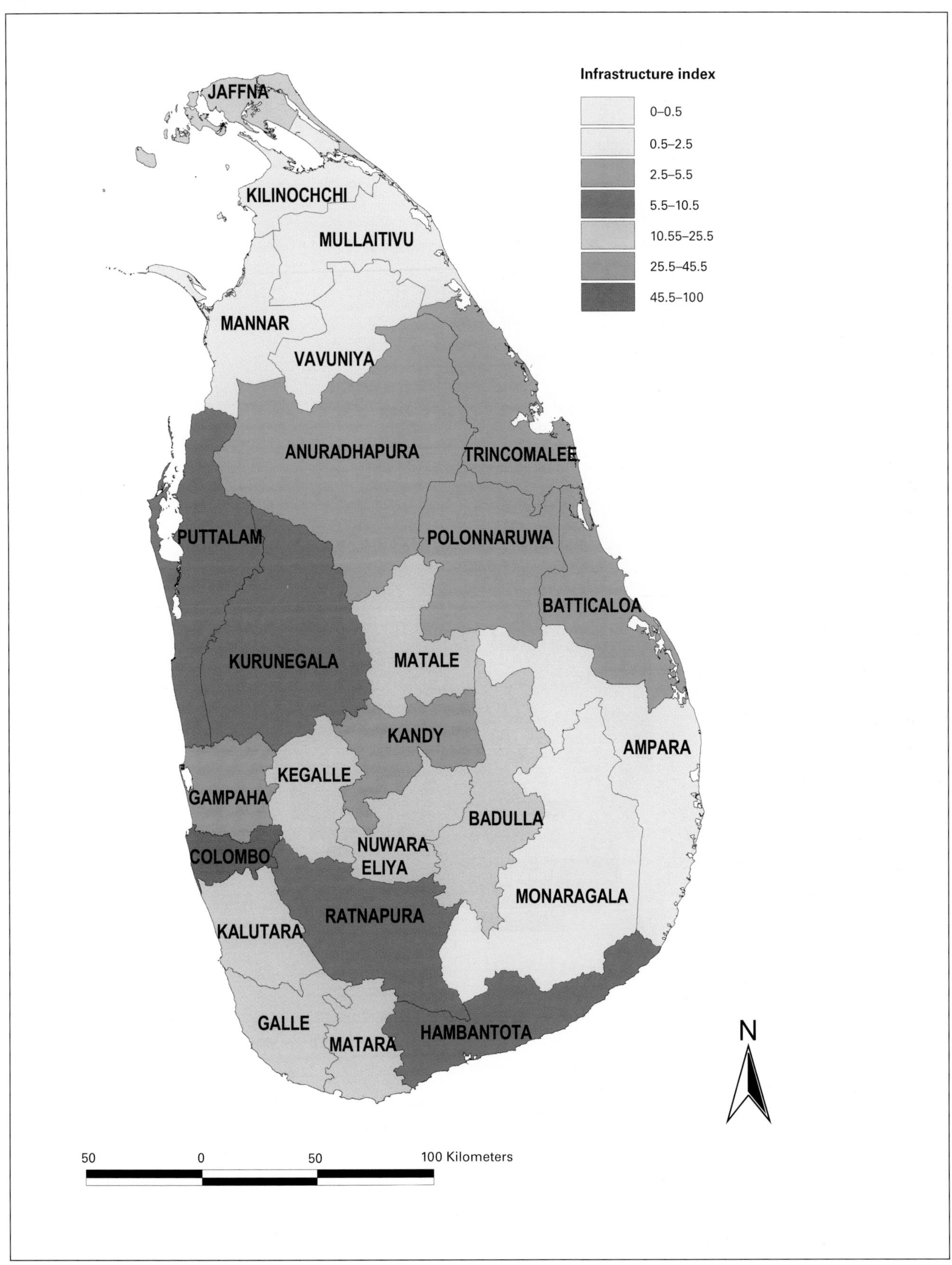

Figure 4.9. The drought hazard was estimated using a modified WASP index. The details of the WASP index are provided in the text. The negative WASP values (dry) were averaged over a 12-month period to identify drought prone regions. The hazard values were normalized so that they ranged between 0 and 100.

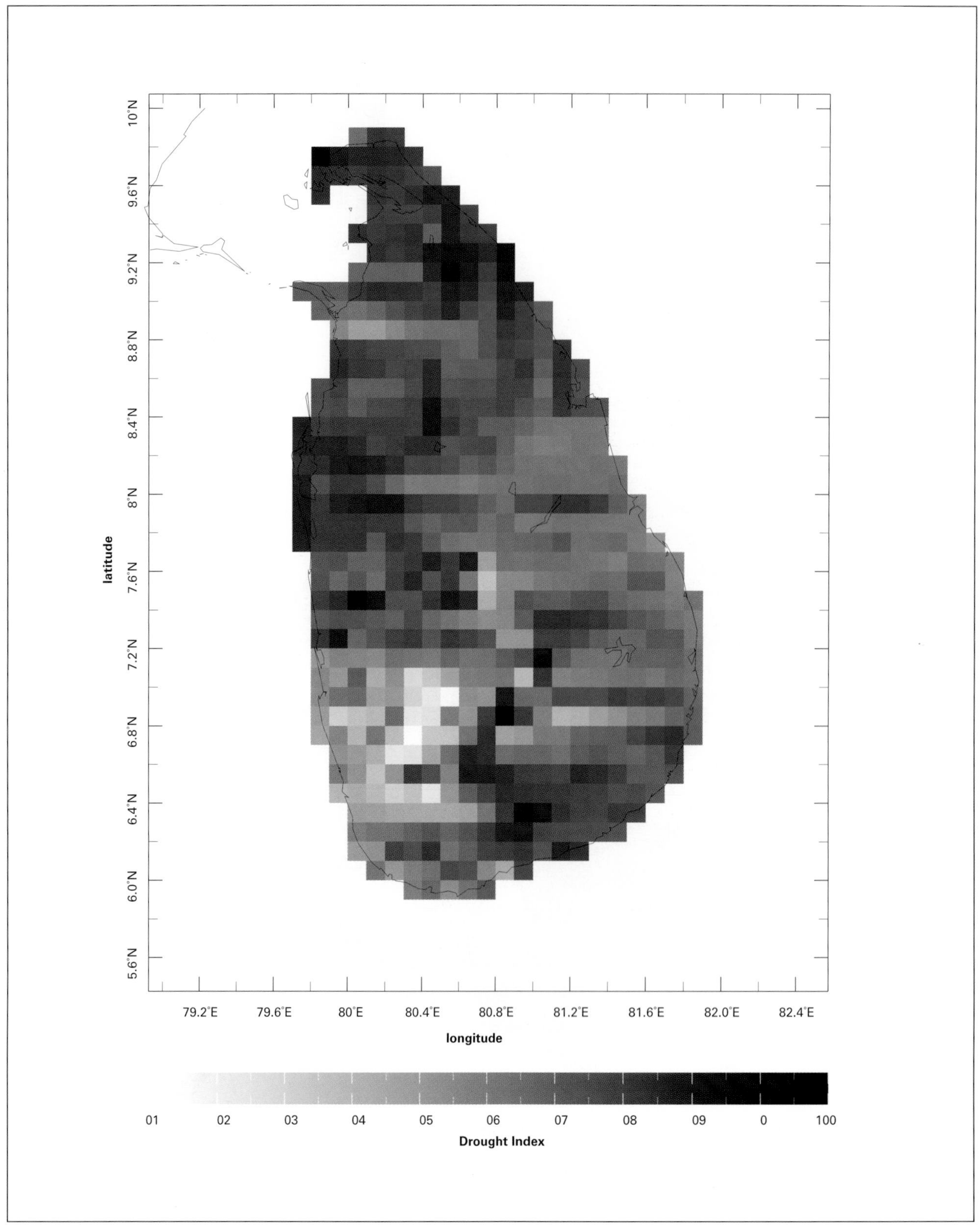

Figure 4.10. Drought disaster incidence frequency was constructed by aggregating the numbers of droughts that have been recorded in each district. Major droughts as categorized by the Department of Social Services were weighted by 1.5, medium droughts by 1.0, and minor droughts by 0.5

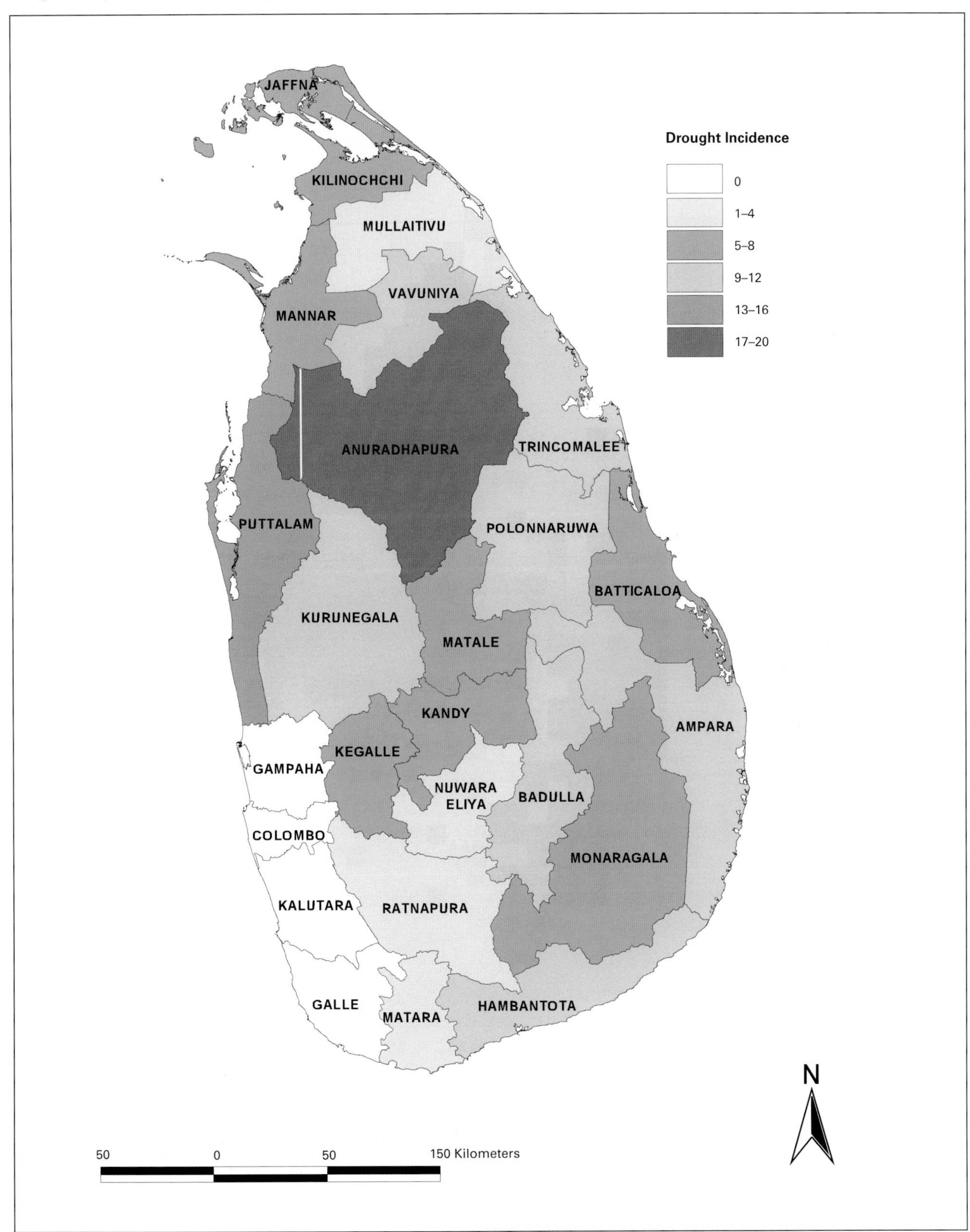

Figure 4.11. The flood hazard estimate based on the frequency of months of extreme rainfall using data between 1960 and 2000. The threshold chosen for extreme rainfall was 600 mm per month.

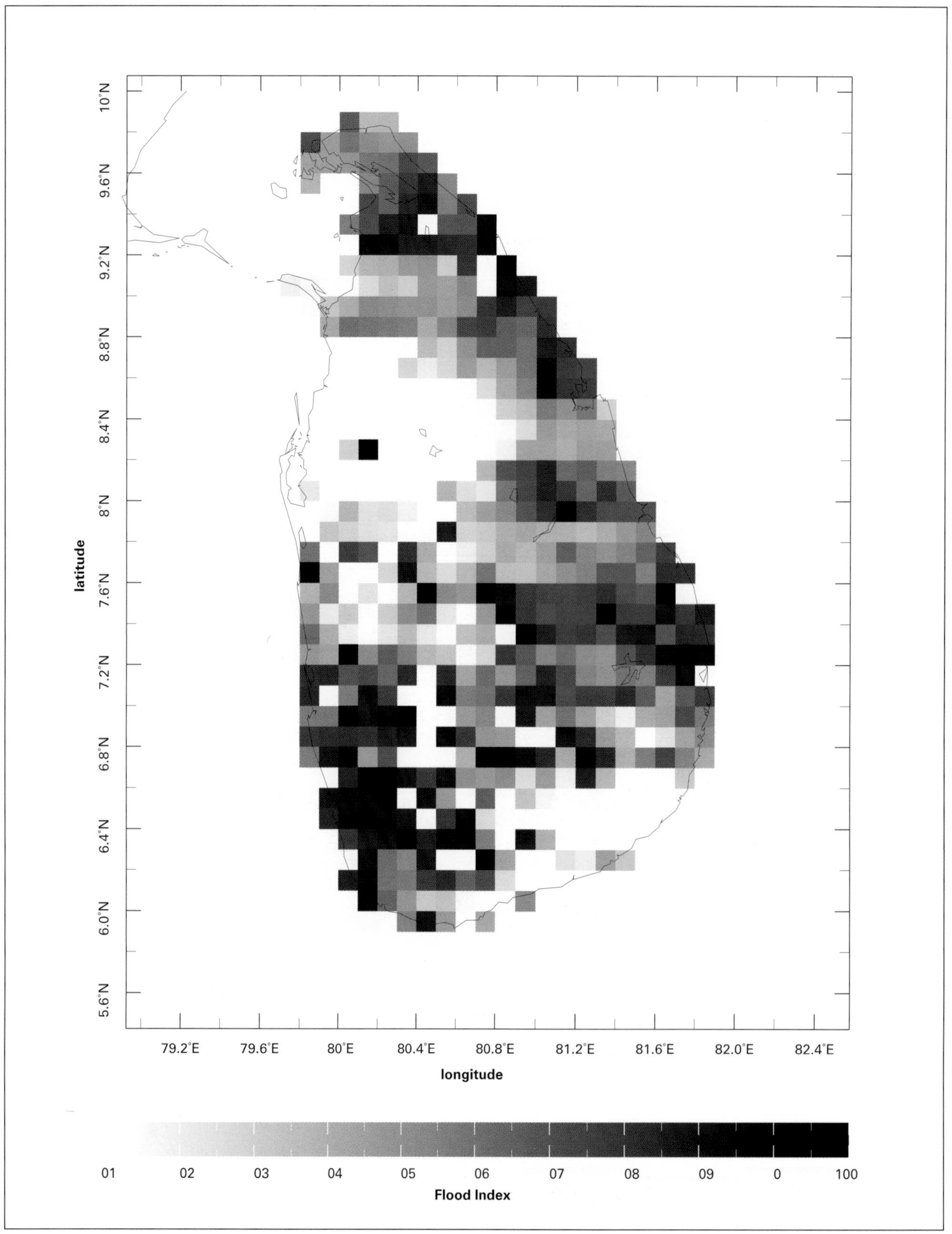

Figure 4.12. Frequency map of flood disaster incidence created by aggregating the numbers of floods recorded in each district between 1957 and 1995. Major floods, as categorized by the Ministry of Social Services, were weighted by 1.5 and minor floods were given a weight of 0.5. The index was normalized by area.

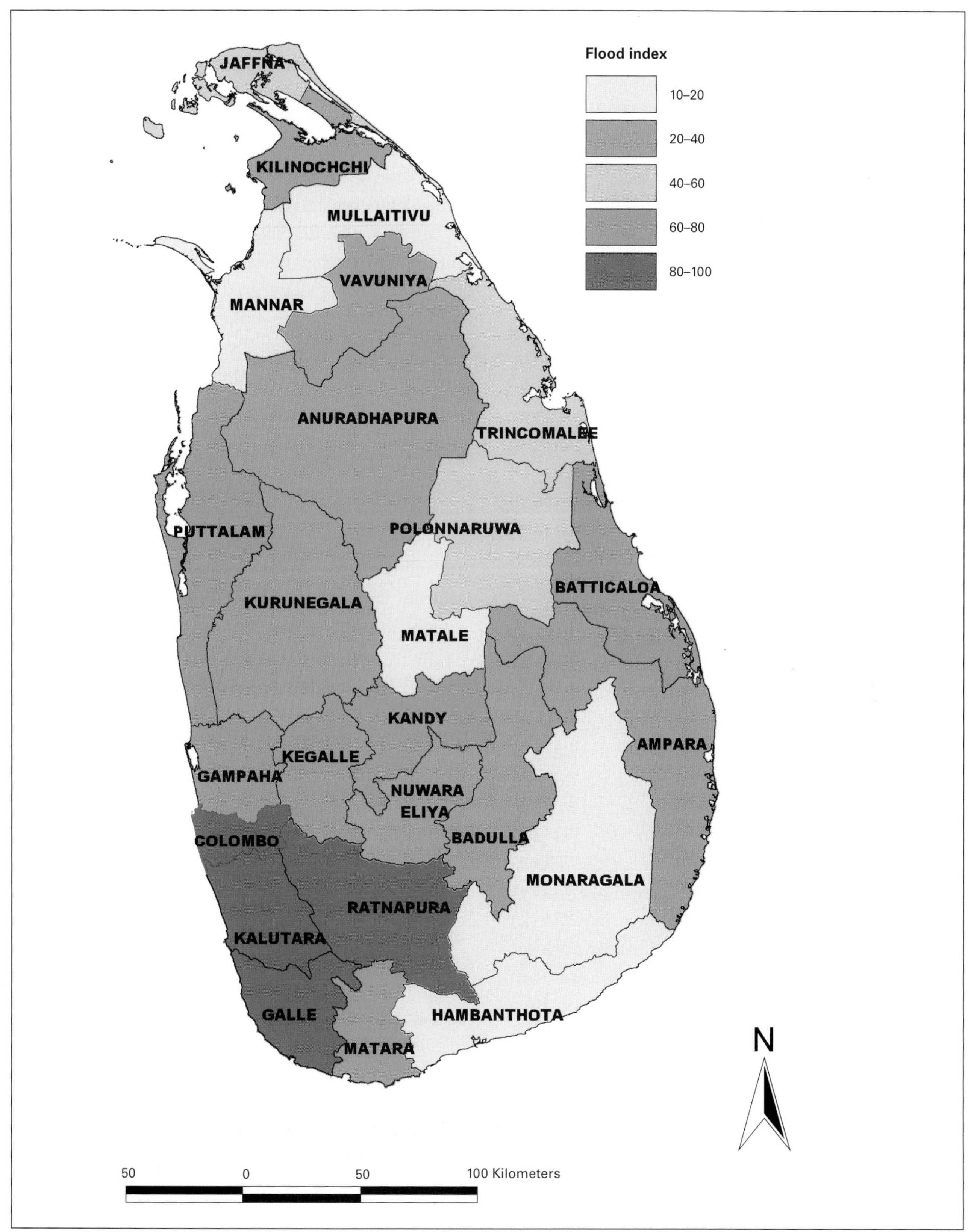

mates based on rainfall data and the above disaster incidence estimate.

We estimated the seasonal distribution of floods in the western and eastern regions separately (figure 4.13) based on 33 flood events in the EM-DAT database that had records of months of occurrence.

The flood hazard and disaster maps show high risk in the western, southwestern, northern, northeastern, and eastern parts of the country. The western slopes show the highest risk followed by the Batticaloa and Badulla Districts. The most flood-prone districts are Kegalle, Ratnapura, Kalutara, Kandy, Colombo, and Galle. These districts are located in the southwest part of the island. Flood occurrences in the eastern slopes and the northern plains coincide with the period of heavy rainfall (September to January) during the *Maha*. In the western slopes, floods do occur during the *Maha,* but are more common in the mid-*Yala* season, which lasts from May to August. These trends are also reflected in both hazard-risk and seasonal maps. Of the 33 flood events in EM-DAT, 20 events occurred in the November–January period (during the *Maha* rainfall season), including 3 cyclone-induced events. These flood events affected both the western and eastern parts of the island. Eleven events occurred during the May–July period (*Yala* rainfall season), which affected only the western slopes (figure 4.13).

Heavy rainfall in the eastern and southwestern slopes is a principal cause of the flood risk. The drainage and topography of certain districts and the land use patterns are also significant factors. For example, in the districts of Kegalle and Ratnapura, people have settled in flood plains and steep hill slopes. The eastern slopes receive most of the rainfall during the *Maha* season. This is also the cyclone and storm season that can bring heavy rainfall in short time periods. The Vavuniya District shows a higher flood probability caused by cyclonic storms. Even though their annual rainfall is lower than that of the western highlands, Vavuniya and Mullaitivu in the north have recorded the highest rainfall intensities on the island (Madduma Bandara 2000b).

Floods affect people, economic activities, and infrastructure. The high-risk regions in the western slopes have higher population densities, greater concentrations of industrial activity and infrastructure, and very high GDPs. The north-eastern high-risk region has high food insecurity.

Landslide Hazard

Landslide hazards affect people, infrastructure, and economic activities. Most high-risk DSDs (except in the Kalutara District) are within regions of high food insecurity. There is moderate economic activity in the high-risk regions. Transport by road and railway has frequently been affected, particularly in the hill country.

The National Building Research Organization (NBRO) has undertaken a detailed study of landslide risk in Sri Lanka. Landslide hazard mapping has been completed for five high-risk districts at a scale of 1:10,000. The NBRO methodology takes into consideration various factors, including slope-gradient, geology, soil cover, hydrology, and land use. Enhancement of this methodology is possible through the use of improved datasets for digital elevation modeling and hydroclimatic data and models.

For this study, the potential risk zones were identified at a resolution of 10 km in keeping with the resolutions of the other hazard and vulnerability data. Landslide incidence data from the NBRO was used to map the hazard risk. The event frequency data for each grid cell between 1947 and 1996 was used as the risk factor for landslides (figure 4.14).

Eight districts in the central highlands are at risk. The highest risk is in the Kegalle District followed by Ratnapura and Nuwara Eliya Districts. Even within these districts there is spatial variability at the DSD level. The Kalutara, Kandy, and Badulla Districts have moderate risk, and Matale and Kurunegala Districts have slight risk.

The frequency of landslides has increased in recent years. Changes in land use—including cultivation of tobacco on steep slopes, land clearing in the hills, blocking of drainage ways, and the impact of the large reservoir construction—may be due to the increase. Sometimes, soil conservation programs, such as contour ditches, contribute to increases in landslide hazard risk by increasing soil saturation (Madduma Bandara 2000a).

Cyclone Hazard

Cyclones affect people, infrastructure, and economic activities. The high-risk areas in the north and the eastern seaboard have high food insecurity. Paddy fields are

Figure 4.13. EM-DAT data on floods from 1975 to 2001 were used to estimate the monthly frequency of floods in the Western Slopes and Eastern Slopes regions.

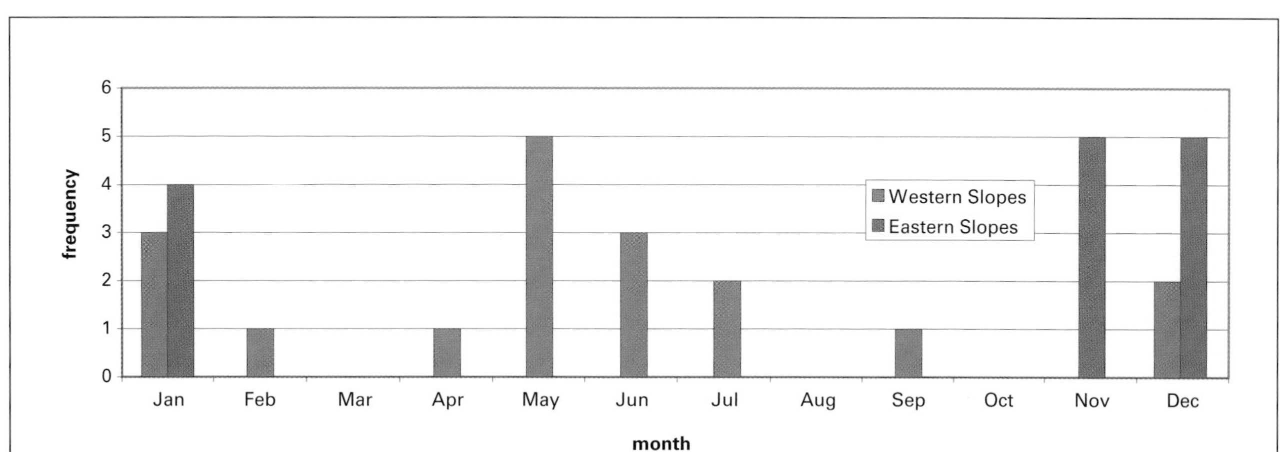

in high concentration in the hazard-prone region. The storm surge at landfall can be devastating. The storm surge of the 1978 cyclone extended up to 2 km inland in some areas. In addition to the storm surge, the intense gusting can be destructive. Intense rainfall that comes along with cyclones creates floods and flash floods.

Cyclones and storms have made landfall only in the eastern coast of Sri Lanka, except for a single storm in 1967. The majority of cyclones and storms pass through the northern and north-central parts of the island. The cyclones that pass through Sri Lanka originate from the Bay of Bengal during the northeast monsoon. Incidences of cyclones that pass through Sri Lanka in other seasons are rare due to geography and the regional climatology. There have been four severe cyclones during the last 100 years as well as a number of severe and moderate storms.

The available cyclone tracks from 1900 to 2000 were used to construct a map of cyclone hazard (figure 4.15). The frequency with which storms passed through a grid point was estimated. The immediate adjoining grid points were given an impact factor of half that given to grid cells that lay on the storm and cyclone track. Cyclones were weighted three times as heavily as storms. The northeastern seaboard has high hazard.

A cyclone seasonality graph was constructed by plotting the number of cyclones and storms that occurred in each month (figure 4.16). Cyclone incidence shows a strong seasonality, and 80 percent of all cyclones and storms occur in November and December.

Note that cyclone hazard mapping can be improved. Wind-speed modeling techniques that estimate deceleration after landfall can account for the diminishment of the intensity of storms over land. Wave and tidal models can be used to identify the risks from storm surges. Elevation maps and hydrological analysis can be used to identify flood-risk areas.

Assessing Multihazard Hotspots

A multihazard map was constructed by aggregating the hazard indexes for droughts, floods, cyclones, and landslides, with each hazard weighted equally (figure 4.17). This map shows the high risk of multiple hazards in the north. The Anuradhapura, Polonnaruwa, Batticaloa, and Trincomalee Districts in the northeast also feature high risk, as do the southwestern districts of Kegalle, Ratnapura, Kalutara, and Colombo. Regions with sharp gradients along the mountain massifs (Nuwara Eliya, Badulla, Ampara, and Matale) also show high risk of multiple hazards.

Disaster risk maps may be constructive by taking into account exposure and vulnerabilities in addition to hazards. Exposure and vulnerability are more difficult to quantify than hazards. A proxy for the combination of hazards and vulnerability may be constructed if it is assumed that the history of hazards provides a representation of future spatial variability. Such an approach needs long records of disasters and is based on the

Figure 4.14. A landslide hazard risk index was estimated based on frequency of incidence.

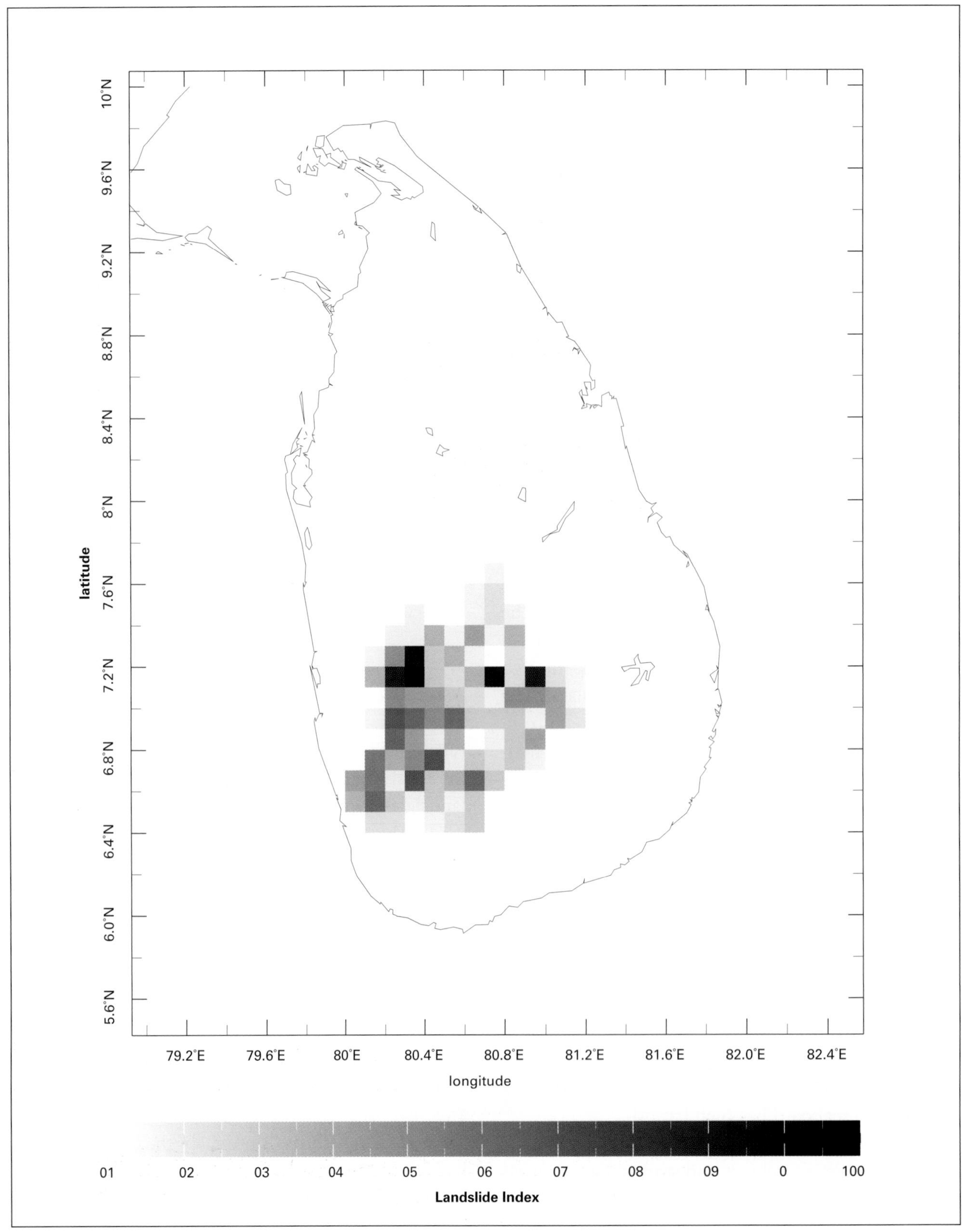

Figure 4.15. The storm and cyclone tracks for the last 100 years were used to create a cyclone hazard risk map.

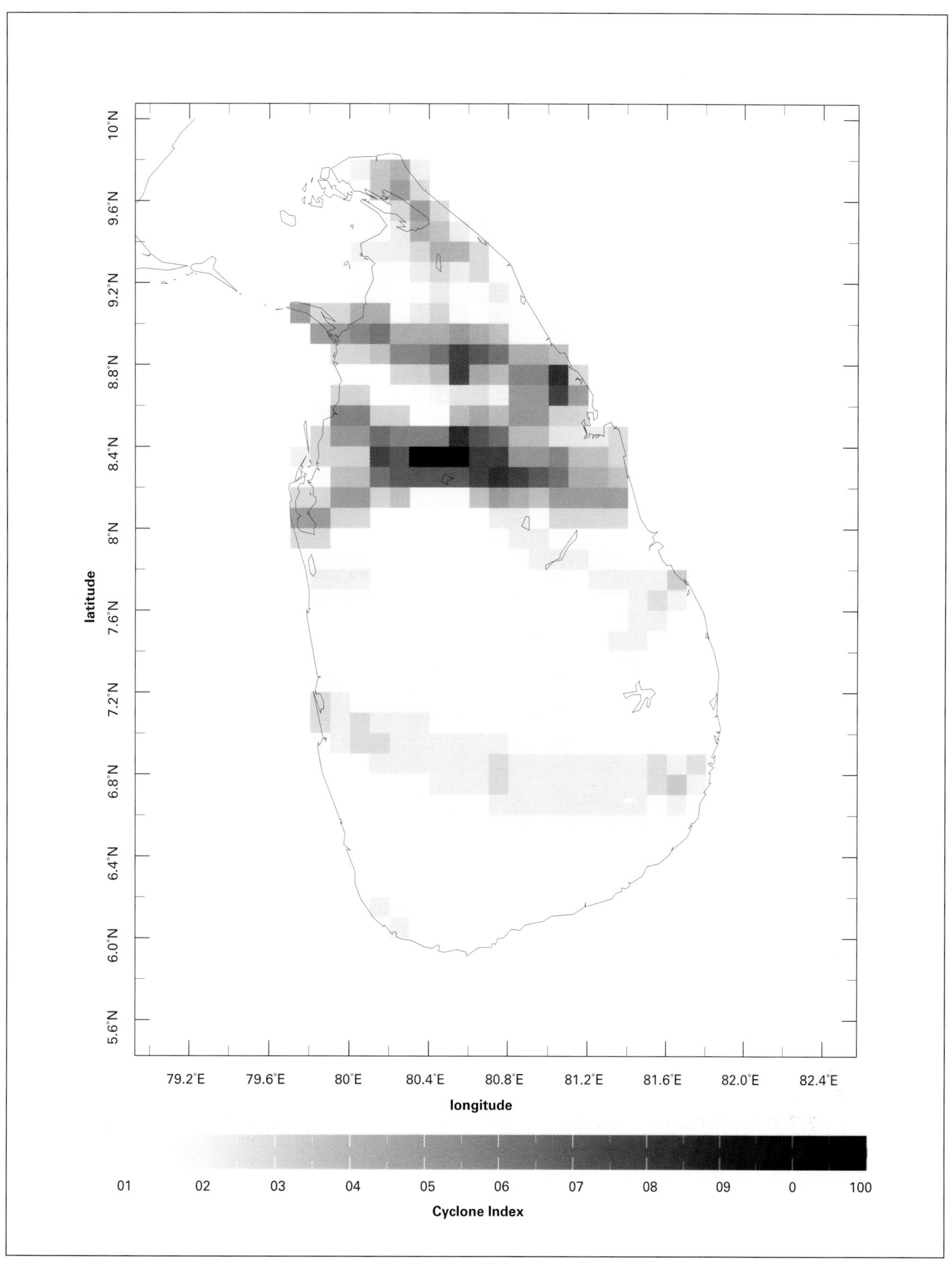

Figure 4.16. The monthly count of storms and cyclones between 1887 and 2000

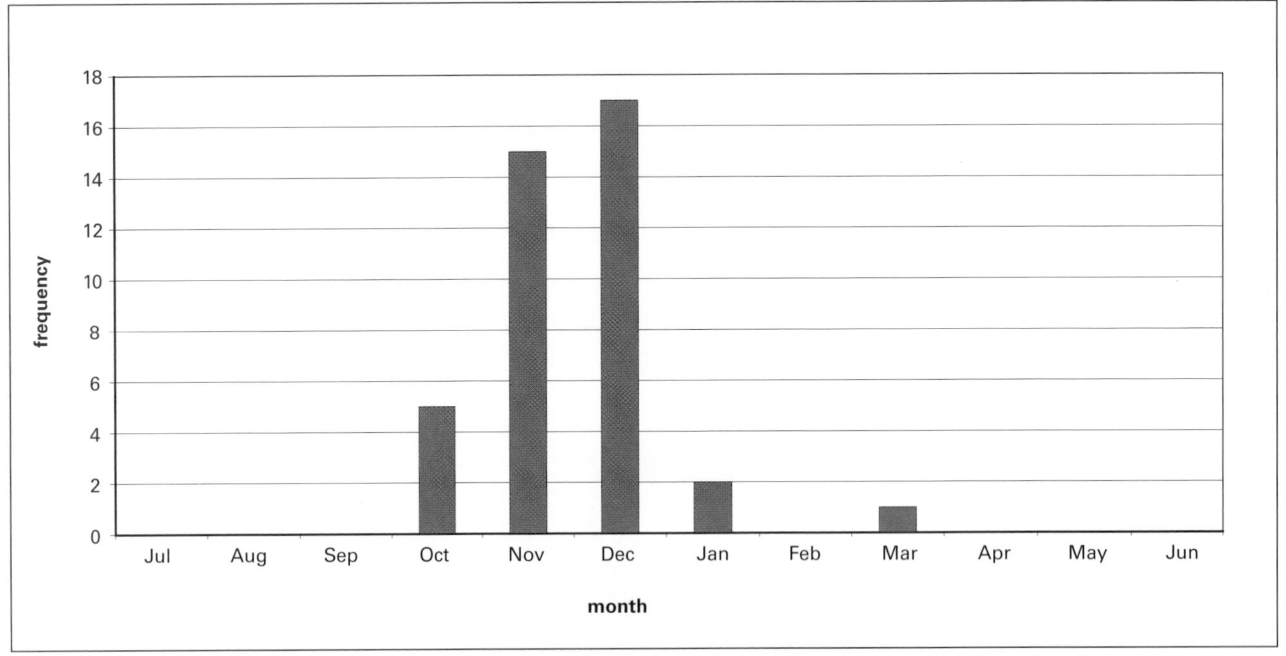

assumption that the future occurrence of hazards, exposure, and vulnerability is similar to past occurrences. This assumption, while not precise, does enable us to provide an estimate of the variability of risk. More precise estimates must await more long-term data that have good spatial and temporal resolutions.

Subject to the highlighted limitations, records of disasters may be used to weight for exposure and vulnerability to particular hazards. Figure 4.18 shows the multihazard map with weights for each hazard based on the number of occurrences of each hazard from 1948 to 1992. Multiple landslides within a single year were treated as one event. This map gives greater weight to droughts and less weight to floods. The result, however, does not significantly differ from that produced with equal weight. There is high risk in some regions in the north and east in addition to the regions with the sharpest hill slopes in the south. The risks are also enhanced in the region around the Hambantota District in the south-east and around the Mannar District in the north-west.

The next figure (figure 4.19) is identical except that the data for the frequency of hazards were obtained from the EM-DAT database. There is high weight toward floods in this dataset. This map shows very low risk in the south-east and north-west and high risk in the north-eastern tip as well as the eastern and western slopes regions.

Note that for the period from 1948 to 1992, the EM-DAT data are weighted toward floods (Weights—Droughts: 9, Floods: 30, Landslides: 2, Cyclones: 3), whereas the data obtained from the Department of Social Services were weighted toward droughts and cyclones (Weights—Droughts: 27, Floods: 24, Landslides: 17, Cyclones: 10). The difference may arise from differing perceptions and criteria for identification as a disaster.

The final multihazard risk map (figure 4.20) was calculated by weighting each hazard index by the disaster relief expenditure for each hazard. This hotspots map is heavily weighted toward droughts and cyclones, with landslides receiving a meager weight. This hotspots map shows higher risk in the north and north-central regions and in the Hambantota District (south-east) compared with previous maps.

The various multihazard maps have differences but also show commonalities. Three regions emerge as having high risk in all maps. One is the region with sharp slopes in the south-west: the Kegalle District is the most risk prone, with significant risk of landslides and floods and moderate risk for droughts. The Ratnapura and Kalutara Districts also have high risk of floods and landslides. A second region is in the north-east: the Batticaloa, Trincomalee, Mannar, Killinochchi, and Jaffna Districts along the north-eastern coast show high multihazard risk.

Figure 4.17. Multihazard index constructed by aggregating the hazard indices and scaling the result to range between 0 and 100 (Weights: droughts: 1, floods: 1, landslides: 1, cyclones: 1)

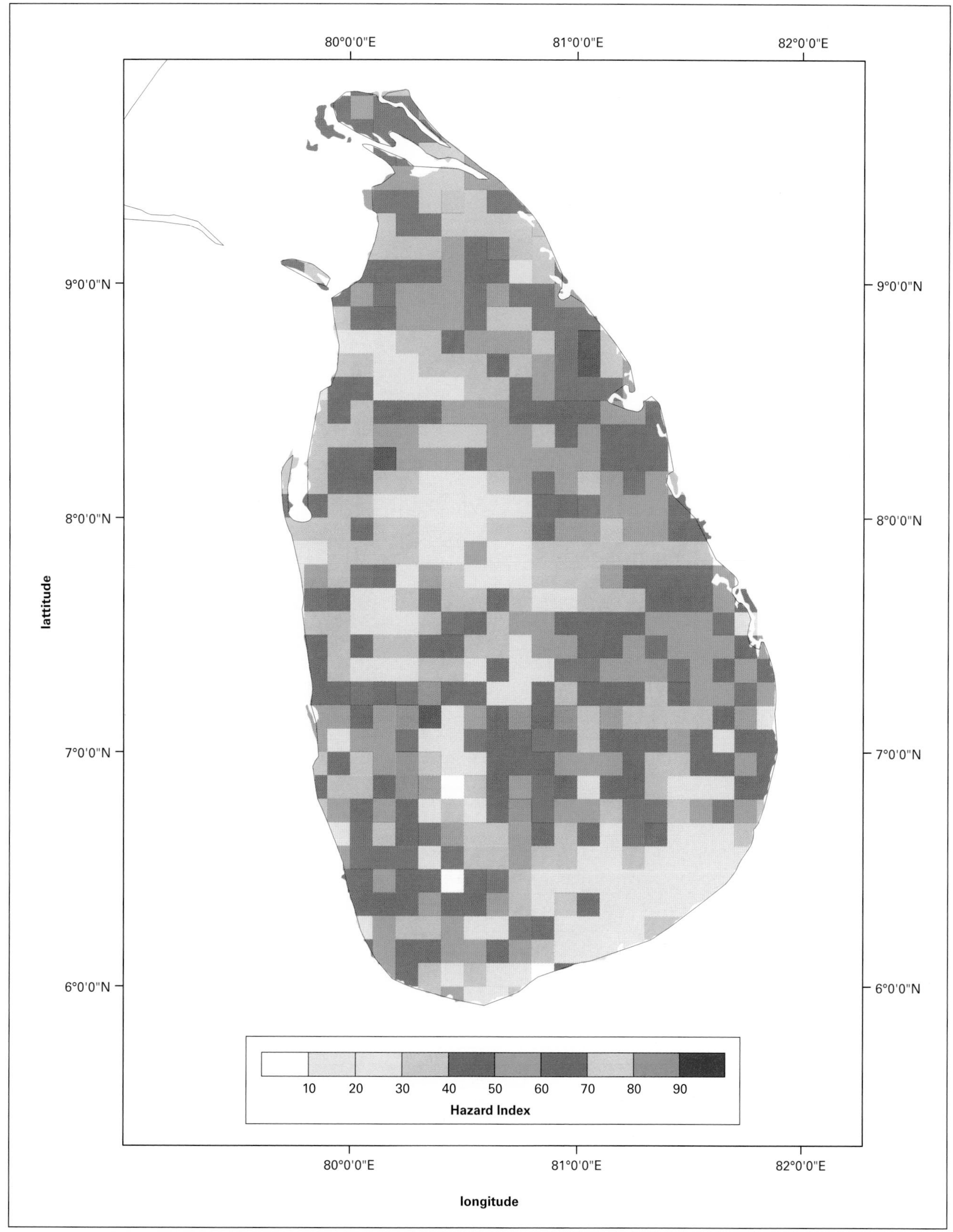

Figure 4.18. Multihazard risk estimated by weighting each hazard index by its frequency from 1948 to 1992 and rescaling the result to range from 0 to 100. The hazard incidence data was obtained from the Department of Social Services. (Weights: droughts: 27, floods: 24, landslides: 17, cyclones: 10)

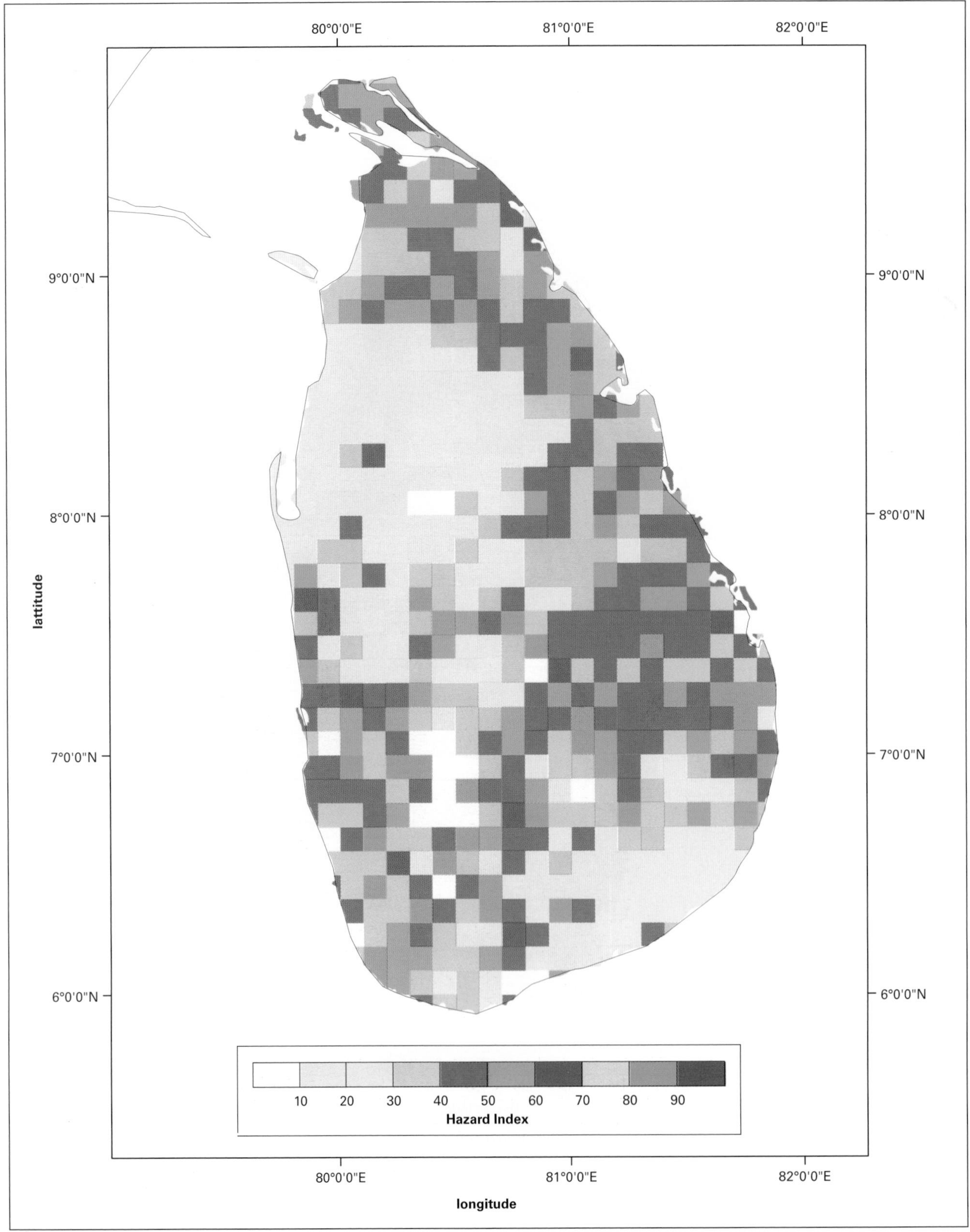

Figure 4.19. Multihazard risk estimated by weighting each hazard index by incidence frequency. (Weights: droughts: 9, floods: 30, landslides: 2, cyclones: 3) The result was rescaled to range between 0 and 100.

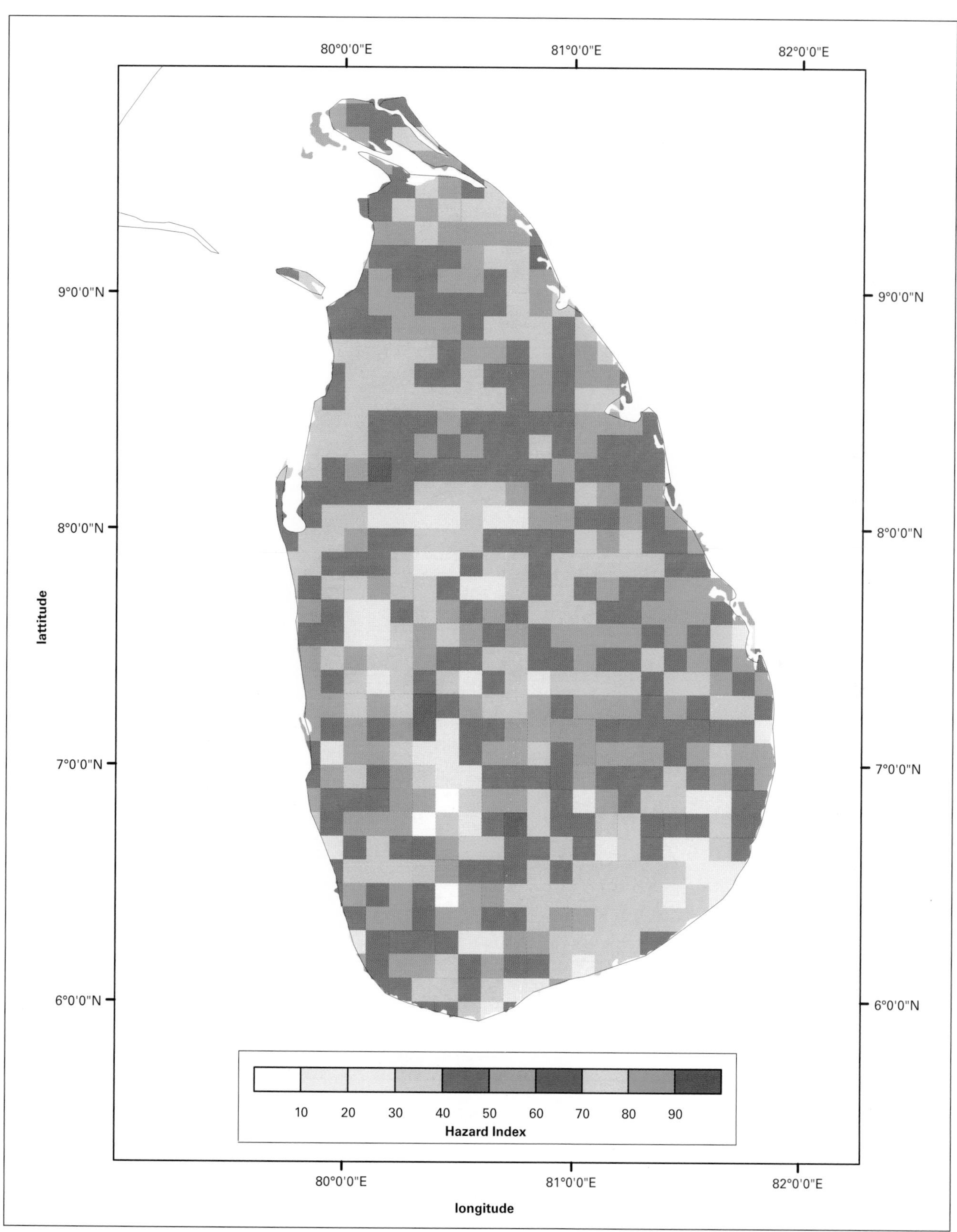

Figure 4.20. Multihazard risk estimated by weighting each hazard index by the associated relief expenditure between 1948–1992. (Weights: droughts: 126, floods: 25, landslides: 0.06, cyclones: 60)

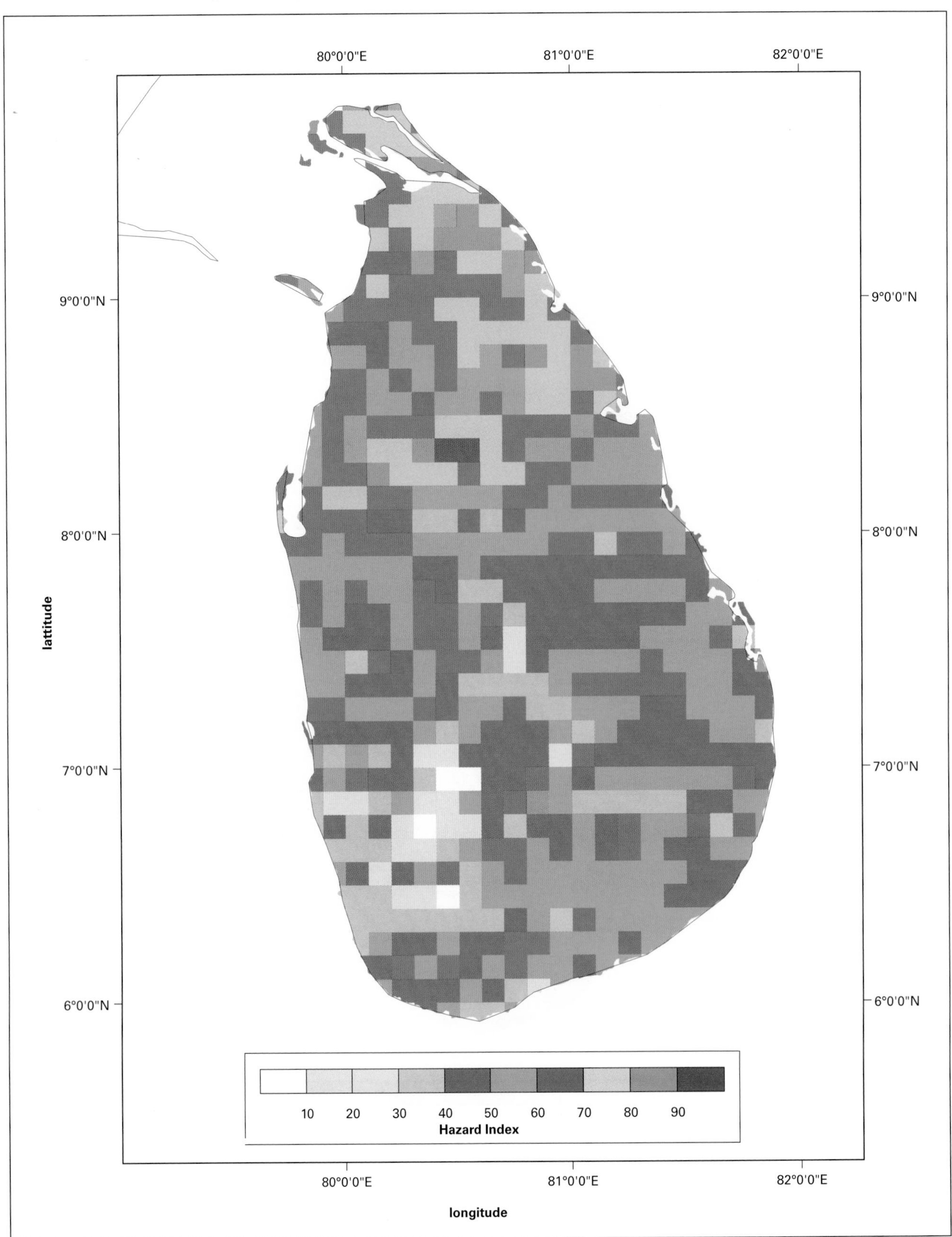

A third region is along the mountain massifs with the sharpest hill slopes—this includes parts of the Nuwara Eliya, Badulla, Ampara, and Matale Districts.

Some of the high-risk regions have concentrations of economic output, agriculture, and industrial concentrations. Some regions in the southwest with high multihazard risk also have high food insecurity. The north shows high multihazard risk as well as high food insecurity. Rice cultivation in these regions is particularly vulnerable to drought and flood hazards.

Discussion

Spatial Variability

The use of data available in Sri Lanka enabled the construction of detailed hazard maps and the investigation of trends. The spatial hazard and disaster risk-mapping should be useful for local authorities as well as international relief organizations.

Hazard Mapping Methodology

The hazard mapping methodology at the local scale needs to be fine-tuned to take advantage of the finer resolution of data and finer resolution of the results. An example of a good use of multiple datasets is the landslide hazard-mapping project carried out by the Sri Lanka NBRO.

Vulnerability Analysis

Hazard-specific vulnerabilities are needed at high resolution. Vulnerability analysis is more constrained by data limitations than by hazard analysis. Notwithstanding these limitations, the vulnerability analyses provide a broad initial assessment of the nature of hazard risks and vulnerabilities at a national scale.

Seasonality

Strong seasonality was evident in drought, flood, cyclone, and landslide risks in Sri Lanka. Information about the seasonal risk levels of different disasters is useful for disaster risk management and should be provided. Our work has shown that the risk factors change with climate variability (such as the effects of El Niño). The ability to predict shifts in climate up to six months in advance provides an opportunity to engage in predictive risk-mapping, as the climate of Sri Lanka is relatively predictable.

Long-Term Climate, Environmental, and Social Change

Both the climate and environmental change, such as deforestation and urbanization, affect the hazard analysis and, in ideal conditions, should have been included in the analyses. Such work is needed in the future. Here, we note that climate change is already making parts of Sri Lanka more vulnerable to drought. This is a development that shall have far-reaching ramifications.

Further investigation is required to build comprehensive drought maps that take into account hydrological and physical conditions that contribute to drought. Our vulnerability analysis, too, can be improved by taking account of long-term changes in demographics, urbanization, migration, and the consequences of civil war.

Conclusions

We have presented an example of the use of physical and social data for fine-scale hazard and vulnerability analyses. This case study has demonstrated that the use of such fine-scale analyses recognizes crucial regional variations and is more useful than relying on currently available global-scale data.

We have presented methodologies for using fine-resolution gridded climate data to estimate droughts and floods and for using past-incidence data to estimate cyclones and landslides. Seasonal climate predictions can be factored into this methodology to yield hazard-risk predictions that exploit the emerging technology of seasonal climate predictions.

Vulnerability analysis is much less precise than hazard analysis. The approach adopted here considers the specific elements of people, economic activity, and infrastructure, and estimates these elements based on proxies, which has been shown to be viable with locally available data. Crucial spatial variations in vulnerability emerged in the higher-resolution maps that were not evident at coarser scales. Estimates of hazard-specific vulnerabilities had to be based on the assumption that sufficiently long records of the past give an indication of future spatial variability. This is a reasonable assumption when one considers that the topography, climate, and terrain, which are the basic causes of regional variability, do not change substantively. However, long-term climatic, environmental, and social change needs to be investigated in the future and factored in the analyses.

Multihazard mapping is subject to limitations in the types of data that are available, particularly for exposure and vulnerability. There were multiple ways to weight the different hazards, each of which has arguments in its favor. These different maps can suit different purposes. Given the limitations in the methodology, it is useful to focus on the commonalities from the maps.

References

Department of Census and Statistics. 2001. *Statistical Abstract of the Democratic Socialist Republic of Sri Lanka,* Department of Census and Statistics, Colombo.

De Silva, Soma. 1997. Population. In: *Arjuna's Atlas of Sri Lanka,* S. Somasekeram (ed.). Columbo: Arjuna Publishers.

Gunaratne, Lalith. 2002. Rural Electrification of Sri Lanka, presentation at World Bank Energy Sector Management Assistance Program (ESMAP) Energy and Poverty Workshop, Addis Ababa, Ethiopia, October 23-25, 2002.

Lyon, B. 2004. The Strength of El Niño and the Spatial Extent of Drought, *Geophysical Research Letters.* 31: L21204.

Madduma Bandara, C.M. 2000a. *Land Resources. Natural Resources of Sri Lanka 2000.* Colombo: National Science Foundation, p. 53-73.

Madduma Bandara, C.M. 2000b. *Water Resources, Natural Resources of Sri Lanka 2000.* Sri Lanka: National Science Foundation, p. 75-109.

Puvaneswaran, K.M., and P.A. Smithson. 1993. An Objective Classification of Homogeneous Rainfall Regimes in Sri Lanka. *Theoretical and Applied Climatology.* 48: 133–145.

Tissera, C.H. 1997. Natural Hazards. In: *Arjuna's Atlas of Sri Lanka,* S. Somasekeram (ed.). Colombo: Arjuna Publishers, p. 76-78.

United Nations Development Programme. 1998. National Human Development Report 1998: Regional Dimensions of Human Development, Sri Lanka: United Nations Development Programme.

World Food Programme. 2002. Identification of DS Divisions Vulnerable to Food Insecurity. Vulnerability Analysis and Mapping Unit. Sri Lanka: World Food Programme.

Zubair, L. 2002. El-Niño-Southern Oscillation Influences on Rice Production in Sri Lanka. *International Journal of Climatology* 22(2): 249–260.

Chapter 5

Multihazard Risks in Caracas, República Bolivariana de Venezuela

Kristina R. Czuchlewski, Klaus H. Jacob, Arthur L. Lerner-Lam, Kevin Vranes, and Students of the Urban Planning Studio: "Disaster Resilient Caracas"

Catastrophic risk management associated with natural hazards has developed over the last few decades into a mature, quantitative discipline. This preliminary case study employs quantitative methods where feasible, but time and resource constraints have prevented a more systematic application. Nevertheless, we present a brief overview of these methods as they are used in this report.

General Definitions Used in This Report

Perils. Perils refer to the different natural processes that can potentially provide hazards and cause losses. Such perils can be earthquakes, floods, and land- or mud-slides, for instance. In other areas, cyclones, coastal storms, volcanoes, hail, tornados, or snow avalanches may be important perils. For Caracas, the most important perils are earthquakes, mudflows and landslides, and stream flooding.

Hazards. Each peril poses hazards that are more or less quantifiable. For example, earthquake shaking can be measured on the Modified Mercalli Intensity Scale (MMI, based on damage to structures), by peak ground acceleration (PGA), or by some other measurable ground motion variable. In the case of river flooding, the "flood stage" (that is, the height to which a river may rise) or the flow rate (volume of water passing per unit of time) could become the measure for the severity of the hazard. Similar units could be used for mud- or debris flows. For winds, the hazard may be characterized by wind speed.

Once a hazard parameter is chosen it can be traced back to the interaction of many contributing factors. For instance, *flood height* may depend on the amount of rain that has fallen over time and space. Other contributing factors are the topography of the landscape and river network: the degree to which the ground surface can absorb and retain the precipitation (types of soils and ground cover, such as vegetation versus urbanized parking lots); and the shape, gradient, and smoothness of drainage and river channels. *Mud- or debris flows* require, in addition to the variables mentioned for floods, the availability and size distributions of solid materials that can be mobilized. The nature and severity of the debris flow hazard is different when tree trunks and house- or room-sized boulders are available, as compared to when only clays, silts, sands, or perhaps gravel make up the suspended solid bulk of the fluidized debris flow. Large boulders and tree trunks contributed to the severe damage during the massive debris flows observed during the Vargas disaster that killed many tens of thousands of Venezuelans in December 1999.

In the case of seismic shaking, the magnitude of causative earthquakes, their depth and distance, and the firmness of ground (rock versus soil, among other factors) will determine the level of ground shaking. The frequency of earthquakes as a function of their magnitude determines the probability with which set levels of ground shaking will be exceeded.

Risk. The risk to a region or community is the expected future loss defined in terms of probability of losses vs. their magnitude. Since risk implies future losses, it is inherently uncertain because hazard and other risk-contributing elements are uncertain. Generally, risk is defined in terms of the value of assets, their fragility (in terms of direct loss or loss of function) in the face of particular hazards, and the exposure of those assets to multiple hazards. In general, while quantitative risk assessment provides a motivation for implementation of specific interventions, the identification of critical assets and a qualitative, experience-based assessment of their fragility and exposure constitute the bulk of this report. We use empirical methods to estimate the occurrence of perils, and geographic analysis to identify the exposure of assets. This report makes qualitative assessments of the potential fragility of structures and infrastructure. This analysis supports preliminary recommendations on the inclusion of risk management interventions in a Caracas urban plan. In concluding remarks, we develop a set of recommendations on quantifying the risk analysis.

The Caracas Urban and Environmental Context

Natural Hazards

Located at the intersection of the South American and Caribbean Plates (figure 5.1), the northern area of República Bolivariana de Venezuela faces extreme seismological hazards. Perez et al. (2001) report a 2-cm per year rate of plate motion at the offshore boundary. Half of this boundary is accommodated by the San Sebastian fault, which likely comes ashore under the Simon Bolivar International Airport in Vargas State (Audemard et al. 2000). The fault zone is diffuse, containing the Tacagua-El Ávila and La Victoria fault systems that surround Caracas to the north and south. Major earthquakes have destroyed the city three times in the last 400 years. The last large earthquake (Mw=6.5) came in 1967, killing an estimated 300 people and destroying four modern structures built for earthquake resistance (Papageorgiou and Kim 1991).

The natural hazards faced by this area are not limited to earthquakes. The position of the northern coast near 10°N ensures frequent heavy rainfall events with strong erosion potential. In December 1999, a month of rain on the north-central coast of the country—including over 900 mm of rain in a 72-hour period between December 15 and 17—triggered landslides, mudflows, and debris flows on the north face of the El Ávila range that killed an estimated 25,000 residents of the coastal state of Vargas. (Estimates of this number vary by one order of magnitude between the national government and nongovernmental organizations.) The heavy rains also caused fatalities in the Caracas basin.

High slope angles along El Ávila (some up to 80 percent) allow for immediate acceleration of surface fluids. The December 1999 event saw evidence of hyper-concentrated flows, alluvial fan reactivation, and some evidence of prior, larger flows (Salcedo 2000, 2001). The Vargas coast is lined with extensive alluvial fans, nine of which reactivated during the December 1999 event (Larsen et al. 2001). The Caracas basin contains at least three alluvial fans with clear signs of earth movement in the past 100 years. Larsen et al. (2001) present an excellent overview of El Ávila geology and mud flow processes during the December 1999 disaster.

Although rainfall data are sparse, historical records compiled by Salcedo (2000) show that either the Caracas or Vargas area has been severely affected by debris flows roughly every 25 years since the start of recorded history. Previous empirical work by local geologists illustrates that any rainfall exceeding 100 mm in 24 hours will cause damaging mud- and debris flows; any rainfall exceeding 300 mm in 72 hours is considered catastrophic. An analysis of 25 years of regional rainfall data produced during the Columbia University Urban Planning Studio extrapolates a frequency of recurrence of 100 mm per 24 hours to once every 5 to 10 years; the probability of 300 mm per 24 hours is once in 25 years.

Built Environment

Since the last major earthquake in 1967, the population of Caracas has doubled to 5 million people, with a population density of 12,000 persons per km^2 and growth of 3.1 percent per year. Eighty-six percent of the Venezuelan population is urban, making it the seventh most urbanized country in the world. The valley floor is well developed, with high-rise buildings and densely packed apartment blocks scattered unevenly throughout the city. These buildings are generally concentrated in the deepest part of the basin (where shaking is expected to be highest during an earthquake).

Barrios, or informal squatter settlements, dominate the landscape on the low-lying, rugged mountains to the east and west of the city center, where rainfall-induced debris flows are expected to be greatest. To the south exists a mixture of *urbanazacions* (similar to suburbs)

Figure 5.1. Regional elevation map of Caracas and Vargas State

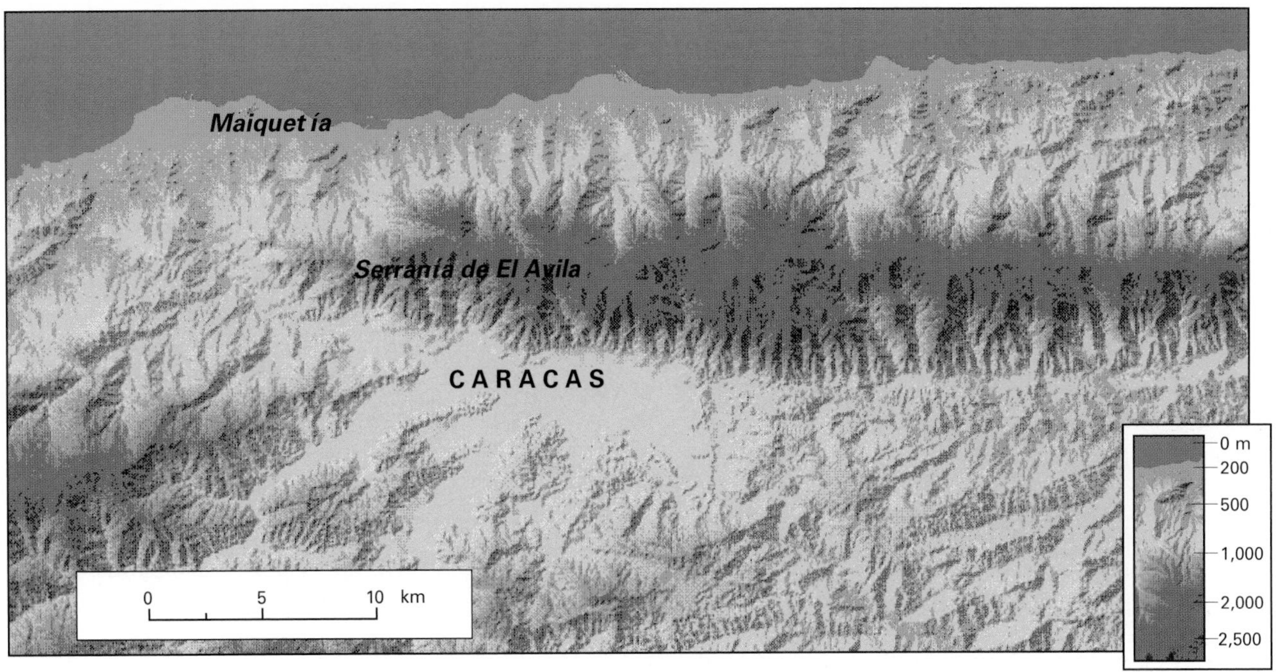

and *barrios*. The individual building blocks of the *barrios*, known as *ranchos*, are constructed of unreinforced masonry, making them particularly vulnerable to earthquakes. The *ranchos* are highly visible from every point in the city as they carpet the hills, creating a starkly contrasting landscape of a dual urban fabric (figure 5.2).

While the formal city averages 6,000 persons per km², similar to the average urban density worldwide, the *barrios* approach 25,000 persons per km². Vargas State is isolated physically from the Caracas basin by El Ávila (figure 5.1). However, Vargas is inextricably linked to Caracas. It serves as Caracas' economic connection to the rest of the Caribbean, and acts as the social "relief valve" for the city by offering weekend recreation for residents. Although separated geographically, Vargas and Caracas are economically and culturally intertwined.

Collision of the Built Environment and Natural Hazards

Centuries ago, Caracas was purposefully built away from the coast and through steep terrain to deter sea-borne attacks on the city. However, this distance creates major transportation and utility infrastructure problems that are exacerbated by natural hazards. Caracas is linked to the world through its airport and seaport, both of which are located across El Ávila on the Vargas coast (figure 5.1). The only road between Caracas and the airport and seaport is a single highway that travels through steep, landslide-prone valleys crossing secondary faults of the active San Sebastian fault.

Uncontrolled building and lack of enforcement of building and zoning codes in this hazardous environment have led to human disasters and potential problems of great magnitude. A lack of building code and enforcement allowed Vargas residents to build on active (but quiescent for the previous 50 years) alluvial fans, which reactivated during December 1999. Although various groups are working to repair and rebuild Vargas State with new housing built in safe locations, a general lack of planning and enforcement is allowing squatters to return to the alluvial fans and stream beds where most of the December 1999 destruction was concentrated.

Addressing the Risk: Results of the Urban Planning Studio

It is clear that natural hazards affect the Caracas urban environment. To address this complex problem, a strategic planning process, designed to identify the city's ability to cope with the forces of nature, was initiated. In order to accomplish this, certain critical facilities (for example,

Figure 5.2. Map of the Petare barrio of Caracas, illustrating the dual nature of the city. On the left is the open spacing of the planned "formal" city. On the right are the densely packed squatter barrios of the "informal" city.

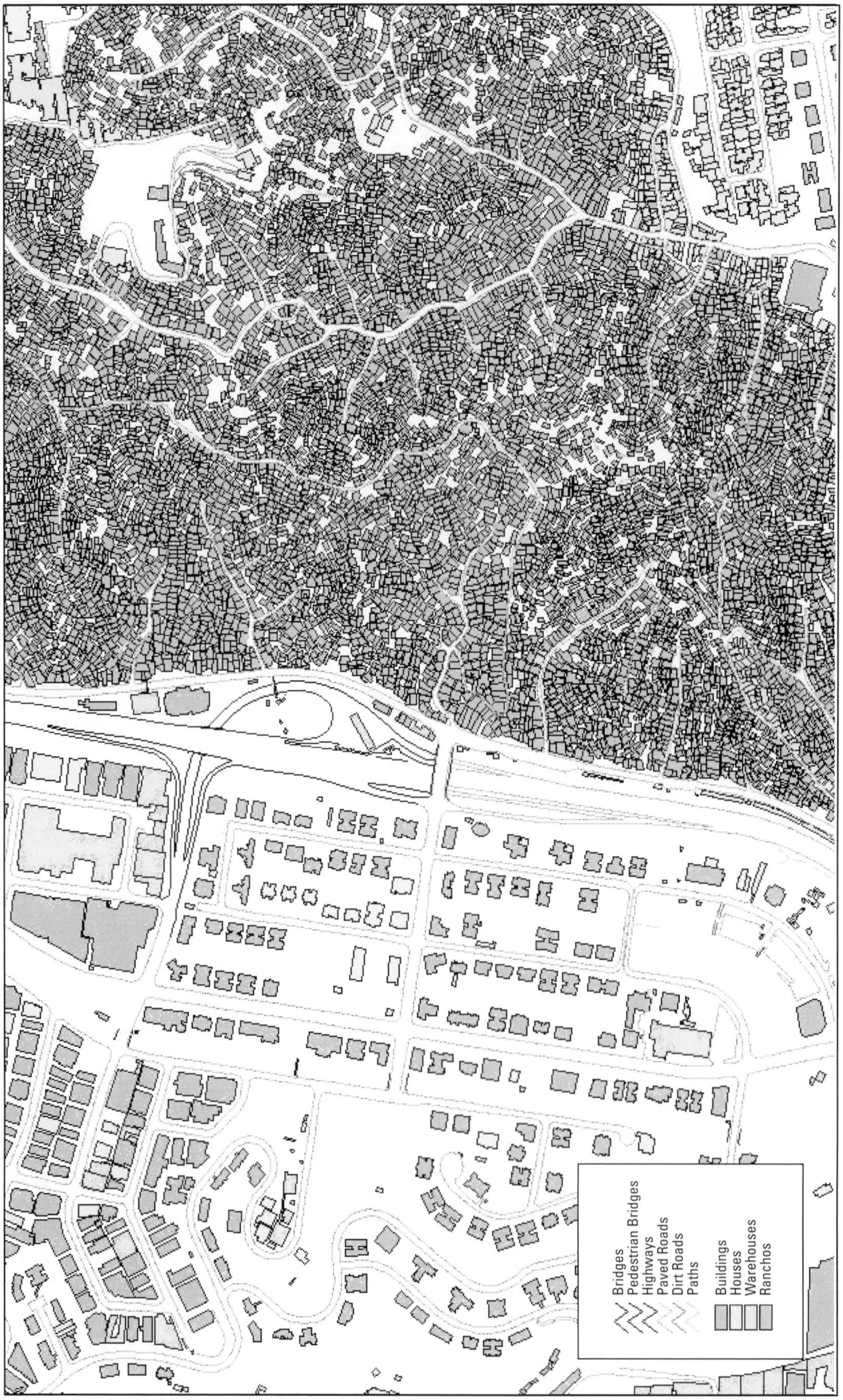

the Caracas-Vargas highway) were identified based on their importance both during and after a potential natural disaster. These facilities can be overlaid on top of hazard maps to identify specific locations in need of special attention. By analyzing such maps, it is possible to determine a city's strengths and weaknesses pertaining to natural disasters. This allows decisions to be made about both large-scale systems and individual entities.

Table 5.1 and accompanying explanations act as the foundation for the recommendations made in the Urban Planning Studio action plan. They were developed through a series of discussions that analyzed the city's utility and public service infrastructure—facilities critical for survival in the event of a natural disaster.

Ranking Explanations

Tier I

Tier I facilities are critical for human survival immediately after a natural disaster. The extent and severity of human casualties and injuries as well as property damage will depend primarily on the quality of these facilities.

Medical: The ability of existing medical facilities to absorb a massive influx of triage and the ability to create temporary overflow space in the immediate aftermath of a disaster will be crucial for the survival of the city. Early indications are that up to 60 percent of the existing medical facilities in the greater Caracas region are in some state of disrepair. Unknown factors include the availability of temporary medical facilities (that is, field hospitals), the stockpiling of medicine and medical supplies, and the training of medical personnel in responding to a disaster (which will likely displace them from their normal place of work). However, these functions are critically needed in any large city, such as Caracas, in the event of a disaster.

Water: Should the city become cut off from its water supply, it will have less than one full day of stored water. The water supply system is extremely fragile, considering that the three incoming supply routes, Tuy 1, Tuy 2, and Tuy 3, originate in one general location to the south of the city (Tuy Valley) and that the current maximum supply rate barely exceeds current consumption levels. Blockage or destruction of even one aqueduct will cause a severe water shortage. After a disaster, water is considered essential to human survival, medical response, fire fighting, and infrastructure/services recovery. In addition, a contaminated water supply system could lead to widespread disease.

Transportation: The surface vehicular transportation network is considered to be extremely fragile. The system lacks redundancy, and current critical links may be rendered useless in a natural disaster. Survival of a catastrophic disaster within Caracas may require immediate and then continued evacuation out of the Caracas basin and Vargas. There is a strong possibility that a large natural disaster affecting Caracas will also cut its link with the airport and seaport and possibly cut the secondary supply routes to the west (Valencia). In addition, the airport and the seaport are fragile facilities due to their location, potentially rendering them useless in the event of a large earthquake (for example, on the San Sebastian Fault). Clear transportation is essential for evacuation, fuel importation (assuming cut pipelines), food distribution, fire and hazardous materials (HAZMAT) response, as well as the movement of temporary sanitary and medical facilities.

Shelter/housing: Much of the housing in Caracas is considered extremely fragile due to the quality of construction in residential areas. Therefore, there will be a need for the absorption of large numbers of displaced people after a natural disaster. The facilities for temporary shelter must exist, be ready for deployment, and be fully accessible by emergency response teams. Current open spaces (parks, stadiums, and reinforced auditoriums) must be able to absorb large numbers of people. Designated shelters and controlled security will discourage people from returning to precarious structures immediately after a disaster.

Communication: Open communication is essential for coordinated response and recovery following a disaster. This includes radio/CB/cellular lines as well as TV and commercial radio. The fragility of these facilities is largely unknown, but it is assumed that the robustness and location of communication transmission sites (towers and antennae) will determine the quality of the system. People need to be informed on a continuous basis.

Table 5.1. Critical Facilities and Systems (Categories and Definitions)

TIER I	
Medical	Hospitals, ambulances, clinics, Red Cross installations, depots of supplies (medicine and equipment), mobile equipment (field hospitals)
Water	Water supply infrastructure, aqueducts, storage tanks, water trucks, water treatment plants, impoundments
Transportation	All roads, rail lines, airports, bridges, heliports, seaports, evacuation routes, trucks
Shelter/housing	Existing structures, including barrios and inner-city apartment blocks (for fragility), that can serve as secure shelters. Tents, cots, blankets, gas lamps, camping equipment (for response)
Communication	Emergency broadcast system, cell phone/ radio/CB/TV transmission towers and infrastructure
TIER II	
Fuel	Fuel storage tanks, delivery mechanisms, pipelines
Fire/HAZMAT	Fire stations, hydrants, fire equipment/apparatus, HAZMAT equipment/apparatus, response system
Electricity	Power generation stations, transmission stations/nodes/infrastructure, backup generators, batteries
Food	Storage warehouses, distribution points
TIER III	
Reserved space	Stadiums/parks/fields for construction of temporary tent cities, field hospitals, and central gathering points
Sanitary facilities	Treatment facilities, temporary facilities
SYSTEMS	
Management system	Competent, cohesive command and control center with high-level authority (mayor or president) in central location
Search and Rescue	Trained personnel, dogs, heavy lifting and clearing equipment, truck evacuation system, boats, and building inspection teams
Law enforcement/ Security	Military, police, National Guard

Tier II

Tier II facilities may not directly impact civilian lives in the immediate aftermath of a natural disaster. However, these facilities are key components of a coordinated and efficient emergency response system, aimed at minimizing the severity of the disaster in terms of human loss and property damage.

Fuel: Fuel will be critical for emergency electricity generators, general transportation, and recovery vehicles. The fragility of the supply is considered high, due to the presence of fuel storage facilities in hazardous areas; however, not much is known about this factor. The availability of mobile supply equipment is also unknown. It is assumed that the current supply for the Caracas area is via fuel pipeline, which should be considered fragile.

Fire/HAZMAT: Most formal homes in Caracas use natural gas for heating/cooking, so it is assumed that extensive fires could occur after an earthquake. The HAZMAT situation is unknown. The fragility of fire stations, fire fighting equipment, and HAZMAT apparatus is also unknown. The fire authority is assumed to play a leading role in disaster response, but it is unknown whether they currently accept and practice for this role.

Food: The supply of food is important but not as critical as other basic needs such as water and shelter. It is assumed that food is not stored within the city, but rather follows some dynamic market path where food in the city is replaced as it is consumed (much like the water situation). Food supply is also not centralized, but rather spread among many thousands of grocers and possibly some warehouses. The fragility of the food supply is therefore considered low. The reintroduction of food into Caracas will require a functioning transportation system, including airport access.

Electricity: Electricity will be critical for some missions (medical, police, and rescue coordination) and unnecessary for others (basic personal survival). It is assumed that temporary and mobile generators will fill inevitable gaps in the power supply, but the availability of these facilities is unknown. The fragility of the existing power supply in terms of generation and distribution is also largely unknown. Since most earthquake disasters involve extensive loss of electricity, this must be assumed for Caracas as well. However, much of the electricity for Caracas originates in southern Venezuela, and the supply might not be affected in a natural disaster, although distribution may be.

Tier III

Tier III facilities are not critical to human survival in the event of a natural disaster; at least, they are not immediately necessary in an emergency response situation. However, these facilities are important parts of a coordinated response system.

Reserved space: The evacuation and subsequent sheltering of displaced persons will require available open space. This will likely include parks, stadiums, and any other open areas. These areas must absorb temporary shelters (tent cities) and field hospital facilities. These areas will become central locations for information dispersion, missing persons/split family reunions, and social services.

Sanitary facilities: Some provision for temporary sanitation must be made before a disaster occurs. Public sanitary facilities are few or non-existent, so they are not considered fragile facilities. Without such provision, conditions can become untenable after a few days, and may cause outbreaks of disease.

Systems

Systems refer to operational organizations that require effective coordination between decision-making personnel and a corps of trained workers.

Management system: Survival after a disaster will require highly coordinated management of emergency response and recovery. This should be staged from a hardened, robust central location, staffed by trained personnel and run by an official in the upper government level (that is, a mayor or higher). Staffing must consist of well-trained government employees whose job requirements will immediately be shifted to emergency response. All groups of personnel—police, fire, military, emergency medical service (EMS), search and rescue (SAR)—must be under the control, and be totally responsive to, the central command authority. This system does not exist, but its importance cannot be overstated.

Search and rescue (SAR): There must be in place a deployable, trained volunteer SAR force pulled from all sectors of the community. SAR cannot rely solely on one branch of government service (that is, fire or military), as each will have other duties to fulfill. SAR will save lives in the days after the event, but will not be the most crucial component in life-saving (in terms of quantity) immediately following the event. The fragility of SAR should be low to allow heavy moving equipment to be dispersed and undamaged by the event.

Law enforcement/security: Control of the security situation will be challenging, requiring coordination by all departments. The fragility of stations and barracks is unknown. This will require an intact backup electricity supply and functioning communication lines, as well as a working central management system. However, the military, National Guard, and police are functioning entities that may be mobilized in the event of a natural disaster.

Strategic Planning Process—Development of the Plan

The hazard mitigation plan calls for a targeted and deliberately focused planning methodology. This was provided by the strategic planning process, which assumes a critical situation and seeks an effective and direct path toward solutions. It prioritizes efforts to attain the best possible results with the means available.

The analysis involved with the strategic planning method is focused on identifying strengths, weaknesses, opportunities, and threats (SWOT). The threats examined were possible earthquakes, floods, and landslides/debris flows. Also examined were the strengths, weaknesses, and opportunities in the urban structure as well as the current and future socioeconomic and political conditions that could influence the ability to cope with the threats. The following short lists are examples of the items that were generated.

Strengths

- Moderately diversified economic profile with strengths in the energy sector.
- Modern and efficient public transit system with growth potential.
- Developed intellectual capital based in universities and private institutes.
- Establishment of successful *barrio* intervention models.
- Political receptivity to issues of economic and land-use development.
- Presence of urban airport and military base in Caracas.
- Presence of major seaport to the west of Caracas: disaggregation of wealth and resources.

Weaknesses

- Water system infrastructure is underdeveloped, and supply channels traverse fault lines.
- Highway systems lacks sufficient redundancy to overcome traffic congestion and are vulnerable to closure. Parts of the Cota Mil, a major highway along the northern rim of the city, are incomplete, and the bridge that connects Caracas with the Vargas coast is experiencing structural duress.
- Communication technology lacks a public emergency broadcast system.
- The sanitation and water run-off system is underdeveloped, lacking sewage treatment and possibly posing a health risk.
- Pervasive fear of crime and corruption.

Opportunities

- Newly consolidated metropolitan government.
- Mixed-density development allowing for in-fill and promotion of open space.
- El Ávila National Park acts as a natural growth boundary to the north.
- Investment in rail transportation infrastructure opens regions of the Tuy Valley and points west for development.

Threats

- Branches of the San Sebastian and Tacagua-Ávila faults traverse the Caracas region, posing a threat of both minor and major earthquakes in the region in the next few decades.
- Climatic variability and steep terrain presents an ongoing threat of small and large landslides and debris flows to populated areas of the region.
- Extensive rainfalls could result in flooding conditions.

Based on the SWOT analysis, a hazard mitigation plan was developed that addressed critical weaknesses and leveraged strengths and opportunities present in the Caracas region. Using ARCView, a geographic information system (GIS), base maps were prepared of regional land-uses, service infrastructure, housing typologies, and critical emergency facilities (such as police stations, fire stations, and hospitals). These base maps were then overlaid with maps identifying hazards risks—specific areas where steep topography suggested that landslides might occur, and low-lying areas that were prone to flooding. In addition, maps of soil depth, indicative of earthquake shaking periods, were created and overlaid on maps of the city. The composite map resulting from the layering process highlights, at the metropolitan level, neighborhoods with specific vulnerabilities that might require targeted intervention (figure 5.3).

The studio did not develop micro-level plans for each of the vulnerable areas of the facilities, but rather focused on creating a comprehensive schematic plan for the Caracas metropolitan area that addressed cited critical weaknesses. In addition, the studio selected a few examples of micro-interventions as demonstration models of the broader concepts. The development of small open-spaces in select urban neighborhoods is one such example. The bi-level approach of the plan and

Figure 5.3. An example of the multihazard map produced by the Urban Planning studio. The map is a compilation of urban-facilities research and natural-hazards research. This map relied upon existing estimates of ground shaking period from FUNVISIS and estimated flooding extent, based on local topography.

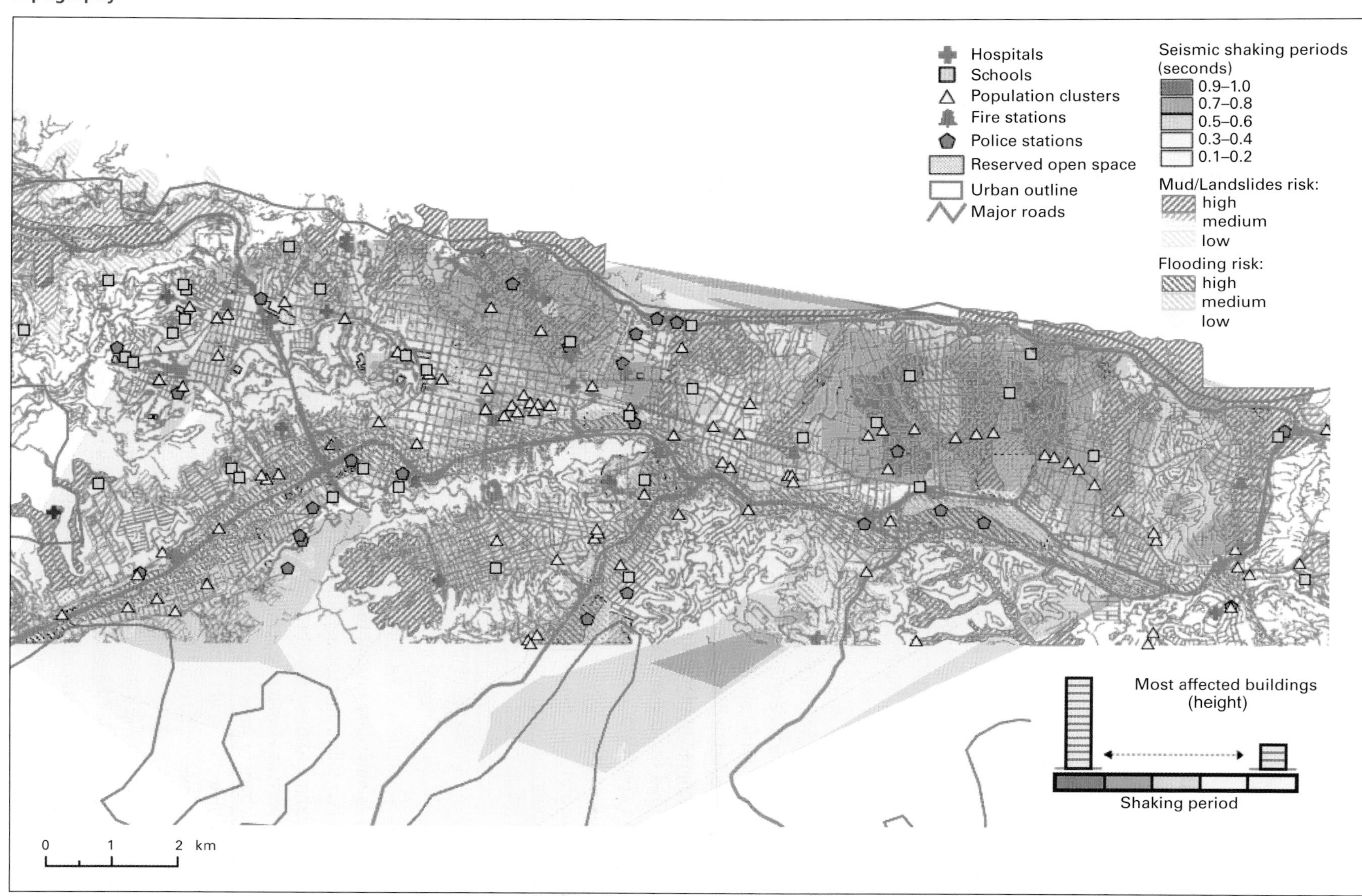

recommendations, also referred to as "mixed scanning," was best suited for the large region under consideration. The broad scope was intentional—at the onset of the project the studio participants understood the limitations they faced as "foreign specialists." It was felt that the broad plan was a platform from which local planning professionals could develop specific project plans using a more participatory planning approach that included the direct stakeholders from each area of intervention. The principal aim was to develop the methodology within which detailed intervention could be introduced and the obtained outputs perhaps modified interactively with stakeholders.

The plan focused primarily on physical facilities that required additional assessment, but also touched upon social and administrative programs that would build resiliency in the community. These included aspects of a land tenure program that would stimulate improved building construction and insurance coverage, as well as a public hazards awareness campaign, which would occur in the popular media and through education (primarily at the school level).

The plan was outlined in a flexible 20-year time frame to allow for a phased implementation. The timing of the plan considered the present condition of any specific factor under consideration, the resources required for improvement, and the extent of development time needed for implementation. Qualitative factors such as economic and political conditions also influenced the phasing sequence.

Facilities

Emergency facilities are crucial to minimizing loss of life immediately following a natural disaster. Their importance is heightened in situations where the entire city is affected, such as after a large earthquake. New facilities must be built in areas where populations are underserved, and all facilities, whether located in a high-hazard area or not, must be structurally sound to withstand powerful earthquakes. (See table 5.1 for a list of needed facilities during a disaster and for the locations of the existing facilities [figures 5.4 and 5.5].) In order to determine the structural integrity of existing facilities, all buildings in Caracas should be inventoried based on their age and assessed based on their earthquake-resistance (by reviewing their previous performance during earthquakes). This information can be used for determining the disaster response capabilities of key systems and to assist in the decision-making process for retrofitting critical facilities.

Reserved Space

Reserved spaces are open spaces such as parks and recreational fields as well as buildings like community centers and school gymnasiums. In the event of a natural disaster, these places will serve a dual function as evacuation centers, providing temporary emergency services to surrounding residents. Therefore, reserved spaces must be created and/or enhanced in areas that can be easily accessed by people and vehicles. Additionally, they should be equitably dispersed throughout the city so that every neighborhood has a predetermined evacuation site. Larger spaces, such as Parque del Este, Parque Central, and Universidad Central, could serve as evacuation areas for large populations for long stays (figure 5.4).

Smaller spaces, likely located in *barrios,* are intended to accommodate a designated neighborhood for a few days. Because of the smaller scale of reserved spaces in *barrios* and the high population density of *barrio* neighborhoods, a larger number of reserved spaces must be strategically created there.

Open spaces may be the facilities that could be located in high earthquake risk areas. However, the same cannot be said for their location within areas subject to hydrological hazards.

Buildings used for evacuation centers must be reinforced to withstand the strongest of earthquakes and may be a better option in *barrios,* considering the scarcity of land. Regardless of their location, reserved spaces must be large enough to allow for temporary shelter, hospitals, and information centers. A key concept in both hazard mitigation and disaster response for Caracas is the proposal to create *Plazas de Seguridad.* Similar to a traditional Latin American *parroquia* in design—an open space surrounded by civic buildings and community facilities—the *Plaza de Seguridad* is a practical option, primarily in *barrios,* where public services and neighborhood centers are lacking (figures 5.2 and 5.6).

The *Plazas de Seguridad* should include police and

Figure 5.4. Reserved open space in the Caracas Valley. The box to the lower right indicates the location of the Petare District.

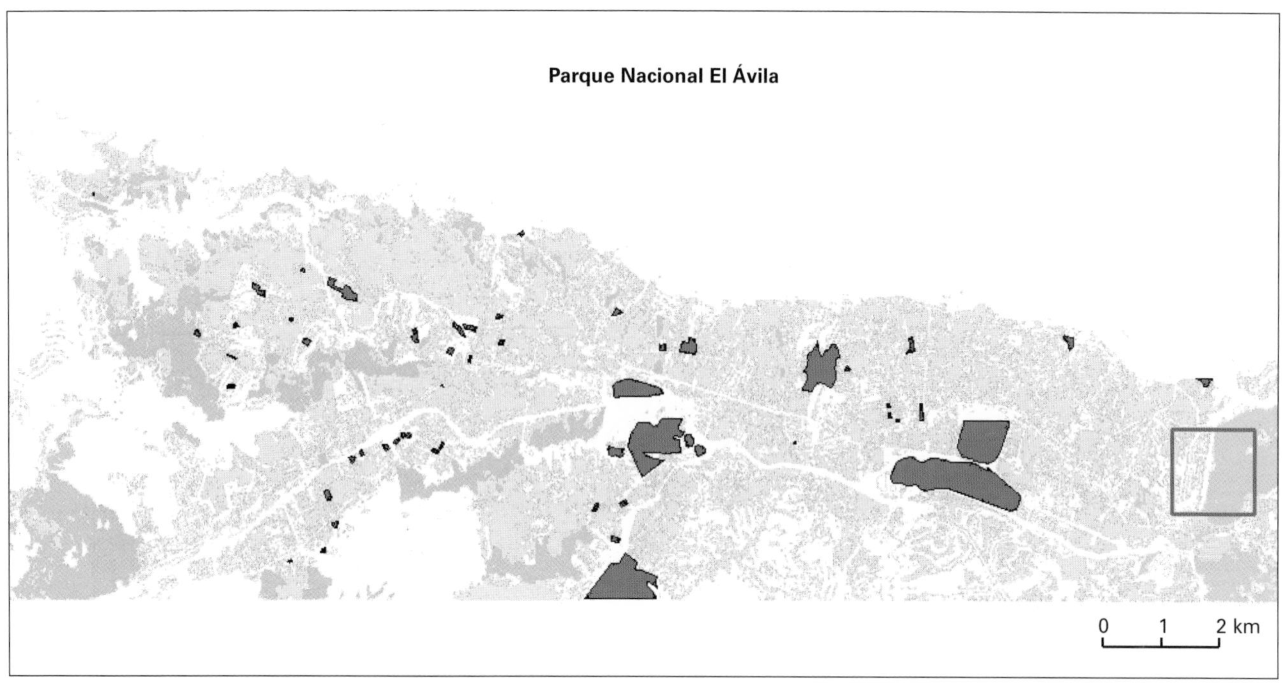

Figure 5.5. Hospitals, police stations, and fire stations in the Caracas Valley

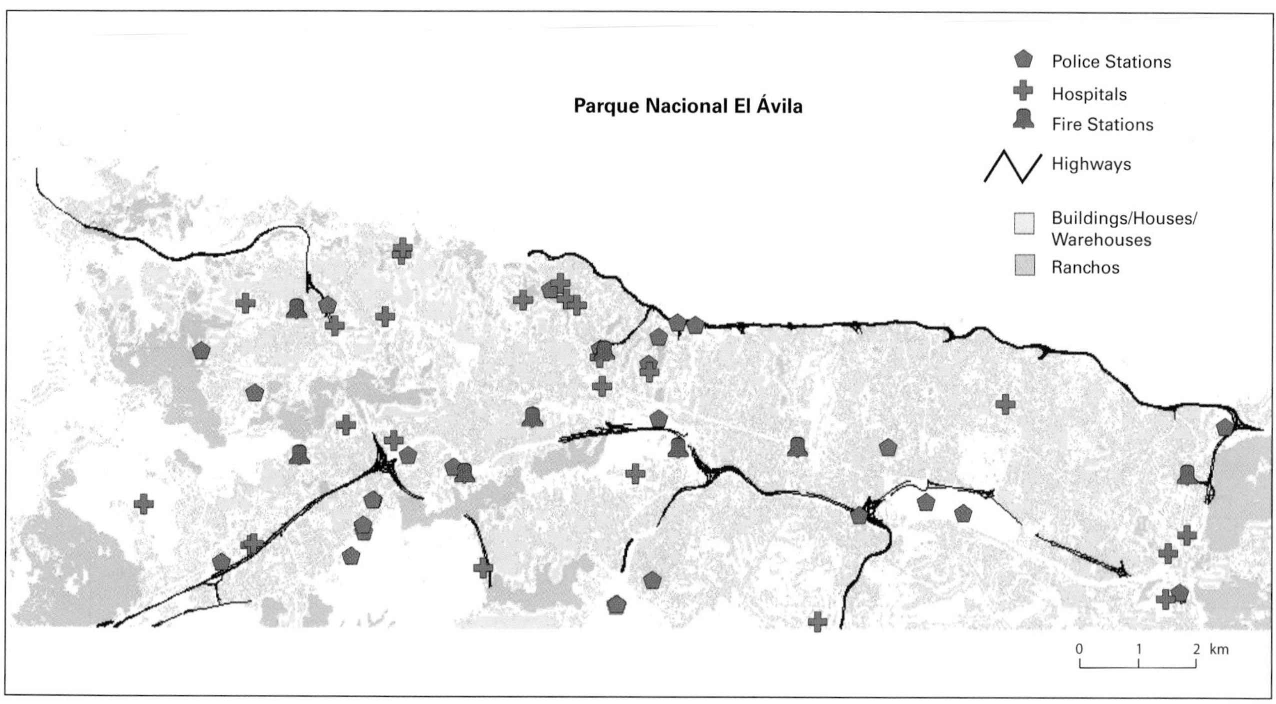

fire stations, a medical facility, a community center, and technical units when possible. Therefore, while the *Plazas de Seguridad* would function regularly in the absence of a natural disaster, supporting the community and enhancing the quality of life, their clustered design would help facilitate coordinated emergency response efforts when an earthquake or flood strikes.

Plazas de Seguridad should be located in low hazard

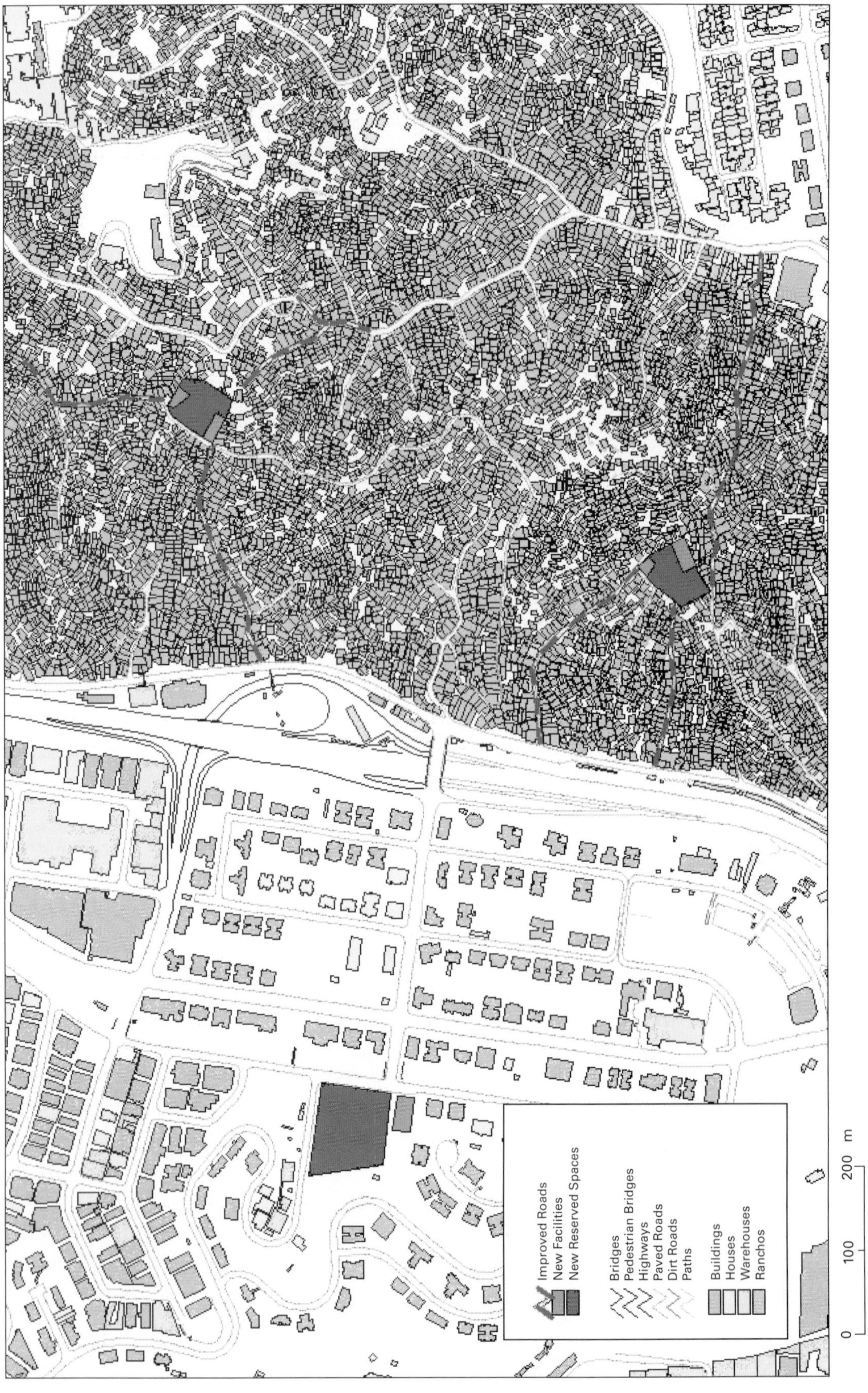

Figure 5.6. Proposed interventions in a section of Petare to improve disaster preparedness with the allocation of reserved space

zones if possible. Nevertheless, the civic buildings that accompany the plazas should be strong enough to withstand the strongest of earthquakes. At varying capacities, both open spaces and buildings used as evacuation centers will function as:

- temporary shelters, equipped with a supply of tents if necessary;
- field hospitals, possibly in existing buildings with stored supplies and basic medical equipment;
- information centers, with uninterrupted linkages to the central communications system;
- supply distribution points for basic survival supplies, such as water, food, and blankets; and
- sanitary facilities, including toilets, showers, and waste disposal units.

Medical, Police, and Fire Buildings

These critical facilities have to be self-sufficient structures, able to withstand strong earthquakes and remain functional. Therefore, they should have structural integrity, backup electrical generators, and a separate and sufficient water supply and storage space. As with the *Plazas de Seguridad,* their effectiveness in terms of disaster mitigation depends, to a large extent, on their proximity to populations. Thus, proportionate distribution of hospitals, police stations, and fire stations based on population should be encouraged. Where this is not feasible, smaller medical facilities can fill in gaps as long as they have access to locally stored medical equipment and supplies. The hardening or relocating of critical facilities must be considered on a case-by-case basis, as the decision would depend upon factors such as accessibility and need in the case of a disaster.

Storage Depots

It is necessary to construct major assembly points for the maintenance and storage of equipment and supplies that will be utilized during the post-disaster period. This equipment includes heavy machinery such as cranes, bulldozers, and trucks; hazardous materials cleanup apparatus; a fleet of helicopters and buses; and temporary shelters and hospital equipment. The storage depots should be placed in strategically located and secured areas such as military bases. Access to major transportation links should be a major factor in determining their locations.

Command and Control Center

A command center should be created in a central location. It must be a self-sufficient structure, capable of absorbing and disseminating massive amounts of information in a short period of time. The center will be used to coordinate immediate emergency relief efforts and long-term disaster relief programs; it should also serve as a permanent installation able to manage routine emergency situations.

Cultural Buildings

Cultural buildings such as museums, libraries, government buildings, and universities hold the country's history and heritage within their walls. They are important symbols of national identity and pride, and many government buildings and libraries store official records, legal documents, and personal identification information. These buildings should receive high priority for retrofit efforts.

Water Distribution System

As mentioned previously, the water distribution system in Caracas is inadequate, considering that current supply lines provide insufficient amounts of water to the valley and are susceptible to earthquakes. As a result, more distribution pipes and aqueducts built to withstand seismic events must be constructed, and the system must be made more redundant in case of malfunction of one of the lines. Additionally, all existing lines must be hardened, particularly at the points where the aqueducts intersect seismic faults (figure 5.7). While these measures will help to ensure that Caracas has a sufficient and consistent water supply, the critical function of water, both during and after a natural disaster, necessitates extra precautionary measures.

Because water must be pumped up into Caracas, which is located ~900 meters above sea level, water distribution capability is directly tied to the robustness of the electrical power system. As a result, backup power is critical to ensuring continued water delivery in the

Figure 5.7. The Caracas water supply system, showing key infrastructure crossing fault lines

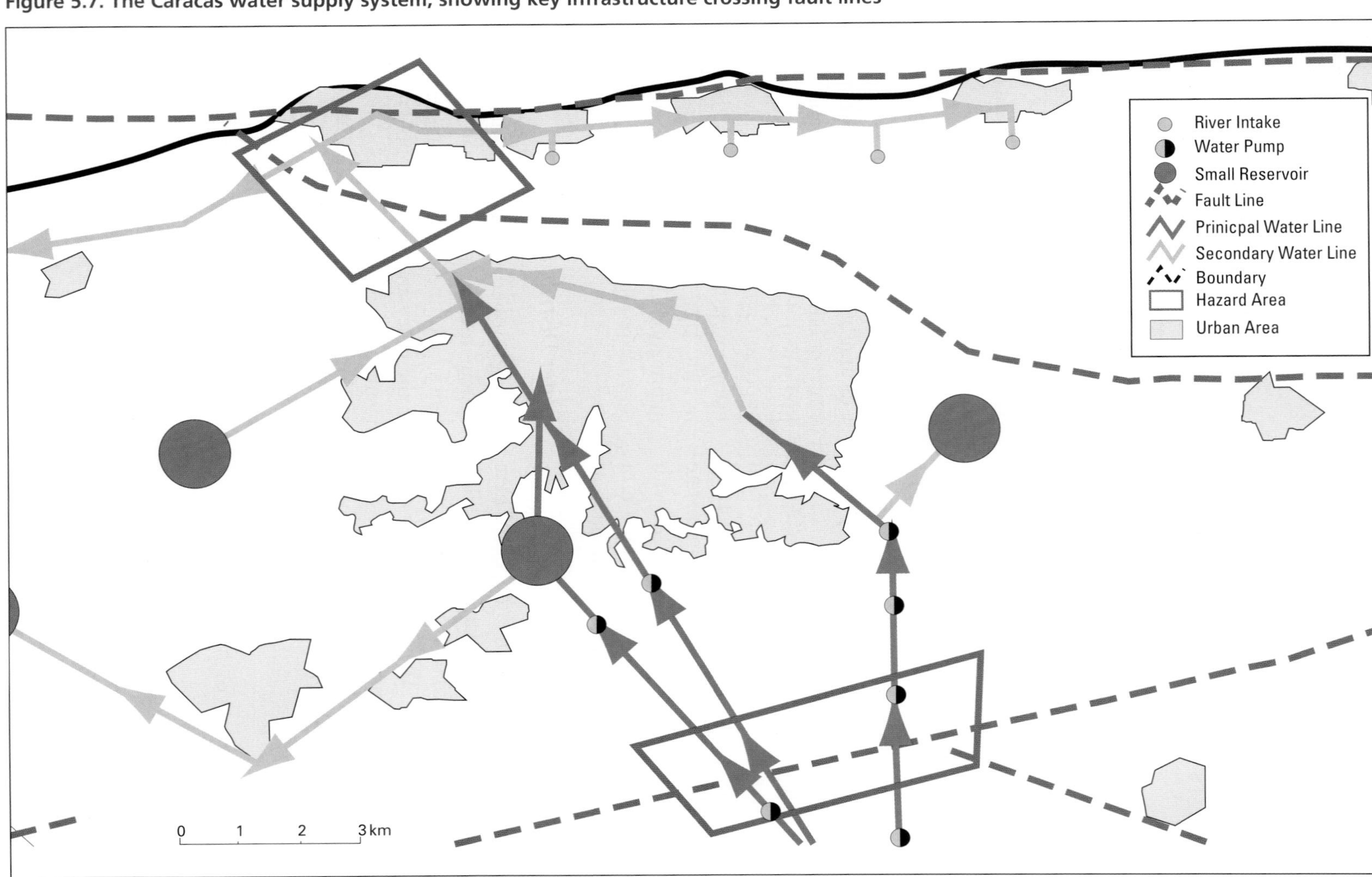

case of a general power failure. All water pumping stations should have individual generators and be provided with additional alternate electrical lines, as appropriate.

Additionally, since one or more of the water supply lines may fail during a strong seismic event (even if they are well built), ample water storage must be available within the city. Currently, there is less than a one-day supply of water on reserve, and the major storage facilities are located outside of the valley. Consequently, sites should be found, within the city, where large holding tanks or reservoirs can be built. The total water reserve capacity should be no less than the equivalent of three days worth of potable and fire-fighting water.

Surface Transportation

Surface transportation is a critical infrastructure system that must be functioning well at all times, but is especially crucial in case of emergency. Many lives will be saved directly following a major disaster if emergency vehicles carrying personnel and supplies are able to move efficiently throughout the city.

Therefore, the key network should be planned to withstand natural hazards and to handle emergency responses (figures 5.8–5.10). Sections of the road network under risk must be well engineered to handle both earthquake shaking and mudslides/debris flows caused by heavy rains. Elevated sections are under highest threat during an earthquake, and should be hardened to prevent major structural failure. Some sections of the highway built at grade are under threat of flooding. The river must be channeled and controlled in these areas to prevent water from blocking all vital movements.

A road network with a high degree of redundancy should be in place both within the Caracas valley and along the major highways that connect Caracas to the rest of the region so that alternate paths may be open under the most serious disaster conditions. Many of these major connectors are under threat, and a robust network must be created and emergency routes established to prevent gridlock should one of these main arteries fail. Without redundancy, the entire city could be paralyzed following a major event, preventing assistance from reaching victims.

Bridges should be given special attention, as they are the most fragile elements of the surface transportation system and are under heavy seismic threat. The bridge connecting the Caracas valley to Maiquetia/La Guaira should receive immediate attention, considering it is the only connector to the coast and to the major international airport and port. Its vulnerable status has been documented for some time, and structural failure could occur, even without a major disaster event.

Communication

In the minutes and hours directly following a major emergency, communication can be a matter of life or death. The general public must be able to receive information about what has happened, as well as instructions for further action. An emergency broadcast system should be created so that information is disseminated as quickly and efficiently as possible.

Television and radio broadcasts as well as announcements over public address systems and megaphones are all effective means of disseminating information. The system should be set up with a strict hierarchy of decision making focused on what information is to be distributed and what personnel should be responsible to avoid confusion.

The general public should be made aware of where to receive information and instructions immediately following a disaster. Public education and awareness campaigns, along with regular drills, can help to acquaint residents with the sources and processes, and particularly with the emergency broadcast system.

Authorities responding to an emergency need to be in constant communication, as well. A unified and permanent emergency communication center should be created that will handle all communication between the police, civil defense, fire fighters, medics, and other authorities in case of an emergency. A clear hierarchy of instruction, procedure, and personnel should be established to avoid mass confusion and wasteful duplication of effort following the disaster.

Finally, the city should adopt software systems to prevent communication gridlock, maintain a protocol, and give priority to the appropriate personnel. Gridlock happens during post-disaster periods when the use of tele-

Figure 5.8. Seismic hazard affecting the city's transportation network. Five points of vulnerability to shaking were identified in the major transportation infrastructure.

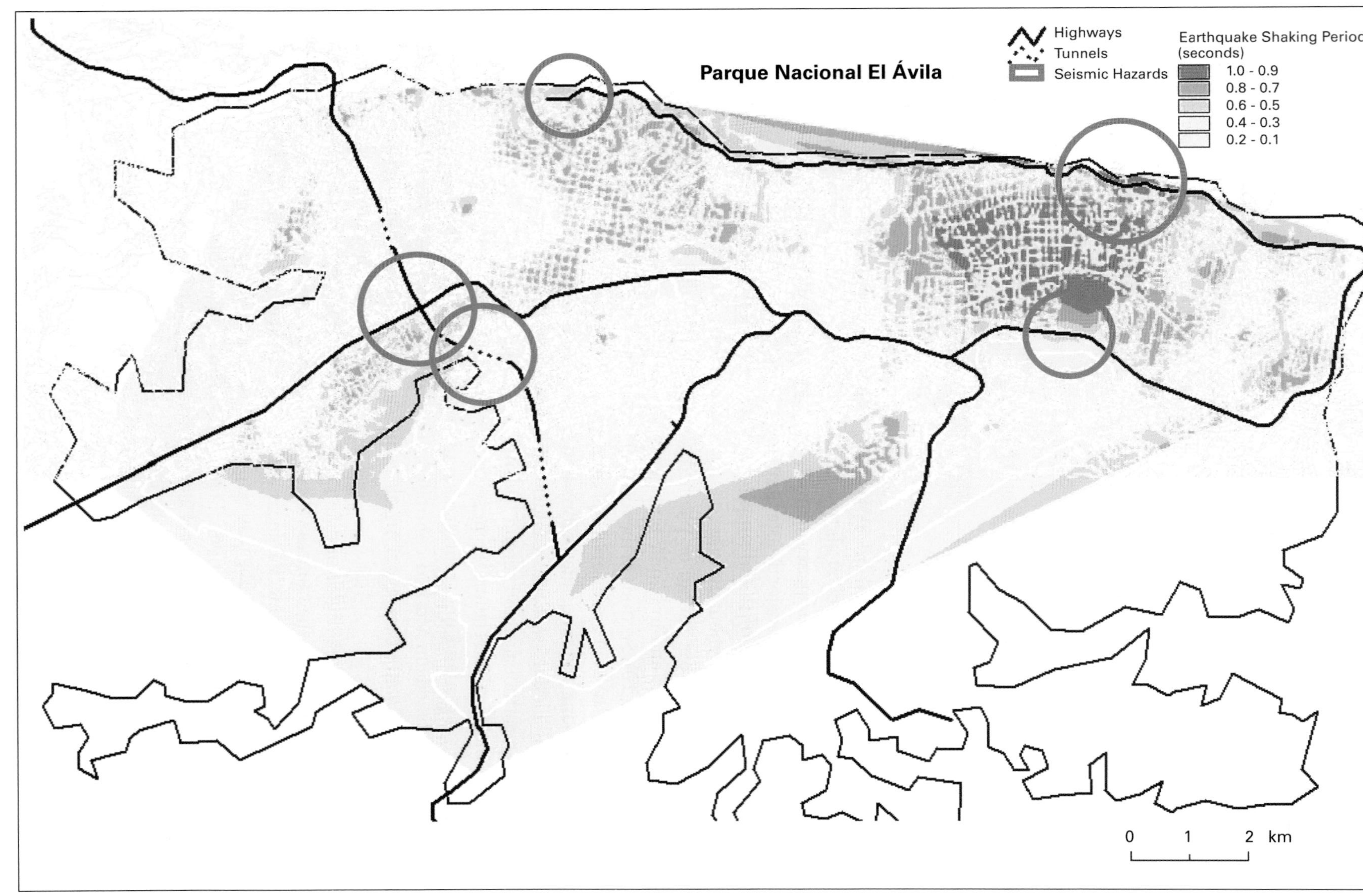

Figure 5.9. Debris flows affecting the city's transportation network. The Cota Mil highway is especially vulnerable to debris flow as it traces the southern border of the steep El Ávila mountain range. The Caracas-Vargas highway is also threatened by landslides.

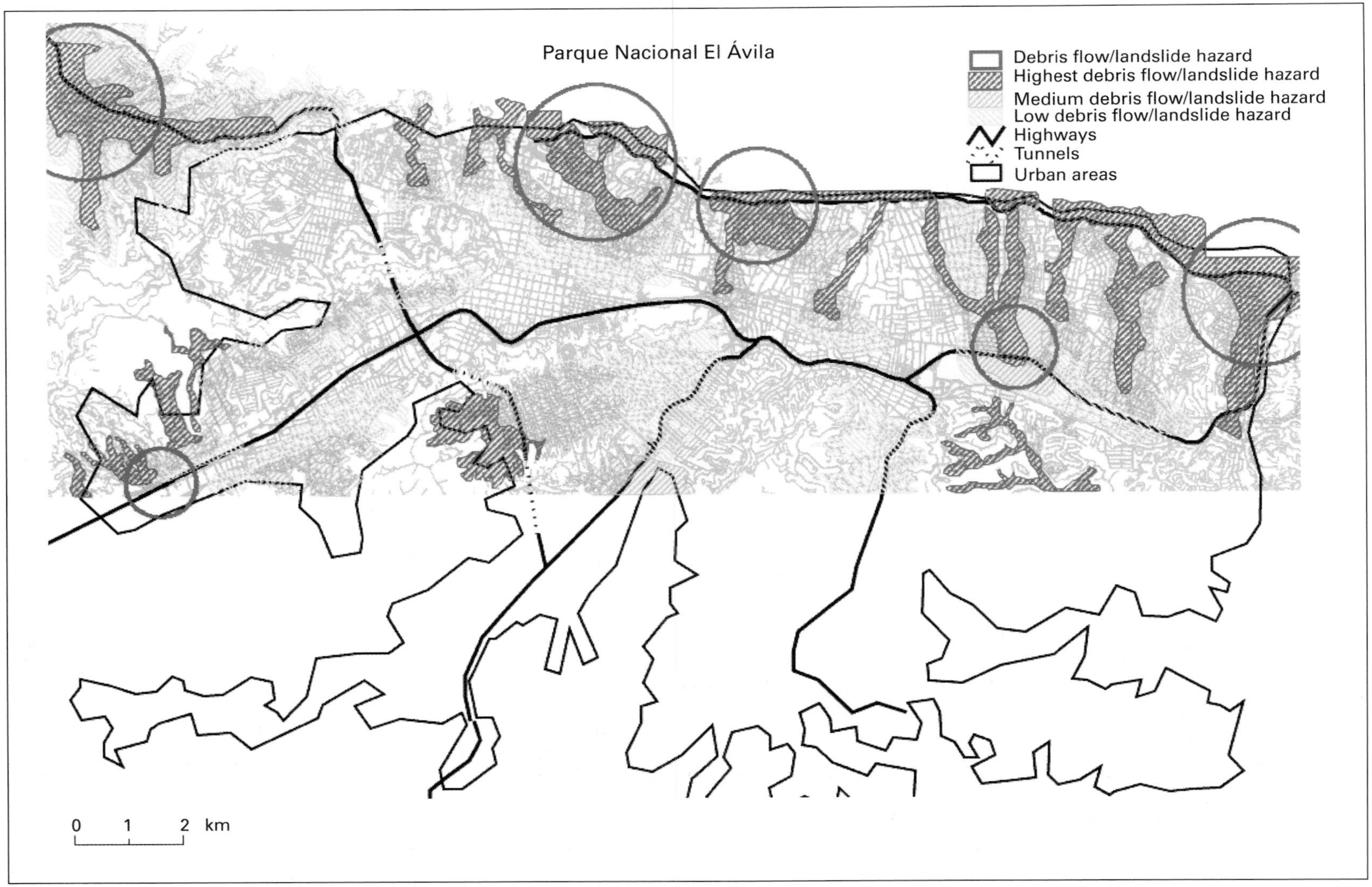

Figure 5.10. Flood hazard affecting the city's transportation network. The main east-west thoroughfare through the city is paralleled by the main, channelized river.

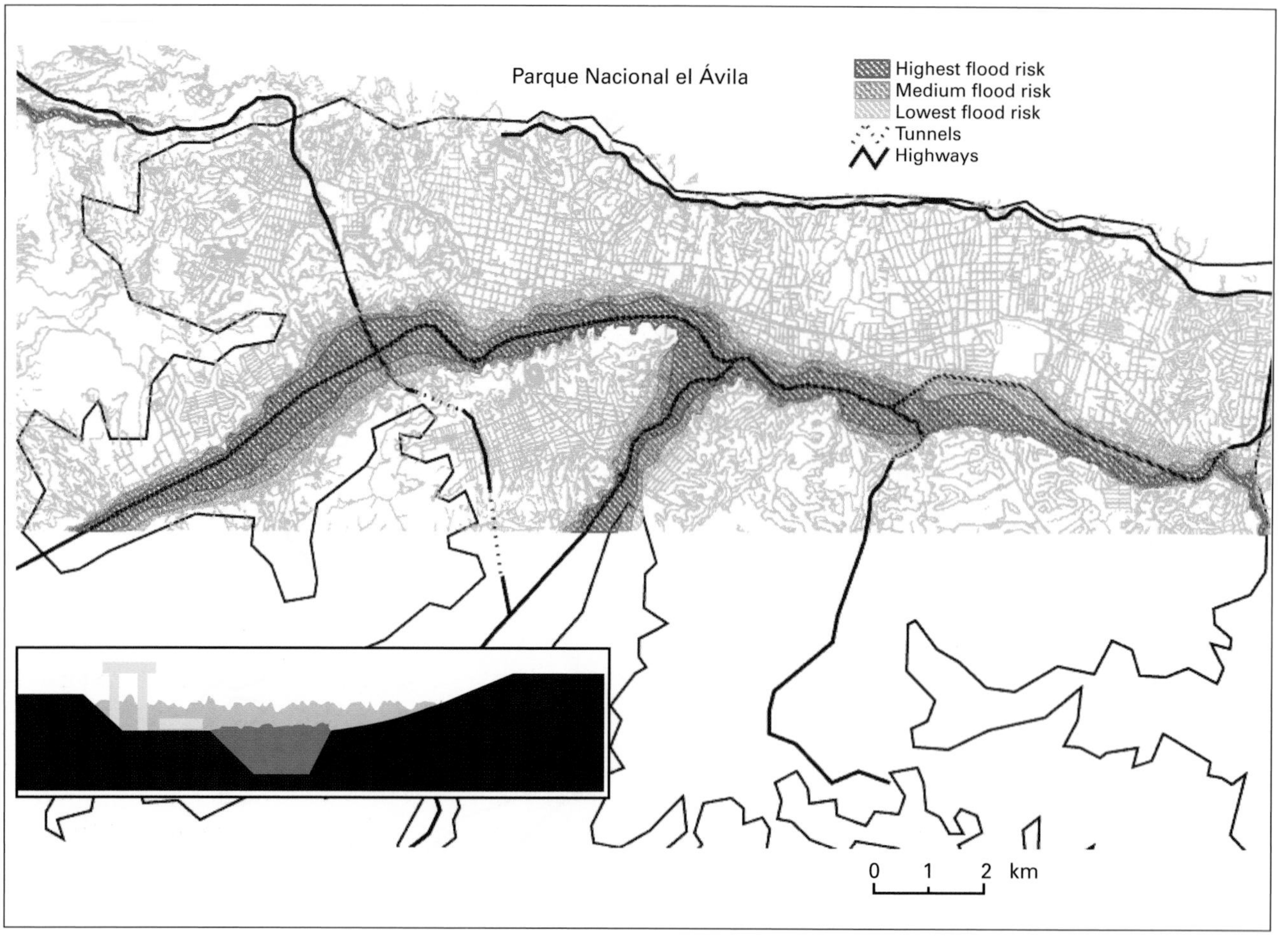

phone lines and other communication links increases drastically. Some lines must be reserved for official emergency use only in order to prevent a complete breakdown.

METRO System

The structural strength of the METRO system is most important in terms of earthquake risk. Operational elements must be engineered to handle these forces. Operational safety of the system is also crucial in case of a natural disaster. The METRO system should be prepared to move and protect its users by providing clear and unobstructed emergency escapes and evacuation routes. These routes should be equipped with communication devices connecting it to the emergency broadcast system.

Since the METRO was built recently, it can be assumed that proper safety factors have been incorporated in its design. Many light and heavy rail lines are currently being built or proposed for the valley of Caracas. Among them are the Railroad Cua-Tuy Medio, the new METRO lines, and the Los Teques line. To prepare these systems for a natural disaster, it is necessary to assure that structures are built robust enough to withstand an earthquake.

It is also necessary to assure that the operational problems the systems may encounter during a natural disaster, including issues of citizen safety, availability of evacuation routes, and accessibility for repairs, are anticipated. All these issues should be taken into account in the design and construction phases so that time and money can be saved later.

Air and Seaports

Air and seaports become critical in the event of a disaster. They are the major ports of entry and exit for personnel and equipment. They must be fully operational in order to absorb national and international relief assistance, and to evacuate people out of the area if necessary.

Power System

The power system must be designed to withstand a disaster, and to be operational should one occur. Particularly during large earthquakes, it is common to have massive power failures in multiple locations, making restoration efforts difficult. To prepare the system for a natural disaster, it is necessary to make an assessment of the existing conditions and to reinforce the available infrastructure in relation to its importance in the system. This includes insuring the structural stability of power generation stations, transmission towers, transformer stations, switchyards, and distribution lines. The control and related communication systems must be hardened and redundant.

Natural Gas Distribution

Caracas has a natural gas distribution system that serves most of the valley, yet only limited information has been obtained so far on the specific location and condition of these lines in the city. They carry a highly flammable substance, thus representing a major fire threat in the case of disaster. The system should be analyzed to assess its structural soundness, identifying possible leakage and break-up scenarios. In some cases, retrofitting may be necessary. In order to reduce fire risk, emergency shut off valves—which would allow authorities to stop the flow of gas from the source—should be considered. These valves should exist at least at central distribution nodes, but may be considered at major consumption points as well.

Sewage

Although sewage is not an essential element in disaster preparedness and mitigation, it becomes a danger to human health if raw sewage enters the water supply or the environment. It is necessary to strengthen the sewage system, especially the major outflow pipes, to prevent leakage in case of earthquake or flooding. Concrete and steel are generally used for sewage pipes. Concrete has poor tensile strength and can be highly vulnerable to ground shaking. Steel has much better tensile force, but the joints can be vulnerable and may have to be retrofitted to handle earthquake stress. Cast iron pipes are brittle and perform poorly during earthquakes.

Housing

The overarching goal of housing policy is to equip all existing residential structures for hazard resiliency and to guide future disaster-resistant housing development. Housing is at once both inherently physical and social, and the programs presented here reflect this duality.

Physical Programs

Appropriate building codes: these should be developed based upon a complete hazard assessment of the given area as well as information about the existing structures. Requirements should include building and site-grading ordinances along with design and construction regulations. All categories of local housing and the array of local materials used in its construction have to be considered. Mortgage lending, permits, training, and quality control inspections can be tied into the administration of building codes as well. A failure to include disaster-resistant standards for low-cost housing increases the vulnerability of citizens, and further excludes them from the formal housing market. Strict codes not only ensure that existing structures will have a better chance in the event of a major disaster, but they also guide future hazard-resistant building. Enforcement is critical, and a well-trained, well-staffed agency is needed to accommodate demand.

Structural reinforcement: Hazard maps and building history can be used to establish priority structures for hazard abatement programs. In the most hazardous areas, local governments can adopt mandatory retrofit programs. Retrofitting measures may include the insertion of walls on the outside or in the interior of buildings, buttresses, specially anchored frames or the construction of a new frame system, covering of columns and beams, portico fill-in walls, and tie-rods and safety "wraps." Government subsidies may be necessary to promote this program in the form of low-interest loans, to ensure that people are not displaced by rising rents.

Land use and zoning: Hazard risk mitigation should be a deciding factor when choosing new building sites. These issues should be considered at the early stages of site selection to ensure that hazards will be weighed against the strategic advantages of a given location. Thus, in addition to abiding by building codes, structural design considerations should include the location and height of the building, the structural system, building materials, functional relations between various sections and building composition, vulnerability to specific disasters, possible impacts of disasters on occupants, and special needs of residents.

Training: A great number of homes in Caracas are built outside of the formal construction process without the involvement of lending institutions, trained architects, or experienced builders. Therefore, building codes must be supplemented by a training program that teaches disaster-resistant building techniques to all builders within the private and informal sectors, as well as to self-help labor (those who build their own homes). The most important component of a training program is local participation. People must be aware of the hazard risks, believe that the implementation of certain construction techniques will add to the safety of their homes, and be offered the opportunity to either build or improve their homes to meet building codes at affordable costs.

A higher level of training is necessary for architects, builders, masons, and other construction personnel. Trainers from this pool may be selected to instruct other builders or to provide technical assistance to local communities. They also can be certified as building inspectors. A second level of training should focus on self-help builders. This may include specific training in basic building techniques, as well as raising awareness of the importance of hazard-resistant building. The success of any housing improvement program is dependent upon the extent to which communities seek to increase the safety and stability of their homes. Maintaining high performance standards in workmanship is crucial (possibly more effective than building codes) in assuring that structural standards are met. Programs should be monitored to ensure that the instruction is effective. Testing and licensing procedures should be instituted, and appropriate quality control standards should be in place. Cooperative building groups, material subsidies, or community work programs will benefit low-income families who cannot afford extensive home improvements or construction loans.

Social Programs

Land title: The Housing Policy Law of 1989 recognizes *ranchos* as a legitimate form of housing, and mandates the granting of property rights to established *barrios* as a part of the process of *barrio* upgrading. *Barrio* upgrading has become the focal point of national housing policy, and hazard risk mitigation should be fused into these programs. Several government agencies, states, and municipalities contribute to *barrio* upgrading, including the *Comision Nacional de Equipamento de Barrios* (National Commission on Barrio Upgrading), which was created in 1995 with a mandate to coordinate policies and investments in *barrios*. Granting land tenure to *barrio* residents explicitly acknowledges that city growth and improvement will be linked to *barrio* development. As such, the immense informal housing stock can be transformed from a problem to be resolved into a resource to be utilized. Additionally, the provision of property rights can facilitate the community participation necessary to pursue effective hazard-resistant planning. Land title not only gives legitimate value to investment, but also can be used to leverage home improvements, loans, and disaster insurance.

In Caracas, 58 percent of *barrios* are located on public lands; 27 percent are on lands with a mixture of public and private ownership; and 15 percent are located on private lands. The process of transferring public lands to agencies involved with *barrio* improvements must be streamlined and made more efficient. Private land owners should be reasonably compensated for relinquishing their land, and a government agency in cooperation with local communities should oversee the transfer of land titles to residents. The extensive involvement of each community is essential for legitimizing the ownership structure, thereby reducing subsequent property-related disputes. It also will encourage community policing of further invasions. The Housing Policy Law has begun this process, but it should be modified and given additional legal and institutional support if it is to successfully incorporate disaster-resistant measures.

Hazard risk mitigation is an underlying factor in the transfer of land rights. Landowners and real estate brokers should be legally responsible for full disclosure of hazard assessments of the property.

Housing finance: Volatile conditions within the financial sector have direct and adverse effects on the housing sector. The high annual inflation rate (averaging 52 percent between 1990 and 1997) hinders the development of the mortgage market; overdependence of the economy on oil leads to the fluctuation of housing subsidy levels. This causes stagnation in the private financial sector and the deterioration of real income levels. All these factors serve to cripple the efficient development of a strong housing sector. Unfortunately, housing loans will continue to be in limited supply as long as interest rates continue to be subsidized, and many of the proposals suggested here require a supply of low-interest loans. To reconcile these conflicting trends, attention must be given to finding ways to introduce greater competition into the housing finance market.

One possible solution is to eliminate direct housing subsidies and, instead, to subsidize loans for safe housing construction and disaster-resistant upgrading. These loans should first be made available to those with the greatest need, such as low-income *barrio* or "vertical" communities (in low-income, multi-story residences). Low-interest loans can also be tied to training programs as an added incentive for builders to undergo training in the construction of hazard-resistant buildings.

Insurance: Disaster insurance should be introduced and tied to housing finance. Real estate agents could be required to generate risk disclosure statements, offer special insurance coverage and policy riders, maintain affordable premiums, and introduce mandatory purchase requirements in lending agencies. Insurers could provide premium reductions for policy-holders who undertake loss prevention measures. Structures that meet certain criteria would qualify for financial incentives from banks, contractors, and insurers. Group insurance schemes can be incorporated into the training and education programs aimed at low-income communities. Incentives to exceed minimum safety standards can be built into the rate structure. The government could provide tax incentives to companies who insure very low-income communities.

Planning and provision: New *barrio* development is constantly underway and must be targeted for immediate planning for service provision to prevent the problems with lack of access, services, and extreme hazard risk that affect many existing settlements. Service and infrastructure provision in newly emerging *barrios* will be far more cost effective than late interventions. Municipalities can work together with these new communities to develop good design ideas and to establish effective zoning codes.

Land Use Regulations and Relocation Principles

Regulating land use, both in built and open areas, is a crucial component of hazard risk mitigation. In open areas, good urban design guidelines, enforceable building codes, and limits on population settlement in high hazard areas can ensure that the city is a less risky place, even as population grows. In built areas, attention to the adequate provision of public services and space, as well as the identification of particular facilities that need structural reinforcement or relocation, can help reduce the vulnerability of large sectors of the city's population. Finally, attention to land use regulations can make Caracas a more livable city, both before and after a natural disaster strikes.

Enforcement

At the outset, it needs to be emphasized that no regulation should be enacted unless there is an immediately workable enforcement procedure (including adequate funding and involvement of the local community in both drawing up the regulations and implementing them.) Regulations enacted without the consent of the community are likely to be challenged or ignored, while unenforced regulations can actually increase overall risk, as they lead to complacency on the part of government officials and the affected population; such a circumstance gives the sense that the problem had been solved when it was actually worsening during periods of perceived safety. Land-use regulations that involve community policing and enforcement efforts should receive priority.

Open Areas

For the open areas of the Caracas metropolitan area—particularly at the edges of *barrios* and in locations subject to formal private real estate development—high-risk areas, as determined by thorough hazard assessments, should be off limits to residential construction and to nearly all commercial activity. Such areas can still be used; potential uses include agricultural production, recreation, and other open spaces with activities that do not place people and significant investments in danger. Areas of medium risk should be reserved for roads and other access routes, manufacturing and industrial activity, and low-density commercial uses. Low-risk areas should be open to residential construction and serve as the sites of *Plazas de Seguridad,* higher-density commercial activity, schools, hospitals, and other critical facilities. However, they, too, should be built recognizing potential dangers. Additionally, it is possible to consider the construction of some non-vital structures with an expected short life span and limited investment, recognizing that they may be destroyed.

Built Areas

For the built areas of the Caracas metropolitan area, there is likely to be tension between the hardening of existing structures in high-hazard areas and the relocation of people and buildings out of those areas. No blanket rules can be established to resolve this difficult choice.

Nevertheless, certain guidelines can be recommended. Areas that are high risk both for seismic and hydrological reasons ought to have a bias toward relocation. Areas of high risk for either, but not both, should have a bias toward hardening, with an emphasis not only on traditional engineering techniques, but also on the use of alternative materials. No relocation should take place in areas of moderate risk, except where it is related to the introduction of new infrastructure.

When buildings are removed to introduce roads and other access routes into the *barrios,* moderate-risk areas should receive priority—ensuring that the people are relocated out of risky areas, but that new infrastructure is not located within the areas of highest risk. Such roads and access routes should lead to newly established *Plazas de Seguridad,* which should be located within areas of low risk, if possible. This will not be feasible in many instances because these plazas must be easily accessible to the population that they are expected to serve.

Relocation Principles

In some areas of Caracas, only extremely costly engineering techniques can save the lives and property of many people living in risky areas. Where it is a matter of life and death, relocation of people and buildings should be considered. Relocation may also be warranted where the entire community would benefit—that is, for the introduction of access roads and services into *barrio* areas.

In these cases, it is recommended that certain principles be followed. First, the members of the population at risk should be active participants in the relocation process. This population should be involved not only in determining who needs to be relocated, but also determining what constitutes a risky area. Different populations have different perceptions of risk, and this needs to be taken into account. Often low-income populations, in particular, knowingly bear risks in order to satisfy immediate living and work objectives.

Second, priority should be given to maintaining the familial, social, and economic support networks of the people who are moved. Experience with natural disasters and relocation both in Repúplica Bolivariana de Venezuela and around the world has shown that if these networks are disrupted, people will move back into risky areas. Residents of Caracas should be allowed to remain in Caracas, preferably within their existing neighborhoods.

This can be achieved by increasing density through appropriate housing design within the lower-risk parts of neighborhoods affected by relocation. Finally, relocation for natural-hazard mitigation should not be used as an excuse for mass relocation or to justify "urban renewal" programs. If the above principles are followed, only a small percentage of the population at risk will need to be moved.

Education and Outreach

Education is one of the most fundamental and important hazard mitigation strategies. It is also an area where innovation, creative thinking, and experimentation can be employed at a low cost to raise the collective awareness about the dangers posed by natural hazards. A population that is cognizant about the risks associated with their environmental surroundings is more likely to be willing to accept and participate in the implementation of an overall hazard risk mitigation plan.

Hazard education in Caracas should generally fall into two categories: emergency response, or what to do when disaster strikes; and the teaching of basic mitigation techniques, or what to do to lessen the impact of a natural disaster.

Crucial for both of these areas is the introduction of a mandatory natural-hazard curriculum into the schools of Caracas. Children can be taught both what to do in a disaster and how to prepare for it ahead of time. Such instruction can eventually be mainstreamed into the overall school curriculum so that subjects such as science and history can take on disaster-related themes.

Raising awareness and preparing the population in general to respond to natural disasters is a crucial task for the mass media. Public service announcements and short instructional messages on television and radio and in the print media can go a long way toward educating the public about their city and its dangers. These messages should be incorporated into the preparation of hazard drills and the formulation of family, school, community, and business hazard response and mitigation plans.

Yet, even deeper than such traditional methods, natural hazards and disasters can become a theme in popular culture. Incorporating disaster subject matter into soap operas, movies, and advertisements—most any domestic story line could accommodate formulating a family hazard drill and plan—would be both an entertaining and effective way of making all those who live in Caracas aware of the dangers that surround them.

Penetrating people's consciousness in such a creative way can take many different forms. Since so many homes in Caracas are built by the residents themselves, it is crucial to link some form of education in proper building techniques to the sale of home-building materials. Such an effort should be just a small part of an overall education and outreach scheme targeting the professional community (who both prepare for and respond to natural disasters), including builders, architects, health care professionals, emergency response technicians, and so on.

Much of this specialized education could be administered by technical units, which should be established throughout the entire metropolitan area. These units would not only provide education and training at the grassroots level, but also could serve as an operations base for a trained volunteer corps such as the Red Cross and other nongovernmental support groups.

If all these tasks can be accomplished, not only will Caracas be a safer place in which to live, but also the city could become a regional center for hazard education and research, attracting international attention and funding for further innovation and experimentation in hazard education and outreach.

Management Structure

An effective management structure is crucial to planning and implementing hazard mitigation plans as well as for preparing for disaster response. While some of the recommendations here are important independent proposals, if implemented in their entirety, the sum will be greater than the parts. Thus, coordination and oversight are essential. Nevertheless, it is not the intent to propose additional layers of bureaucracy, both for fiscal and programmatic reasons. Many of the policies called for in this plan can be implemented by existing government departments—they simply need to be properly oriented to undertake current and new programs with disaster mitigation and prevention in mind. Furthermore, a new bureaucracy could inhibit many of the community-based initiatives proposed in this plan.

When governments are forced to respond to natural disasters, agencies and organizations must quickly cooperate to enact coordinated actions. This type of cooperation could work for the planning for natural-hazard mitigation as well. Therefore, a Presidential Commission on Disaster Preparedness and Response should be created that would signal and provide leadership from the top, but assign both planning and response largely to existing organizations.

At an organizational level, the Commission would be run by an executive director, who would have two assistant directors—a civilian official responsible for hazard mitigation (that is, continuous long-range planning), and a military officer responsible for disaster response (that is, action under emergency conditions). While in many cases mitigation and response measures can overlap, one aiding the other, in terms of planning and implementation they are largely separate activities. In the Venezuelan context, the programs needed for mitigation are generally implemented by civilian government agencies and local community groups, while the manpower and logistics needed to respond adequately to natural disasters are largely located within military institutions and domestic and international nongovernmental organizations (NGOs).

Aiding the executive director would be two independent offices—one focusing on research and information (and linked with those doing hazard awareness and disaster preparedness education, as well as with those working on *barrio* integration), and the other on finance and fundraising, with an emphasis on securing monies from the international community and suggesting ways to raise funds internally for mitigation and preparedness. It is in these two broad areas, information and funding, that mitigation and preparedness often overlap.

The section of the Commission responsible for hazard mitigation should work directly with the various government ministries and independent government agencies responsible for the built environment and social policies and welfare. Each one of these ministries and agencies would create a department of hazard mitigation, which, upon direction from the Commission, would ensure that all activities of the ministry are consistent with proper hazard-mitigation procedures. In addition, this sector would have an office expressly dedicated to ensuring that NGOs and community groups are fully integrated into the planning and implementation of hazard-mitigation policies.

The section of the Commission responsible for disaster response should have at its disposal the resources of both Defensa Civil and Guardia Nacional. It would also, through an NGO/Community Group liaison office, be able to integrate the expertise and abilities of these types of organizations as well as call upon, in the event of a disaster, experts from other government departments through an additional liaison office. Within this sector it is crucial that clear lines of authority, responsibility, and procedure be established, practiced, and monitored.

Cost-Benefit Considerations

Preparing a city for a disaster is a major task, requiring a serious investment in preparedness, mitigation, and emergency response measures. Before undertaking such a project, a full cost-benefit analysis would allow priorities to be defined and effective programs to be structured. Such an effort was not possible to accomplish in this preliminary study, but should be considered in a full-scale disaster preparedness effort. In the meantime, based upon past experiences in other cities, some estimates can be made as to the losses incurred by major earthquake events, both in terms of property damage and loss of life. This point can be illustrated by exploring the impact of magnitude 5, 6, and 7 earthquakes in a city whose physical assets are valued at US$100 billion (table 5.2).

These figures are limited to physical losses as well as losses associated with suspended use and service after a seismic event. They do not address the loss of life, which can be much more difficult to estimate. Though the benefits of preparedness, mitigation, and emergency response are nearly impossible to quantify, the costs associated with these activities can be estimated. In order to make the process more cost effective, it is necessary to first inventory all existing buildings and infrastructure.

These structures and systems, summarized in our action plan, can then be prioritized for retrofitting and other mitigation measures. A system of "rapid screen-

Table 5.2. Studio estimates for the order of magnitude of losses for a generic city whose assets are valued at US $100 billion. Approximate losses are given for three earthquake magnitudes. Actual losses can vary widely depending on geology, fragility of structures, and the location of the earthquake relative to the center of the city. Estimates are based on observed losses from recent earthquakes in several countries.

Assumed Asset Value: US $100 billion

earthquake magnitude:	*recurrence period:*	*percent loss:*	*dollar loss:*
5	10 years	< 0.1%	< $0.1 billion
6	10–100 years	1-5%	$1–5 billion
7	100+ years	10-20%	$10–20 billion

ing," which is now underway in the United States, allows qualified professionals to observe any structure from the outside and to enter information into a standardized form via portable computer. This allows an engineer to cover a lot of territory in a short period of time, and information is directly transmitted to those making systems decisions. This is a relatively low-cost approach that has enormous long-term benefits.

Constructing new buildings to withstand natural disasters is essential to lowering the future cost of preparing a city for natural disaster or of rebuilding it. On average, the added cost associated with building seismic resistant structures from the start is estimated at 4 percent. This figure varies depending upon location, hazard, and type of structure. This can be compared to the cost of retrofitting, which can be as high as 25–30 percent of the replacement value.

Instituting a system of disaster insurance means that the financial burden of a disaster is shifted away from the victims themselves alone. The insurance industry could be tied in to mortgage lending, permits, and financing in order to insure that each new structure built in Venezuela is properly insured in the event of a disaster.

Studio estimates for the order of magnitude of losses for a generic city whose assets are valued at US$100 billion. Approximate losses are given for three earthquake magnitudes. Actual losses can vary widely depending on geology, fragility of structures, and relative location of the earthquake to the center of the city. Estimates are based on observed losses from recent earthquakes in several countries.

Future Disaster Risk Management Tasks for Caracas

The Urban Planning Studio has made largely qualitative assessments of the most important hazards to which Caracas is exposed, and it has provided some sense of the social, economic, and physical risks that need to be managed to transform Caracas into a disaster-resilient metropolis for the 21st century. But before realistic disaster risk management policies for this region can be implemented, it will be necessary to repeat this effort in a fully quantitative mode. Such an effort will require fully probabilistic methodologies of hazard and risk assessment; cost-benefit analyses; and the use of improved, more comprehensive datasets on the physical, demographic, social, and economic characteristics of the region. We briefly list some of the key methodologies that will need to be applied for such an effort.

Quantitative Risk Assessment

Risk is generally defined as the product of three locally varying factors, integrated or summed over the region or subjects of interest. The three elements are assets, hazard, and fragility of the assets to the hazard. As an equation, one can write this definition of risk:

Risk = Regional Sum of the Local Products of
(Assets x Hazard x Fragility)

The assets are taken as the (dollar) value of any of the objects or subjects at risk. They can be lives lost, or they can be the replacement value of built structures such as buildings, their contents, or infrastructure. It is easier to estimate the value of physical structures, and, hence, compute the losses from physical damage to the built environment. It is much harder to estimate the indirect economic losses that follow from physical damage, not to speak of the even more difficult estimation of the intangible losses such as loss of lives or the impact on the culture and social fabric from natural catastrophes.

The *hazard,* as described above, is the level of the hazard parameter at each location of an exposed asset, likely to be exceeded at a given probability level. If there are multiple perils (floods, earthquakes, landslides), then the above risk equation has to be computed for each hazard and chosen exceedance probability separately, and the losses from the different types of hazards must be added to obtain a combined multihazard risk at this exceedance probability. When the losses are calculated at different exceedance probabilities, one can construct a *probabilistic loss or risk curve* (Loss vs. Annual Probability of Exceedance). The averaged total of annualized losses[24] is related to the area under the risk curve.

The third variable is the *fragility* of a given asset to the given hazard. Fragility is defined as the fraction of the asset's replacement value that was damaged and, hence, lost. A fragility of 1 represents a total loss, and a fragility of 0 means no damage, and, hence, no loss. The fragility varies for each hazard and hazard level, and as a function of the type of asset. For the same shaking level, an adobe building may collapse, a concrete building may show cracks, and a well-built steel building may have no damage. But for the most severe shaking, all three types of structures may collapse.

Modern computer-based techniques have been developed to quantify the risks according to the above relation for risk. The losses can be quantified either for given scenario events, or as annualized average losses to the region. Physical losses, economic losses, and demands in terms of emergency resources needed (for example, available versus needed hospital beds; amount of debris to be removed; functionality of infrastructure systems as a function of reconstruction time; and so on) are useful outputs of these computer-aided risk assessment tools.

Developing Optimal Risk Management Plans

Once the risks from natural hazards to the region are quantified, then one can develop informed plans to manage these risks and to mitigate them. Many options are available, ranging from just waiting and then dealing with the *consequences* of *unmitigated* events; to a mixture of disaster preparedness and mitigation; to trying to largely eliminate the risks through radical rebuilding and restructuring the communities in a truly disaster-resilient way at obviously high up-front social and financial costs. In reality, some optimization will take place that attempts to balance affordable costs to the community with the achievable benefits of risk and loss reduction.

To achieve such optimization in disaster mitigation on sound scientific/technical grounds, it will be necessary to:

- Build the institutional and personal knowledge infrastructure for risk assessment and management so it can become effective in those populated regions of a country that are most threatened by natural hazards and disasters.
- Establish sound data acquisition and data management programs on the natural environment and processes that are needed to quantify at least the most important hazards (that is, meteorological, hydrological, seismic, and geological data).
- Assemble databases for the exposed assets (or future planned assets) and their current (or planned) fragilities to the various hazards.
- Based on the quantitative risk assessments, develop indigenous, cost-effective policy options to advance optimized, region-specific, natural-hazard, and risk-mitigation procedures that are worth financing and that contribute to disaster-resilient sustainable development.

Specific Recommendations for Caracas

As can be seen from the previous section, those who are planning, building, and administering the city of Caracas and the country of Venezuela have many tasks ahead of them if they are to realize the goal of creating a city that is prepared to withstand natural disasters. It is difficult to argue that certain tasks are more essential than others. It is hard to imagine a resilient and strategic road network being built without the issues of access and land use in the *barrios* being adequately addressed, for example. Yet we are certain that one thing needs to be done first. This planning exercise needs to be duplicated, in Caracas, on a larger scale, and by those who

[24] Summing up the annualized loss contributions from all probability levels.

have a better understanding of the issues surrounding implementation than we do. It cannot be stressed enough that the plan offered here is more an example of the issues that need to be addressed than a prescription that should be followed. Our data were limited—terribly so in some cases—and the numerous assumptions that we have had to make to conclude this plan may have caused it to have some fatal flaws.

Because of these data inadequacies, such a full-scale, natural-hazard, mitigation-planning task would have to begin with a better set of data. In the science section of this publication, we have already outlined some of the issues that need to be addressed in this area, such as obtaining more accurate measurements of current plate motion and rainfall rates, a better historical record of major earthquakes and debris flow events, and a more complete methodology for determining the relationship between soil type and the magnitude of earth shaking and debris flows.

Similarly, the city's infrastructure and housing need to be completely inventoried, with particular attention paid to building conditions and how they intersect with the hazard risks for each individual location. This data collection is just the beginning of what we see as an integrated implementation timeline that simultaneously works on many levels in a diverse set of areas. Each of these areas—infrastructure, housing and land use, scientific inquiry, education, administration—should be addressed immediately; furthermore, each area has some short-term goals that both address particular problems and further the completion of some medium- and long-term goals as well.

The recommendations and goals we have arrived at require many people to begin to make hazard planning a part of their daily lives at both work and home. They also call for important steps to be made in areas that are not in the traditional domain of hazard planning. But in this way, all those concerned with the health and welfare of the entire population of Caracas can be part of achieving the overall goal of building a safe and livable city.

Goals and Time Frame

For the different sectors below we propose the following short-, medium-, and long-term goals.

Infrastructure

1–5 years: Inventory existing infrastructure; harden and retrofit the most critical infrastructure such as the road between Caracas and the Vargas coast; develop appropriate building codes considering hazard conditions, building history, and building location; determine the location and programming of new open spaces, critical facilities, and other needed infrastructure.

5–10 years: Harden and retrofit second-tier-risk infrastructure; begin relocation/redundancy schemes for risky areas; strengthen water infrastructure, including the construction of water storage facilities within the valley; construct new open spaces.

10-plus years: Achieve a redundant and resilient road network, water system, power grid and communications infrastructure; relocate all critical facilities currently located in high-risk areas; create open space in all areas where needed; establish critical facilities in all areas where needed.

Housing

1–5 years: Inventory existing structures; develop appropriate building codes; streamline transfer of land tenure; organize technical design units and the distribution of safe materials; begin hardening and retrofitting of residential units; plan and organize relocation strategies.

5–10 years: Continue *barrio* and infrastructure upgrading; fully integrate the work of technical units; development of hazard-based zoning code; complete relocation; continue transfer of land title; begin to establish a real estate market in tandem with title transfer.

10-plus years: Legitimate land title; low-interest-loan options; working real estate market.

Scientific Inquiry

1–5 years: Data mining; exchanges between professionals and technicians; purchase of appropriate technology.

5–10 years: Complete set of accurate hazard maps; established system for ongoing data gathering, hazard mapping and data analysis; ongoing information exchange.

10-plus years: Hazard information clearinghouse for scientific community and others interested in the field.

In the area of scientific inquiry, we propose the following short-, medium-, and long-term goals.

Public Education and Outreach

1–5 years: Establish hazard curriculum in schools; begin public outreach/education programs; mainstream the hazard message into pop culture; begin public service announcements via mass media; hazard drills, family, school, community, business hazard plans; Begin training for professionals (builders, architects, health care, and legal) on hazard-specific issues.

5–10 years: Hazard message mainstreamed into schools; develop training programs for the technical design units, the public and other professionals; establish trained volunteer corps.

10-plus years: Make Caracas a regional center for hazard education and research.

Administration

1–5 years: Establish constitutional and legal legitimacy for disaster management; convene meetings of experts in all related fields; establish a funding authority for disaster management; mobilize grassroots community groups; train military and civil defense forces in disaster response.

5–10 years: Establish a hazard-coordination authority with clear legal and organizational authority; set up hazard mitigation groups within each government ministry; streamline funding through centralized system.

10-plus years: Clearly organized management system in place with active participation of elected officials, military, community groups, local and international nongovernmental organizations, the scientific community, and the general public.

References

Audemard, F. A., et al. 2000. Map and Database of Quaternary Faults in Venezuela and its Offshore Regions. United States Geological Survey Open File Report 00-018. Reston, VA: USGS.

Larsen, M. C., et al. 2001. Venezuelan Debris Flow and Flash Flood Disaster of 1999 Studied. *Eos Trans., American Geophysical Union:* 82: 572–573.

Papageorgiou, A. S., and J. Kim. 1991. Study of the Propagation and Amplification of Seismic Waves in Caracas Valley with Reference to the 29 July 1967 Earthquake: SH Waves. *Bulletin of the Seismological Society of America* 81(6): 2214–2233.

Salcedo, D., and J. Ortas. 1992. Investigation of the Slide at the Southern Abutment Hill of Viaduct No. 1, Caracas-La Guaira Highway, Venezuela. *Proceedings of the Sixth International Symposium, Landslides,* 189–198.

Salcedo, D. 2001. Aspectos Socio-económicos y Socio-ambientales de los Flujos Catastróficos de Diciembre 1999 en el Estado Vargas y el Area Metropolitana de Caracas. *Proceedings of III Panamerican Symposium on Landslides,* Cartagena, Colombia, 291–317.

Salcedo, D. 2000. The December 1999 Catastrophic Debris Flows at Vargas State and Caracas, Venezuela, Characteristics and Lessons Learned. *Proceedings of the XVI Seminario Sociedad, Venezolana de Geotecnia,* 28–175.

Chapter 6

Reducing the Impacts of Floods through Early Warning and Preparedness: A Pilot Study for Kenya

Hussein Gadain, Nicolas Bidault, Linda Stephen, Ben Watkins, Maxx Dilley, and Nancy Mutunga

Kenya is a drought-prone country and is reasonably prepared for drought emergencies. However, Kenya is also prone to very serious flood risks, especially in the lowlands in northeastern Kenya—particularly, the Garissa, Ijara, and Tana River districts; the areas surrounding Lake Victoria (Nyanza Province); and Nairobi. Despite warnings of strong El Niño-related weather anomalies in 1997, Kenya was unprepared for the floods that occurred in 1997 and 1998. The magnitude of flooding necessitated a massive relief operation. Ironically, floods are often more destructive in a low-rainfall environment where drainage infrastructure, control, and coping strategies tend to be under-developed. In the Tana River basin, El Niño 1997–98 floods displaced thousands. Properties were destroyed and the livelihoods of the riverine population were severely impacted.

An impact analysis of the El Niño flood event clearly demonstrates that Kenyans were inadequately prepared to cushion these adverse impacts. Up to that point, the Government of Kenya (GoK) had neither a flood disaster management policy nor an institutional framework to monitor and manage flood disasters. This has had serious implications as floods have recurred, especially in western Kenya, causing displacement and death on an annual basis.

The Government of Kenya is trying to strengthen its disaster management capability, with an emphasis on preparedness and risk management. A flood contingency planning activity for Kenya is already underway. Data resources are reasonable, but data management and analysis remain weak. While much has been achieved in modeling floods and predicting climate, less is known about the potential impacts of floods on people and livelihoods.

The Tana River basin (figure 6.1) is one of the biggest river basins in Kenya, with an estimated river length of 1,000 kilometers (km) and a drainage area of approximately 126,000 km^2. It runs from the Aberdare and Mount Kenya ranges of central Kenya through the arid and semiarid lands in the eastern part of the country and into the Indian Ocean through a fan-shaped Delta, which covers approximately 1,300 km^2. The Delta has unique, fragile, and vulnerable ecological characteristics. The Tana basin supports the livelihoods of more than four million people; most of them are pastoralists, farmers, and fisher folk. It is the only permanent river in this extremely dry region and constitutes a vital water resource for all sectors of the human population. At the middle and lower parts of the Tana basin lies a flat flood plain, 20 km wide. Irrigated agriculture is practiced along the river with pastoralists occupying the rest of the basin. The lower reaches of the river pass through semiarid land populated by pastoralists and riverine people. The delta also has a high tourism potential.

Over the last 50 years, the Tana basin has undergone major changes in land use and cover. The loss of forest in the headwaters to smallholder farming and timber harvests has increased surface runoff and flooding during the rainy seasons and sediment deposition in the storage reservoirs, drastically decreasing dry-season flows. The construction of dams for hydropower generation in the late 1960s, 1970s, and 1980s resulted in decreased outflows downstream during the dry period with high outflows during the high-flows period. This resulted in spill-water levels that severely compromised

Figure 6.1. Location map of Tana River basin in Kenya with the river gauging stations

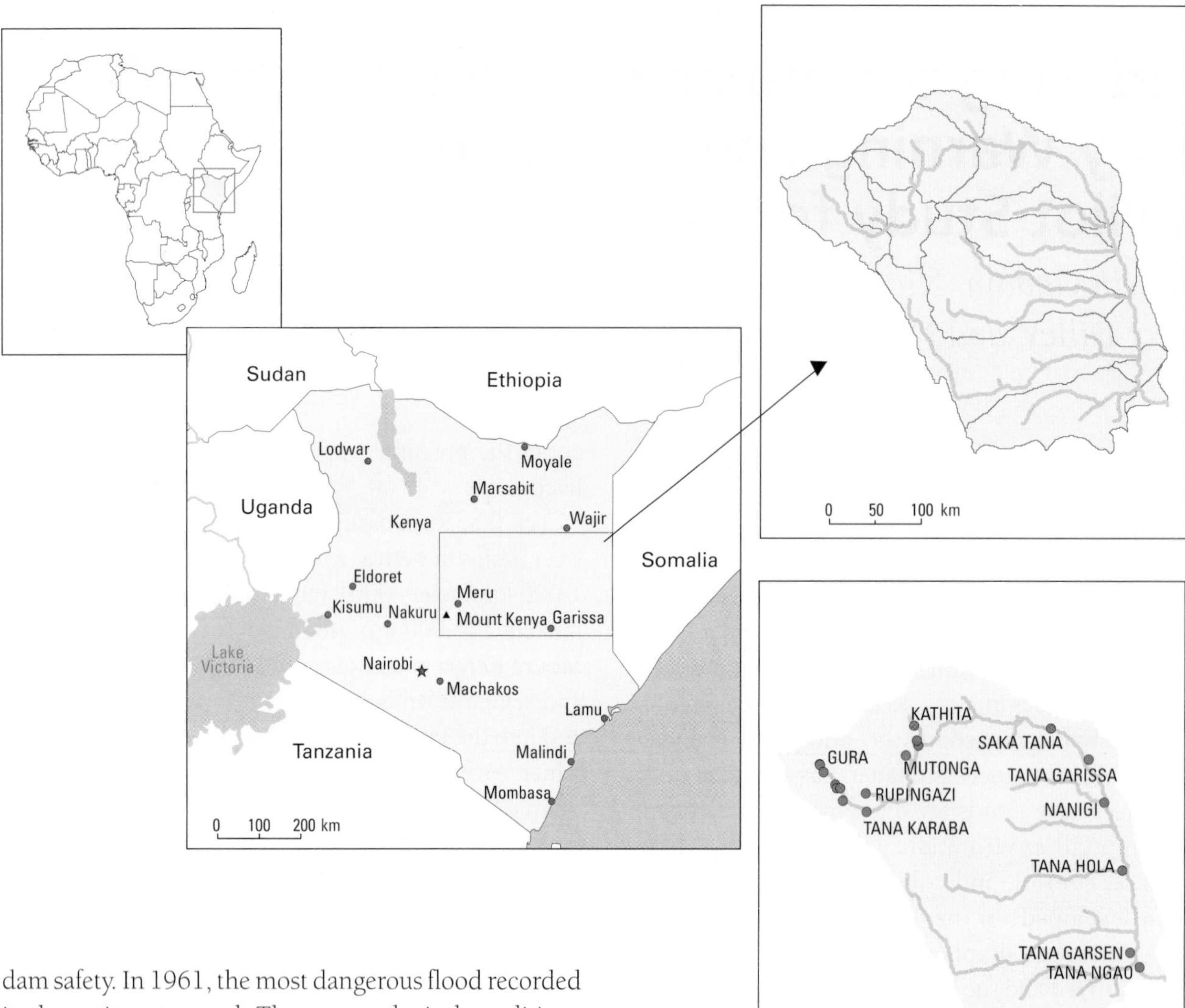

dam safety. In 1961, the most dangerous flood recorded in the region occurred. The meteorological conditions associated with this extremely wet period were experienced over a wide area. In the middle and lower sections of the Tana basin, however, the impacts of the flood were probably more severe, with the Tana River district considered as the most seriously affected Food and Agriculture Organization ([FAO] 1967). The impacts of the 1997–98 El Niño events were less than those of the 1961 flood. This is mainly attributed to the dam construction process that took place in the 1970s and 1980s.

Watershed planning and management in the Tana basin has traditionally been initiated and implemented at the national level with little subnational-level input. In 1967, the Government of Kenya initiated development of Tana River water resources for hydropower development, flood control, and irrigation (FAO 1967). Some of these activities were not fully implemented, however. Only hydropower potential was fully investigated. To date, five major reservoirs have been built on the upper reaches of the Tana: Kindaruma (1968), Kamburu (1975), Gitaru (1978), Masinga (1981), and Kiambere (1988). Dam construction has had a major influence on the river's downstream flow and physical characteristics, most notably through regulating water flow and decreasing the frequency and magnitude of flooding. The Masinga dam is the biggest storage reservoir for hydropower generation in Kenya, and also is the main cause of downstream flooding during the high-flow periods. When the dam spills, a huge amount of water is released. The spill waters from the dam cause flooding downstream in Garissa town and parts of the Ijara and Tana River districts. The question of "who will be flooded downstream?" still remains, despite efforts in recent years by the Kenya Power Generation Company (KenGen) to issue warnings to the downstream settlements through radio, TV, and newspapers; through daily dissemination of information on dam levels; and through provision of data on spill levels to the disaster management unit in Kenya.

This study focuses on the middle and lower parts of the Tana River basin that are prone to recurrent floods: mainly the Tana River and Garissa districts. Using a semidistributed hydrologic model, this study aims to quantify the economic losses arising from flood events using flood mapping as an input to livelihoods and economic analysis. The outcomes of this study are flood hazard maps linked with different livelihoods for use in future flood-contingency planning and preparedness in the Tana River and Garissa districts. The case study uses a semidistributed stream flow model and flood hazard maps to generate flood-level scenarios for the lower Tana River Basin, where emergency assistance is frequently required due to flood events. Flood impact risks to the population and livelihoods are assessed using a livelihood zoning dataset that includes populated places. The results are interpreted for use in contingency planning and preparedness.

Objectives

The overall objective of this study is to contribute towards sustainable flood preparedness for improved livelihoods protection against any future flood events. The target beneficiaries are local communities that live along the *riverine* and flood plains in the Tana River and Garissa districts. This includes farmers, pastoralists, and other stakeholders in the basin. The study aims to provide better tools for contingency and response planning; management of water, agriculture, and livestock; and awareness creation.

Other specific objectives include the following:

- Generation of flood hazard maps using a semidistributed hydrologic model and high-resolution terrain and satellite data;
- Linkage of the flood hazard maps with livelihoods along the flood plains in the Tana River and other infrastructure data to assess differential flood impacts;
- Scientifically tested strategies to guide policy, contingency, and response planners in the flood early warning process in the Tana River basin; and
- Increased capacity among local and national institutions for sustainable planning and management of the Tana River waters. This objective is running in parallel to this study and being handled by the U.S. Geological Survey and the Drought Monitoring Center in Nairobi (DMCN).

Study Area

The study area encompasses the Tana River and Garissa districts in Kenya (figure 6.2).

Tana River District

The Tana River District in the Coast Province is divided into seven administrative divisions with a total area of 38,694 km^2. The topography, drainage pattern, and soil contribute to a potentially large areal extent of flooding. The district is generally an undulating plain, which slopes southeast with an altitude ranging between 0.0 and 200 meters above sea level. The main geographical feature of this district is the Tana River. The large flood basin, which ranges from 2 to 40 km in width, provides fertile arable land and is the economic backbone of the district. The hinterland has seasonal streams (lagas), which provide wet-season grazing areas and serve as sources of inlets for earth pans. Soils in the Tana River district are divided into two groups: well-drained, sandy soils ranging in color from white to red, and silty, clayey, poorly drained soils that are gray and black in color. The nomadic pastoralists—who keep large herds of cattle, goats, and sheep—are the main inhabitants of the hinterland. In 1997, during a three-month period, the district received over 1,200 mm of El Niño-related rainfall, which was triple its annual average. The resultant floods destroyed many houses, damaged infrastructure, swept away crops, and killed livestock.

Figure 6.2. Location map of the Tana River and Garissa Districts with coverage of the Tana River basin in the Garissa District

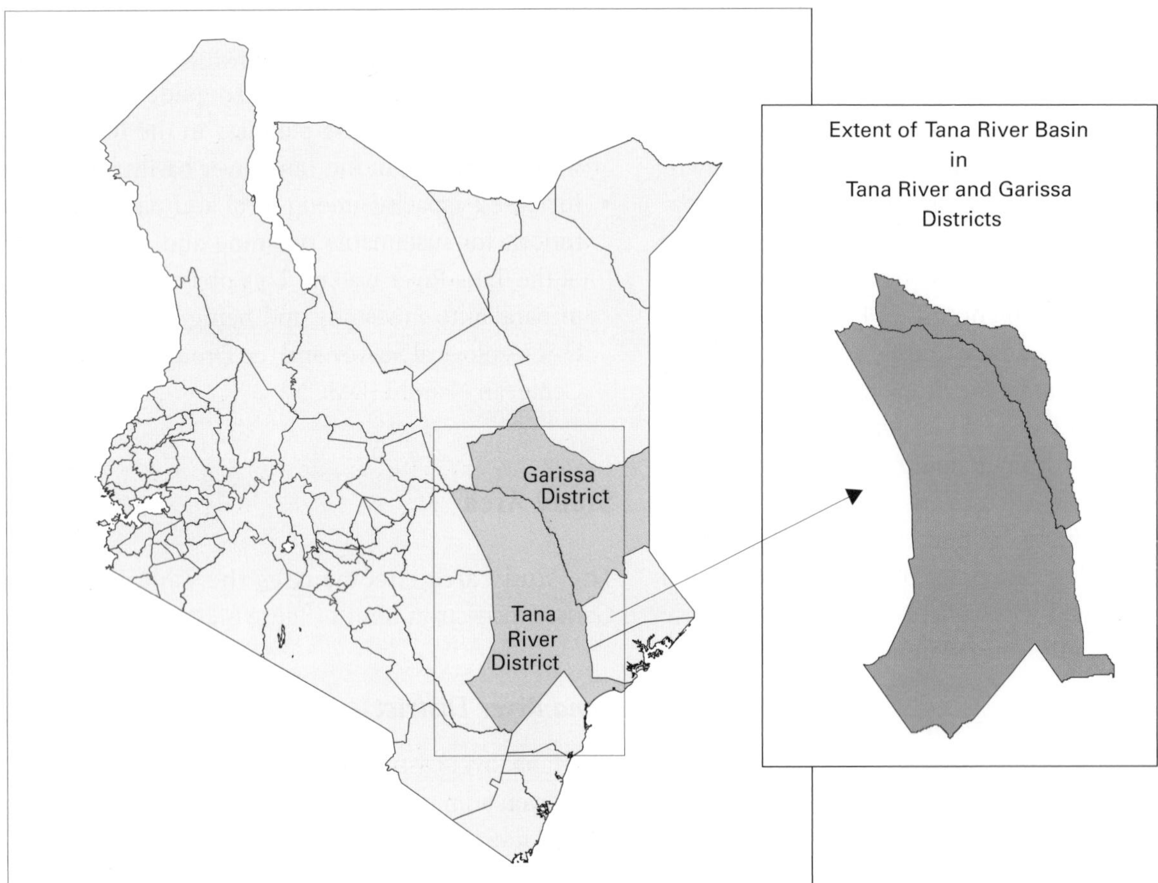

Garissa District

The Garissa district is one of three districts that make up the North Eastern Province of Kenya. The total area of the district is 43,931 km^2, and it is divided into 14 administrative divisions. Most of Garissa consists of nearly level and featureless plains. The plains generally slope toward the southeast and south from about 300 m above mean sea level to gradients of 0.5 to 0.7 meters per kilometer. Most of the district is drained by broad, shallow, and poorly defined streams that flow for only a few hours at a time, once or twice per year. The Tana River crosses the district to its outlet in the Indian Ocean. Soils in Garissa are divided into two groups: well-drained, sandy soils ranging in color from white to red, and silty, clayey, poorly drained soils that are gray and black in color.

The total population of the district is 231,000, according to 1999 census population projections. Almost 60 percent of the population is below 20 years of age, and about 40 percent of the population resides within the environs of Garissa town. The district is predominately inhabited by Somali people who traditionally practice livestock-keeping.

The climate of Garissa is semiarid, and the long-term average rainfall is about 300 mm. Rainfall normally occurs in high concentrations and intensities, allowing temporal accumulation of excess moisture for drought-adapted vegetation and surface-water storage. Since 1961, average annual rainfall has been above the mean rainfall of the previous 30 years (UNICEF 1998). Prior to the 1997/98 El Niño rains, the greatest rainfall events occurred in 1961 and 1968, when an average of 920 mm was measured. Unusually heavy rains occurred in 1997, totaling 1,027 mm; 925 mm occurred between October and December 1997. This was a huge amount of rainfall for an area receiving an annual average of 300 mm.

Impacts of the 1997 El Niño Floods

During El Niño-related floods in the month of October 1997, the catchments of the Tana River received heavy rainfall. As a result, the river levels rose within the first 10 days of October. By the end of the first week of November 1997, the river had risen by more than 4 meters to three times its average level (UNICEF 1998). The peak of the flood wave was in December when the river reached 6.65 meters and eventually covered the measuring staff. The effect of this forced the riverine people to flee for their lives. The river maintained flood levels for more than three months. In southern Garissa, most of the flooding was caused by direct rainfall (figure 6.3). Virtually all the farms along the river, pump- and flood-receding irrigation systems, and water supply systems were swept away during the peak floods. Traveling was extremely difficult; people were marooned in camps for more than three months; and health conditions were very poor, with high outbreaks of rashes and cholera, which severely effected on children.

Hydrologic Model

The U.S. Geological Survey Earth Resources Observation Systems Data Center (USGS/EROS/EDC), through its support to the U. S. Agency for International Development (USAID), Famine Early Warning System Network (FEWS NET), is implementing activities related to hydrological modeling and flood forecasting in the Greater Horn of Africa (GHA). The activity is being implemented by a number of international organizations and other partners in the region.

FEWS NET, in cooperation with the USGS/EROS, has undertaken efforts to enhance flood preparedness. With hydrologic modeling techniques, it is possible to better predict and react to such events. The FEWS NET Geo-Spatial Stream Flow Model (GeoSFM) (Artan et al. 2001) is a geo-spatial model based on the use of satellite remote sensing, numerical weather forecast fields, and geographic datasets describing the land surface. The model is currently operational in Eastern and Southern Africa. Since the severe flooding in Kenya that resulted from the El Niño rains in 1997/98, USGS and FEWS NET have begun to regularly monitor flooding in Eastern Africa. The Tana River has been monitored in this process since 2001.

The FEWS NET hydrological model was built to provide a continuous simulation of stream flow, on a daily time step, for approximately 5,600 basins on the African continent. The model is a physically based, catchment-scale hydrologic model (semidistributed hydrologic model). It consists of a GIS-based module used for model input and data preparation, and the rainfall-runoff simulation model. The rainfall-runoff model is comprised of a module for soil water accounting that produces surface and subsurface runoff for each subbasin, an upland headwater basins routing module, and a major river routing module. The model also generates flood inundation maps for specified river depths at different cross sections. To allow for evacuation and relief services, the maps can easily be linked with livelihoods and infrastructure to provide hazard maps that indicate, three days in advance, which areas and population centers would likely be inundated.

Data and Methodology

Data

The data used in this study to create the flood hazard maps consist of approximately 150 topographic maps at a 1:50,000 scale. The maps were scanned, digitized, and geo-referenced in a GIS to form a mosaic of contours, spot heights, and rivers at 20-meter intervals (figure 6.4). Using procedures developed by the Environmental Systems Research Institute (ESRI), finer terrain data were generated from the mosaic to form a Digital Elevation Model (DEM) containing a 100-meter spatial resolution (figure 6.4). The DEM was further processed to remove topographically incorrect sinks to obtain a hydrologically corrected DEM for use in the creation of the flood hazard maps.

Although the DEM was created from 1:50,000-scale maps, the contour interval is coarse (10-m interval near the coast). This caused outliers in the SFM analysis in low-lying areas due to the flat terrain toward the ocean in relation to the contour interval.

Data on observed stream flow were available as gauge-height observations at Garissa through the Department of Water in the Ministry of Water Resources covering

Figure 6.3. Rainfall for selected stations during El Niño 1997–98

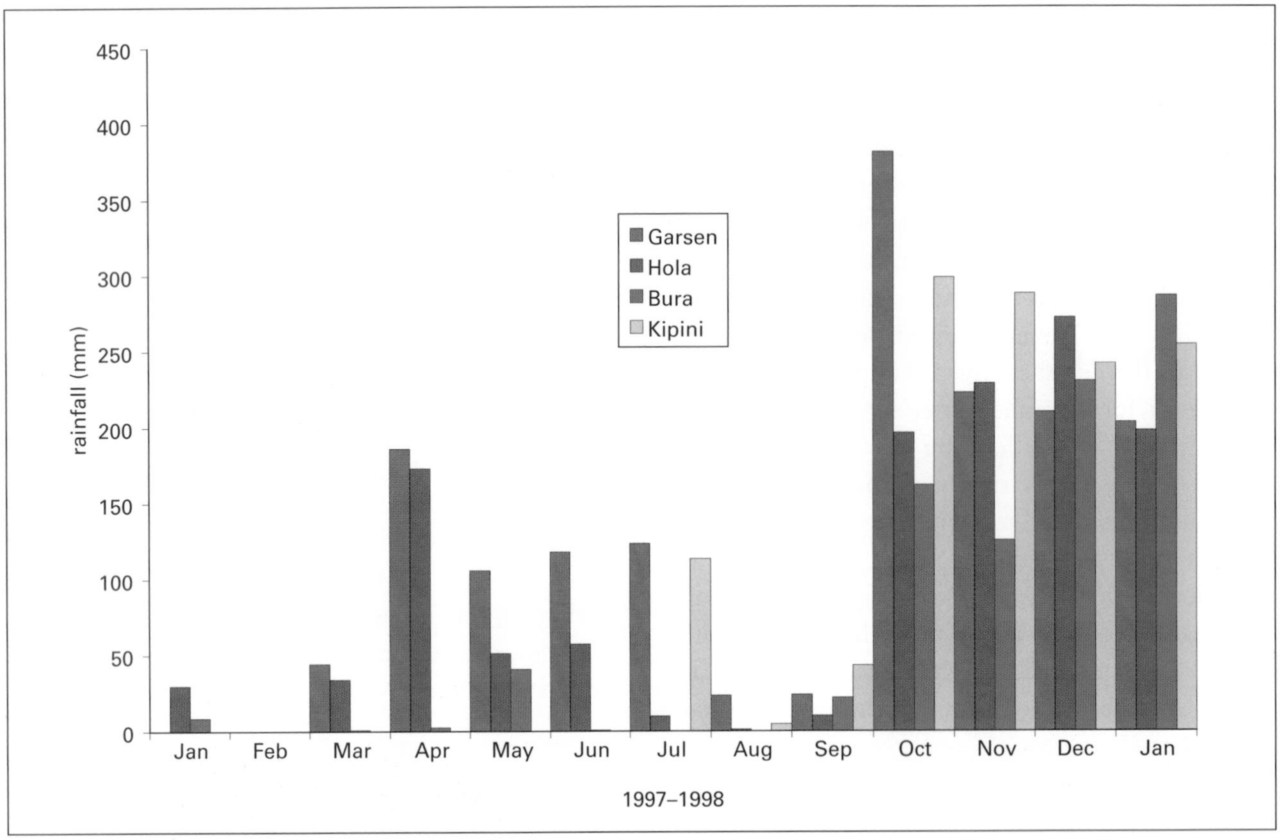

Source: Kenya Meteorological Department

the period 1933–2001. These data (figure 6.5) show the historical variability of river levels before and after the construction of the dams upstream of Garissa. From the figure, it is clear that the river recorded high levels during the 1961 and 1997/98 periods, when severe flooding occurred in the middle and lower reaches of the river. Satellite Rainfall Estimates (RFE) for the same period were available through USGS. The U.S. National Oceanic and Atmospheric Administration Climate Prediction Center (NOAA/CPC) developed these data for the USAID-funded FEWS NET project starting in 1995 (Xie et al. 1998). Other spatial data on terrain, soils, land use, and land cover were available through USGS as well.

The data used for impacts analysis were obtained from the World Food Programme Vulnerability Assessment and Mapping unit (WFP/VAM). These data were comprised of a GIS layer on livelihood zones developed by WFP/VAM, FEWS NET Kenya and the Arid Lands Resources Management Project (ALRMP) in the Office of the President (OP) for the whole of Kenya. Data on population centers and schools were digitized by WFP/VAM, and data on administrative boundaries and population came from the latest census in 1999. (These were updated during the 2002 elections by the Central Bureau of Statistics [CBS].)

Stream Flow Modeling

Stream flow modeling was done using the USGS GeoSFM to generate forecast stream flows at Garissa. The model was calibrated for the period from 1995 to 1998. The modeled stream flows mimicked the observed situation to a reasonable level of accuracy, suggesting predictive skill by the model for use in the future for flood forecasting. Model flow estimates were converted into equivalent river stages for mapping of inundated areas, since inundation is more directly related to river stage than to flow. The model efficiency criterion used to judge the model performance was the coefficient of determination, R2, proposed by Nash and Sutcliffe (1970). An R2 of 0.72 was obtained for the calibration period. Since

Figure 6.4. Data used in the creation of the DEM for flood-hazard mapping

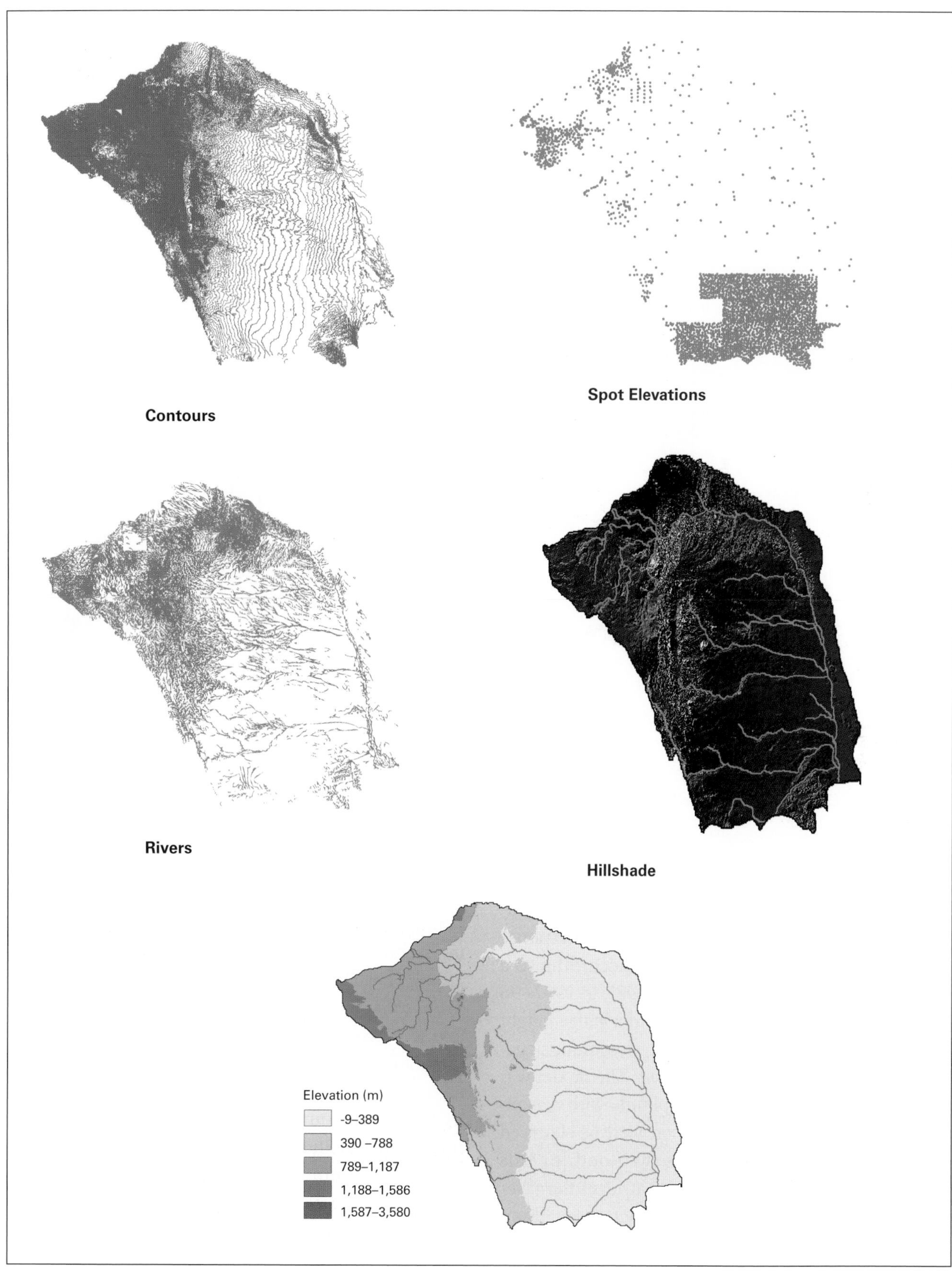

Figure 6.5. Variability of river stages at Garissa Town (1933–2001) with special focus on El Niño 1997–98 heights

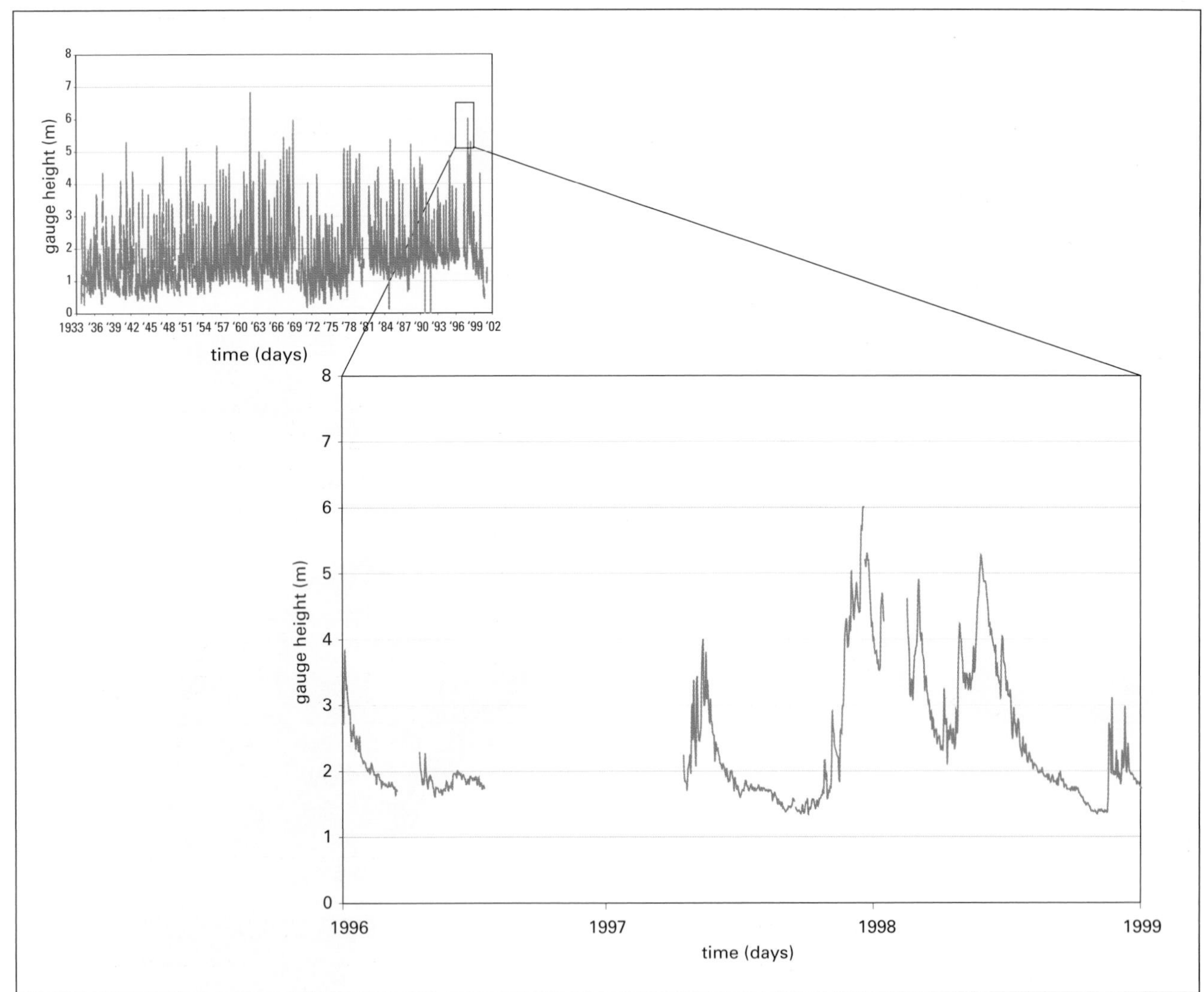

the river is controlled at a series of dams upstream in Garissa, the modeled observed flows are more influenced by the dam releases than by the actual response of the catchment to rainfall events. According to a Ministry of Water report (UNICEF 1998), in 1997–98 the gauge at Garissa washed away and a gauge height of 6.65 meters was observed before the hydraulic structure measuring the water levels failed. The model was able to predict this high flood amplitude with reasonable accuracy (figure 6.6). Since there were no observed gauge heights available during the flood for this period, it is difficult to predict what level the river reached. For this purpose, we restricted our flood mapping to an arbitrary height as is presented below.

Flood Hazard Mapping

Rapid progress has been made in the use of remote sensing techniques for flood inundation mapping. Applications of satellite imagery from optical sensors, including SPOT (Blasco et al. 1992), AVHRR (Zhou et al. 2000), and LANDSAT (Mayer and Pearthree 2002), for flood inundation mapping are well documented. The key limitation of these remote-sensing techniques is their inability to estimate inundation for areas for which there is no existing satellite imagery of the river in a flooded state. Flood inundation maps based on topography are, therefore, useful for flood-warning purposes. One example is the USGS experience in flood forecasting and mapping for Mozambique. In Mozambique, where

Figure 6.6. Stream flow modeling at Garissa (1995–1999)

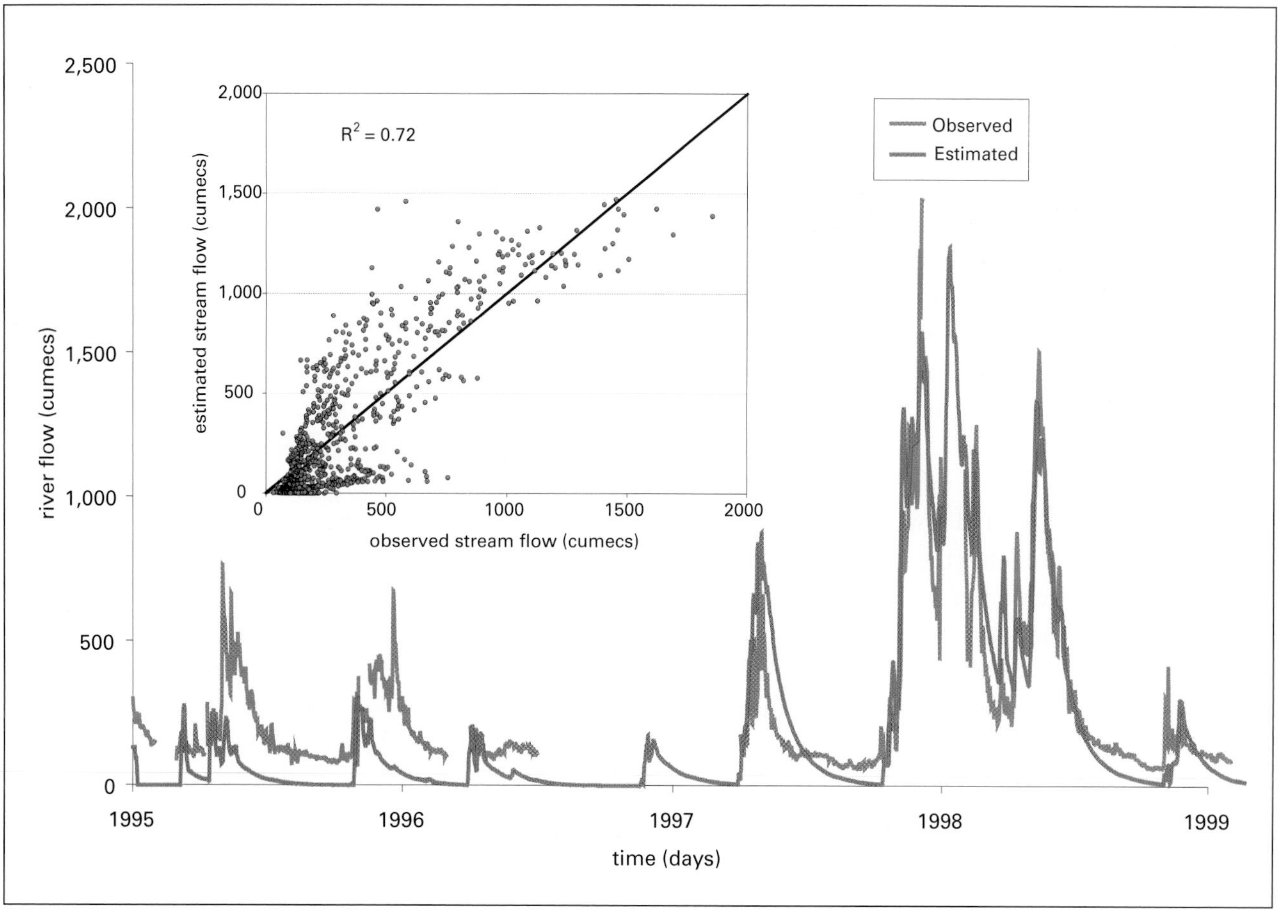

a high resolution DEM was available, a detailed flood-forecasting system was implemented by the local water agency (ARA-Sul) and USGS. Fine-resolution DEM data (90-meter resolution) were created from topographic sheets by the local remote-sensing lab (CENACARTA) and USGS. With the high-resolution DEM data, inundation maps were created and linked with model forecast river levels for flood early-warning purposes. Mild, moderate, and severe flood scenarios were generated and linked to data for settlements, schools, and other livelihood zones. The result was comprehensive information for flood contingency planning, preparedness, and response in Mozambique.

The methodology adopted and implemented in this study was developed and implemented by USGS in Mozambique after the two devastating floods events in 2000 and 2001 (USGS 2003). Most of the analysis and methodology presented in this study is taken from USGS (2003). After correcting topographic sinks in the DEM, the DEM is used in the USGS GeoSFM interface to generate hazard maps for various depth increments in the channel.

The method maps flood inundation from a one-dimensional flow routing model onto a digital elevation model assuming hydraulic connectivity, while respecting the effects of impediments to flow within the area of inundation. The method makes use of the three-dimensional topographic information contained in the DEM. The user identifies the level of water that must be attained in the river channel before increments of the adjacent land surface become inundated.

The DEM is the main data input for terrain analysis. The analysis begins with the establishment of the raster equivalent of the river line, which is the imaginary line connecting the lowest points along the river channel. The direction of flow, characterized by the eight-direction pour-point scheme (Jenson and Domingue 1988), is computed. Each DEM grid cell is assigned one of the eight compass directions based on the assumption that water flows in the direction of steepest descent. River cells are identified by computing flow accumulation— defined as a grid cell count of the upstream area—followed by an application of a minimum threshold of the contributing area to differentiate between river cells and non-river cells. The grid cells along the flow path represent the minimum extent of inundation required for creating a raster representation of the river. Assigning an increment depth to all non-river cells within the analysis area creates an incremental flow depth grid. The incremental flow depth grid is then added to the original DEM to create a flow stage grid.

An increment value that is more than the vertical resolution of the original DEM, that is, a 1-meter elevation, results in a disruption of the hydraulic connectivity over the DEM surface through the formation of flow sinks adjacent to the raised river cells. A method is then applied that allows water to be distributed over the land surface in a manner that approximates a natural maintenance of hydraulic connectivity, taking into consideration the newly incremented river stage relative to the ground surface elevation of all surrounding cells.

After each river depth increment is applied, disruptions to hydraulic connectivity are identified by computing flow direction based on the new flow stage grid. This follows the same basic process that was initially used in computing the flow direction grid and the flow path of least topographic resistance from the original DEM. The algorithm assigns a flow direction from a given cell toward whichever one of the neighboring grid cells has the lowest potential energy, whether or not it is a river cell. A disruption to flow (flow sink) is identified whenever a grid cell cannot be assigned a flow direction because all neighboring cells have a higher flow stage or ground surface elevation. The disruption is resolved by simulating the accumulation of water in the flow sink until its stage rises sufficiently for it to discharge to one of the neighboring cells (Hutchinson 1989). A new flow path of least resistance is traced and a raster representation is created.

The depth of flow on each grid cell is subsequently determined by subtracting the original DEM elevations from the hydraulically connected, sink-filled flow stage grid. All cells with flow values of flow depth greater than zero are identified as inundated, while those with values of zero are classified as dry cells. The cells along the flow path of least resistance are also identified as minimally inundated, since the newly established hydraulic conductivity requires flow through these cells. The procedure is done iteratively for multiple depths.

Livelihood Data Collection and Mapping

The livelihood zoning of Kenya was undertaken through interagency collaboration with the objective of collecting, in a cost-effective way, basic livelihood data at the smallest, workable administrative unit: the sub-location (administrative unit six). The sub-location unit covers approximately three kilometers by three kilometers, in which only three to four settlements, on average, can be found.

Three teams were sent to cover a total of 30 districts. In each visit to the districts, the district officials were met, including the District Agricultural Officer (DAO), the District Livestock Officer (DLO), and the District Crops Officer. The officials were given a questionnaire and an A3 map of their district showing the boundaries of the divisions, locations, and sublocations.

The questionnaire was designed to gather basic livelihood data, including the following:

- Main sources of income and food
- Crop production per season
- Livestock and poultry ownership
- Labor patterns
- Expenditure patterns
- Market(s) serving the livelihood zone
- Settlement and migration patterns of the inhabitants of the livelihood zone
- Society and ethnicity
- Historical patterns of hunger
- Hazards and constraints to main economic activities

The officials were asked to identify the different livelihood zones in their respective districts and to answer the questionnaire for each livelihood. This was done in consultation with experienced field staff at sublocation levels. Answers relied on available data, especially for questions concerning crop production. When the data were not available, officials were asked to use their "best guess." This particularly applied to questions on patterns of hunger, hazards, and constraints to main economic activities. For each sublocation, officials were also asked to identify on the map that was provided to them the main livelihood system representative of that sublocation.

Two weeks were given for the completion of the exercise, and the data were sent back to the WFP Kenya office, where they were entered into a database. Mapping outputs were produced with ArcView GIS software.

A total of 78 different and highly specific livelihoods were identified in the 30 districts visited. Data collection for mapping livelihoods in the remaining 40 districts of Kenya is currently underway. The livelihood zoning exercise serves national and district planning in a number of ways. It helps to identify a new unit of analysis—the livelihood zone—at the sub-location level; it improves the ability to analyze and assess the impact of floods, droughts, and other hazards on the population living in the livelihood zone; and it allows more meaningful analysis of price-related, agricultural, and socioeconomic data.

Results

In this analysis, two severe floods were investigated: the 1961 flood and the El Niño of 1997–98. River depths associated with the 1961 flood were the highest river depths recorded over a 70-year period, with a maximum depth of 7.0 meters. The deepest El Niño 1997–98 recorded river depth was 6.65 meters. This occurred on the night of December 3, 1997. According to the Water Department, the river level rose rapidly to three times its long-term average (figure 6.5), forcing people to flee for their lives. A second flood came in January 1998. The river maintained flood levels for more than three months. Although rainfall levels associated with the 1997–98 El Niño were much higher than was the case in 1961, lower river depths were recorded. This is mainly attributed to the Masinga dam, which controls river flow upstream of Garissa town. Massive rainfall associated with the 1997–98 El Niño resulted in severe floods in many parts of the country, including the Tana River basin.

Using the methodology described above for the Tana River basin application, flow depths of 1 to 15 meters were applied in 1-meter increments, resulting in 15 inundation polygons associated with 15 different depths of flow at the channel centerline. These flood maps are not associated with a specific flood; the user can identify the bank levels and generate depth-specific maps. In the Tana River case, flood inundation maps associated with the river depths for the 1961 and El Niño floods were generated. Considering the 1997–98 levels as the highest recorded and comparing this level to the GeoSFM results, hazard maps from the GeoSFM results were generated and considered to be the worst-case scenario for the past 35 years after the construction of the dams upstream in Garissa. A more moderate flood event, taking into consideration the presence of the dams, was also generated.

Historical Floods

To model the impacts on the Tana River and Garissa districts, we intersected the basin boundaries with the two district boundaries. This resulted in a smaller portion of Garissa district contained within the Tana River drainage boundaries (figure 6.2). As explained in the background section, the floods in the Tana River basin are the results of the rainfall runoff from the Mount Kenya area. Before 1968, when the first dam was constructed at Kindaruma, the absence of dams downstream from Mount Kenya resulted in severe flooding in the Tana River basin. Using the stream-flow model, the 1961 flood depths were mapped, as shown in figure 6.7. In order to give an idea of the impact of these severe floods, locations of settlements from the Central Bureau of Statistics (CBS) 1999 census, schools, and roads—which have been recently digitized from the 1:50,000 topographic maps—were overlaid onto the flood map as shown in figures 6.7, 6.8, and 6.9. It is clear that the flooded areas are more contained in the Tana River district, and that the floods due to Tana River flows had less impact in the Garissa district. The floods of the Ewaso Nyiro River, which passes through most of Garissa and drains into the Indian Ocean, had more of an impact in Garissa than did the Tana River (UNICEF report 1998). The low elevation in the middle and lower parts of the basin allows the floods to spread widely,

Figure 6.7. Flood hazard map for the 1961 flood (the case of a severe flood before construction of the dams)

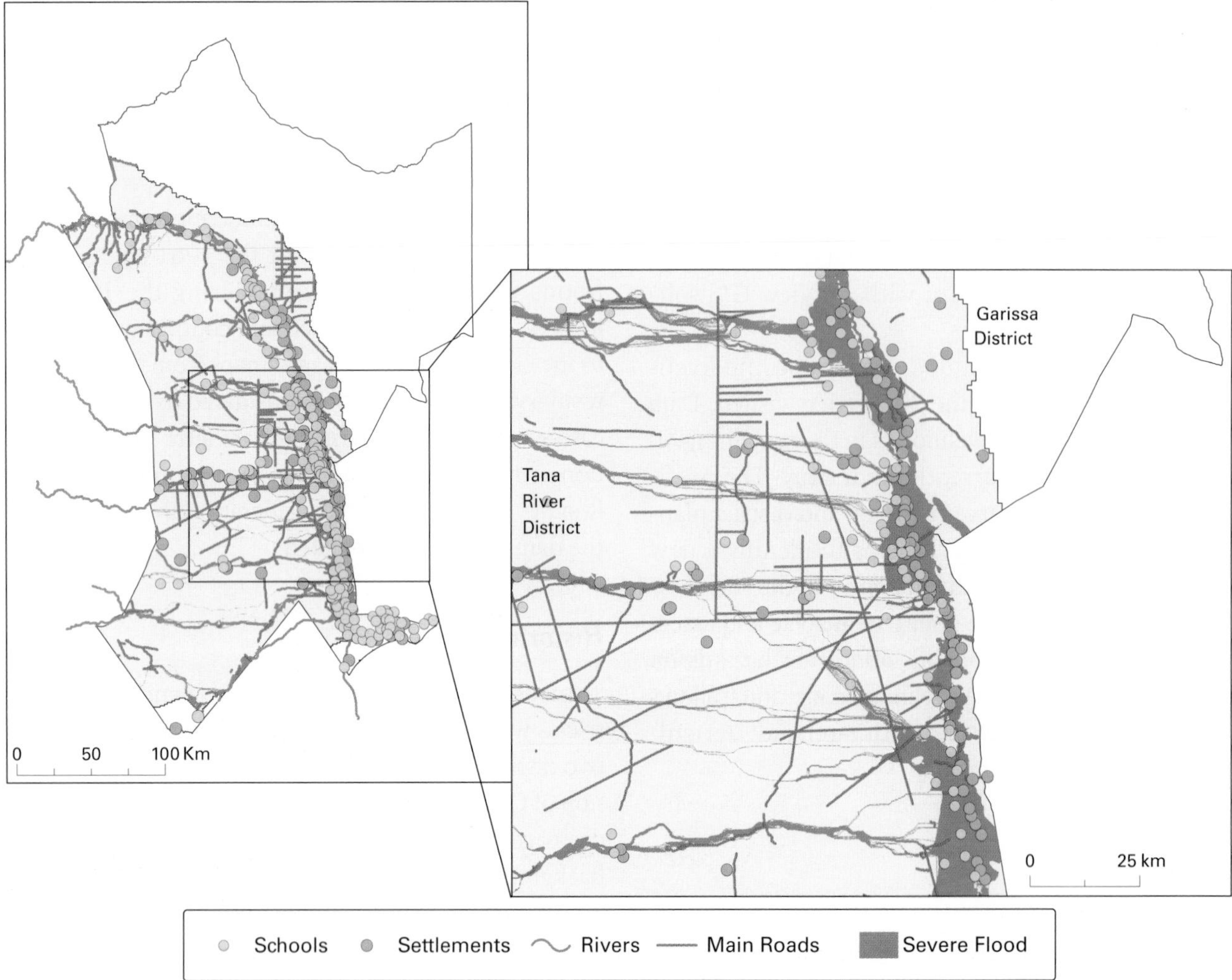

reaching a maximum extent of more than 10 km across at its maximum width in the Tana delta. The wide extent of these floods resulted in a large number of settlements being entirely underwater, as well as main roads being completely submerged, rendering access by road to these areas extremely difficult for emergency-assistance personnel.

El Niño-related flood levels for 1997–98 were also mapped and overlaid with the data for settlements, schools, and main roads, as was done for the 1961 floods (figure 6.8). These floods were quite severe, and a large number of settlements, schools, and portions of main roads were once again underwater. According to the Kenya Meteorological Department, more rainfall was received during the 1997–98 El Niño (figure 6.3) than in 1961. Comparing the two maps, we can observe that the overall flooded area of El Niño was significantly reduced compared to that of the 1961 historical floods. The presence of the dams managed to minimize the extent of El Niño floods in the basin in 1997–98, avoiding an even more serious disaster. However, flooding in the Tana River has become recurrent, with a return period of 1 to 2 years, constituting shocks that hamper sustainable development along the river. Better control of the water spilling over at the dam to minimize the floods would help plan more sustainable use of the land, thus decreasing vulnerability for the groups living in the area.

Flood Scenarios

Areas and Population Affected

As previously mentioned, flooding is a regular occurrence in the Tana River basin, as almost every year inhab-

Figure 6.8. Flood-hazard map for the El Niño 1997/98 flood (a worst-case scenario after the construction of the dams)

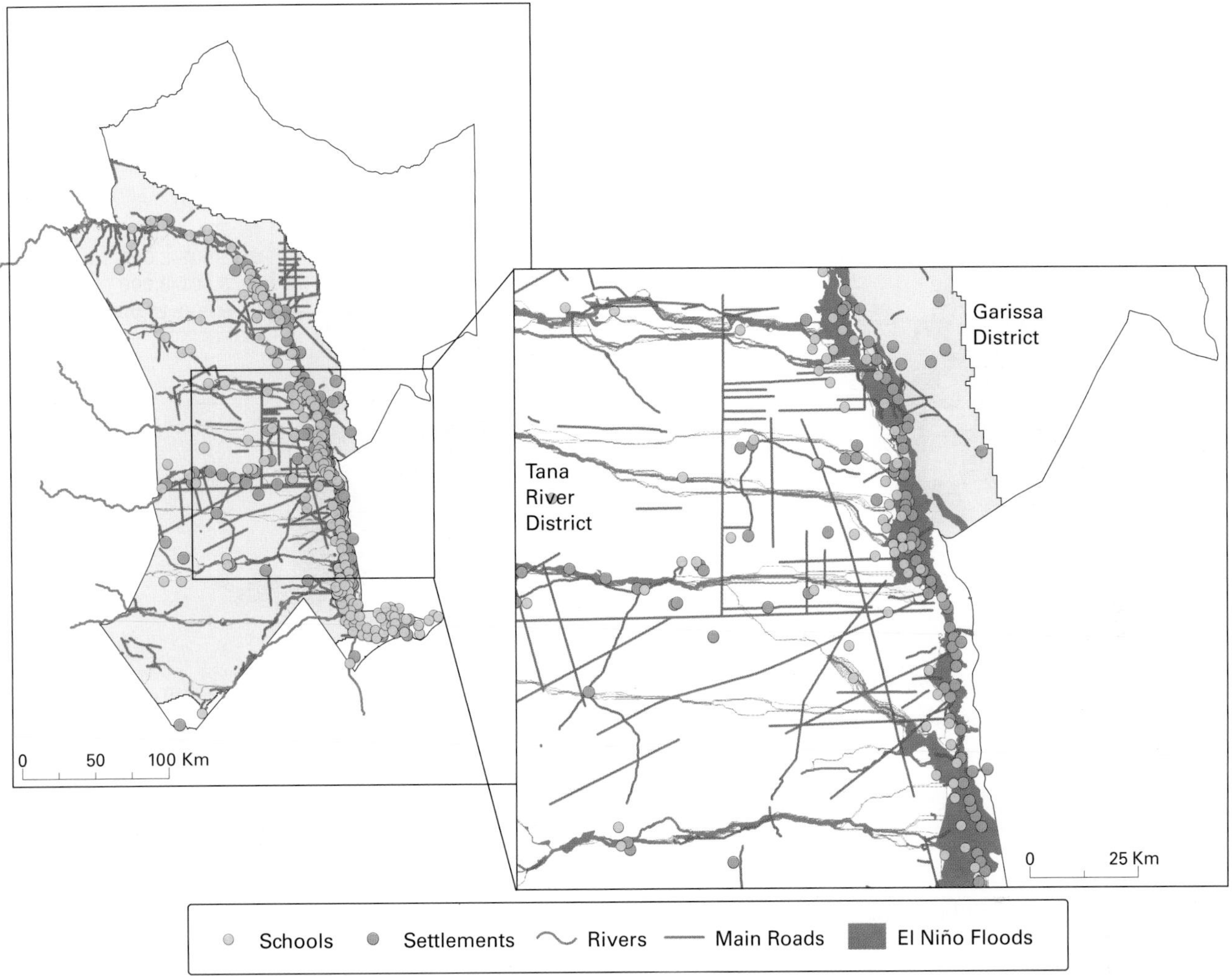

itants of the basin have to prepare for losses to property, livestock, and crops. However, the amplitude of the floods is not the same from year to year. Floods of the magnitude experienced during the 1997–98 El Niño are, fortunately, a rare occurrence and unlikely to happen more than once every 35 years, given the cascade of dams upstream. On the contrary, moderate floods, characterized by a maximum water level of approximately 5 meters on the river gauge at Garissa, could strike at a frequency of once every 2 to 5 years. Figures 6.8 and 6.9 show the effects of moderate and severe floods.

Considering the 1997–98 El Niño as the worst-case scenario, the map in figure 6.8 shows the flooded area as modeled by the SFM and the impact on the populations. For each scenario, we computed the total flooded area. Villages that are underwater and the total number of people affected by the floods were identified. We assumed the total population in a sub-location is contained in the villages located in that sub-location. One drawback in this methodology is that the data on villages and schools were digitized from old maps. The school locations, therefore, are different from the village locations. In reality, these schools are associated with certain villages. We subdivided the population by the total number of villages in the sub-location and computed the average population per settlement (table 6.1). These figures are only for riverine areas; in contrast,

Table 6.1: Flood scenarios for a worst case and a moderate case

Flood type	*Villages*	*People*	*Area Km²*
Severe	73	70,000	5,377
Moderate	51	47,000	4,612

Figure 6.9. (a + b) Livelihood zones overlaid on El Niño floods case

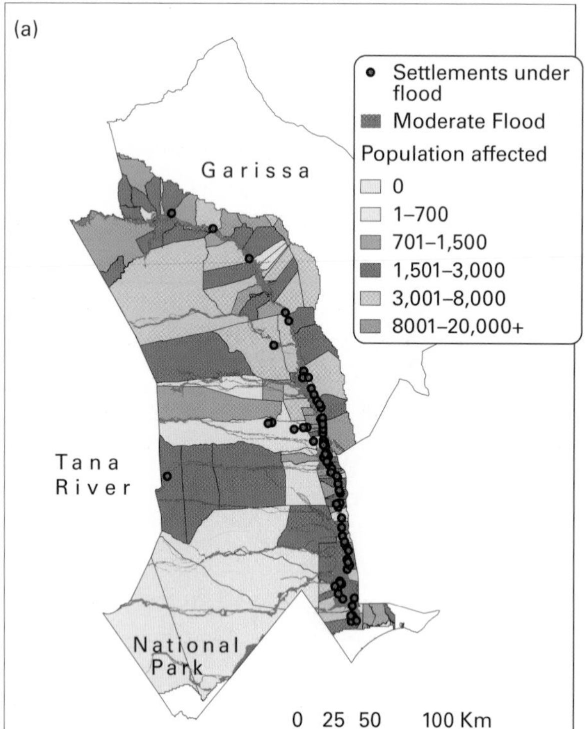

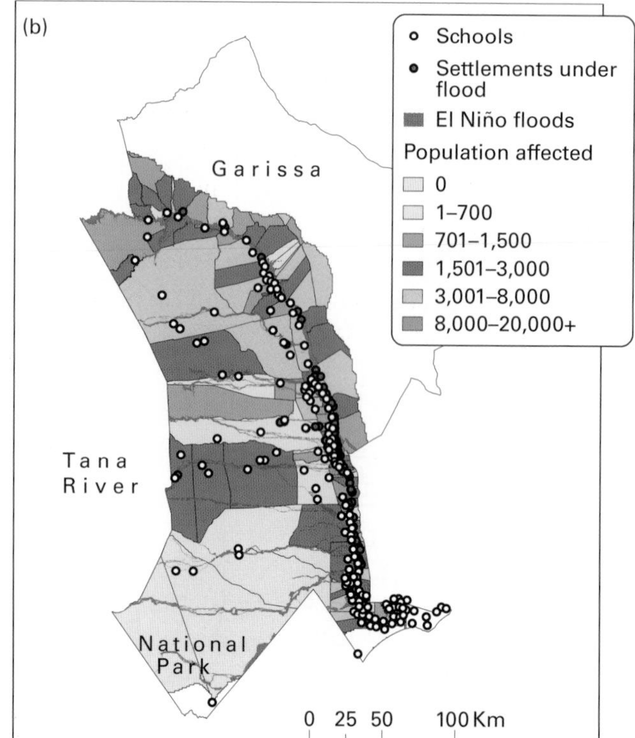

the 1997–98 El Niño floods occurred due to direct and high rainfall on non-riverine areas.

In a moderate flood, the total riverine area that would be flooded was found to be 4,600 km^2. Out of a total number of 148 villages located in the flood plain, 51 villages would be under water, resulting in approximately 47,000 people affected by these kinds of floods. In a severe flood, the impact would obviously be larger, with an approximate total flooded area of 5,400 km^2 (17 percent higher than a moderate flood); 73 villages would be underwater and a total of 71,063 people (50 percent higher compared to a moderate flood) would be affected.

General Impacts of the 1997–98 El Niño Floods

The 1997–98 El Niño floods drastically affected livelihoods in the area, especially along the river in both the Garissa and Tana River districts. The floods caused major infrastructure damage, and all roads were severely damaged. Most roads were gullied and silted, becoming impassable. Some roads became part of the riverbed and some bridges were washed away. This resulted in some communities being completely isolated, with no access to food other than through food aid relief brought by helicopters. Pockets of population in Dujis and Modogashe (Garissa district) were marooned for more than two months as result of roads being cut off.

For most communities, access to markets was highly reduced, resulting in decreased food access. This circumstance was aggravated by lower purchasing power due to loss of income and conjugated high commodity prices resulting from increased logistical costs.

Most schools were damaged, resulting in high dropout rates (65 percent of the boys and 50 percent of the girls in primary school in the Garissa district). A large number of water sources were washed away, submerged, or rendered unsafe for drinking through contamination, mostly from the destruction of latrines. This was especially the case in the permanent settlements along the river.

During the 1997–98 floods, there was a change in the overall physical environment, resulting in an increase in humidity to above 80 percent of saturation in both districts, with a peak of 97 percent humidity in December 1997. This resulted in a drastic increase in human and livestock diseases, an increase in vectors (mosquitoes, tsetse flies), and a severe outbreak of Rift Valley Fever. There were massive outbreaks of malaria, diarrheal disease, skin disease, ARI, worms, and cholera. Malnutrition rates of children under five years of age reached incredibly high levels, with reported overall rates of 56 percent and 48 percent, respectively, in the Garissa and Tana River districts (using mid-upper-arm circumference [MUAC] measured at <13.5cm).

Disease had a considerable economic impact on livestock exports. Saudi Arabia banned the import of livestock from the east Africa region. According to a flood emergency assessment report in Kenya prepared by UNICEF, GoK, and UNDP (1998), immediately after the 1997–98 El Niño floods, shoats died in masses in the Garissa district, which accounted for an unbelievable 70 to 95 percent of dead shoats reported. This predominantly affected the pastoralists' communities in the basin. Figure 6.11.a shows the number of livestock before and after the floods. The loss of livestock in the Tana River district was reported to equal 50 to 90 percent of all animals (depending on particular areas), with an average figure of over 70 percent for the whole district. Larger animals did not die in as large numbers as small animals. Some 10–20 percent of camels and 0–5 percent of cattle were reported to have died as a result of the floods in the Garissa district. However, in some areas of the Tana River district, the reported cattle loss was as high as 70 percent. The ground became saturated with water, which meant that large animals had to stand or lie in water, resulting in increased livestock mortality from foot rot or pneumonia. Moreover, the stress on livestock resulted in mass abortion rates, reportedly affecting 80 to 100 percent of pregnant animals of all species in both districts. This, together with the high morbidity, resulted in low milk production.

Crops were destroyed en masse. Up to 1,200 hectares of bananas, tomatoes, and vegetables were reportedly washed away in the Garissa district, while 100 percent of the bananas, mangoes, rice, maize, and pulses were destroyed in the Tana River district. The destruction of crops resulted in a drastic increase in commodity prices, as indicated in figure 6.11.b. The prices of most commodities doubled, making these essential commodities out of reach for most of the population.

The overall impact on the livelihoods has been impoverishment of the population, hunger stress, displacement, destitution, and increased insecurity; reports of these maladies have been especially prevalent in the Tana River district.

Impacts of Floods on Livelihoods

The impacts of floods on populations differ depending on the members' livelihoods and wealth-group affiliations. In order to better identify the impacts of the floods on the different livelihoods in the Tana River and Garissa districts, we mapped the main livelihoods using the data described above at the sublocation levels in both districts. The result is shown in figure 6.10. These two districts are characterized by several livelihoods. On the Garissa district side, three livelihood groupings can be distinguished: fishing and subsistence cropping, urban (around Garissa town), and pastoralist. On the Tana River district side, three livelihoods zones can also be found: dry riverine zone (in the north and covering a great length of the river), agro-pastoralists, and Tana Delta zone (in the south). The floods affected all of these zones.

Among the different livelihood groups in both districts, the ones most exposed to flooding are pastoralists, agro-pastoralists, dry riverine, and the Tana Delta livelihood system. For that reason, we have focused our analysis on these groups. The analysis begins with a description of the baseline livelihood. The key characteristics considered are cash income, expenditure sources, income diversification, food consumption sources, livestock ownership and its contribution to cash income and food consumption, and market dependency. A wealth breakdown was applied for agro-pastoralists, pastoralists, and dry riverine livelihoods to highlight disparities within these groups. The analysis aims at building a picture of the impacts of floods on the different elements that constitute the livelihoods of the exposed populations taking into account the immediate, short-term and long-term impacts.

The livelihood zones directly on the river (dry riverine zone, Tana Delta zone, pastoralists, and agro-pastoralists, as they are mostly located in the hinterland except in the south part of the basin) are likely to be affected through the direct destruction of their properties (houses, crop fields, pumps, and so on). The population in the urban area (especially at Garissa town) is likely to be mostly affected through the indirect impacts

Figure 6.10. Livelihood zones overlaid on El Niño flood cases

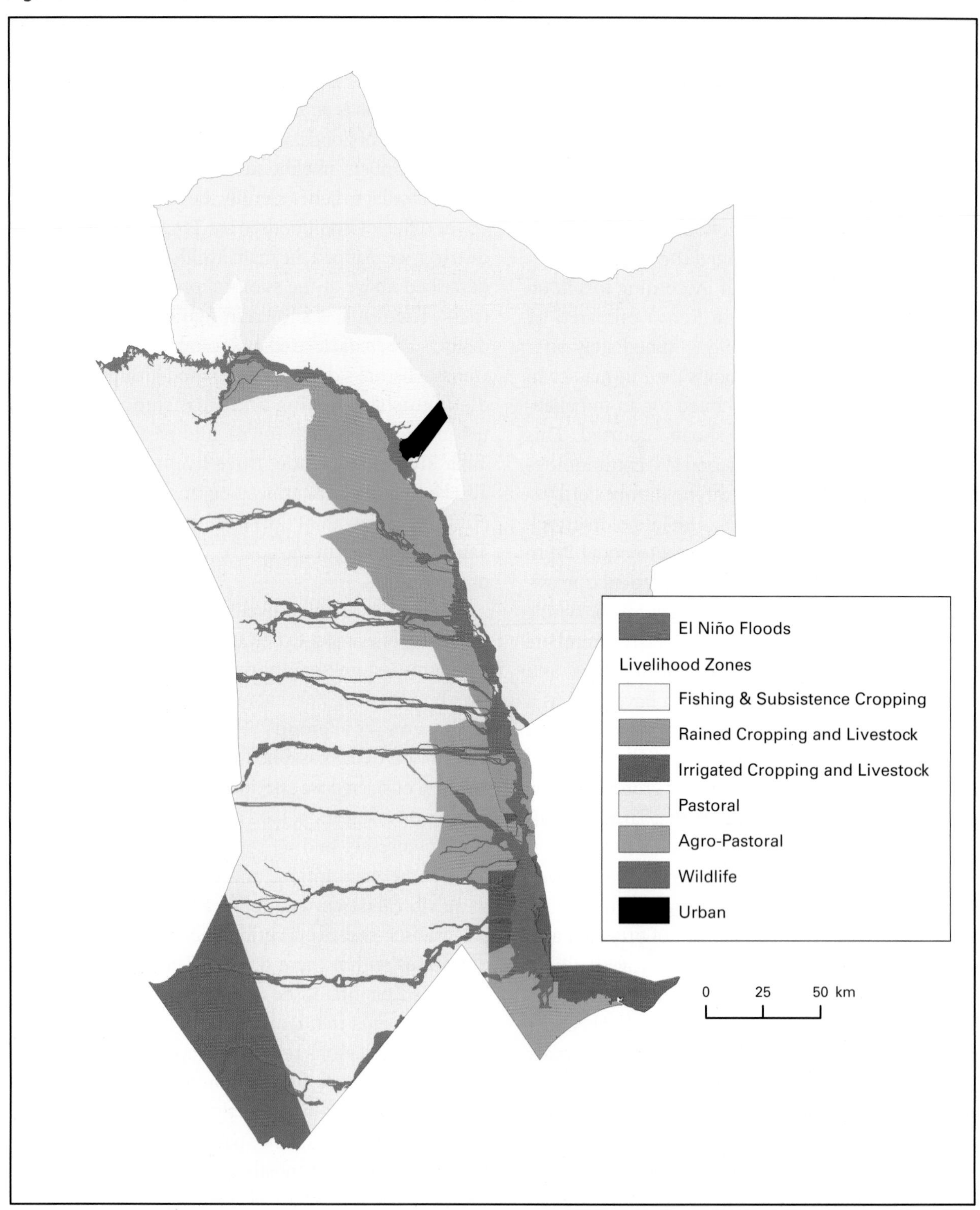

Figure 6.11. Impacts of floods on market prices and livestock: (a) commodity prices (b) livestock losses

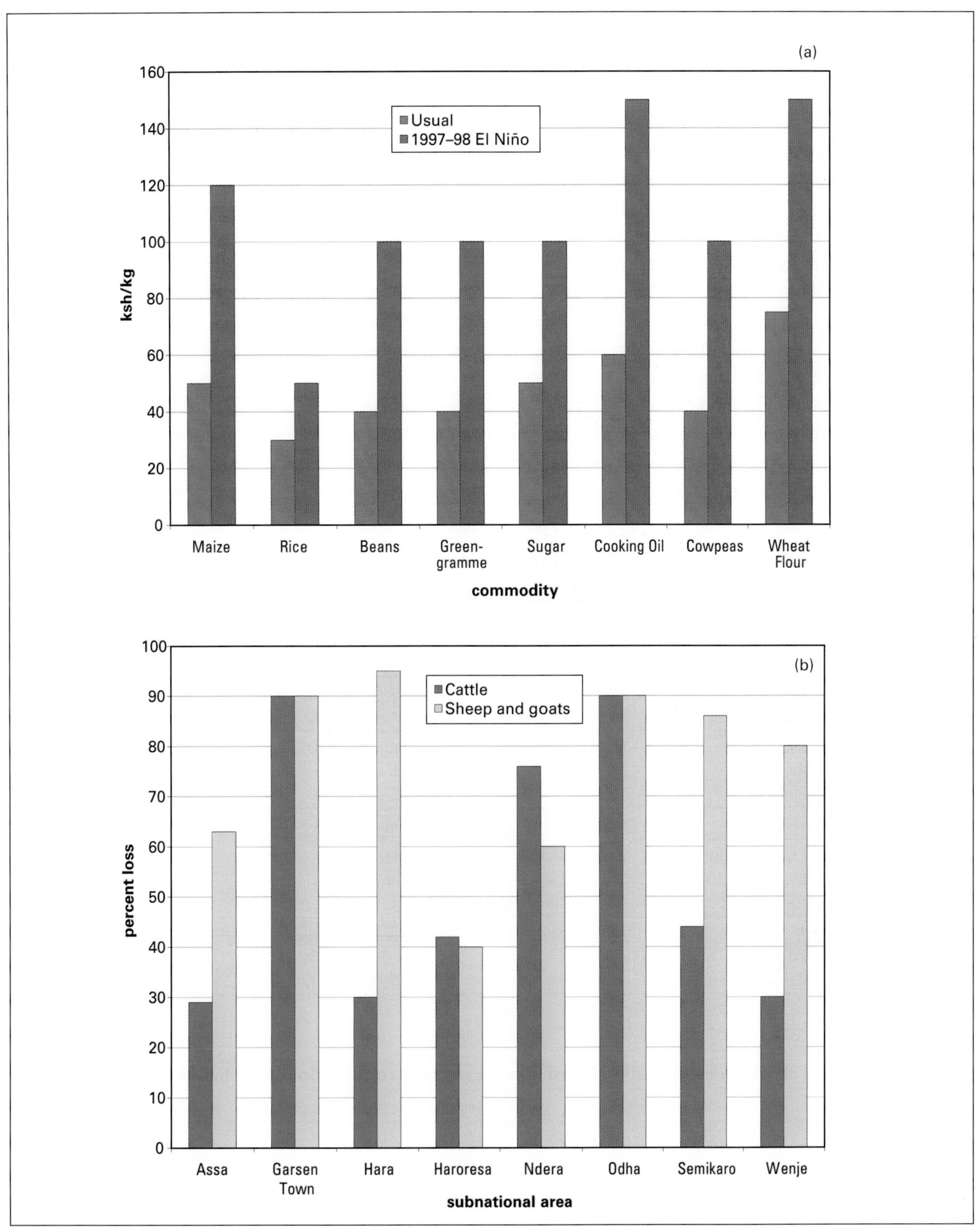

Source: UNICEF 1998

of the floods, such as through an interruption of access to markets and concomitant loss of income, though some may also encounter loss of properties. However, people in urban areas are more likely to have resources to cope and, therefore, are less at risk of a complete collapse of their livelihoods. The population in fisheries and subsistence cropping may find benefits in the floods thanks to the likely increase in fish production, though they are also likely to see their subsistence cropping resources being affected.

The different characteristics of the livelihoods are summarized in table 6.2. Unless specified, the data represent an average.

As we can see in table 6.2, the main income source of the pastoralists, agro-pastoralists, and the people from the dry riverine communities comes from livestock. This is also a major source of food consumption. Table 6.3 summarizes the percentage of livestock contribution to cash income and food consumption.

As described earlier, during the El Niño floods close to 90 percent of shoats died in the Garissa and Tana River districts, resulting in a complete collapse of the main source of income. Shoats represent close to 15 percent of the total income for the agro-pastoralist, dry riverine, and pastoralist groups. In addition, in both the short and long term, mortality and morbidity among larger animals increased drastically as a result of diseases such as foot rot and pneumonia. On top of direct loss of animals, the decrease in livestock marketability has also hurt income. Due to the fear of Rift Valley Fever, animals were not bought on the markets, and income from animal sales was lost. The impact on livestock has hurt equally the "very poor," "poor," and "middle income" groups, who have seen their income from livestock reduced to zero. Most of the "very poor" and "poor" have moved to the destitute category, while only the "middle income" group, featuring larger cattle sizes, may have avoided destitution.

Table 6.2. Characteristics of the different livelihood zones analyzed

Characteristics	*Agro-pastoralists*	*Dry riverine zone*	*Pastoralists*	*Tana delta zone*
Cash income sources	Livestock prod: 40%, Food crop prod: 10% (Maize: 30%), Poultry prod: 10%	Livestock prod: 22%, Firewood collection: 12%, Food crop prod: 10% (Maize: 30%) Hunting and gathering: 10%	Livestock prod: 68%, remittances and gifts: 10%, Firewood collection: 5%	Food crop prod: 40% (Mangoes: 37%), Formal wage labor: 15%, Livestock prod: 10%
Expenditure of poor HH	Maize: 50% Rice: 10% Milk: 10%	Maize: 50% Rice: 10% Milk: 10%	Milk prod: 40% Meat: 20%	Maize: 47% Pulses: 10% Vegetables: 10%
Food consumption	Maize: 40%	Maize: 50%	NA	Maize: 41%
Maize sources for consumption	Own farm: 40% Market purchase: 40%, Gifts and food aid: 40%	Own farm: 30% Market purchase: 10%, Gifts and food aid: 60%	Market purchase: 60%, Gifts and food aid: 40%	Own farm: 60% Market purchase: 20%, Gifts and food aid: 20%
Livestock ownership: Cattle Shoats	Poor Middle 20–50 70–100 25–40 75–125	Poor Middle 0–2 2–5 5–10 10–20	Poor Middle 5–20 30–50 15–60 70–120	 2 5

Source: Livelihoods data base 2004 (FEWS NET Kenya, WFP/VAM and GoK)
HH = Household

Table 6.3. Percentage of livestock contribution to cash income and food consumption of the livelihood zones analyzed

Percent		*Agro-pastoralists*	*Dry riverine zone*	*Pastoralists*	*Tana delta zone*
Cash income	Cattle	15	33	70	20
	Shoats	40	65	20	70
	Camels	15	-	-	-
Food consumption	Cattle	15	15	40	40
	Shoats	60	80	40	53
	Camels	10	-	-	-

The loss of livestock also had an important impact on food consumption. Food intake was reduced due to the direct loss of animals, from which people were getting meat and milk. Secondly, the loss of income translated into a loss of purchasing power that, when combined with higher commodity prices, put basic commodities out of reach for these communities. As a result, their access to food was drastically reduced.

Moreover, these populations depend highly on maize as their major source of food, either from their own farm production (40 percent agro-pastoralists, 30 percent dry riverine, 60 percent delta Tana) or from market purchase (60 percent pastoralists). The direct destruction of crops reduced availability of maize in the area, with the consequence of very high prices for available maize on the market. In all cases, maize has become unavailable for these populations. As a result most people in these livelihood zones require food aid to survive. It is interesting to note that all the livelihoods in the Tana River basin seem to be heavily dependent on food aid. This is the result of consecutive years of drought in the area. Up to 60 percent of the maize consumption for the dry riverine people already comes from food aid distribution. However, due to the difficulties in shipping food into the areas and the increased competition for food aid, the threat of starvation for these populations is drastically increased.

The population less likely to see a complete collapse of livelihoods is that of the Tana Delta zone, where 40 percent of the income comes from crop production, especially from mangoes (37 percent), tomatoes (20 percent) and bananas (10 percent). Any impact on these products will negatively impact this group. Through more diversified income sources, however, with only 10 percent linked to livestock production, these people are more likely to be able to cope. For example, 15 percent of their income comes from formal wage labor. Yet even this income may not be guaranteed, as, after a flood shock, there is likely to be increased competition for this income source. Similarly, this population is also dependent on maize as a source of food consumption, with 20 percent coming from food aid; so they are likely to require immediate and short-term food assistance to survive.

Conclusions

The above discussion has demonstrated that some sectors of the population will be more affected than others during flood events in the Tana River basin. This finding is critical for contingency planning, in which the objective is to anticipate and therefore better manage a potential crisis. The central components of a contingency plan are to understand ***who*** (who is affected?), ***where*** (where are they located?), ***what*** (what types and modalities of emergency assistance are needed?), ***how*** (how, if roads are impassable, will food be delivered and people evacuated?), and ***how much*** (how much are the associated costs for implementing an emergency operation?).

Drawing from our analysis here and past experience, under the worst-case scenario, pastoralists and dry riverine communities are expected to experience the worst losses. Therefore, a response directed toward these groups of people, and the pastoralists in particular, would be advisable. Assistance should take the form of free food distribution and income generating activities, as the analysis has shown that for all of the groups, income, daily food consumption, and nutrition are tied to livestock and crop production, both of which may completely collapse in any flood scenario. Furthermore, assessments during the 1997–98 El Niño floods showed that relief food enabled pastoralists to save their remaining livestock and to start rebuilding herds and livelihoods. For planning purposes, we know from our hazard maps that food assistance in the short term and income regenerating activities in the long term would be required for up to 70,000 persons. In the moderate case scenario, the population in need would be 47,000 people. This provides core data for calculating costs and the volume of food commodities required.

On the logistical side, a workable solution to providing timely assistance in both worst-case and moderate-case scenarios would be to deliver commodities and evacuate by air, although accessibility from the airstrip may not be guaranteed. During December and January of 1997–98, WFP was able to use helicopters to airlift food to over 60 sites within the Garissa district. Due to the limited capacity of the helicopter (payload of 2.5 tons) and the large number of needy sites, the amount delivered per site was very limited.

Even so, the relief food probably averted total famine.

One way of alleviating the logistical burden would be to gather the affected people into displacement camps located in easily accessible areas. This requires moving large numbers of people at once, which was not possible during the 1997–98 El Niño floods due to the status of the roads. Affected people in the Garissa area poured into town, increasing the stress on the local population.

Given the analysis presented here, it is also possible to estimate logistical costs should air transport be the only option. As an example, during the 1997–98 emergency (which serves as the worst-case scenario here), the operational cost to the World Food Programme was US$1,100 per ton for each airdrop. A total of 7,414.23 MT was distributed at a cost of US$4,117,734. This food reached up to 641,451 beneficiaries in Garissa, Wajir, Mandera, Isiolo, Marsabit, Moyale, and the Tana River.

For policy makers, planners, and the humanitarian aid sector as a whole, the value of this analysis, which has linked flood forecasting and livelihood zone data, is a forecast of the scale of a hazard, estimated costs, and, most important, an identification of vulnerable groups. This information will improve emergency preparedness, response, and assistance.

References

Artan, G., J. Verdin, and K. Asante. 2001. A Wide-Area Flood Risk Monitoring Model. Proceedings of the Fifth International Workshop on Application of Remote Sensing in Hydrology, Montpellier, France.

Blasco, F., M. F. Bellen, and M. U. Chaudhury. 1992. Estimating the Extent of Floods in Bangladesh Using SPOT Data. *Remote Sensing of Environment* 39: 167–178.

FAO (Food and Agriculture Organization). 1967. Survey of the Irrigation Potential of the Lower Tana River Basin. Prepared by ACRES International Limited, Canada; International Land Development Consultants N. V., the Netherlands; and the Government of Kenya.

Hutchinson, M. F. 1989. A New Procedure for Girding Elevation and Stream Line Data with Automatic Removal of Spurious Pits. *Journal of Hydrology* 106: 211–232.

Jenson, S. K., and J. O. Domingue. 1988. Extracting Topographic Structure from Digital Elevation Data for Geographic Information System Analysis. *Photogrammetric Engineering and Remote Sensing* 54(11): 1593-1600.

Mayer, L., and P. A. Pearthree. 2002. A Method for Mapping Flood Inundation in Southwestern Arizona Using Landsat TM Data. In: *Ancient Floods, Modern Hazards: Principles and Applications of Paleoflood Hydrology,* vol. 5, P. K. House, et al. (eds.), Washington, D.C.: AGU, 61–75.

Nash, J. E., and J. Sutcliffe. 1970. River Flow Forecasting through Conceptual Models. Part 1: A Discussion of Principles. *Journal of Hydrology* 10: 282–290.

UNICEF (United Nations Children's Fund), UNDP (United Nations Development Programme), and Government of Kenya. 1998. A Flood Assessment Report. Prepared after the El Niño 1997/98 Floods.

USGS (U.S. Geological Survey). 2003. U.S. Geological Survey Technical Support to the Mozambique Integrated Information Network for Decision-Making (MIND). Project Completion Report, submitted to the U.S. Agency for International Development. Prepared by K. Asante and J. Verdin.

Xie, P., and P. A. Arkin. 1998. Global Precipitation Estimates from Satellite Observed Outgoing Long Wave Radiation. *Journal of Climate* 11: 137–164.

Zhou, C. H., et al. 2000. Flood Monitoring Using Multi-temporal AVHRR and RADARSAT Imagery. *Photogrammetric Engineering and Remote Sensing* 66(5): 633–638.